James Joyce and the Irish Revolution

James Joyce and the Irish Revolution

THE EASTER RISING
AS MODERN EVENT

Luke Gibbons

The University of Chicago Press   CHICAGO AND LONDON

The University of Chicago Press, Chicago 60637
The University of Chicago Press, Ltd., London
© 2023 by The University of Chicago
All rights reserved. No part of this book may be used or reproduced in any manner whatsoever without written permission, except in the case of brief quotations in critical articles and reviews. For more information, contact the University of Chicago Press, 1427 East 60th Street, Chicago, IL 60637.
Published 2023
Printed in the United States of America

32 31 30 29 28 27 26 25 24 23   1 2 3 4 5

ISBN-13: 978-0-226-82446-8 (cloth)
ISBN-13: 978-0-226-82447-5 (paper)
ISBN-13: 978-0-226-82448-2 (e-book)
DOI: https://doi.org/10.7208/chicago/9780226824482.001.0001

Library of Congress Cataloging-in-Publication Data

Names: Gibbons, Luke, author.
Title: James Joyce and the Irish revolution : the Easter Rising as modern event / Luke Gibbons.
Description: Chicago : The University of Chicago Press, 2023. | Includes bibliographical references and index.
Identifiers: LCCN 2022027214 | ISBN 9780226824468 (cloth) | ISBN 9780226824475 (paperback) | ISBN 9780226824482 (ebook)
Subjects: LCSH: Joyce, James, 1882–1941. Ulysses. | Joyce, James, 1882–1941—Criticism and interpretation. | Literature and revolutions—Ireland. | Modernism (Literature)—Ireland. | Ireland—History—Easter Rising, 1916—In literature. | Ireland—History—War of Independence, 1919–1921—Literature and the war.
Classification: LCC PR6019.O9 U4223 2023 | DDC 823/.912—dc23/eng/20220727
LC record available at https://lccn.loc.gov/2022027214

♾ This paper meets the requirements of ANSI/NISO Z39.48-1992 (Permanence of Paper).

For Dolores, Laura, and Barry

In Memoriam
Seamus Deane (1940–2021)
George Coyle (1954–2021)

If Joyce's novel is the city's *Odyssey*, then the Easter Rising is its *Iliad*.

ROBERT CREMINS

Contents

List of Figures — xi
Preface — xiii
Abbreviations — xxi

INTRODUCTION:
James Joyce and the Irish Revolution — 1

1. "OLD HAUNTS":
   Photographic Memory, Motion, and the Republic of Letters — 21

2. MODERN EPIC AND REVOLUTION:
   Montage in the Margins — 45

3. "A WORLD THAT RAN THROUGH THINGS":
   Ulysses, the Easter Rising, and Spatial Form — 67

4. THE EASTER RISING AS MODERN EVENT:
   Media, Technology, and Terror — 91

5. "PAVING OVER THE ABYSS":
   Ireland, War, and Literary Modernism — 111

6. "THROUGH THE EYES OF ANOTHER RACE":
   Ulysses, Roger Casement, and the Politics of Humanitarianism — 135

7. TRANSATLANTIC "USABLE PASTS":
   America, Literary Modernism, and the Irish Revolution — 159

8. ON ANOTHER MAN'S TEXT:
   Ernie O'Malley, Politics, and Irish Modernism   181

9. BEYOND DISILLUSIONMENT:
   Desmond Ryan, *Ulysses*, and the Irish Revolution   203

Acknowledgments   225
Notes   229
Index   287

Figures

1.1 "Plan of Dublin" from *How to Enjoy James Joyce's "Ulysses"* (1934) 23

1.2 Thomas W. Pugh (1883–1968) 25

4.1 "A New Form of the Chaplin Craze" (1916) 92

4.2 *The Only Way* (1899; 1942) 98

4.3 Military checkpoint, Mount Street Bridge (1916) 104

4.4 Coliseum Theatre, Henry Street (1916) 104

4.5 Count Plunkett speech, Loopline Bridge (1917) 105

4.6 John Martin-Harvey as Sydney Carton on scaffold, from a poster by John Hassall, R.A. (1907) 109

6.1 Doctore Joachimo Laurentio Villaneuva, *Phœnician Ireland* (1833) 140

6.2 Thomas Jones Barker, *The Secret of England's Greatness* (1863) 152

Preface

> Array! Surrection. Eireweeker to the wohld bludyn world.
>
> JAMES JOYCE, *Finnegans Wake*[1]

Commenting on the influence of James Joyce on Irish writers who have "to some extent treated the national revolutionary movement," the Irish-American novelist and activist James T. Farrell noted: "It is not unsafe to prophesy that, when and if a novel dealing with the revolutionary movement is written . . . it will be shown to have been influenced—most likely profitably—by Joyce's *Ulysses*."[2] That novel has never appeared but in its absence, it may be that critical and historical accounts of the Irish revolution would benefit considerably from being recast in the light of Joyce's revolution of the word.

This is what is proposed in the present study, not to overwrite multiple interpretations that already exist of Joyce or events in the period, but to find innovative, even discordant, narrative structures capable of doing justice to the heterogeneity of forces that went into the making of the Irish revolution (1916–23). In an aside, Farrell refers to a British official who, in his testimony to an inquiry into the Easter Rising of 1916, claimed that "the rebellion might have been averted if the Abbey Theatre in Dublin might have had a longer period in which to influence the Irish people."[3] This is not to deny the obvious contribution made by incendiary plays and specific members of the theater to the "imagination of an insurrection" (as it has been called), not to mention those who participated directly and lost their lives in action, such as the leading Abbey player Seán Connolly.[4] The point, rather, is that myths of the Celtic Twilight and related aspects of Abbey productions were perfectly compatible with keeping the king's peace, and more radical disruptive interventions were required to sever the connection with empire. In a famous misreading, W. B. Yeats was taken to have heralded the mystic George Russell (pseudonym Æ) in 1898 as "the poet of the people, perhaps the poet of a new insurrection," but the accolade was erroneously transcribed: what Yeats had written, in keeping with the idealism he shared with Russell, was "the poet of a new inspiration."[5]

It is not too difficult to see how a heroic past of chivalry and nobility of the kind fostered by Standish O'Grady and other purveyors of Romantic Ireland posed no threat to the order of the day. Romantic nostalgia looks back to a golden age, suitably located in a distant past but easily transposed in period dress to the present, as with the return to Camelot to temper the crass commercial realities of Victorian Britain. The charm of the golden age lies in an illusory perfection that casts its glow down the centuries, ruling out any need for change in the here and now, and imbuing tradition with an aura of continuity. By contrast, what Walter Benjamin termed "left-wing melancholia" refers to strands of modernism that look back to previous eras precisely for their capacity for change, to propitious pasts that continue to have a future. According to Joyce's friend John Francis Byrne, the most important words in Thomas MacDonagh's address before his execution as a leader of the Easter Rising were "Yet it could have been otherwise."[6] In his poem "Of Ireland," MacDonagh wrote of "present joy broken with old regret / Or sorrow saved from hell by one hope yet."[7] Though the 1916 rebellion did not succeed in its immediate military objectives, it was not *destined* to fail, still less in the long run, and viewing it through Joyce's narrative techniques challenges any sense of linear trajectories or foregone conclusions, particularly in times of convulsive social change.[8] Subsequent perceptions of the Rising as "doomed to failure," prompting disavowals of the whole delinquent project, feed into the conventional bildungsroman of a character chasing foolish ideals, only to mend the error of their ways and rejoin settled society (or else rue the day, succumbing to disillusionment and despair).

Viewed in conventional narrative terms, the Easter Rising did not bode well for happy endings, but as readers of Joyce's fiction from *Dubliners* onward realized, it is often the dispelling of illusions that proves most emancipatory in the end. It is in the nature of revolutions, as Michael Denning has observed, to "exceed their scripts" and take off in directions despite the best-laid plans of their organizers, not to mention the odds stacked against them.[9] Artworks, too, are of their moment, and yet their remit extends far into the past and the future, picking up on what was not always available to the present. "When he was with us," Joyce's school friend William Fallon remarked, "he sometimes appeared to be peering into the future."[10] At moments of acute social upheaval, aesthetic form, particularly a disruptive avant-garde, may be seen as providing glimpses of alternative worlds, and new ways of seeing things, while acknowledging the risk that a vista that looks to the future may also be cast aside peremptorily before its time. Using Joycean terms, Theodor Adorno explained the only crime of the defeated is that they did not appear to have the forces of history on their side, but it is the epochal function of art to address the extent to which these forces themselves may be called into question: "Art is the epiphany of the hidden essence of reality ... an unconscious form of historiography, the memory of what has been vanquished or repressed, perhaps an anticipation of what is possible."[11]

It is striking that one of the revolutionary novelists introduced by James T. Farrell to the English-speaking world was Victor Serge (1890–1947), a survivor of many imprisonments and uprisings, and himself a great admirer of Joyce. Just as melancholia, in Freud's view, is characterized by a refusal to let go of the past, Serge is notable among key figures in the Russian Revolution for his subsequent condemnation of the tragic betrayal of socialism under Stalin, but yet holding on, like Trotsky, to the unrealized promise of the Revolution. Writing of Serge, Susan Sontag noted that his is "a voice that forbids itself the requisite tones of despair or contrition or bewilderment—literary tones as most people understand them" that lack a certain liberal appeal, since they are "not as attractive to us as a more anguished reckoning."[12] For many Irish republicans, coming to terms with the conservatism of the new Irish state, the note of defiance and candor in Joyce's writing may have offered a similar reprise of the hopes that drove the Irish revolution. It was the repressive aspects of the new Irish state, including the "new censorship," that led John Eglinton to note in 1929 that "Joyce is, I should think, the idol of a good many of the young men of Ireland," if by that was meant those who looked to a writer who "has reached for the first time in Ireland a complete emancipation from Anglo-Saxon ideals."[13] In *A Portrait of the Artist as a Young Man* (1916), Stephen Dedalus looks back to an "Ireland of Tone and of Parnell" that "seemed to have receded in space," but to the post-revolutionary generation, the world of Joyce's fiction, and the open-ended narrative vistas of *Ulysses*, recalled an era in which anything was possible, including the breadth of vision of the novel itself.[14] Serge wrote in 1923, in words that could apply to *Ulysses*, "The revolution which has broken all the old social disciplines has also broken the all-too-conventional ones of literature": "No linear story-line.... No 'plot' (what a poor thing, what a poor word!). No unique central characters. Crowds in motion—in which each individual is a world, an end in himself—events crowding, intertwining, colliding, overriding each other, multiple lives which appear and disappear, all of them rare, unique, central, because human, all insignificant."[15]

Accounting for the interweaving of representation and reality in what he termed the literary "chronotope" (time/space), Serge's contemporary, the critic Mikhail Bakhtin, analyzed how specific understandings of space and time within a story are framed in turn by wider configurations of space and time at work in society itself: as social "objective forms," Bakhtin wrote, they "enter literary works, sometimes almost completely bypassing the subjective individual memory of their creators."[16] On these terms, the artist's stepping back from his handiwork as outlined in *Portrait* (P, 233) allows for the creation of life-worlds in which the "conscience" of the race, not only of characters in the novel or even the author, is forged "in the smithy of the soul" (P, 276). To be sure, Joyce's personal views on Irish politics and current affairs are of considerable interest, particularly as contained in his correspondence and journalism, where Sinn Féin sympathies are evident from the earliest years of the movement, but they should by no means be taken as the limits of his creative endeavors, any more than we should expect other aspects of his personal life to be simply mirrored in his fiction. When Henrik Ibsen wrote that "revolutions in externals, in politics, etc." are not sufficient for the artistic purpose of going all the way down into "the spirit of man," he was enunciating what attracted Joyce to his writing—"the opening up of a great question, or a great conflict which is almost independent of the conflicting actors."[17]

According to Declan Kiberd, "The Easter Rising, like *Ulysses*, was an answer to a question which had never exactly been asked. It was a gesture out of an uncertain future, an act whose meaning would become clear only in retrospect when people learned to decode it."[18] This book does not set out to answer clear-cut questions, as in a factual historical record, nor does it provide a purely literary analysis of Joyce's work, attentive only to what is within the text. Rather, it attempts to reclaim what was radical in the Irish revolution for a modernist project akin to that of Joyce's, both of them responding to Ireland's position on a fault line in the imperial world system of the early twentieth century. "*Ulysses* is a revolutionary work that seizes the day without ever simply settling for it," writes Joe Cleary, and it is in this sense that Ireland's "modest desire," as Leopold Bloom would have it, "to be just another bourgeois nation" is cut across by the "epic ambition" of a culture, on Stephen Dedalus's terms, "to take on the world's greatest empire."[19] When the astute French critic Simone Téry envisaged, as early as 1925, that "within the next hundred years James Joyce will have his statue in Dublin,"[20] it still left open the question whether the society that hosted it would live up to imaginative range of Joyce's modernist vision, as against the "split little pea" (*FW*, 171.6) of the new Irish Free State, whose birth coincided with the publication of *Ulysses*.

"The political writer," according to Joyce Carol Oates, "is obliged to be ever more subtle, and his/her fictions ever more reflective of our contemporary fracturing of consciousness, to express this tragic disparity. For me, therefore, the great model of the political novel is James Joyce's *Ulysses*."[21] In the introduction below, Joyce's stylistic innovations are considered in the light of the crisis in representation under modernity that called for new artistic interventions in reality, not least relating to notions of time, place, and the body under duress. The paralysis that Joyce diagnosed in Ireland, and which took on a new intensity in the traumatic experiences of the Great War, itself gave rise to symptomatic modes of expression at odds with the mimetic order of realist representation. That Joyce's writing attracted the interest of combatants in the Irish revolution is outlined in chapter 1 through his friendship with the socialist veteran of the Easter Rising, Thomas W. Pugh (1883–1968), and the subsequent engagement with Joyce's work by many leading republicans, whether in criticism, journalism, or private reading. "Photographic memory" linked both Joyce and Pugh, and the extent to which Joyce's fiction translates the "paralysis" of the still image into a more dynamic moving image may account for the manner in which the modernity of Dublin in *Ulysses* was perceived as moving on from *Dubliners* to capture structures of experience that laid the basis of insurrection. Though the Easter Rising is often framed in exclusively Romantic or Catholic nationalist terms, chapter 2 contends that the Romantic epic as fashioned by Revivalists such as Standish O'Grady was compatible with colonial and confessional rule, and a greater break resetting the Irish past in distinctively modern terms was required to confront the power of empire. The montage principle underlying modernist practice lent itself to this, and as figures as diverse as Bertolt Brecht, Ernst Bloch, Alfred Döblin, and Hermann Broch testified, Joyce was central in re-creating the modern epic in this form. If the novel addressed the imagined community of the nation, the scale of the epic was in keeping with forces that challenged empire, preeminent among them being the Easter Rising, which "blast[ed] the widest breach in the ramparts of the British Empire since Yorktown."[22]

Chapter 3 examines how the "shock" or convulsion of the Easter Rising was perceived as bringing a comatose Irish culture to its senses in the midst of the Great War. Wyndham Lewis admonished Joyce for the "dissolution" of things in his work and the tendency to undo the fixity of space by the permeable flow of time. It was through this capacity to reconfigure the city, common to both the Paris Commune and the Easter Rising, that strategies of revolution reenacted new modalities of space and time in modernist narratives, including the heterogeneity of the volatile forces that came together in the insurrection. As shown in chapter 4, the modern infrastructure of Dublin that set the stage for the Easter Rising of 1916 was in keeping with the material setting of many of the stylistic innovations in *Ulysses*. In this light, the Easter Rising itself is better conceived as a modern event, and this chapter looks at how emergent media technologies of photography, radio, and cinema impinged on events—in particular, the recasting of the modern hero in terms of the cult of the celebrity actor John Martin-Harvey as Sydney Carton in popular theatrical and cinematic adaptations of Charles Dickens's *A Tale of Two Cities*.

Reframing the Easter Rising within the wider catastrophe of the Great War brings debates about shell shock, and modernist techniques designed to deal with shattered worlds, into dialogue in chapter 5. This chapter looks at how activists and writers during the Irish revolution used experiments in style to articulate extremes of experience, including hunger striking, in times of war—in effect, using techniques Joyce was developing at the same time in *Ulysses*. Chapter 6 discusses how Roger Casement, executed for his part in the organization of the Easter Rising, features in the "Cyclops" chapter of *Ulysses* in a manner that links his indictment of crimes against humanity to critiques of imperialism. In *Ulysses*, the universalism of Homer's *Odyssey* is not conceived as an abstract model but reworked in terms of Irish historical links with the Levant and North Africa, and in a related idiom, the universalism of human rights is situated by Casement in historical challenges to empire that led to his participation in the Irish revolution.

Joyce's determination to have *A Portrait of the Artist as a Young Man* published in 1916 ensured that reception of his work was coupled, initially by Ezra Pound, with *Literature in Ireland* (1916), the posthumous publication of the executed leader of the Rising, Thomas MacDonagh (1878–1916). The international implications of this in the intellectual ferment of the United States of the period are discussed in chapter 7, the association of Joyce and MacDonagh encouraging a perception of the Rising as essentially modern in American letters, whether in the writings of F. Scott Fitzgerald, Marianne Moore, H. L. Mencken, Van Wyck Brooks, Ludwig Lewisohn, W. E. B. Du Bois, Marcus Garvey, or Claude McKay.

One of the most prominent guerrilla leaders of the Irish revolution, Ernie O'Malley (1897–1957), devoted a considerable amount of time to the study of, and lecturing on, Joyce in the course of writing his two classic memoirs of the Anglo-Irish War and the Civil War: *On Another Man's Wound* (1936) and *The Singing Flame* (1977). By examining his unpublished notebooks on Joyce, chapter 8 examines what might have attracted a gunman to these modernist works, looking in particular at how avant-gardes in both literature and politics, though "ahead" of their time, were dedicated to transforming the future to bring about conditions of their own reception. Another key figure in the Irish revolution, Desmond Ryan (1893–1964)—a combatant in the General Post Office fighting and secretary to Patrick Pearse, the most prominent leader of the Easter Rising—wrote some of the most notable firsthand historical accounts of the period, including a classic memoir, *Remembering Sion* (1934), using narrative techniques (and a title) greatly indebted to Joyce's breakthroughs in style. Commenting in late 1921 on *Ulysses* just before its publication, Valéry Larbaud claimed that Joyce "did as much as did all of the heroes of Irish nationalism to attract the respect of intellectuals of every other country toward Ireland," and this distills many of the disparate arguments running through *James Joyce and the Irish Revolution* as a whole.[23]

Abbreviations

BL   *Broken Landscapes: Selected Letters of Ernie O'Malley, 1924–1957,* ed. Cormac K. H. O'Malley and Nicholas Allen (Dublin: Lilliput Press, 2011).

BMH   Bureau of Military History, Witness Statement.

BSW   Walter Benjamin, *Selected Writings, 1927–1934*, vol. 2, trans. Rodney Livingstone et al., ed. Michael W. Jennings, Howard Eiland, and Gary Smith (Cambridge, MA: Harvard University Press, 1990).
Walter Benjamin, *Selected Writings: 1938–1940*, vol. 4, ed. Howard Eiland and Michael W. Jennings (Cambridge, MA: Harvard University Press, 2003).

CC   Standish O'Grady, *History of Ireland: Cuculain and His Contemporaries*, vol. 2 (London: Sampson, Low et al., 1880).

CWPP   *Collected Works of Padraic H. Pearse*, ed. Desmond Ryan (Dublin: Phoenix, 1924).

D   James Joyce, *Dubliners*, introduction by Terence Brown (1914; repr., London: Penguin, 1992).

DF   Frank Gallagher, *Days of Fear: Diary of a 1920s Hunger Striker* (1928; repr., Cork: Mercier Press, 2008).

DM   Michael North, *The Dialect of Modernism: Race, Language, and Twentieth-Century Literature* (New York: Oxford University Press, 1994).

FB   Kathleen Coyle, *A Flock of Birds* (New York: Dutton, 1930).

FW   James Joyce, *Finnegans Wake*, introduction by John Bishop (1939; repr., London: Penguin, 1999).

GZ   Hermann Broch, *Geist and Zeitgeist: Six Essays*, ed. John Hargreaves (1932; repr., New York: Counterpoint, 2002).

HI Standish O'Grady, *History of Ireland: Critical and Philosophical* (London: Sampson, Low & Co., 1881).

HT Ernst Bloch, *Heritage of Our Times* (1935), trans. Neville and Stephen Plaice (Cambridge: Polity Press, 1991).

IA Desmond Ryan, *The Invisible Army: A Story of Michael Collins* (London: Arthur Barker, 1932).

JCPD Joseph Campbell, *"As I Was among the Captives": Joseph Campbell's Prison Diary, 1922–1923*, ed. Eiléan Ní Chuilleanáin (Cork: Cork University Press, 2001).

JJ Richard Ellmann, *James Joyce* (Oxford: Oxford University Press, 1982).

JJCH Robert H. Deming, ed., *James Joyce: The Critical Heritage*, vols. 1 & 2 (London: Routledge & Kegan Paul, 1970).

JJL *James Joyce: Letters*, ed. Richard Ellmann (New York: Viking Press, 1966).

JJQ *James Joyce Quarterly*

LI Thomas MacDonagh, *Literature in Ireland: Studies Irish and Anglo-Irish* (1916; Dublin: Talbot Press, 1919).

OAMW Ernie O'Malley, *On Another Man's Wound* (1936; repr., Dublin; Anvil, 2002).

OCPW James Joyce, *Occasional, Critical, and Political Writing*, ed. Kevin Barry (Oxford: Oxford University Press, 2000).

OT Hannah Arendt, *The Origins of Totalitarianism* (1951; repr., New York: Schocken Books, 2004).

P James Joyce, *A Portrait of the Artist as a Young Man* (1916), ed. Seamus Deane (London: Penguin, 1982).

RS Desmond Ryan, *Remembering Sion* (London: Arthur Barker, 1934).

SF Ernie O'Malley, *The Singing Flame* (Dublin: Anvil, 1977).

SH James Joyce, *Stephen Hero* (1907), ed. Theodore Spencer (London: Paladin, 1991).

"SRS" Desmond Ryan, "Still Remembering Sion," *University Review* 5, no. 2 (Summer 1968).

TSP F. Scott Fitzgerald, *This Side of Paradise* (1920; repr., London: Penguin, 2000).

U James Joyce, *Ulysses* (1922), ed. Hans Walter Gabler (New York: Vintage Books, 1993).

Introduction

JAMES JOYCE AND THE IRISH REVOLUTION

> Revolutions never run on time.
>
> DANIEL BENSAÏD[1]

In Tom Stoppard's play *Travesties*, set in Zurich in 1917, a character asks James Joyce on his contribution to the Great War and receives the caustic response: "I wrote *Ulysses*. What did you do?"[2] When similar questions were raised of Joyce's contribution to the Irish revolution in the same period (1916–23), answers were sometimes provided by combatants themselves, most notably the veteran of the 1916 Easter Rising Desmond Ryan: "When Joyce wrote *Ulysses* he shook the world, and to many of us left the most eloquent prologue to the Irish revolution ever written."[3] "Prologue" refers to the fact that *Ulysses* is set in the Dublin of 1904, twelve years before the Rising, and Ryan is drawing attention to its capacity to depict a city, and a nation in general, on the verge of revolt. It is often forgotten that though magisterial in scope, Tolstoy's *War and Peace* (1869) was conceived as a prologue to a story set over a decade later, that of the Russian Decembrist revolt of 1825, when liberal revolutionaries, inspired by the ideals of Republican France, sought to overthrow the czarist regime. Tolstoy originally began work on a novel, *The Decembrists*, but soon left it aside to devote attention to the conditions that gave rise to the uprising in the first place, proposing to stop with "the first forewarning of the movement that led up to the events of 14 December 1825."[4] The magnitude of *War and Peace* provided that forewarning.

Joyce never set out to deal directly with Ireland in a time of war but was acutely conscious as he was writing *Ulysses* (1914–21/22) of the events that were transforming the country from which he had emigrated in 1904. "Coming events cast their shadows before" is a theme that runs through the novel, and Stephen Dedalus, taking his bearings in the National Library, allows his mind to drift through space and time in a distended present: "Hold to the now, the here, through which all future plunges to the past."[5] *Ulysses*, writes Paul K. Saint-Amour, "hints that a given present is constituted of other moods and tenses, including the past tense of memory, the future tense of prophecy, the future conditional of forecast, and the subjunctive moods of the counterfactual."[6] A conception of the present as a thin membrane barely separating past from future is also a feature of the Easter Rising, itself an act staging the conditions of its own legitimation in years to come. Though the Rising was proclaimed in the name of "the dead generations," its leaders looked to a future they were determined to bring about through the shock of the rebellion on public opinion: as Patrick Pearse remarked in the General Post Office (GPO), the headquarters of the Rising, in the midst of military bombardment: "When we are wiped out, people will blame us for everything, condemn us. . . . After a few years, they will see the meaning of what we tried to do."[7] It is striking that even with a mandate from the Dáil and the electorate for the Anglo-Irish Treaty in 1921–22, Michael Collins still looked to the future for vindication, seeing the settlement optimally as a stepping-stone toward an ultimate republic.[8] Writing in 1917 of the future orientation of literary work that preceded the Rising, the librarian and critic John Eglinton noted: "Mr James Joyce had not yet published his highly instructive studies in the life of those young men who have chiefly to be reckoned with nowadays in arranging or forecasting the future of Ireland."[9] Little did Eglinton realize that he would have a speaking part in this future, as Joyce was soon to write him into the "Scylla and Charybdis" chapter of *Ulysses*, set in the National Library where he worked.

In the Great War, the assault on the senses through the mass production of death induced a radical dissociation with the present, not only through "shell shock," sometimes characterized as male hysteria, but also through grief on an unprecedented scale that stopped time in its tracks for hundreds of thousands of families. In Dublin, the word "shock" first came into diagnostic use at the Richmond Asylum in the month following the Easter Rising "where the rebellion was deemed to be central to the presentation." In St. Patrick's Hospital, admissions at the height of the rebellion were also "produced by shock and terror caused by the Insurrection."[10] Unable to describe the sundering of time in trauma, psychologists and medical experts eventually drew on the newly coined lexicon of film practice, in particular, the jump-cut device of "flashback," to render intelligible sudden irruptions of the past in the present: "flashbacks were virtually nonexistent among veterans who fought before the age of film."[11] There may be a temptation to speculate which came first, the experience or the mode of representation, but both are interwoven to the extent that one does not fully make sense without the other.[12] Historians of psychology have traced versions of post-traumatic stress disorder (as shell shock came to be known) to the American Civil War, and even to Homer (where literary form is indistinguishable from mythic history).[13] Likewise, precursors of flashback techniques are found in literature and drama (again going back to Homer), recurring with increasing frequency as the nineteenth-century novel sought to address rapidly shifting landscapes of migration, the machine age, and urban life.[14] The point, however, is that traumatic experiences, whether at an individual or cultural level, involve problems of representation from the outset, and the relationship between the two—and the corresponding search for form—is part of the process itself.[15] This is bound up with the displacements of form under modernism, at once closing and yet opening (for nothing is complete) the gaps between experience and expression. According to Walter Benjamin, "It has always been one of the primary tasks of art to create a demand whose hour of full satisfaction has not yet come," and it is through *form* that art addresses unresolved pasts, and gestures toward futures, beyond the horizons of things as they are.[16] The birth of cinema is often attributed solely to technological innovations, but its stylistic signatures of crosscutting, panning and tracking shots, dissolves, close-ups, even rudiments of flashbacks, had already been introduced tentatively in theater and the novel, as noted by Sergei Eisenstein in his essay on anticipations of D. W. Griffith's film effects in Charles Dickens,[17] and migrated readily into the practice of writers like Joyce. This has important consequences for understanding how narrative forms, and particularly the disjunctive techniques of modernism, find their way from avant-garde practice into everyday life, becoming, in effect, "equipment for living" (in Kenneth Burke's phrase) in a rapidly disorienting world.[18] Avant-garde does not mean out of touch but *ahead* of its time: "The technological reproducibility of the artwork changes the relation of the masses to art," wrote Benjamin. "The extremely backward attitude toward a Picasso painting changes into a highly progressive reaction to a Chaplin film" (*BSW*, 4:264).

Though Joyce is often perceived as set apart from events in Ireland, in this book I try to show multiple points of intersection between the literary avant-garde and the Irish revolution. This is not to imagine Joyce on the barricades, or to read the 1916 Proclamation through the lens of *Ulysses* (though Raymond Queneau, as will be discussed below, wrote a surrealist novel to this effect), but rather to show the Ireland that created the "conscience" (*P*, 276) of Joyce's modernist sensibility was in many respects the same culture that produced the Easter Rising and the Irish revolution. On being asked by a French publication in 1918 to write about events in Ireland, Joyce demurred, making it clear he had no illusions about the challenges it presented to even his imaginative resources: "The problem of my race is so complicated that one needs to make use of all the means of an elastic art to delineate it—without solving it.... I am restricted to making a pronouncement on it by means of the scenes and characters of my poor art."[19] This allows for a possible answer to a question raised by Fredric Jameson: How did it come about that societies marked by "incomplete modernization" produced breakthrough works in modernism?[20] If, as will be seen, the modern epic extended beyond the imagined national community of the novel to address crises in empire that culminated in the Great War, so the scale of *Ulysses* is in keeping with an insurrection that was not a sideshow but intrinsic to the globalization of war, the Easter Rising setting a precedent in striking the first major blow for independence against the British empire. The first writer to introduce James Joyce to Russian readers, Douglas Goldring, visited Dublin in the aftermath of the Rising and embarked on an anti-imperialist novel, *The Fortune* (1917), objecting to the Great War against this backdrop: "when the first chapters were being written the Easter Week rebellion in Dublin, like forked lighting, illuminated the war's inky sky."[21] Extending his stay in Ireland, Goldring wrote in 1918 as news from Russia was also raising radical hopes: "At present it looks as if these two races, the Irish and Russians ... alone can save Europe. The attitude first of rage, then of bewilderment, finally of interest mixed with a certain respect, which has been the English attitude towards the Russia of Lenin and Trotsky, might, I believe, have been paralleled in the case of Ireland, but for its deceptive proximity and 'familiarity.'"[22] In this heady climate, it is not surprising that on hearing of the execution of the leaders of the rebellion, Cecil Spring-Rice, the English ambassador in Washington, DC, declared: "These shots signal the end of the British Empire," to which John Quinn, the American lawyer and art collector who had dealings with both Joyce and a number of the Rising leaders, added: "These will be the shots heard around the world."[23]

It is in this light that the Easter Rising may be redefined as a modern event, in contrast to traditional interpretations that reduce it to a futile gesture of Romantic Ireland, destined from the outset to take the eventual conservative turn of the new Free State. Realigning the revolution toward the modern extends its vision beyond mythic elements in the Celtic Revival inspired by Yeats and the Abbey Theatre, the Victorian Gael of Standish O'Grady, or the insular Catholic nationalism of faith and fatherland: "The political rebellion and even the cultural resurgence led by Yeats," as Seamus Deane notes, "seemed to Joyce insufficient (though notable) attempts on the part of the Irish to break from the psychological dependency that they manifested towards the British and the Roman imperiums."[24] The constellation of forces that drove the Irish revolution did not lend itself to conventional poetics or narrative form but to the heterogeneity of the modern epic. Some of the leading figures in the revolution feature (even if somewhat precociously) in *Ulysses*, such as Arthur Griffith and Roger Casement, and in a reciprocal movement, many advanced republicans looked to Joyce's writings to make sense of their own shattered worlds following the Irish Civil War (1922–23)—most notably, the guerrilla leader Ernie O'Malley as well as Desmond Ryan, Patrick's Pearse's closest confidant, but also many others discussed below with modernist tendencies who took part in the revolution. "The coincidence of Irish secession from the British Empire and the development of modernism," writes Nicholas Allen, was due in part to the open-ended nature of both projects: "The conditional unfinished spaces of the modernist novel or the abstract painting were an unfinished civil war that maintained the dissident energies of the revolutionary period into the new dispensation."[25] It is not surprising that many individuals of a modernist temperament faced with the suspension of the republic in the formation of the new Free State, looked to restructurings of narrative to disabuse them of any desire for easy resolutions, but the lack of closure tying up all the loose ends also meant that defeat need not give way to despair. The scale of *Ulysses* was part of this recuperative process for it helped to recast the Irish revolution in a wider international frame, viewing it in the light of the Great War, other anti-colonial movements, and the Paris Commune. This also extended to particular cultural responses to events in Ireland examined below, among them strands in British modernism relating to Ezra Pound, the Imagist movement, and Wyndham Lewis, and transatlantic influences on writers as diverse as F. Scott Fitzgerald, Marianne Moore, H. L. Mencken, W. E. B. Du Bois, Claude McKay, and others. Urban modernity—commodity relations, mass culture, the latest energy and transport technologies, and new configurations of time and space, state and society—informs both Joyce's work and the Irish revolution, leading writers such as Bertolt Brecht, Ernst Bloch, Alfred Döblin, Hermann Broch, and others to extol Joyce's avant-garde practice as challenging the stasis of the cultural consensus that presided over the global catastrophe of the Great War.

Though Marxist critics Georg Lukacs and Theodor Adorno disagreed radically on their responses to modernism, both agreed that "the truly social element of literature is its form."[26] It is in this sense that the Dublin of 1904 in *Ulysses* prefigures events taking place in Ireland during the later composition of the novel, Joyce's stylistic innovations registering what had not become manifest as content, but which was stirring beneath the surface calm of an ordinary day in June. Recalling his early acquaintance with the young Joyce, John Eglinton wrote that "forecasting" (as he described it above) was already under way,

> for his art seems to have found in this period the materials on which it was henceforth to work. Dublin was certainly at this moment a centre of vigorous potentialities. . . . Political agitation was holding back its energies for a favorable opportunity, while the organization of Sinn Féin was secretly ramifying throughout the country. There was hardly anyone at the time who did not believe that Ireland was on the point of some decisive transformation.[27]

Many of the formal breakthroughs in *Ulysses* lie in its capturing forces that were eddying in Irish society at the time in which it is set, but which only surfaced at the time of writing. Artistic form, by means of its autonomy, stands back from the present but does not step outside time: in what Adorno called "the recollection of the possible," it transcends the present to point toward alternative pasts, other futures.[28] This prospective hindsight is what distinguishes art from journalism even if, as in *Ulysses*, it simulates the accumulation of detail and (seemingly) random juxtaposition of items in a disposable daily newspaper. Art begins where the documentary archive leaves off, articulating areas of experience beyond present-day or conscious representation, whether through over-familiarity and lack of awareness, restricted codes, official silencing, or simply elusive by their nature—in short, areas deprived of permission to speak, notwithstanding the profusion of speech in everyday life. Understanding an artwork draws, of course, on the historical record and is contextualized by it, but its artistic value does not lie in what is known already, or what can be accessed by other means: it is concerned ultimately with what cannot be stated directly but which must be enacted in form. Commenting on blind spots in the self-images on an age, the historian Marc Bloch observed, "We are nevertheless successful in knowing far more of the past than the past had thought it good to tell us," and it is the task of the novel to address aspects that cannot be negotiated without attention to form or considerations of style.[29] No doubt letters, journals, and diaries also open up "backstage" experience, and the lived texture of public affairs lost in official documents or reports, but even at that, much of their ability to communicate with subsequent generations depends on the manner in which they invite reading skills and ways of knowing derived from artistic works.[30]

Keats's letters, as has been remarked, are works of art in themselves; Edmund Burke's *Reflections on the Revolution in France* (1790) was written as a letter to a correspondent in France and maintains this epistolary address in the published version. The interdependence of literature and history is clear in the meticulous attention paid to discernible real-life events in *Ulysses*, but is also evident in the recourse to modernist idioms in a number of diaries, memoirs, and autobiographical fiction of the period examined below, written under duress by participants in the Irish revolution such as Ernie O'Malley, Desmond Ryan, Kathleen Coyle, Frank Gallagher, and Joseph Campbell.[31]

As Joyce was bringing antiquity to bear on the modern epic, a contemporary, the art critic and collector Aby Warburg (1866–1929), was drawing on new directions in psychology and anthropology to suggest that aesthetic form provides not only connective tissue between art and antiquity, but also attends to what cannot be said, intractable issues in society not amenable to overt representation in the present. In his funeral address on Warburg's death in 1929, Ernst Cassirer observed: "Where others saw definite, circumscribed forms, where they saw forms in repose, he saw moving forces: he saw there what he termed the great 'emotive formulas' [*Pathosformel*] that Antiquity had created as an enduring legacy for mankind."[32] Warburg coined the term *Pathosformel*, "extremes of gestural and physiognomic expression, stylized in tragic sublimity," to convey the sense in which an emotional charge of the past surfaces in fragmented forms, outliving the built-in obsolescence of linear conceptions of progress.[33] As an example, he cited painterly aspects of Botticelli's *Birth of Venus* (1484–86) such as gestures, flowing drapes, and windblown hair, seemingly incidental to the story but which animate the still image, setting in motion reverberations from previous usages of similar forms in literary sources and antiquity.[34] For Warburg, suppressed pagan or Dionysian elements from the classical world found their way into works at a formal level, notwithstanding the content being governed by the ostensible Christian ethos of the era. In this, Warburg is picking up on what Carlo Ginzburg examined in a related context of Renaissance Italy, the clash of registers between state—or church—sanctioned orthodoxies and divergent profane or vernacular histories from below, often coming in at an angle.[35] Instead of form establishing order and cohesion in art, moreover, as in later ideals of neoclassicism, refractory elements upset surface composure, constituting, in Goethe's famous description of the *Laocoön*, "a frozen lightning bolt, a wave petrified at the very moment it was about to break on the shore."[36] For Warburg, lightning bolts in artistic terms were flashes of inspiration, discharges of latent cultural energy activated and transformed "by contact with the new age."[37] Where neoclassical critics such as Johann Winckelmann and G. E. Lessing looked for stasis, unity, and equilibrium in aesthetic form, exemplified by the powerful statue of *Laocoön* unearthed from antiquity, Warburg saw the dynamism of the statue as unearthed in a different sense, charged with pent-up energies of emotion and pain exceeding the constraints of its particular moment.[38] Carried over from other works and extending beyond conscious influences, such forms are concentrates of time that have risked being lost in oblivion, functioning as *symptoms* rather than signs, "revealed through *the intensity generated by a displacement.*"[39] In his symptomatic readings, Warburg was laying the ground for what became a truism in the age of psychoanalysis: that the meaning of a work is not confined to intentions or conscious deliberations but is also relayed through complexities of form, the material qualities of style and medium in their cultural milieus—in Georges Didi-Huberman's formulation, "a transindividual notion of the psychological in the study of images within a cultural field."[40] For the Portuguese modernist writer Fernando Pessoa, this was the condition of *Ulysses* itself: "Even the sensuality of Ulysses is a symptom of intermediation. It is an hallucinatory delirium—the kind treated by psychiatrists—presented as an end in itself."[41]

The kaleidoscopic picture in *Ulysses* of a city at odds with its imperial fate is effected through dynamic and, to many contemporaries, bewildering experiments in form. There are certain writers, wrote Joyce, who address not only unknown aspects of "human consciousness" but also "the more questionable virtue of embodying in themselves the thousand conflicting tendencies of their age, of turning themselves into, so to speak, storage batteries of the new energy."[42] As with Warburg, imaginative power is conceived of in electrical terms, as, in effect, stored lightning in the idioms of *Finnegans Wake*, "where flash becomes word" (*FW*, 267.12): "This bolt in hand be my worder" (*FW*, 483.16). In keeping with Warburg, moreover, the capacity of artistic form to act as a conductor is connected to shell shock—"Shallburn Shock" (*FW*, 377.7)—and trauma, as in the association of lightning with electrical ("allucktruckall") transport and tram conductors: "The lewdningbluebolteredallucktruckalltraumconductor!" (*FW*, 378.9–10).[43] Though relayed in literature, these charged forms of storage—as in the case of flashbacks noted above—extend beyond artworks to lay the grounds for new structures of experience required by rapid, and often disconcerting, changes in society. The narrative device of stream of consciousness comes into play here, at one level an innovation in literary style but also a term used by William James in psychology to capture the flow of thought in everyday life.[44] Notwithstanding its semblance of normalcy, however, it emerged as a literary technique to catch minds thrown off balance, or "occasional states of mind of normal individuals bordering on obsession or delirium."[45] As Stephen Greenblatt notes of a passage in Shakespeare's *Julius Caesar* (1599), one of the earliest recourses to inner life in drama capturing Brutus's "molten state of consciousness" as he resolves finally to murder Caesar, the assassin likens his thoughts "to a little kingdom" which "suffers then / The nature of an insurrection."[46]

According to Paul K. Saint-Amour, "*Ulysses* is the stream that forks around the [Easter] Rising, lapping along both its leading and its trailing shores," as its techniques were deployed by many combatants to make sense of events, both during and after the revolution.[47] There may be no real contradiction here between normal and extreme situations, for the shock value of *Ulysses*, according to Mary Colum, suggested a different zone than the Celtic Twilight, "a method of revealing the subconscious and the twilight stage between the conscious and the unconscious."[48] The reactions of many early readers to what goes through the mind of Stephen, and of Leopold and Molly Bloom, bore out its interpretation as a response to the jolts of modern life, quite apart from the particular shadows of loss and grief thrown across the pages of Joyce's novel. When Umberto Eco questions the image of a stream conveying a smooth flow of impressions, and instead pictures the mind as a screen registering "stimuli that bombard it from all directions," it is uncannily appropriate for characters that walk through a city center facing demolition in just over a decade.[49] One of those who walked through the streets in the immediate aftermath of the Rising was, as noted above, Douglas Goldring, intent on writing the war episodes of his novel *The Fortune*: "such intellectual stimulation as he received during his stay," writes Guy Woodward, "perhaps accounts for the heightened intensity of the second half of *The Fortune*, which he completed in Dublin," and which drew praise from T. S. Eliot, among others.[50]

The motto "God is in the details," favored by Warburg, could have been enunciated with *Ulysses* in mind, not only in its elliptical links with *The Odyssey* but also its attention to the ephemera of everyday life.[51] The reference points here are Sigmund Freud's critical psychopathology—the seemingly throwaway accidents or "parapraxes" through which the unconscious reveals itself—and the diagnosis of hysteria conducted by Freud's teacher Jean-Martin Charcot (1825–1893), whose symptomatic readings of bodily gestures and poses provided the basis of his clinical practice.[52] The dynamics of form for Warburg has more to do with the arc of a gesture than aesthetic repose, and a similar animation of structure through rhythm is envisaged by Stephen Dedalus in *Ulysses*: "So that gesture, not music not odour, would be a universal language, the gift of tongues rendering visible not the lay sense but the first entelechy, the structural rhythm"

(*U*, 15.106–9). In hysteria, what is not admitted to the mind is lodged in the body, and experiences that prove recalcitrant to language or signs reemerge as symptoms, expressions all the more charged on account of their displacement. "It might be maintained," Freud wrote, "that a case of hysteria is a caricature of a work of art," for in each case, the material form of the sign becomes the vehicle for what cannot find expression by more direct means.[53] Hence "the return in the image of something that has been repressed": what is muted as content comes back as form.[54] The paralysis or "hemiplegia" associated with hysteria was an abiding concern in Joyce's writing from the first story in *Dubliners*, "The Sisters," and his sustained artistic endeavor can be seen as putting words on a culture, as Freud said of hysterics, that "suffers from reminiscences," or in Joyce's own words, "a batlike soul waking to the consciousness of itself in darkness and secrecy and loneliness" (*P*, 239–40).

It is striking that Joyce continually speaks of paralysis as both an individual and cultural malaise: indeed, its cultural expression, due to the control of church and state, prevents the development of a private sphere as the preserve of the individual and domestic life: "The economic and intellectual conditions of his homeland do not permit the individual to develop.... Individual initiative has been paralyzed by the influence and admonitions of the church, while the body has been shackled by peelers, duty officers and soldiers" (*OCPW*, 123). Joyce's readiness to apply medical terminology relating to hysteria—"paralysis," "hemiplegia"—to the Ireland of his day is not simply a recourse to analogy on his part, but a more profound reading of the pathologies of social life in a period of acute political breakdown. Joyce's familiarity with this terminology was given a more precise focus by his study of medicine, which at one point he had contemplated briefly as a career, and in particular by his acquaintance with the writings of Dr. George Sigerson (1836–1925), whose biology classes he attended while at the National University.[55] Sigerson, by means of his poetry and translations from Irish over several decades, was a leading figure in the Revival but in his professional career was a neuroscientist of international standing, with his English translation of Charcot's major work, *Lectures on the Diseases of the Nervous System* (1877, 1881) and his own contributions to medical journals establishing his reputation as an authority on nervous disorders such as hysteria and paralysis.[56] Sigerson attended Charcot's courses on pathology in Paris in 1873, just before the arrival of a more famous student, Sigmund Freud, and his friendship with Charcot led to the great neuroscientist visiting the Sigerson family home at 4 Clare Street, Dublin, during his stay in Ireland in 1879, while Sigerson in turn visited the Charcots in Paris.[57] Charcot acted as Sigerson's referee in his pursuit of a hospital appointment, but as J. B. Lyons points out, Sigerson's rise in the medical profession in Ireland was greatly hampered by his political persona as one of the most articulate liberal champions of the nationalist cause in the late nineteenth century. When Charcot wrote to Sigerson at one point, seeking his views on "agitation," he made it clear that it was not hysterical fits he was interested in but rather the political agitations convulsing Ireland during the Land War (1879–91). As Sigerson himself expressed the relation between the two:

> Nations sometimes suffered from diseases, and required remedies not less by the surgeon's knife than by the mental or intellectual aid of the physician. When that great patient—one's country—suffered, let it not be accounted odd that the physician took part in what he considered his duty to relieve pain, to heal wounds, to cultivate hope and assure her of a happy future.[58]

The connection between hysteria and history in the Land War is picked up in *Finnegans Wake*—"Hystorical" (*FW*, 564.31)—in relation to the assassination of Chief Secretary Cavendish and Under Secretary Burke in the Phoenix Park by members of the secret society the Invincibles in 1882. Charles Stewart Parnell ("pimparnell") was falsely implicated in the conspiracy by the London *Times* but in keeping with Joyce's investing the Phoenix Park in the Fingal district of Dublin with Irish historical links to the ancient Phoenicians (discussed below) and the invention of letters, pagan (i.e., pre–St. Patrick) ascriptions of language to trees and standing stones in ancient Gaelic Ogham writing bear witness to (or eavesdrop on) the primal scene in *Finnegans Wake*:

> A scarlet pimparnell now mules the mound where anciently first murders were wanted to take root. By feud fionghalian. Talkingtree and sinningstone stay on either hand. Hystorical leavesdroppings may also be garnered up with sir Shamus Swiftpatrick, Archfieldchaplain of Saint Lucan's. (*FW*, 564.28–33)

In the absence of a functioning private sphere in Ireland, the civilizing process in Britain and mainland Europe that siphoned off the emotional excesses of carnival and vernacular culture into the confines of the home, often to reemerge as individual hysterical symptoms, was not tenable. There was no shortage of control of the body, as Joyce avers, but discipline was not maintained by a Puritan inner self but by the more overt policing of church and state. As a number of recent scholars have argued, following the pioneering analyses of Norbert Elias and Mikhail Bakhtin, the nineteenth century witnessed the culmination of concerted efforts by liberal reformers to purge vernacular culture of its festive or carnivalesque elements, and to release prospective citizens and rational subjects from dependence on what were considered grotesque communal rituals.[59] Through fragmentation, marginalization, sublimation, and suppression, traditional practices involving bodily excesses such as feasting, violence, drinking, processions, fairs, wakes, superstition, rowdy spectacles, and so on were brought under scientific observation and subjected to systematic social regulation. These controlling mechanisms sought not so much to eliminate the practices as to sanitize and refine them, in particular redirecting and privatizing the sexual energies associated with carnival within more manageable domestic spaces. The often macabre raw material of Grimms' fairy tales, staples of folklore among the German peasantry, migrated to the nursery and the child's imagination, to "old wives' tales," or else were relegated as archaic survivals to the remote periphery. The difficulty with Ireland was that, notwithstanding its advanced modernity at several levels, the whole country was a remote periphery in imperial eyes, subject to hysterical symptoms that had not been interiorized and which thus continued to circulate in the public arena.

Much of the animus against superstition and irrationality directed by liberal reformers at medieval survivals found its ultimate bogey in the Catholic Church and the affront presented by its mystique and credulity to the march of intelligence. It is not surprising, therefore, that the Irish were considered to be in particular need of rational enlightenment, if they were to take their place in the modern world. Writing from Trinity College, Dublin, the eminent historian W. E. H. Lecky drew a character sketch of his country, preceded by an image of barely literate priests and monks "flitting to and fro among the mud hovels":

> In the absence of industrial and intellectual life, and under the constant pressure of sufferings that draw men to the unseen world, Catholicism acquired an almost undivided empire over the affections and imaginations of the [Irish] people. The type of religion was grossly superstitious. It consecrated that mendicancy which was one of the worst evils of Irish life. Its numerous holidays aggravated the natural idleness of the people. It had no tendency to form those habits of self-reliance, those energetic political and industrial virtues in which the Irish character was and is lamentably deficient; but it filled the imagination with wild and beautiful legends, it purified domestic life, it raised the standard of female honour, it diffused abroad a deep feeling of content and resignation in extreme poverty . . . which

has preserved it from at least some of the worst vices that usually accompany social convulsions and great political agitations on the Continent.[60]

Lecky's confidence that Ireland would escape social agitations proved unfounded, but it is not too difficult to see in his diagnosis outlines of the forces that convulsed Ireland from the Land War of the 1880s to the Anglo-Irish War and Civil War period. As the author of the highly successful *History of the Rise and Influence of the Spirit of Rationalism in Europe* (1865), Lecky's ambitious attempt to demonstrate the triumph of reason over irrationality and to secularize the public sphere exerted enormous influence on European contemporaries, not least the young Freud.[61] According to William McGrath, it may indeed have been Freud's reading of Lecky that first stimulated his interest in hysteria.[62] Though Freud persisted at one level in construing nervous disorders as the result of purely individual problems, his early psychological researches were part of a general European movement, spearheaded by Charcot, that applied scientific, medical explanations to hitherto inexplicable forms of social and religious behavior. This intellectual trend was aligned to a wider political project that sought to liberalize society by challenging the influence of religion, and particularly the Catholic Church, in schools, hospitals, and other areas of public life. The irony once more of social reform in Ireland was that whereas the Catholic Church was the main target of progressive movements in metropolitan Europe, and of the rationalizing project of reformers such as Lecky, the task of modernizing Irish society after the Great Famine fell onto the Catholic Church and a debilitated middle class, both coming out from under the shadows of the Famine and centuries of colonial rule.

Hysteria represented vividly the manner in which forms of impropriety that "had been excluded at the level of social identity (the 'symbolic') returned at the level of subjective articulation, as both phobia and fascination, in the individual patient."[63] Displaced energies also found their way into other errant forms, particularly those concerned with the art of indirection itself—literature, visual culture, and the performing arts: "the *exclusion* necessary to the formation of social identity at level one is simultaneously a *production* at the level of the Imaginary."[64] It is not too difficult to discern in this the conditions that give rise to artistic forms, akin to Warburg's *Pathosformel*, that resisted evolutionary schemes of progress, acting more, in Didi-Huberman's words, as cross-currents in which different eras ebb and flow across the centuries: "No longer imaginable as an unbroken river, where accruals are carried from up- to downstream, tradition should, after Warburg, be conceived as a tense dialectic, a drama that unfolds between the river's flow and its whirling eddies."[65] As the Renaissance engagement with "the 'posthumous life' of pagan culture" demonstrates,[66] the clash of Christian and pagan influences attests to disruption in history, "a play of 'pauses' and 'crises,' of 'leaps' and 'periodic reversions,' that together form, not a narrative account of the history in question, but a web of memory—not a succession of artistic facts, but a theory of symbolic complexity."[67] By narrative here is meant the well-plotted story of the conventional novel but of course, as Warburg and his protégés were writing, and as Didi-Huberman recounts elsewhere, narrative itself was undergoing fundamental changes in the early twentieth century, not least in terms of the crises, leaps, and montage used by Joyce in *Ulysses* to bring Christian, classical, and Irish pasts into the modern world.[68]

Crises in representation, whether political or aesthetic, arise when maps no longer fit the territory and are unable to chart underlying shifts, at first barely discernible but eventually shaking the foundations of the social order. One of the most trenchant critiques of *Ulysses* was directed by Wyndham Lewis at the novel's propensity to dissolve matter, the apparent stillness and solidity of objects belying forces that opened the ground under one's feet, much as Stephen Dedalus sinks under the weight of his own meditations on Sandymount strand in the "Proteus" chapter of *Ulysses*. Taking issue with the tendency of historians to believe that "the *sole possible form* of historical narration was that used in the English novel as it had developed in the late nineteenth century," Hayden White questions why, in relation to the new century, narrative techniques "uniformly eschew the techniques of literary representation which Joyce, Yeats and Ibsen have contributed to modern culture."[69] It is not only writing that is at stake here but pictures of society by which people are held captive at a given time, and, in opposition to these, dissident forms (akin to Joyce's "poor art") that challenge or dispel these pictures "given to the imaginary, dominated by the actual," in Seamus Deane's phrase.[70] The modern epic, wrote Walter Benjamin, "used montage to turn daily life into its ally," an activity that "explodes the framework of the novel, bursts its limits both stylistically and structurally" to take effect in street culture, the material texture of the city "rain[ing] down on the text."[71]

To consider history as narrative in these circumstances is not to tell the story after the event, but to see it emplotted in history *as it is lived*, the stories through which people—"as both teller and actor (or agent and character)"—make sense of their lives.[72] To be sure, history is not a text but what lies "outside" the text, yet this is not to say it is inchoate and unfathomable, devoid of form: if "the case histories I write should read like short stories," Freud noted of his studies on hysteria, this is because "the nature of the subject is evidently responsible for this, rather than any preference of my own."[73] Insofar as the present is informed by the past and opens onto the future, experiences and actions assume narrative form, or rather many disparate or contesting narratives, as some are in more of a position to gain adherence than others.[74] These are not necessarily of people's own making but even if, as Marx asserted, they represent the ruling ideas of a society, they are not omniscient or omnipotent: they do not close off other histories, still less stories relegated to the margins of society or the political underworld. However obvious ways of life at a given time may seem to contemporaries (including views on class, race, gender, and religion), they are contingent on power structures, and open to change in the future: when this happens, "it is not as if a story was being imposed on or invented for events that originally had none, rather events that were lived in terms of one story are now seen as part of another."[75] This was the position of the abject loyalty to colonial rule in early twentieth-century Ireland, and as life seemed to unfold at the leisurely pace of a Victorian novel, it is not surprising that insurgent politics coincided with the emergence of dissonant narrative forms, seen to telling effect in *A Portrait of the Artist as a Young Man*, *Ulysses*, and other works more directly related to the revolution examined below. Joyce's determination to have *Portrait* published in 1916 (even if it just managed to make the deadline, issuing a few copies on December 29) ensured reception of his work was coupled in reviews, initially by Ezra Pound, with Thomas MacDonagh's *Literature in Ireland* (1916), the posthumous publication of one of the executed leaders of the Rising.

At a political level, a contrast between myth and event—what J. M. Synge colorfully described as the "gap between a gallous story and a dirty deed"—opens up dramatically in the case of the Easter Rising.[76] Backlit by the Celtic Twilight, Romantic Ireland and visionary messianism inspired perceptions of a "poet's rebellion" but do not account for the modernity of the event. "Today," Marc Bloch wrote during the Second World War, "even in the most spontaneous and voluntary testimonies, what the text tells us no longer constitute the primary object of attention."[77] As Carlo Ginzburg elaborates, this presents "the possibility of isolating within voluntary testimony an involuntary deeper core," a task for which the skills of art/literary criticism are preeminently suited to read between the lines of history: "By digging into the text, against the intentions of whoever produced them, uncontrolled voices can be made to emerge."[78] Among the "uncontrolled voices" driving the Irish revolution were Fenian republicanism, the class politics of a Labour movement mobilizing under James Larkin and James Connolly in the wake of the 1913 Dublin Lock-Out, the rise of internationalism and anti-imperial sentiments in protest against the Great War, the challenging of patriarchal gender roles by Cumann na mBan and the Suffragette cause, collective energies organizing nationwide under the Co-operative movement, and, not least, the urban mise-en-scène of colonial Dublin itself, linked arterially, as shown in Joyce's fiction, to a countryside poised between the end of the Land War and the outbreak of armed insurrection.[79] The rebellion cannot be identified with any one of these: the point is that only accounts riven with heterogeneity could address the complexity of such events. As Emer Nolan notes, "The theatricality of the Rebellion may have signaled its success as modernist artifice," but whereas *Ulysses'* formal innovations found lasting expression in literary form, the Easter Rising and the War of Independence, though setting a precedent for other challenges to empire, failed to live up to their radical potential, settling for a confessional state that was precisely the target of Joyce's satirical vision.[80]

That montage effects are not confined to art but work through history itself throws into relief Stephen Dedalus's pronouncement that history "is a nightmare from which I am trying to awake" (*U*, 2.377). This is often cited without attending to its implication that history may call for types of reading applied to the latent and manifest forces of "dream-work" in psychoanalysis, or to the psychopathology of social life.[81] One of the more insightful turns in early twentieth-century political philosophy was an extension of psychopathology to symptoms, inhibitions, and repressions of the body politic, and slippages in masks of power—pathology itself bearing witness to the word "pathos."[82] In Daniel Bensaïd's words, "revolutionary theory has something in common with psychoanalysis" and thus with mechanisms of repression akin to those of the psyche: "Political class struggle is not the superficial mirroring of an essence [i.e., the power relations of a system]. Articulated like a language, it operates by displacements and condensations of social contradictions. It has its dreams, its nightmares and its lapses."[83] It is precisely breaks in the pattern, "the politics of the improbable event," that ensures existing narratives lose their claim to normality, just as happened in Ireland in the aftermath of the Easter Rising.[84] By the same token, as against faithfully reproducing reality, what Joyce termed the "[c]racked lookingglass of a servant" (*U*, 1.155) holds up a more revealing mirror to the nation, displaying the "crises, leaps" and fissures in society prized open in revolutionary moments. As in the layers of meaning in works of art, revolutions look not only to the future but also build on displaced strata in society, the cast-offs of sedimented traditions and habits of authority consolidated over centuries.

Considered in this light, the relation of Homer's *Odyssey* to Joyce's

Ulysses is not one of mere analogy, or a model on which to base a contemporary story, but is better understood as the interplay of forms and motifs deposited through the ages, *Pathosformeln* in literary terms, drawing on what Joyce termed "the broken lights of Irish myth" (*P*, 195). As will be seen in chapter 6 below, *Ulysses* weaves a complex web of texts and cultural crossings bearing on narratives as various as Ireland's being the original of Calypso's isle at the edge of the Homeric world; fables of Ireland as founded by the Phoenicians; the reimagining of Odysseus as a Phoenician in Victor Bérard's revisionist account of *The Odyssey* admired by Joyce; or views of Ireland as a second Troy—all making for vestigial forms mediating Irish cultural links to classical antiquity, Africa, and, in the process, world literature. The resuscitation of the epic is bound up with this, addressing a modernity whose unsettling of life as portrayed in the bourgeois novel culminated in the mass destruction of war and crisis of empire in the early twentieth century. If the ocean was the basis of the classical epic, the global expansion of the world economy required, in Benjamin's terms, "the reinforcement of radical epic" to extend the national boundaries of the novel, a process facilitated by Ireland's precarious position in the imperial order.[85]

Bakhtin's concept of "chronotope" is helpful at this point in understanding the complex relations between literary form and society: "a literary work's artistic unity in relation to an actual reality is defined by its chronotope," writes Bakhtin. "That is, we get a mutual interaction between the world represented in the work and the world outside the work."[86] As experiments in fictive worlds answer to the pressures placed on them by recognizable shifts in social relations, these historical forms are also redefined in the process. When the cerebral Stephen Dedalus imagines "[a] very short space of time through very short times of space" (*U*, 3.11–12) in "Proteus," he is questioning the separation of space and time in Newtonian physics but also the aesthetic theory of G. E. Lessing's *Laocoön*, which clearly demarcated word from image, and movement (time) from stillness (space). Stephen has Lessing's treatise in mind as he walks the strand, but its thesis that images can only be realized in spatial terms, and narrative in time, is contested by Joyce, not only in the person of Stephen, who is aware of these categories, but also in new emplotments of space and time on the streets and in the lives of ordinary individuals. One chapter in *Ulysses* ostensibly mapped in space, "Wandering Rocks," is conceived in visual terms as an exercise in parallel action or simultaneity, but the crosscutting does not quite keep pace with the action, and throws conceptions of both place and the present into doubt.[87] Maps of sites of military conflict during the Easter Rising resemble the dispersal of action in "Wandering Rocks," and it is striking, as will be shown in chapter 3 below, how strategies of urban warfare such as street barricades blocking linear progression, and tunneling through buildings facilitating lateral, clandestine movements, enact the displacements of both time and place under modernism.

As Stephen imagines "walking into eternity along Sandymount strand" (*U*, 3.18–19), the most pedestrian movements provide glimpses of futures emanating from unrequited pasts. Setting out from the north side of Dublin in *Portrait*, Stephen's "morning walk across the city had begun, and he foreknew that as he passed the sloblands of Fairview" (*P*, 190) his mind would summon the shades of Cardinal Newman, Cavalcanti, Ibsen, and Ben Jonson: as Camille Bourniquel describes it, "These labyrinths of streets, dead ends, and vague territories have been used by Joyce ... with strange foreknowledge, as if he understood, in a kind of prophetic vision of Dublin, how to join the myths of the past with the eternal journeyings of Stephen Dedalus and Leopold Bloom."[88] Similar sentiments were echoed by the republican activist and writer Dorothy Macardle in her poem "The City," written in response to the ruins of Dublin following the Easter Rising: "There is memory in the stones, / And prophecy in the shadows; the houses know, — / They know but they are dumb, — / Things were dreamed in the city ages ago, / And things will come."[89]

For Benjamin, the present in such circumstances is better conceived as "now-time" (*Jetztzeit*), in which reactivated pasts open onto new futures, as in the "optical unconscious" of the camera that picks up on the inadvertent detail, "the inconspicuous spot where in the immediacy of that long-forgotten moment the future rests so eloquently."[90] It is no coincidence that contingency in *Ulysses*, the throwaway handout announcing "Elijah is coming" (*U*, 8.14), is cast in the shadow of the future, as is the horse "Throwaway" running the same day in the Ascot Gold Cup. Bantam Lyons misinterprets Bloom's use of the term discarding his newspaper—"I was just going to throw it away" (*U*, 5.537)—as the name of the horse on the racing page, imagining it as a surefire tip, and when the horse wins, he calls on Bloom's powers again to look into the future: "Prophesy who will win the Saint Leger" (*U*, 15.1840).[91]

Writing of the persistence of memory in Joyce, Shiv Kumar has noted how the past is all too present: "Stephen and Bloom do not go, like Proust's Marcel, in search of a lost time: memory is co-extensive with their perceptions, manifesting itself in a thousand elusive forms. It may be said that *memoire involontaire* is a permanent aspect of their mental processes, and it's rarely that they have to evoke past images by a deliberate effort of the will."[92] Nowhere is the working of involuntary memory as an ethical resource more evident than in bringing our own moral histories (however buried) to bear on the present, altering both in the process.[93] In the moving classroom sequence in "Nestor," Stephen initially looks askance at the miserable boy Cyril Sargent unable to complete his school exercises: "His thick hair and scraggy neck gave witness of unreadiness and through his misty glasses weak eyes looked up pleading. On his cheek, dull and bloodless, a soft stain of ink lay, dateshaped, recent and damp as a snail's bed" (U, 2.124–27). Yet no sooner has Stephen reflected on the plight of the hapless pupil than he remembers even an "[u]gly and futile" boy could elicit material love: "someone had loved him, borne him in her arms and in her heart. But for her the race of the world would have trampled him underfoot, a squashed boneless snail. She had loved his weak watery blood drained from her own. Was that then real? The only true thing in life?" (U, 2.140–43). Universal as these sentiments are, Stephen's awareness of *Amor matris* is prompted by memories of his own past (perhaps recalling the bullying and injustices he suffered at Clongowes): "Like him was I, these sloping shoulders, this gracelessness. My childhood bends beside me. Too far for me to lay a hand there once or lightly. Mine is far and his secret as our eyes. Secrets, silent, stony sit in the dark palaces of both our hearts: secrets weary of their tyranny: tyrants, willing to be dethroned" (U, 2.168–73). Aspects of maternal bonding, a capacity to love with candor and without illusions, informs Joyce's attachment to Dublin as viewed by Desmond Ryan in his memoir, *Remembering Sion* (1934), discussed in chapter 9, a love shorn of the sentimentalism of popular romances in "Nausicaa" but all the more enduring for that. As in the ghost's injunction to "remember me" in *Hamlet*, Bloom's compassion for both his dead father and son is also summoned by memory, and the revenant of Stephen's dying mother gives birth to the ethical impulse of conscience itself, "Agenbite of inwit": "She is drowning. Agenbite. Save her. Agenbite" (U, 10.875).

In "Cyclops," the connection between Roger Casement's Irishness (he would have been known primarily as a British diplomat in 1904) and his humanitarian responses to atrocities in the Belgian Congo is underpinned by historical affiliations between Ireland and Africa, dating back to the ancient Phoenicians in Joyce's writing. If the best way of doing justice to the past is to treat it as an object lesson for the present, these pivotal crossings inform Casement's indictment of "crimes against humanity" (and his being one of the first to use that term in human rights discourse). For Casement, "In these lonely Congo forests where I found Leopold, I found also myself, an incorrigible Irishman," and it is clear from this that an encounter with the other instills or activates a moral awareness within.[94] Casement's refusal to separate his universalist humanitarianism from his political allegiances led to his execution following the Easter Rising, an unwitting demonstration that the threat presented by the Rising was international as well as national in scale. The understanding of aesthetic form in Adorno and Warburg is akin to this ethical stance: though grounded in a particular cultural moment, it is not confined to it, and by means of "an exemplary universalism, typical of the realm of aesthetics," transcends its immediate local contexts.[95] Just as the reverberations of the Easter Rising were felt in decades to come in the post-colonial world, so also *Ulysses* spoke "through the core of the local" to literatures emerging from their own marginalization, serving as "inspiration for writers who have put Istanbul, St. Lucia, New Delhi or Tokyo as their own centres, and from these have ventured out onto the wider stage of world literature without losing a sense of their place or origin."[96]

According to Æ (or "A.E.," as Joyce writes it) in *Ulysses*, "Any object, intensely regarded, may be a gate of access to the incorruptible eon of the gods" (*U*, 14.1166–67). Though no Prometheus, the god of revolution, the Joyce of *Ulysses* was, according to Ernst Bloch, closer to Proteus, the god of metamorphosis, who presides over a world (and a chapter in the novel) in which things that appear fixed and immutable undergo constant change.[97] Storytellers in the premodern world told stories in an environment "that showed hardly any trace of rupture; [and in which] the social hierarchy was fixed and apparently stable," whereas the present age no longer "emits the false luster of an *ordo sempiternus rerum* (eternal order of things)."[98] For Bloch, the task of modernism is to dispel an "idealistic and rhetorical totalization of the world":

> It was Joyce, above all, who provided the means of engagement here . . . [who] reveals objective "misspellings," as well as objective montage, wherein distantly related things are no longer viewed as being fixed in place, susceptible to an orderly arrangement for the purpose of [realist] representation. This no doubt, entails a collapse of some sort, and honest depiction of the rubbish piles.[99]

On this reading, *Ulysses* might be seen as reassembling Dublin from the rubbish piles of the Easter Rising, not just in architectural terms (as Joyce liked to envisage, half in jest) but from the point of view of a nation whose epic had still be written. In Joyce's play *Exiles* (1918), the character Richard Rowan (based on the author himself) returns to Dublin and reads an account in a national newspaper welcoming his being called back to Ireland "on the eve of her longawaited victory." To which his confidante Beatrice answers: "You see, Mr Rowan, your day has dawned at last."[100]

❋ 1 ❋
"Old Haunts"

PHOTOGRAPHIC MEMORY, MOTION,
AND THE REPUBLIC OF LETTERS

> Mr Bloom is a very live person, and in his company we wander about the streets of Dublin seeing the Ireland of 1904, the bleak, shiftless, sordid, soulless Ireland that came to an end catastrophically in 1916.
>
> EIMAR O'DUFFY, "'Ulysses,' by James Joyce" (1922)[1]

Memoirs of James Joyce abound with stories of how guests from Dublin were subjected to endless interrogations about the city, or to astonishing feats of recall by Joyce of the buildings and streets he had left behind. "When any visitors came over from Dublin," Mary Colum wrote, "he would invite them to dinner at a restaurant: he was so happy when any Dubliner understood his work and liked it, especially if he was a nonliterary personage":

> Once when we were in a café in Montmartre, a Dubliner who recognized my husband [the well-known Irish writer Padraic Colum] came over and spoke to him. He was over in Paris to attend a football match between an Irish and a French team ... like many Dubliners he was soaked in *Ulysses* though he made no pretence of literary sophistication. Immediately we knew he was the very type Joyce would like, and I telephoned to ask if we might bring him round. Joyce was alone in his apartment; it was Sunday and the family had gone somewhere. "Bring him right over." The Dublin citizen was dazzled but he was delighted to come. What particularly fascinated Joyce was that this guest belonged to a family of old Dublin glassmakers, the Pughs, and represented an item he wanted for *Finnegans Wake*; the careful reader can find it there. He handed a copy of *Ulysses* to the guest and asked him to read a chapter out loud in the accent of a lower quarter of the city, the Coombe. The visitor produced something that enchanted

Joyce and showed that he must have read parts of *Ulysses* out loud many times and could reproduce the exact low-down accent necessary for this particular episode. Joyce, obviously delighted, felt that here was a simple citizen for whom *Ulysses* was a national masterpiece.[2]

Adding to this account in the memoir *Our Friend James Joyce* (coauthored with Padraic Colum), Mary Colum noted that it was—not surprisingly—the "Cyclops" chapter of *Ulysses* that lent itself to the performance: "After a while Joyce handed the Dubliner a copy of *Ulysses*. Selecting the barroom episode, Mr Pugh read from it with an accent so low-down that the very speech of the collector of bad debts who relates the episode came into the Paris apartment. As if put to the challenge, Joyce remarked: 'I can read in a more low-down accent than that.'"[3]

The importance of Joyce's visitor, Thomas W. Pugh (1883–1968), in striking a Dublin note did not end with a Coombe accent. During his visit Mary Colum related how "Joyce and his visitor soon got talking of haunts they had frequented in Dublin. 'What sort of person really knows Dublin?' my husband asked. Mr Pugh answered categorically: 'The man that knocks about.' The creator of Mr Bloom was sure he was right."[4] That Pugh knocked about in a more than casual fashion is clear from his being perhaps the first to follow systematically in the footsteps of Bloom and Stephen Dedalus, compiling the earliest photographic record of key locations in *Ulysses*. Joyce requested Pugh to forward his photographs for a circular devised by the American publishers of the book: "My American publisher would like to have for a circular he publishes some photographs of scenes mentioned in *Ulysses* so I wonder if you would consent to have some of yours reproduced? I remember [Barney] Kiernan's but he would also like to have the Martello Tower (Sandycove), Holles Street Hospital and the view of the Strand at Sandymount showing the Star of the Sea Church."[5] It is unclear from this whether Joyce had actually seen the pictures by then (is it the original Barney Kiernan's he remembers, or Pugh's photograph of it?) but within a few weeks, copies of the photographs were with Joyce, accompanied by a thank-you note from Pugh for a copy of an early sequence from *Finnegans Wake*, published as *The Mime of Mick, Nick and the Maggies*.[6]

Joyce's request for accurate photographs was at odds with the unfortunate illustrations that accompanied the original Random House fold-out brochure published in January 1934, *How to Enjoy James Joyce's "Ulysses,"* designed to make the novel more accessible to readers. In this misguided brochure, an ancient round tower at Glendalough was used to illustrate the Martello Tower of the Napoleonic era at Sandycove, accompanied

"Old Haunts"   23

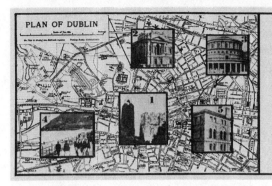

FIG. 1.1 "Plan of Dublin" from *How to Enjoy James Joyce's "Ulysses"* (1934). Random House brochure displaying mistaken images of (1) "Round Tower" for Martello Tower, Sandycove, and (4) "The Beach," depicting Bray promenade as Sandymount beach. Photograph: Private collection.

by the text: "ROUND TOWER (Part 1, Chapter 1) like the one where Stephen Dedalus and Buck Mulligan have breakfast," while a picture of citizens strolling on Bray promenade, in County Wicklow, was used to illustrate "THE BEACH: Dublin Bay (Chapter 13) where Bloom goes to rest from his day's wanderings." One can only imagine Joyce's bemusement when this reached him, not to mention his dismay on discovering that Random House has mistakenly used Samuel Roth's inaccurate copy of *Ulysses*, pirated in 1927, on which to base the otherwise beautifully designed first popular edition. One week after sending his request to Pugh, Joyce wrote to his son, Giorgio: "I had a reply from Mr Pugh in Dublin. For some weeks now I have been hoping to have a series of six authentic photographs which could be substituted for photographs of the present day. Matisse telephoned me this morning from Paris for some details. I gave them to him and I am to meet him in Paris in five weeks' time."[7]

The mention of Matisse brought Pugh in contact with Joyce for another related reason. When Henri Matisse agreed to illustrate a deluxe edition of *Ulysses* in 1934, Joyce requested Pugh to find illustrated Dublin periodicals for the year 1904 to help impart an Irish quality to the images: "[Matisse] knows the French translation very well but has never been to Ireland. I suppose he will do only the human figures but even for that he would perhaps need some guidance.... If I could have some back numbers (the picture pages only) to show him when he gets back to Paris he might be able to conjure up the past better."[8] Pugh sent material relating to the *Evening Telegraph* of June 16, 1904—the paper for which Leopold Bloom worked as a canvasser—but it was of little interest to Matisse.[9] The artist ended up bypassing both *Ulysses* and Dublin by sketching figures from Homer's original *Odyssey*, a measure of the gap, perhaps, between Joyce's perception of local resonances of his work, and the initial critical reception of the novel that lauded its modern use of myth to attain a classic universalism.[10]

Pugh's initial meeting with Joyce in Paris long predated the request for photographs: by 1931, he was among the few Dubliners with whom Herbert Gorman was in regular contact in preparation for the second edition of his biography of Joyce, a role Pugh replayed for Richard Ellmann's biography, answering queries about personalities and other details in Joyce's works.[11] It is intriguing that notwithstanding his lasting engagement with Joyce's work, Pugh as a native Dubliner still felt the need to recreate visually the actual sites in *Ulysses*, as if the physical features of the locations took up, as it were, where Joyce's words left off. As made explicit in the stage directions/screenplay format of the "Circe" chapter of *Ulysses*, the text of *Ulysses* as a whole might profitably be seen less as a self-contained work than as a set of cues for endless performances of walking the city, much as Bloom, Stephen, and other characters wander the streets, following what seem like hidden scripts of their surroundings.[12] In the climactic passage of "Cyclops" read in Joyce's apartment, the citizen in Barney Kiernan's bar hurls a Jacob's biscuit tin at Bloom, and it is hard to imagine Pugh not mentioning that he was among the Irish Volunteers who fought in Jacob's biscuit factory under the command of Thomas MacDonagh during the Easter Rising of 1916. One of Pugh's fellow Volunteers in Jacob's, Vinny Byrne, recalled that "we threw a lot of empty tins out through the windows which were spread out over the roadway, so that if any enemy came along in the dead of night, he would hit the tins and we would know there was someone on the move."[13]

Thomas Pugh was born at 85 Talbot Street, Dublin, in August 1883, a member of the distinguished flint glass manufacturing family of Richard and Thomas Pugh situated in Liffey Street and, later, Potter's Alley.[14] Joyce's willingness to strike common cause through his fascination with coincidences led him to remark of Pugh's blindness in one eye ("with more friendliness than accuracy," according to Ellmann): "We are much alike both of us blind in one eye, and both born in the same year" (*JJ*, 635). Given Joyce's interest in forging the conscience of his race (*P*, 276), he would perhaps have valued the discovery that much of the highly prized glass associated with the first Irish Volunteer movement and Grattan's Patriot Parliament in the late eighteenth century was, in fact, a later forgery, produced by a master craftsmen, Franz Tieze, who came to Ireland to work with the Pugh brothers.[15] In an uncanny coincidence, the Pugh name is associated in *Finnegans Wake* with the forger Richard Pigott, whose misspelling brought about his downfall in the attempt to frame Parnell

TOMÁS W. PUGH

FIG. 1.2 Thomas W. Pugh (1883–1968). Photograph: Christian Brothers Province Centre Archives, Dublin.

for complicity in the Phoenix Park assassinations: "Mind your pughs and keaoghs, if you piggots, marsh!..." (FW, 349.2–3). Elsewhere in Finnegans Wake, HCE is buried in a "teak coffin, Pughglasspanelfitted, feets to the east" (FW, 76.11–12) under Lough Neagh, that launches him on his voyage through the underworld.

Thomas Pugh attended secondary school at St. Joseph's, Marino, a cradle of republicanism, where he met his lifelong friend Peadar Kearney, author of "The Soldier's Song," the future Irish national anthem, and uncle of Brendan Behan.[16] As Kearney later recounted, Pugh's socialist leanings led to his joining the Socialist Party of Ireland and attracted him initially to the Irish Citizen Army: "Thomas W. Pugh was what one would call a Social Revolutionist. He avoided joining the Volunteers because he believed it was a capitalist movement to throw dust in the eyes of the workers. He considered the issue was economic and not national."[17] A chance meeting, however, with Irish Volunteer organizer Richard Mulcahy in the National Library led to Pugh joining the national movement, as well as becoming secretary of the John O'Leary Literary Society in the underground Irish Republican Brotherhood.[18] Having worked as a clerk in the Labour Exchange, his extensive knowledge of trade unionism and union leaders proved a valuable asset in linking the Volunteers to the Labour movement. On receiving word of the countermanding order that canceled the Rising planned for Easter Sunday, 1916, Pugh relates nonchalantly that he "went into town and went to an exhibition of pictures, in the Royal Hibernian Academy. I was the last man to leave the exhibition. I returned home from the exhibition and was mobilized next morning... for St Stephen's Green."[19] Pugh must have been among the last visitors to the RHA, for the building and its contents were demolished in the bombardment of Dublin city center during the following week of the Easter Rising.

The unit of Volunteers joined by Pugh assembled on Easter Monday at St. Stephen's Green in front of "the four posts marking the foundation stone (since disappeared) whereon a memorial to Wolfe Tone was to have been erected"[20]—the vacant space commemorated in *Ulysses* as the site "where Wolfe Tone's statue was not" (*U*, 10.378), which will be looked at in greater detail in chapter 2.[21] In the eyes of many leaders of the Rising, the insurrection set out to undo this historical void, completing the legacy of the republican uprising planned by Wolfe Tone and the United Irishmen in 1798 but crushed ruthlessly by the British government. In the course of the occupation of Jacob's factory, Pugh was among a group of Volunteers who found a bookcase in the library that they used to form a study circle to combat fatigue, "quotations from 'Julius Caesar,' the battle of Pharsalis [*sic*], etc.... remind[ing] one of a school rather than a war camp."[22] Imprisoned in Richmond Barracks after the Rising, Pugh furnished one of the last accounts of Patrick Pearse before his execution.[23] He was transferred to Knutsford jail in England in the company of Richard Mulcahy (his friend from the National Library) and Arthur Shields (later to become a Hollywood film star), and while at Knutsford met his future wife, Cork-born Margaret Dilworth, who visited Irish prisoners while working as a teacher in Manchester.[24] Pugh eventually ended up among the two thousand prisoners interned at Frongoch camp in North Wales, where he managed to gain an appointment as aide to the prison censor, a role he used, as one of "[Michael] Collins's men," to remove mail before the censor could read it.[25] Pugh's autograph book, compiled throughout his imprisonment in various jails, is filled with pictorial sketches and contributions by fellow prisoners such as Arthur Shields, Terence MacSwiney, Desmond Ryan (of whom more in chapter 9 below), and a humorous parody by Alistair Connolly promoting Frongoch prison camp as a tourist resort, "The Rebel's Tour," that would not be out of place in the "Cyclops" chapter of *Ulysses*:

> Delightful scenery by sea and rail. Corridor carriages with attendants on all rail journeys. Board and lodging free. Fatigue parties always at hand. Length of tour extended if necessary. Travelling parties collected at and returned to their own districts. Permits obtainable from the Home Sec-

retary, to enable tourists to visit Frongoch. Date of return dependent on climatic conditions. For Voucher apply to Box _____ at this paper.[26]

During the War of Independence, Pugh continued his intelligence work under Michael Collins, representing the Clerical Workers' Union on the Irish Republican Brotherhood (IRB) Labour Board, which was established to mobilize trade union support for the insurgent campaign, to identify trade unionists suitable for military purposes, and to gain "important key positions, such as Power Stations, Railways, and Transport Dockworkers, etc.; and most important of all, to undermine the Amalgamated or Cross Channel Unions, and where possible to organize a break away from these unions"—part of a wider effort to counter the perceived lack of sympathy for Irish independence among leading British trade unions.[27]

In the interwar years, Pugh underwent a series of operations to save his sight before eventually going blind. His meetings with his friend Peadar Kearney became a fixture on the margins of Irish literary life. As Seamus de Burca notes, it was through Pugh that Kearney was introduced to *Ulysses*:

> Having got out of the habit of visiting the National Library, renewing acquaintance with Pugh gave Kearney the opportunity of reading books like James Joyce's *Ulysses*. Joyce was a friend of Pugh, and Pugh often visited him in Paris and corresponded with him. He is the repository of more Joyceana than any living man. Of *Ulysses*, Peadar said: "It would be an excellent book for a theological student in a seminary because every mortal sin is mentioned in it."[28]

In later years Pugh lost his sight but was far from losing his memory, as de Burca recounted from firsthand experience: "Although Thomas Pugh has been blind for some years, his amazing retentive memory stands to him, and he can repeat the name of every shop that did business in Talbot street or Henry street in the 'nineties. More than that, he can pause and describe a shop photographically down to the last detail. He is an excellent authority on old Dublin."[29]

"Yet It Still Moves": Photographic Memory

> Blinding in Paris, for his party-piece
> Joyce names the shops along O'Connell Street.
> SEAMUS HEANEY, "Gravities"[30]

It is striking that such prodigious feats of recall were also performed by Joyce in the presence of visitors from Dublin, Talbot Street again providing the theater of memory. Kenneth Reddin recounted how on visiting the writer in Paris with the painter Patrick Tuohy, Joyce challenged them "to name all the shops from Amiens Street to the Pillar. First one side and then the other. When Tuohy or I left a gap, he filled it. When we named a new proprietor, he named, and remembered the passing of, the old."[31] Whether Pugh had sharpened Joyce's memory by his recall of the shops in Talbot Street is open to debate, but other streets were also etched in time for Joyce. His former school friend William Fallon recounted, "One of the most notable things about him at school was his flair for observation linked to an uncanny memory":

> He was preoccupied with memories of Dublin. He enquired about my former house in Fitzwilliam Street, and the college boys who lived in the same line of houses. Then he invited me to check the accuracy after naming and numbering the households on both sides of that residential street in those far off years. He didn't overlook mention of a broad passageway that led to the residence and horse-training establishment of one Rogers, who, if we are to believe Joyce, wore "leather leggins and a sports jacket day and night in mitigation of an iron-grey beard sprouting from a florid complexion." (On my return to Dublin I checked Joyce's memory with the aid of a Thom's Dublin Directory, and found that he was correct in every item. At the same time I learned that the habit of listing a series of business names in shopping centres was one of Joyce's devices to retain pictures of his Dublin.)

Hence, Fallon concludes, "incidents, not even of passing interest... were all imprinted on his mind with photographic accuracy."[32]

According to Graham Smith, "[E. M.] Forster did not name Joyce among writers employing 'the snapshot method,' but he might well have done so, for there is much in *Dubliners*, *A Portrait of the Artist as a Young Man*, and *Ulysses* that may legitimately be termed photographic."[33] Though unusually accurate recording of the past is often attributed to photographic memory, in its more traumatic form it relates to "flashbulb memory," a meticulous recall of superfluous details, or the setting of an event, that engraves experiences of acute pain or loss on the back of the brain.[34] "Every mean shop legend," *A Portrait* relates of Stephen Dedalus, "bound his mind like the words of a spell and his soul shrivelled up, sighing with age as he walked on in a lane among heaps of dead language" (*P*, 193). The vivacity of the image links it to the recall of memory—and, indeed, if the acoustic effects of the phonograph are added—to spectral memory from beyond the grave. Bloom's meditations on the headstones of Glasnevin Cemetery pass imperceptibly to those who once walked the city streets and worked in its stores: "How many! All these here once walked round Dublin. Faithful departed. As you are now so once were we":

> Besides how could you remember everybody? Eyes, walk, voice. Well, the voice, yes: gramophone. [...] Remind you of the voice like the photograph reminds you of the face. Otherwise you couldn't remember the face after fifteen years, say. For instance who? For instance some fellow that died when I was in Wisdom Hely's. (*U*, 6.960–69)

Many critics, taking a lead from Joyce's friends, have drawn attention not only to his remarkable powers of recollection but his systematic cultivation of the art of memory, based on his classical training under the Jesuits, and fascination with the mnemonic systems of Giordano Bruno and the hermetic tradition. Joyce considered memory to be inextricable from the imagination, and accounting for his prodigious feats of recall, Sylvia Beach explained that Joyce had practiced memory exercises since his early youth such that, while recovering from an eye operation later in life, he memorized Walter Scott's book-length poem *The Lady of the Lake* to keep his mind occupied.[35] It is not too difficult to see how such a training would have benefited Joyce's later creative method for, as Francis Yates points out in *The Art of Memory*, the cultivation of memory advocated by Cicero and Quintilian involved a mnemonic system of images and places, or *loci memoriae*. According to this system, memory is structured spatially like a building through which the mind proceeds from room to room, alighting on mental objects or "furniture" it seeks to recall (it is, ironically, a piece of furniture out of place in the bedroom that jogs Bloom's memory in the early hours on his return to Eccles Street at the end of *Ulysses*). For Quintilian, it was possible to recast a more expansive memory along the lines of a collection of buildings, reenacting in the imagination the experience of walking through a city: "What I have spoken of as being done in a house can also be done in public buildings, or a long journey, or in going through a city, or with pictures. Or we can imagine such places for ourselves."[36]

There is little doubt that whatever about the physical exercises endorsed by the bodybuilder Eugen Sandow in *Ulysses*, Joyce engaged in mental exercises along these lines. The classical source of memory as a spatial form lay in a story related of Simonides, who recited a poem at a banquet in favor of his host, Scopas, but also included passages praising two others. Scopas refused to pay for these sections, but when Simonides temporarily left the table to answer a request to meet two young men outside, the roof of the building collapsed, killing all those inside. Such was the mutilation that bodies of victims were unrecognizable but Simonides, by remembering precisely where everyone was seated at the table, was able to identify them. "In the story of Simonides," writes Anne Whitehead, "the two main principles of mnemonics were established: the remembrance of images and the importance of order." But as has been pointed put, Simonides himself had not practiced this system: he had not consciously memorized but rather drew, under force of circumstances at a site of destruction, on the reserves of involuntary memory.[37]

Joyce's way with memory is close to that of Simonides but with one difference: it was the destruction of the entire center of a city in 1916, rather than a single building, that coincided with the production of the "long take" of memory that constituted *Ulysses*. Since flashbulb memory is all background, needless details of the scene attached to events press for attention as the gaze is averted from the source of pain, and displaced onto context and setting.[38] As Daniel Ferrer notes, central to Cicero's or Quintilian's method is the fact that "images somehow must *not* belong where they are stored," and it helps if some remembered objects are out of place for the system to operate: "Adding an extra pillar to a peristyle, or a white object on a white ground, would be self-defeating: to be noticeable and memorable, the image must stand out. This means that in a mnemonic system, a placement is necessarily *and paradoxically a displacement, an uprooting*."[39] While there is no shortage of displacement in Joyce, any more than there was in Dublin city center after the Easter Rising, it was *movement*, not just static positions, that defined the walks down memory lane Joyce shared with visitors such as Thomas Pugh, Kenneth Reddin, or William Fallon. Leopold Bloom, as Wendy Steiner remarks, "is an enemy of stopped action, a proponent of temporal flow," and his coming to see the "freezing of time" as "inimical to both love and successful communication" is in the keeping with the "recuperative temporal flow of *Ulysses* as a whole."[40] The real-life William Fallon found his way into Joyce's fiction: there is a certain irony, as recounted in *Portrait* about the Dedalus family constantly changing houses, that it was "[a] boy named Fallon in Belvedere," who "had often asked him [Stephen] with a silly laugh why they moved so often" (*P*, 177).

In the first story published by Joyce, "The Sisters," the word "paralysis" comes to a young boy's mind as he looks up at the lighted window of a room above a drapery store in which a priest is dying. On hearing of the priest's death, a sense of displacement is evident in his somehow being deterred from viewing the corpse:

I wished to go in and look at him but I had not the courage to knock. I walked away slowly along the sunny side of the street, reading all the theatrical advertisements in the shopwindows as I went. I found it strange that neither I nor the day seemed in a mourning mood and I felt even annoyed at discovering in myself a sensation of freedom as if I had been freed from something by his death.[41]

It is as if the act of walking the city streets brings a welcome release from ruin and death. Much of the story blurs the lines between life and death, the stillness of a photograph and movement, as when the boy's aunt asks the priest's relatives, "Did he ... peacefully?" "'Oh, quite peacefully, ma'am,' said Eliza, 'You couldn't tell when the breath went out of him. He had a beautiful death, God be praised'" (D, 7). Paralysis has indeed set in if one can hardly tell the difference between life and death, but it also works the other way. When the boy eventually views the corpse of the priest, "The fancy came to me that the old priest was smiling as he lay there in the coffin. But no. When we rose and went to the head of the bed, I saw that he was not smiling" (D, 6). It is noticeable that when Bloom presents a photo of Molly to Stephen in "Eumaeus" in *Ulysses*, the composure of stillness is also broken by the possibility of a smile or indeed speech, on account of her looking back: "Her (the lady's) eyes, dark, large, looked at Stephen, about to smile about something to be admired, Lafayette of Westmoreland street, Dublin's premier photographic artist, being responsible for the esthetic execution. [...] As for the face it was a speaking likeness" (U, 16.1434–36, 1444). Even if the camera could not do justice to Molly's "stage presence," there is a liminal zone between life and death, motion and rest, voluntary and involuntary memory, as the photo recalls for Bloom the clutter of her bedroom when he last saw her the previous morning: "he then recollected the morning littered bed etcetera and the book about Ruby with met him pike hoses (*sic*) in it which must have fell down" (U, 16.1472–73; [*sic*] in original).

The fossilization of the past that critics find in the extended case histories of Joyce's *Dubliners* is often opposed by a countermovement, in every sense, that animates the rigor mortis of stillness, whether of the image, the body, or the body politic. While taking full measure of psychic wounds, agency of a kind is restored and invested with the melancholy freedom of movement the young boy feels walking down the street in "The Sisters." Movement is central to the image in Joyce, his stylistic amendments to early drafts of *Ulysses* systematically vivifying pictures so that "the hitherto inert scene has taken on motion."[42] In the famous bird-girl scene on Dollymount strand in *Portrait*, the stillness of the mutual gaze is broken by a stirring action, the girl redirecting her eyes "towards the stream, gently stirring the water with her foot hither and thither. The first faint noise of gently moving water broke the silence, low and faint and whispering, faint as the bells of sleep; hither and thither, hither and thither: and a faint flame trembled on her cheek" (*P*, 186). It is as if, in keeping with Aby Warburg's discerning of motion in the apparent stillness of Botticelli's *Birth of Venus*, the bird-girl functions as a *Pathosformel* charged with the history that surges through Stephen's brain on Dollymount strand: "Now, as never before, his strange name seemed to him a prophecy. So timeless seemed the grey warm air, so fluid and impersonal his own mood, that all ages were as one to him. A moment before the ghost of the ancient kingdom of the Danes had looked forth through the vesture of the hazewrapped city" (*P*, 183).[43]

As Georgina Binnie notes, the *fotodinamismo* movement of the Futurists in Italy, founded in 1911, sought to instill dynamism in photographs through multiple and long exposures, and "would probably have appealed to Joyce given his use of phantasmagoric imagery in the course of his writing."[44] As against G. E. Lessing's insistence in *Laocoön* (1766) that the image is defined in spatial terms and hence not susceptible to time, motion, or action (the preserve of language and narrative), Joyce has Stephen Dedalus from the outset taking issue with the sundering of word and image, or the separation of *Nacheinander* ("one after another") from *Nebeneinander* ("side by side"), in *Ulysses* (*U*, 3.13–15).[45] Oscillations of rhythm place kinesis rather than stasis as the principle of even the still image—"you pass from point to point, led by its formal lines [. . .] you feel the rhythm of its structure" (*P*, 230)—a principle that also applies to sculpture: "It is false to say that sculpture, for instance, is an art of repose if by that is meant that sculpture is unassociated with movement. Sculpture is associated with movement in as much as it is rhythmic. . . ."[46] "Yet it still moves": Galileo's dictum (in defiance of church authority) could be Joyce's credo as well. That stillness may conceal movement is apparent above all in the spectacle of the starry sky as it presents itself to Bloom and Stephen at the end of *Ulysses*, Joyce talking care, moreover, to link the illusion of immobility with the fusion of past and present in cosmic (or Einsteinian) time: "a mobility of illusory forms immobilised in space, remobilised in air: a past which possibly had ceased to exist as a present before its probable spectators had entered actual present existence" (*U*, 17.1143–45).[47]

For Henri Bergson, the philosopher most associated with Joyce in the eyes of contemporaries, photographic memory was precisely that which resisted voluntary effort: "Concentrate your mind on that sensation, and you will feel that the complete image is there, but evanescent, a phantasm that disappears just at the moment when motor activity tries to fix its outline."[48] For Bergson, the photograph is the antithesis of the act of remembering since it arrests the flow of memory and allows inspection of a kind that is impossible for memory images. If traditional theories of knowledge focused on the eye as window, or on single images, Bergson proposed that "the mechanism of our ordinary knowledge is of the cinematographic kind," just as in Joyce it is not the still image but the motion picture that follows Bloom, Stephen, and other characters on their walks through the city.[49] The frozen moment in this reasoning is more an aberration, and in his analysis of time and duration, Bergson argued that "the instant" or "instantaneity" are not functions of time itself, but of the *spatialization* of time, as were indeed the mechanical measurements of clock-time. Hence the emergence in Bergson's thought of what has been called, in photographic terms, the "long now," an extended present interwoven with both past and future: "The psychical state, then, that I call 'my present,' must be both a perception of the immediate past and a determination of the immediate future . . . my present then is both sensation and movement."[50] The difficulty in Ireland is that the immediate past itself had a long duration and, secreted in history, belonged as much to involuntary memory as to the conscious recall of long ago.

It is in this sense that the photograph, in its recording of incidental or involuntary details, militates against the selective operation of memory that retains only what is of significance: "Photography," Geoffrey Batchen concludes, "captures too much information to function as memory."[51] But it is precisely this aspect of photographic memory, the "etcetera" of minor details in Bloom's recall of Molly's bedroom, that recurs in Joyce. Though seemingly total and passive in its operation, there are losses and gaps in the moving picture as in Joyce's concern to name the shops that were no longer there, the sites where old shopfronts were not. As Jacques Mailhos notes, this incompleteness blurs the boundaries between voluntary and involuntary memory, releasing images from a frozen spatial fix: "The fact that not every memory image is thus not necessarily fully developed (either by the writer in the first place, or by the reader) opens up the *play of the possible*: potential stories lie in the gap between the creation and reception of the work, and these *potential* stories account perhaps more for the richness and universality than those that are actually narrated."[52] As George Morrison wrote in *An Irish Camera* of the capacity of seemingly incidental components of an image to speak to the future: "Photographic records preserve many such details which, today, are often of greater interest than the ostensible subject matter consciously recorded; thus the future may look more directly at the past."[53]

It is not just missing storefronts (as many were in Dublin city center after the bombardment of the Easter Rising) that feature in photographic memory: people also tend to be absent, and their presence weighs all the more heavily for that: "Both evoke the presence of people but do so because of their absence: the silence of the image directly reflects the absence of the bustle of the streets."[54] Though registering loss, the photographic recall of Joyce's work overflows the experiences of powerlessness and defeat experienced by individual psychologies in the story, not to mention those of its readers. This kind of counter-memory is uniquely open to contingency, much as the photograph eludes the will of the photographer for many of its telling effects. It is difficult not to suspect that a similar (shutter) release, an openness to possibility, lay behind the imaginative appeal of *Ulysses* to radical combatants in the Irish revolution such as Thomas Pugh and others discussed throughout this book, deprived in the new conservative Irish Free State of the dynamism that drove the struggle for independence. *Ulysses* may thus be conceived as looking back to a time when it was possible to look forward, and from this perspective, the key question to be asked of a novel is not whether it is true but whether it changes the relationship of the reader to the world, even a world one thought one knew already. As Hayden White points out, the scope of fiction follows Aristotle in focusing not on what happened but on *what was possible*: "what were the conditions of possibility of its happening?" and what were the possibilities opened up by the event of its taking place?[55]

Republic of Letters

Though Joyce liked to imagine that *Ulysses* was ignored or rejected in Ireland on its publication, this does less than justice to the excitement produced by its (albeit limited) circulation in Dublin, and the reputation it built up among disaffected radicals such as Thomas Pugh.[56] *Ulysses* was banned and confiscated in Britain and the United States, but at least twenty-five copies found their way to four Dublin bookshops, with one notable outlet, the Irish Bookshop on Dawson Street managed by the former revolutionary P. S. O'Hegarty, ordering six copies.[57] Subscribers also obtained copies through Sylvia Beach's mail-order subscription service, and prominent Free State supporters such as W. B. Yeats and government cabinet minister Desmond FitzGerald were among high-profile subscribers in Ireland.[58] As John Nash notes, other purchasers included the writer Lennox Robinson; the poet Muriel Whitfield of Cabra Park, Dublin; the veteran Sinn Féin editor of the *Kilkenny People*, Edward T. Keane; and the nationalist M. J. MacManus (future literary editor of the *Irish Press*), who wrote an affectionate parody of *Ulysses* in his collection *A Jackdaw in Dublin* (1925). Reviews appeared in magazines and periodicals such as the *Irish Review*, *The Separatist*, *The Klaxon*, and the *Dublin Review* (where it merited two reviews, because its merits were in question).[59] By the end of 1922, as Peter Costello notes, the starring role of Barney Kiernan's pub in the "Cyclops" chapter was well known enough to be mentioned in the *Evening Mail*, and the humorous periodical *Dublin Opinion* carried a cartoon in which a prisoner opted for hard labor rather than the punishment of reading *Ulysses*. A copy of *Ulysses* was delivered to Trinity College Library but it was not cataloged and was held under wraps, except for readers "on exceptional grounds": the National Library did not purchase a copy, though the fact that its edition of *Portrait* had to be rebound in 1928 suggests there was no lack of interest in Joyce.[60]

In 1920 Joyce wrote sardonically of the impending publication of *Ulysses* that "a great movement is being prepared against the publication of behalf of puritans, English imperialists, Irish republicans and Catholics—what an alliance!"[61] All Irish republicans did not, in fact, join in the carnival of reaction, and the circulation of *Ulysses* in revolutionary circles is clear from the memoirs of C. S. ("Todd") Andrews, a former member of Michael Collins's hit squad, who noted that Michael Carolan, acting director of intelligence in the anti-Treaty IRA, had, through his librarian friend Róisín Walsh, "acquired the loan of the first edition of James Joyce's *Ulysses* published by the Shakespeare Press in Paris. He showed it to me with great enthusiasm, thumbing rapidly through the pages until reaching the famous Molly Bloom soliloquy on which he dwelt with shocked surprise which I knew he did not feel—nor did I." Andrews noted that the reputation of *Ulysses* had preceded its circulation: "I had heard something of Joyce and had seen, rather than read, some discussion of *Ulysses* in the *New Statesman*, but it had passed me by. The same could not be said of Molly Bloom. This was my first introduction to Joyce's *Ulysses* which later became for me a source of entertainment and much enjoyable conversation with other Joyce enthusiasts over the years."[62]

Carolan directed his IRA intelligence operations from the house of Walsh at Cypress Grove, Templeogue, Dublin, whose work as a librarian provided access to what might be seen as subversive or indecent literature.[63] Walsh's commitment to republicanism was matched by her lifelong dedication to art, literature, and the women's movement, and an international outlook facilitated by her degree in European languages.[64] The most dynamic figure in building up the Public Library system in Dublin in the early decades of the state, Walsh was appointed chief librarian in Dublin in 1931, a post she held until her death in 1949. Moving in modernist artistic circles associated with Ernie O'Malley and Helen Hooker O'Malley in the 1930s, she was one of the founding editors of *The Bell* magazine in 1940 with Seán Ó Faoláin, Peadar O'Donnell, Maurice Walsh, and her librarian friend Frank O'Connor. Friendship with the left-wing republican O'Donnell went back many years: her house at Templeogue provided the venue in 1931 for the IRA Army Convention that established the left-wing "Saor Éire" initiative led by O'Donnell and David Fitzgerald, the first major shift to the left in the post-Treaty republican movement.[65] That Walsh should have been one of the figures responsible for the circulation of *Ulysses* in Dublin is not surprising, given her internationalism and wide range of literary interests. She was emphatic that building a national culture should not be at the expense of openness to world literature: "Some years ago some people in Ireland wanted to isolate this country from the rest of the world, in order that there would be created a new nation like the ancient Gaelic nation, but now they saw that it is not possible to keep out the rest of the world, and they would not attempt it."[66] At a public lecture in 1940 by Maud Gonne MacBride on the early years of the Revival, Walsh defended the contribution of Anglo-Irish writers to the literary movement. Her speech was followed by Dr. Patrick McCartan, who also spoke against Daniel Corkery's "partition of the mind," suggesting that the achievements of Joyce (along with Yeats and Shaw) "had done more to make the name of Ireland respectable in the American Universities than all the Irish politicians—he would even say more than the martyrs of Easter Week."[67]

Andrews also mentions another reader of Joyce, Seán Dowling (1895–1988), who rose to prominence in the republican movement, acting as O/C of the Fourth Battalion of the Dublin Brigade during the War of Independence, and as director of operations—as well as "Organization and Jail Escapes"—during the Civil War.[68] Andrews writes of his immense debt to Dowling as an intellectual, if not quite as a political, mentor: "This encounter with Dowling, although it was sterile so far as the IRA issue was concerned, was to have important consequences for me.... Dowling seemed to have an extraordinary wide range of interests and I found his conversation fascinating.... He introduced me to art appreciation and in particular to the Impressionists, to Browning, to George Moore, Joyce and to the so-called literary revival generally."[69] Andrews recalls that the intensity of literary debates about the Revival between Dowling and Robert Brennan, who was also conversant with Joyce, was not to everyone's liking in the group: one member (and future Taoiseach/prime minister) Seán Lemass, withdrew from such exchanges to "gaze gloomily" out a window.[70] Dowling was a star pupil at Patrick Pearse's St. Enda's School and acted with his brother Frank in the school dramas produced by Pearse, based on Irish myth and legend. On leaving St. Enda's, Dowling became "the favourite pupil and protégé of Thomas Mac Donagh in the English literature faculty at UCD [and] took his degree in English Literature with such distinction that he was offered a lectureship in the college."[71] His participation in the 1916 Rising and the War of Independence interrupted his studies, though in the end he graduated with a BA in literature, as well as qualifying as a dentist—"Dentist John Dowling," as Samuel Beckett called him.[72] Offered the post of IRA chief liaison officer by Michael Collins during the Truce in 1921, Dowling took the anti-Treaty republican side in the Civil War and was one of the surviving IRA Army Executive, under new Chief of Staff Frank Aiken, that met near Mullinahone, County Tipperary, "to terminate armed resistance to the Free State forces" on April 20, 1923, following the death of the anti-Treaty leader, Liam Lynch.[73] After the war, Dowling briefly emigrated to the United States but returned to Dublin to practice as a dentist. In the 1930s, he acted as art critic for the left-leaning periodical *Ireland Today* and embarked on a series of protracted disputes over the role of modernism, surrealism, and Anglo-Irish hegemony in the cultural life of the state. Dowling remained in the political wings of the republican movement and was a member of the group of IRA members or sympathizers—with Jim O'Donovan, Maurice Twomey, Andy Cooney, and John Joe Sheehy—that met with the American novelist James T. Farrell on his visit to Dublin in August 1938, where Farrell found, to his surprise, that Joyce was a hero in the eyes of rebels:

> The five men talked about literature, politics, and recent Irish history late into the night. The old IRA men explained that they did not want Farrell to get the impression the Abbey [Theatre] crowd was Ireland. They told him that the only Irish writer they liked at all was James Joyce, even though Joyce had repudiated everything they stood for. They saw in Joyce a man of lower middle class origins like themselves, whose feelings and responses to all sorts of things were like theirs. In this sense, he was their writer.[74]

Another advanced republican "who could be counted as among the first Irish Joyceans" was the academic, art critic, and feminist Eileen McGrane (1895–1984), who managed to read *Ulysses* while imprisoned in Kilmainham Gaol in 1922.[75] McGrane was dismissed from a teaching post in Armagh following a speech on a public platform in support of Sinn Féin in the 1918 election, but was subsequently appointed to a temporary post in University College, Dublin, "in lieu of [the poet] Austin Clarke who was ill," and gained a full-time position within eighteen months, following, like Seán Dowling, in the footsteps of her teacher and mentor, the executed leader of the Rising, Thomas MacDonagh.[76] Throughout this period, she worked as an organizer for the women's nationalist organization, Cumann na mBan, becoming its director of publicity, but at a clandestine level was also a key figure in Michael Collins's intelligence network during the War of Independence. Her flat at 21 Dawson Street acted as Collins's secret office, a repository for files and documents, and the rendezvous point for high-level IRA and Sinn Féin personnel such as Ernie O'Malley, Arthur Griffith, and Tom Cullen. The chance recognition of Cullen visiting the apartment on December 30, 1920, led to an immediate raid, the most successful strike by Dublin Castle against Collins's "invisible army." Interrogated by the director of intelligence Sir Ormonde Winter, McGrane was charged with high treason but was eventually sentenced on a lesser charge to four years penal servitude in Mountjoy and Waltham prison, Liverpool.[77] Active in publicity and intelligence for the republican anti-Treaty side during the Civil War, she was again arrested and interned but, following the cessation of hostilities, resumed her academic career at University College, Dublin. She married fellow republican activist Dr. Patrick MacCarvill and was elected to the National University of Ireland Senate in 1934, as well as gaining a later appointment to the Cultural Committee of the Department of External Affairs in 1949. Pursuing her modernist interests, MacCarvill (as she was now known) edited a pioneering book on the writings of the Irish modernist painter Mainie Jellett, *The Artist's Vision*, in 1958, in which Jellett stressed connections between her concept of visual rhythm and Joyce's work.[78] Having completed a doctorate on Joyce at the Sorbonne, Paris, MacCarvill's proposed book "James Joyce: A Documentary"—containing a selection of Joyce's uncollected essays, book reviews, and poems—promised to be the first substantial Irish scholarly engagement with Joyce and, though meeting difficulties with the publisher, went into proof stage at Hely's, Dublin (Leopold Bloom's onetime employers) in 1957.[79] It came into competition, however, with an edition of Joyce's critical writings then under preparation by Richard Ellmann and Ellsworth Mason in the United States and never saw its way into print.[80] MacCarvill was by no means put off in her critical engagements with Joyce and in June 1962 was one of the lecturers, with Padraic Colum, at the first Bloomsday Joyce Week in Dublin. At the inaugural International James Joyce Symposium in Dublin in 1967 (at which Colum again was present), she lectured on "Storiella as she is syung" in *Finnegans Wake*, and at the 1968 "James Joyce, the Artist and the Man" International Summer Course gave lectures on Joyce and James Clarence Mangan, Viconian history, and Geoffrey Keating's *Foras Feasa ar Éireann* in *Finnegans Wake*, as well as the myriad histories of the Liffey and Dublin woven into *Finnegans Wake*.[81] At the 1970 James Joyce School, she lectured on "Composition of Place" and participated in International Joyce symposia in Dublin in 1969 and 1977, as well as being a founding member of the James Joyce Institute established in Ireland in the early 1970s. She also established a reputation as a Swift scholar, speaking at Swift conferences in Ireland on his connections to Gaelic Ireland.

It was not only the republican side of the Civil War that expressed an interest in Joyce's writings, for the new Free State government also sought to avail of his growing international prestige. From different political positions, pro-Treaty figures such as Eimar O'Duffy, Bulmer Hobson, and P. S. O'Hegarty were among the first to grasp the value and complexity of Joyce's engagement with Ireland.[82] Though a leading contributor to the Irish Republican Brotherhood (IRB) organ, *Irish Freedom*, before the Rising, O'Hegarty took the pro-Treaty side in 1922 but still considered his views to be in keeping with the title of *The Separatist*, a publication he took over that year. O'Hegarty's review of *Ulysses* appeared in the magazine and praised Joyce for his reconstruction of the English language in almost military terms: "Mr Joyce has taken English language and has used as never before was used, and used it triumphantly; he has massed it and manoeuvred it as one masses men at army manoeuvres, and do it successfully... remoulded it into a thing which is continental rather than English. He has put into *Ulysses* not merely a story, but an epoch." If the novel is an epic, it is an epic from below:

> I make the assertion, after reading this, that Mr Joyce loves Ireland, especially Dublin. I do not mean that it does it politically, or in any "wrap-the-green-flag" sense. But Ireland is all through him, and in him, and of him; and Dublin, its streets and its buildings and its people, he loves with the whole-hearted affection of the artist.... He may live out of Dublin, but he will never get away from it.[83]

While O'Duffy's praise of *Ulysses* was tempered by a strong disapproval of its "vulgarity" and sexual frankness,[84] O'Hegarty contended that "on the whole, it is justified, and that the two triumphs of the book, the absolutely perfect portrayal of Leopold and Marion Bloom, would be impossible without it." Making a case for the avant-garde, he implies that Joyce more than any writer establishes the separatist ideal in literature, for though rejected by its people, it is because he has the "intellectual daring" to be ahead of them: "Ireland at present will probably not love Mr Joyce. But Mr Joyce has done her honour. No Englishman could have written this book, even if one had the wit to conceive the plan of it. Ireland, Dublin, is all over it, its idiom, its people, and its way, its atmosphere, and its intellectual daring."[85]

In March 1922, Desmond FitzGerald, minister for publicity in the Free State government, visited Joyce in Paris to encourage his return to Ireland and to propose his nomination for the Nobel Prize in Literature.[86] Joyce stated he had no desire to return and was skeptical of FitzGerald's proposal: "He will probably lose his portfolio without obtaining the prize for me."[87] FitzGerald was a member of the nascent Imagist movement in London, 1909–10, which included Ezra Pound, T. E. Hulme, H.D. (Hilda Doolittle), Richard Aldington, Harold Monro, and his friend the Irish poet Joseph Campbell (to whom we shall return in chapter 5). Pound thought highly at this stage of FitzGerald's verse and kept abreast of his activities during the War of Independence. After FitzGerald's arrest and imprisonment by the British authorities in March 1921, Pound wrote: "I am very sorry that Desmond FitzGerald has been copped // but it had to come sooner or later—one has expected it for a year. There was a fine paragraph on him in an article in the Mercure de France (Vepres Irlandaises) some months ago. The Irish have every right to their liberty save what they might have by being more civilized than their despots."[88] Pound attended the final dinner of the Irish Race Convention in Paris in February 1922, but was quick to spot the incongruity of Free State government's ministers hobnobbing with their former despots.[89] He related an "apocryphal" story of FitzGerald, then minister for external affairs, at Buckingham Palace:

[QUEEN] MARY: And what did you do in gt. war?
FITZ: Time
As matter of fact wot happened wuz:
THE EVER TACTFUL GEORGE: Were you in the army?
FITZ (not going to be high-hatted): Not in the British Army.[90]

Five years later, the censorship policies pursued by the Free State government led Pound to send a crude stage-Irish parody to Joyce:

I met Esmond Fitzruggles
And the old souse says to me:
"I fought and bled and died, by Xroist!
That Oireland should be free,
But you mustn't now say 'buggar' nor
'bitch' nor yet 'bastard'
Or the black maria will take you
To our howly prison yard."[91]

Joyce did not reply in a similar tone to Pound and was hardly amused at poor stage-Irish parodies of the kind he excelled in himself. But the attempts by the Free State government to win Joyce's approval did not end with FitzGerald's overtures. Yeats took the initiative in inviting Joyce to Ireland to attend the 1924 Tailteann Games—the Gaelic Olympics, as it were, with a cultural as well as sporting component. Yeats's motivation may well have been to challenge the Catholic censorship that was already exerting its grip on the new state, and as if to reinforce this stance, he declared his public support for Joyce's achievement in *Ulysses* at a student debate in Trinity College, in November 1923.[92] Joyce greatly appreciated the gesture but was not impressed by the fact that Yeats's invitation was issued only in a personal capacity and carried no official weight. Had he known that literary standards at the Games were such that his bête noire Oliver St. John Gogarty received the gold medal for poetry, it is likely he would have been even less impressed.

The Tailteann Games utilized the mass appeal of modern spectacle to fashion a sense of unity in a post–Civil War Ireland. In mass spectacle, the audience is largely passive, spellbound by an image, but as John Nash suggests, Joyce attempts in his work in progress on *Finnegans Wake* to "overwrite" the scene to make it readerly. Converting the one-way gaze of spectacle into the two-way exchange of dialogue, a picture thus *addresses* its spectators so "the event is inseparable from the audience that looks at it": "Reception is already worked into the production of literature. This mutually interpretative spectacle, a sort of textual and historical hall of mirrors, dramatizes and incorporates readers' responses."[93] While spectacle purports to step outside narrative, and to detach itself from engagement with the audience, *time* is reintroduced into Joyce's moving pictures, though with a far from unified linear trajectory. In a passage in *Finnegans Wake* that plays on Stephen Dedalus's view of Dublin in *Portrait* from Dollymount strand (where he views the bird-girl), the "solence of that stilling" in evoked as a faintly audible ("odable") view transmitted by the wireless through the air ("wineless Ere") down the ages:

> It scenes like a landescape Eumaeus from Wildu Picturescu or some seem on some dimb Arras, dumb as Mum's mutyness, this mimage of the seventy-seventh kusin of kristansen is odable to os across the wineless Ere no oedor nor mere eerie nor liss potent of suggestion than in the tales of the tingmount. (Prigged!) (*FW*, 53.1–6)[94]

It is as if the static image of photographic memory—"a fadograph of a yestern scene" (*FW*, 7.17)—is released from its petrified stillness and is set in motion to become, in John Bishop's description, "imperceptible static washed through ether over the wireless air."[95] Aspects of the proto-cinematic diorama in *Portrait* in which "eyes seem to ask me something" (*P*, 272), and Bloom's imagining of the mutoscope in "Nausicaa" in which images queue up to become alive, may also be latent in the "Picturescu... mutyness" of the Dorian Gray ("Wildu Picturescu") picture. This moving picture effect is evoked later in *Finnegans Wake* to capture what seems like footage ("philim pholk") of the ruins of the Easter Rising, with the added, rueful implication that souls were sold ("sould") for a cause that ended in little more than a divided Ireland ("partitional"): "A phantom city, phaked of philim pholk, bowed and sould for a four of hundreds of manhood in their three and threescore fylkers for a price partitional of twenty six and six" (*FW*, 264.22–26).[96]

As Thomas Pugh's encounter with Joyce showed, sporting spectacles such as rugby matches encouraged travel between Dublin and Paris, enabling expatriates to maintain links with the homeland. In the 1920s, William Fallon, Joyce's former schoolmate at Belvedere and future president of the Irish Rugby Football Union (IRFU), arranged to meet Joyce after a rugby international and was surprised on arriving at his apartment to discover Joyce had actually been to see the match. Almost ten years later, Fallon visited Paris as a selector for the Irish team and was amazed to find that Joyce had again attended the game. Though "his eyes had not been strong enough to identify 'our team'":

> He rolled off the names of the Irish players who had taken part in the game and their respective clubs. Then to my astonishment he talked of prominent players in the 1923 side and added that he had attended the alternate games played in the intervening seasons whenever he happened to be in Paris. A substantial part of the conversation was taken up talking about the match and the players.[97]

In the intervening years, Joyce had also sent Fallon copies of *transition* magazine in which *Finnegans Wake* was serialized but that Fallon "hadn't been able to make head nor tail of."[98] It was not the first time Fallon was at a loss to grasp what was said: he was one of the few witnesses to leave a record of hearing Patrick Pearse read the Proclamation of 1916 outside the GPO, reporting that many people "didn't recognize the significance of what Pearse was saying. His voice didn't carry too well and it was difficult to hear him."[99] Decades later, Fallon's friend (and editor of his memoir) Ulick O'Connor linked passages in *Finnegans Wake* to the 1923 rugby game in which two brothers, Bill and Dick Collopy, played for the Irish team: "By the horn of twenty of both of the two Saint Collopys, blackmail him I will in arrears" (*FW*, 457.2–3). As the IRFU overrode Partition in selecting players on an all-Irish basis, Joyce hints that the game in the Stade Colombe in Paris may have provided a brief utopian glimpse of a united state of Ireland—"with shouldered arms, and in that united I.R.U. stade"—and a return of émigrés (the patriotic wild geese) from France to Ireland:

> You will there and then, in those happy moments of ouryour soft accord, rainkiss on me back, for full marks with shouldered arms, and in that united I. R.U. stade, when I come (touf! touf!) wildflier's fox into my own greengeese again. (*FW*, 446.15–19)

❋ 2 ❋
Modern Epic and Revolution

MONTAGE IN THE MARGINS

> The old Irish left no finished epic, but a thousand and one tales, no Celtic Odyssey, but numerous "navigations" of saints and heroes in the Atlantic.
>
> SHANE LESLIE, *The Celt and His World* (1917)[1]

As the viceregal cavalcade led by the lord lieutenant and his wife, "earl of Dudley, and lady Dudley, accompanied by lieutenantcolonel Heseltine" (*U*, 10.1176–77), wends its way through the streets of Dublin in the "Wandering Rocks" chapter of *Ulysses*, "most cordially greeted" (*U*, 10.1182) by crowds of the "gratefully oppressed" (*D*, 35), "[f]ive tallwhitehatted sandwichmen," advertising Hely's stationers and printers where Leopold Bloom once worked, pass by a slab at the corner of St. Stephen's Green "where Wolfe Tone's statue was not, eeled themselves turning H. E. L. Y'S and plodded back as they had come" (*U*, 10.377–79). Such was paralysis under colonial rule that national sentiment could not even rise to the task of building a statue in honor of the founder of Irish republicanism, Wolfe Tone. As Stephen Dedalus notes ruefully in *Portrait* of the legacy of Tone and the 1798 rebellion commemorated in the centenary celebrations of 1898:

> Grafton Street, along which he walked, prolonged that moment of discouraged poverty. In the roadway at the head of the street a slab was set to the memory of Wolfe Tone and he remembered having been present with his father at its laying. He remembered with bitterness that scene of tawdry tribute. There were four French delegates in a brake and one, a plump smiling young man, held, wedged on a stick, a card on which were printed the words: *Vive l'Irlande!* (*P*, 199)

The laying of the foundation stone for a statue of Tone (never in fact erected) at the corner of St. Stephen's Green was accompanied by a stirring rendition of John Kells Ingram's famous poem "The Memory of the Dead," first published in *The Nation* newspaper in 1843. Ingram's verse suggests that even half a century after the 1798 rebellion, a rush of blood to the face was still the embarrassed response of many to the full measure of the calamity: "Who fears to speak of Ninety-Eight? / Who blushes at the name?" It was not the rebellion itself that occasioned shame (though Kells Ingram later in life sought to distance himself from the poem) but the disavowal by subsequent generations of that heroic episode ("When cowards mock the patriot's fate, / Who hangs his head for shame?"). These lines play on what Christopher Ricks terms the "ripples or chain reactions of embarrassment" at an emotion not yet able to name itself.[2] This relationship between the body, memory, and silence is picked up by the citizen in the gallows humor of the "Cyclops" chapter in *Ulysses*, who "was only waiting for the wink of the word and he starts gassing out of him about the invincibles and the old guard and the men of sixtyseven and who fears to speak of ninetyeight and Joe with him about all the fellows that were hanged, drawn and transported for the cause by drumhead courtmartial and a new Ireland and new this, that and the other" (*U*, 12.480–85). When the narrative goes on to recount "the citizen and Bloom having an argument about [...] the Brothers Sheares and Wolfe Tone beyond on Arbour Hill" (*U*, 12.498–99), it is clear from Joyce's own views recorded elsewhere that sympathies were with "the heroes of the modern movement—Lord Edward Fitzgerald, Robert Emmet, Theobald Wolfe Tone, Napper Tandy, leaders of the uprising of 1798," rather than with their detractors.[3] Ingram's poem is again invoked in a passage that alludes to the muting of the Irish language in the cultural breakdown of post-Famine Ireland:

—The memory of the dead, says the citizen taking up his pintglass and glaring at Bloom.
—Ay, ay, says Joe.
—You don't grasp my point, says Bloom. What I mean is....
—*Sinn Fein!* says the citizen. *Sinn fein amhain!* The friends we love are by our side and the foes we hate before us. (*U*, 12.519–24)

The hesitations of speech point in this exchange to a cultural malaise still lodged in the body but awaiting expression. As Stephen goes home on holidays from Clongowes through country roads, "[t]he drivers pointed with their whips to Bodenstown" (*P*, 17), the burial place of Wolfe Tone, "the holiest spot in Ireland" according to Patrick Pearse.[4] This gestural association with Tone is not named in the text, but, as Christopher Woods observes, the hallowed site had passed into the local lore of Clongowes and its surrounding district in County Kildare as early as the 1820s.[5] Instead of displaying monumental history as castigated by Nietzsche, narratives of the past in Ireland had not yet attained the fixity of a monument, and remained in perpetual motion like the sandwich-board men, or Stephen and Bloom, on their endless rounds of the city.[6] As Enda Duffy notes of the negative topography of Joyce's Dublin, a "non-space" is not void but awaits its moment in time, that is, "a truly absent space, whose absence, at all times reiterated, leaves blank a sign of community to come."[7]

If "[t]he Ireland of Tone and of Parnell seemed to have receded in space" (P, 199) and from political articulation, the physical act of 100,000 people moving through the streets of Dublin in the centenary commemorations of 1898 nevertheless helped to reawaken intimations of independence, even among those who, like the Unionist Mr. Tom Kernan in "Wandering Rocks," were far sympathetic to the Irish cause. Some years earlier, in October 1891, a similar traversal of space infused the parliamentary politics of Parnell with the revolutionary ideals of 1798 as the organizers of Parnell's funeral took the roundabout route of directing the vast cortege past Thomas Street, where Lord Edward Fitzgerald was captured and shot dead in 1798, and where Robert Emmet was executed. It is these routes that Mr. Kernan takes on his stroll of the city in "Wandering Rocks," having washed down a "[g]ood drop of gin" to help him on his way. As Michael J. F. McCarthy describes the beginning of the vast parade in 1898, which "first defiled past Tone's house in Stafford-street":

> It then pursued its way, with bands and banners, to St Michan's Church, in the vaults of which lie the remains of the Brothers Sheares—unburied, but marvelously preserved; a gruesome sight!—also the remains of Oliver Bond, Jackson, and, it is said, Robert Emmet.... Moira House, the town residence of Lord Moira in 1798, where many of the United Irishmen were sheltered and entertained by its owner was next passed. It is now called the Mendicity Institution! Next in order came the site of Robert Emmet's execution in Thomas-street; and the house, No. 151, in the same street, where Lord Edward Fitzgerald was arrested on May 19th, 1798.[8]

It is as if this provides a script for "Tom-Gin" Kernan's thoughts as he comes within sight of Thomas Street, the pageantry of the viceregal cavalcade passing nearby being offset by another reason for thinking of the lord lieutenant's wife: "Down there Emmet was hanged, drawn and quartered. Greasy black rope. Dogs licking the blood off the street when the lord lieutenant's wife drove by in her noddy. [...] Let me see. Is he buried in saint Michan's? Or no, there was a midnight burial in Glasnevin. Corpse brought in through a secret door in the wall. Dignam is there now. Went out in a puff" (*U*, 10.764–66, 769–70). As Kernan ambles around Island Street, his mind drifts again toward "Times of the troubles" and Kells Ingram's "Memory of the Dead," lamenting the treachery of the "sham squire" and the fate of Lord Edward Fitzgerald, "[w]hen you look back on it all now in a kind of retrospective arrangement":

> Somewhere here lord Edward Fitzgerald escaped from major Sirr. Stables behind Moira House. Damn good gin that was. Fine dashing young nobleman. Good stock, of course. That ruffian, that sham squire, with his violet gloves gave him away. Course they were on the wrong side. They rose in dark and evil days. Fine poem that is: Ingram. They were gentlemen. Ben Dollard does sing that ballad touchingly. Masterly rendition. *At the Siege of Ross did my father fall.* (*U*, 10.784–94)

For Kernan, the wayward sentiments stirred by the physical act of walking are at odds with his colonial leanings as a returned Indian officer, as if his body doesn't know what his mind is doing. His patriotic reveries distract him from the passing viceregal cavalcade, causing him to miss a close-up view of the lord lieutenant: "His Excellency! Too bad! Just missed that by a hair. Damn it! What a pity!" (*U*, 10.798–99).

In this montage of distractions, it seems history is indeed to blame, even if the past cannot find its way onto a pedestal: "In Ireland we are not a statue-building people," declared *The Nation* in 1888, "few of our immortals live either in stone or in bronze."[9] As memory passes into spectacle, the ceremonial equivalent of monuments, commemorations, lend themselves to the wooden responses of the delegates at the 1798 centenary—the dispiriting French delegate carrying "*Vive l'Irlande!*" wedged on a stick (*P*, 199). Stephen's recoil from the stilted ceremony may be seen as part of a more general indictment in Joyce's work of the deadening impact of mindless repetition on people's lives, itself a form of paralysis. Official commemoration ceremonies, like monuments, reduce memory to force of habit and unthinking acquiescence. Yet this sedentary state may be countered by taking to the streets, stirrings of momentary shocks in which "epiphanies" of sorts—chance encounters, incidental details, random objects—break up, if only temporarily, the paving stones of habit. As Joseph Buttigieg describes this form of counter-memory in Joyce:

> When the past escapes the deadness imposed upon it, when it manifests itself as something new and unknown, when it ceases to be the familiar object of a dull memory, then the past has the power to jolt the Dubliner

into recognizing for the first time what he previously thought he knew so well. This experience is disturbing and painful, like a birth, for it deprives one of mastery over a world rendered comfortable by habit.[10]

Insofar as popular memory is open to chance and contingency, even the most carefully controlled public spectacles and assemblies can get lost in translation. We can assume, given his Unionist sympathies, that Tom Kernan does not consciously call up "the memory of the dead" but such thoughts are prompted by wanderings in space against his own better judgment. For Benedict Anderson, "it is the magic of nationalism to turn chance into destiny," but in the uneven temporality of Joyce's Dublin, this alchemy is reversed and destiny is converted back into the dross of everyday life.[11] Turning a corner can lead to a decomposition of language and signs themselves, and, as if on cue, one of the "tallwhitehatted sandwichmen" in "Wandering Rocks" loses his way as the lord lieutenant's carriage passes by: "At Ponsonby's corner a jaded white flagon H. halted and four tallhatted white flagons halted behind him, E.L.Y'S, while outriders pranced past and carriages" (*U*, 10.1236–38).

The inability of language to transcend what has been termed the "paramnesiac" state of post-Famine Ireland points to a culture rendered mute by its own historical/hysterical symptoms.[12] If the regimentation of both church and state in post-Famine Ireland—the "stationary march" decried by Stephen (*SH*, 191)—dulled the body to the pain of cultural memory, the restless mobility of natives adrift in their surroundings reopen rather than close off the past. For Carle Bonafous-Murat, the different ways in which memory and environment merge in the physical act of walking the city in Joyce's fiction raises the question: "Is it the characters who use the town as a reservoir for their memories, or is it on the contrary the town which makes use of the characters to actualise its memories?"[13] The difficulty with the latter process, as the reception of the viceregal cavalcade indicates, is that it induces habit and "predispositions," depriving the characters of agency in their relationship to the past. For this reason, Bonafous-Murat concludes:

> It appears that most of the Dubliners are more willing to be kept in thralldom that to be liberated from the burden of the past. Indeed, between the community of Dubliners and their memories, there is always the intermediate structure of the Dublin grid, the network of streets and public buildings thanks to which connections are established, and though they may wish to be freed from their history they willingly accept to be imprisoned in the space they are in.[14]

As if in mind of this, responses to commemorations of 1798 and the Emmet insurrection of 1803 act as political forms of involuntary memory, bringing to mind submerged histories of the past. Accounts of the Irish Revival at the end of the nineteenth century point to the literary movement, the founding of the Gaelic League, or sporting organizations such as the Gaelic Athletic Association, as cultural turning points in the resurgence of national sentiment that preceded the Easter Rising of 1916. This is accurate, so far as it goes, but it may be that these formal, institutional initiatives themselves required a deeper shift in the substratum of everyday life, unsettling the sedimented habits of colonial paralysis. These energies were disparate and restless as if putting in place the conditions to lift Robert Emmet's embargo on language in his famous speech from the dock before his execution.[15] One-third of the population of Dublin took to the streets for the procession to lay the foundation stone for the Wolfe Tone memorial, but notwithstanding the rhetoric, only an empty space greeted passersby on June 16, 1904. "For God's sake, try to do something about the Wolfe Tone Memorial," wrote P. T. Daly, a leading IRB organizer, to John Devoy in 1905: "Public promises are being thrown in our teeth every day by the talkers."[16] In the colonial city, it would seem, it was not so much the talking cure as the walking tour that characterized a culture coming to its senses.

Epic, Novel, and Memory

"In every mass movement," wrote the German psychiatrist Emil Kraepelin of the revolutions that swept Europe after the Great War, "we encounter traits which indicate a deep affinity with hysterical symptoms."[17] The Irish had long displayed such symptoms, leading to Tennyson's famous put-down in "In Memoriam" (1850) of the "schoolboy heat" of an unruly temperament, "The blind hysterics of the Celt."[18] It is not surprising, therefore, that a "poets' revolution," one of the popular descriptions of the 1916 Easter Rising, should attract such a description; the historian F. S. L. Lyons wrote of Patrick Pearse, one of the leaders of the Rising, that his behavior left little doubt of the "hysterica passio that lay at the root of his personality."[19] In a note added to an edition of Pearse's letters, Lyons wrote that future historians will have to weigh the record of an "able organizer and the devoted, if sometimes distraught, headmaster," engaged in endless, workaday "pragmatic correspondence" as a journalist and schoolmaster, against "the flamboyance, sometimes even the barely suppressed hysteria of Pearse's published writings from 1914 onwards."[20] These were not only retrospective judgments. Pearse's fellow Volunteer and writer, and early reviewer of *Ulysses*, Eimar O'Duffy, proposed a similar character sketch in his autobiographical novel, *The Wasted Island* (1919), among the few fictional accounts of the Rising and its long gestation written by a participant in the events. In O'Duffy's novel, according to Robert Hogan, "the Rising was a tragic error made by misguided and hysterical idealists": "The hysteria of Mallow's [a composite character in the novel of Pearse and Joseph Mary Plunkett, another leader of the Rising] exhortation to the Irish to fight has much of the flavour of, say, Pearse's oration at the grave of O'Donovan Rossa."[21] For the disillusioned O'Duffy, this is a political malaise, as in the clear association of Max Nordau's *Degeneration* (1893) with "Mallow and his gang" in the novel.[22] These political perspectives suggest that much of what was diagnosed as hysteria was only pathological from a partisan point of view, as was also clear in the gender politics of the period, and for this reason, as Marjorie Howes suggests, other opposing readings of hysteria were also available. In these, "the degenerate, the hysteric, and the revolutionary" were linked to radical politics and insurrection: the tendency of the Celts "to explode on a very slight stimulus" was not unwelcome in conditions of paralysis that sought to throw off the "abject loyalty" of nationalist Ireland under empire.[23]

Before the outbreak of the Great War, the arming of the National Volunteers led one of the main organizers of the Rising, the veteran Fenian Tom Clarke (1858–1916), to observe that the long years of preparation for a rebellion were quickening at last: "it is worth living in Ireland these times—there is an awakening—the slow, silent plodding and the open preaching is at last showing results.... Hundreds of young fellows... are saying things which proves that the right spot has been touched in them by the volunteering."[24] But it was not just the Irish public that required awakening: so did the British government, according to James Joyce, who voiced sentiments close to the 1916 Proclamation in his essay "The Shade of Parnell" (1912): only "a century adorned by seven Irish revolutionary movements... with dynamite, eloquence, boycotts, obstructionism, armed revolt and political assassination, managed to keep awake the slow, apprehensive conscience of English Liberalism" (*OCPW*, 191). When plans finally got underway for the rebellion, Seán Mac Diarmada, Clarke's long-standing IRB co-conspirator, looked to the revolt as shock treatment for sedation under empire: the rebellion was a "forlorn hope to awaken the people," since "the national morale was so low that there was no other way to arrest than by the shock of a Rising."[25] It was left to General John Maxwell to complete the treatment, the "short sharp shock" of summary executions delivering "the most severe sentences on the known organisers of this detestable Rising."[26] In a striking echo (or premonition) of Stephen

Dedalus's invocation of the nightmare of history in *Ulysses* (*U*, 2.37), the Capuchin friar Fr. Columbus, who tended to casualties on the streets of Easter Week as well as visiting rebel leaders before their execution, wrote he had no need for "that torn-note book lying beside me" to remind him of what he had experienced: "I seem to live again through each moment of it. I can best liken it to some horrible night-mare that struck terror into one soul while it lasted; but the awakening light of day; and the assurance of safety obtained thereby, help to dispel and rob it of its gloom and terror."[27]

The use of terms such as "hysteria," "trauma," "shock," or "nightmare" in relation to society bears witness not so much to the transfer of private ailments to public life as to the conditions that give rise to such conjunctions of pathology and politics in the first place. Joyce himself drew connections between individual and national identity, opening his Italian lecture on "Ireland: Island of Saints and Sages" with the statement "Nations, like individuals, have their egos" (*OCPW*, 108). In Ireland at the turn of the twentieth century, national life was as debilitated as the damaged lives of the individuals who people the pages of *Dubliners*, and it is noteworthy that in the initial plan for a collection of stories, Joyce made provision for those dealing with "public life" but none for private life, as if it has not yet constituted itself as an affective sphere. "Home also I cannot go" (*U*, 1.740), Stephen laments at the end of "Telemachus" in *Ulysses*, and this failure to fully interiorize paralysis as a private malady accounts for its functioning in the margins of the public sphere, the clandestine spaces of street culture from which Joyce launched his epic raid on the inarticulate. It is striking that even the ancient hero Cúchulainn who loomed over the epic gesture of the Rising was prone to hysterical excesses in public: "There are passages . . . [in] ancient Gaelic legends, of interest to the physiological psychologist," wrote George Sigerson in his capacity both as neuroscientist and historian, citing as a case in point

> the extreme nervous excitability in Cuchulainn, such as the distortion of his face in battle, his convulsive leaps, his long inexplicable disability . . . from which he rouses suddenly. Symptoms similar, in many respects, are found in cases of 'induced lethargy' or hypnotic trance.

Modern nervous conditions, it would seem, "are quite in harmony with our knowledge of neurotic exaltation in Celtic races."[28]

The relative absence of interior life, both in domestic space and psychology, partly accounts for the failure of the novel, particularly in its nineteenth-century realist mode, to achieve the prominence attained by poetry and drama during the Revival. The novel took over as the main narrative form in eighteenth- and nineteenth-century metropolitan culture and is central to the evolution of imagined communities in Benedict Anderson's conception of nationalism.[29] The novel, for Georg Lukacs and M. M. Bakhtin, maps the secular diversification and disenchanted worlds of commercial societies, in marked contrast to the unified cosmos of antiquity and the Middle Ages that encouraged the *epic* form.[30] In the epic genre, actions and events derived their meaning not from social factors or individual motivation but from a purposive universe, and it was this order in things that allowed for "paratactic" narrative structures: loose ends and digressions, lists and catalogs, magical interventions, all of which were integrated in the end by a cosmos where nothing happened by chance.[31] Of course, religion persists into the modern era but as private belief, and it falls to the novel, as Lukacs argues, to provide the kind of meaning lacking in the cosmos: "The novel seeks, by giving form, to uncover and construct the concealed totality of life."[32] With the expansion of the world economy beyond the nation-state in the age of imperialism, however, new totalizing forms were required and in this lay the basis, according to Franco Moretti, for the resuscitation of the epic in the modern era.[33] For Fredric Jameson, "Whatever his hostility to Irish cultural nationalism, Joyce's is the epic of the metropolis under imperialism.... [P]recisely these rigid constraints imposed by imperialism in the development of human energies account for the symbolic displacement and flowering of the latter in eloquence, rhetoric and oratorical language of all kinds."[34]

As is clear from its totalizing ambitions, the epic carries with it the danger of reintroducing *myth*—"the epic element in primitive society"—into the modern body politic, a project identified, from different standpoints, by Ernst Cassirer and Theodor Adorno with the rise of fascism and the debased hero-worship of the authoritarian leader.[35] If myth in its earlier forms sought to control nature and the physical world through investing it with human traits, modern myth dominates nature through the cult of technology and mass production, regimenting society with a similar mechanical precision. Under this kind of regime, "nothing is left to chance: [and] everything is well prepared and premeditated"[36] under the watchful eye of the state. Passivity and dependency prevail as agency is displaced onto superiors and the organizational efficiency of the factory is replicated in society, with little or no room for maneuvering outside the system. From this it can be seen that *Ulysses*, though aspiring to world literature, breaks significantly with the holism of myth and, though there is a lot of walking, refuses to march in step with church, state, or the existing social order. Instead of an (artificially) unified cosmos, *Ulysses* exploits rather than repudiates chance, and heroism is dispersed into the most desultory actions at street level, or the shadows and corners of society. It helped, moreover, that in Ireland, epic tales were not consigned to a remote organic past but were ready to hand, in fragmented vernacular forms that coexisted uneasily with forces that looked to Ireland as a social laboratory for colonial modernity.

The totalizing reach of the modern world system—"supposing, of course, that such a thing as totality still exists"—prompted the Viennese novelist Hermann Broch to query whether "the more chaotic the distribution of world forces becomes," it will "be forced to forego its total comprehension through the work of art."[37] Faced with this impasse, Broch wrote, "The *Ulysses* epic burst upon the evolution of the new literature with an 'anticipatory reality' of real violence, and thus, despite its hermeticism, has already proven, as least from the standpoint of literary history . . . its capacity for outlasting time." Notwithstanding its epic scale, *Ulysses* constitutes "the strongest attack on myth": "Bloom contains all the religious nihilism of our age and is consciously represented by him" (GZ, 61–62). Joyce's method picks up on one of the qualities of myth, the lack of separation between human and physical world, but runs it through modern theoretical physics in which "both the observer and his act of seeing—an ideal observer and ideal act of seeing—must be drawn into the field of observation" (GZ, 81). There is no God-like view: indeed, it is the failure to grasp the totality of the modern world system that leads to the collapse of representation, a "theism from which God has been banished."[38] In *Ulysses*, the "theoretic unity of the physical object and the physical act of seeing" (GZ, 81) makes it seem as if representation itself intervenes in reality, transforming what is portrays. Extending beyond itself and "decree[ing] a break with art,"

> the work itself must speak, as must also its contemporaneity and universality; and thus the only thing possible is to examine and question the currents themselves that flow through the Joycean world-quotidian of the epoch: *to what extent have they shaped and are they shaping the epoch, to what extent do they give it form and expression, to what extent may they themselves be identified with the spirit of the age and the age itself?* (GZ, 72; emphasis added)

This conjunction of "contemporaneity and universality" finds expression in the striving for simultaneity, "the compression of events into a single day," which nonetheless extends with epic effect beyond a particular time and place: "the demand for simultaneity remains nevertheless the real objective of all that is epical, in fact of all that is poetic" (*GZ*, 76). For Broch, the suspension of time opens the present on to both past and future, just as the apparently still image is charged with succession and movement: "This objective may be defined as follows: to unify a succession of impressions and experiences, to force the current back into the unity of the simultaneous" (*GZ*, 76). For Hannah Arendt, this elaborates a view of multiple temporalities coexisting in epic time: "What is involved here, evidently, is achieving a simultaneity which transforms all sequence into coexistence," but instead of a unified view, the position of the observer within the field of vision imports contingency back into the "unity of memory and prophecy."[39]

These were the grounds of modern epic in Joyce's Dublin, at once integrated and yet sufficiently peripheral to register the disintegration of an imperial world in crisis. In nineteenth-century and early twentieth-century Ireland, the realist novel was not in a position to relate the story of a nation that lacked definition in form. As Thomas Flanagan notes, "Fielding and Richardson and Jane Austen wrote English novels, to be sure, but not novels 'about England'"; by contrast, "That a novel should take as its theme the shape and feel of the culture itself was an assumption" that governed Irish fiction, even if the genre was in no position to meet the challenge.[40] To be sure, there was no shortage of Irish fiction, as writers sought to emulate the example of Scott or Thackeray in an Irish setting, but only those who contributed to national romances or a distinctive Irish Gothic genre attained a metropolitan readership, in a publishing industry that was largely based in Britain.[41] In the genre of the "national tale" that spanned the nineteenth century, the marriage plot itself functioned as an Act of Union, magically resolving warring or cultural divisions through an imperial romance. The bildungsroman had its Irish equivalents, but such resolution of character formation as is achieved at the end was signaled not by self-consciousness and the admission of the hero (through marriage) to settled society, but by the attainment of *national* consciousness, if only by distinguishing Irish social conditions from their (dominant) British counterparts.[42] The *Künstlerroman* was another route for the formation of disaffected youth as in George Moore's *Confessions of a Young Man* (1888), *Hail and Farewell* (1911–14), and Joyce's *Portrait*, but it also vied with the appeal of a religious vocation as the nets of "nationality, language, religion" (*P*, 220) were thrown around the artist. Engaging with the national Revival, even to escape from it, defined personal identity in cultural terms, so that even the most eloquent spokesperson for individualism in the period, John Eglinton, was disposed to argue, "Whenever a man has found himself, the purpose of nationality is fulfilled in him... the gifts of the spirit are no longer from his country to him but from him to his country."[43]

If the novel is concerned with self-fashioning, the task of the epic, in Caryl Emerson's words, is to "bear responsibility" for the task of "founding a city, for realizing justice."[44] The epic did not simply reflect but was directly involved in the making of society so that the entire heroic age, not just Greek literature, basked in the reflected glory of Homer: "To the Greek bards who shaped the mythology of Hellas," wrote the Irish exponent of the Romantic epic, Standish James O'Grady (1846–1928), "we must attribute all the enormous influence which Greece has exercised on the world."[45] For this reason, it is not surprising that O'Grady, as the "Father of the Revival," sought foundational fictions of the nation in ancient myth and legend repurposed in Romantic terms, rather than the more urbane horizons of the English novel. Part of the appeal of the chivalric epic lay in its evocation of the "aristocratic" values of his own declining Anglo-Irish landlord class, faced with the rise of the kind of commercial and democratic society charted by the novel. O'Grady's disdain for the tarnished gloss of commodity culture, shared with Yeats, derived ultimately from Carlyle but, influenced by Ruskin, was led to express a certain solidarity with labor, even if the value placed on it had more to do with the work ethic than class consciousness. O'Grady excoriated the financial policies of "the great Imperial Vampire" of Gladstone's England, and his protests were directed not only at Home Rule but more generally at the reliance of landlordism on British coercion, which had weakened Anglo-Irish claims to act as the natural leaders of Ireland. With this in mind, O'Grady envisioned "an Anglo-Irish Empire" led from Ireland that circumvented republicanism:

> It is no little peasant and pauper Republic, rejoicing in the possession of a toy parliament [i.e., Home Rule] while governed absolutely by a foreign power, that one sees far away down the shining road, but something radiant, nay, Imperial, moving onward in strange ways to the fulfillment of world-wide destinies. The heroic age in Ireland is not a tradition but a prophecy: unfulfilled, but which is to be fulfilled.[46]

The alternative to vampirish capitalism for O'Grady was not socialism but a world of heroes and chivalry along Carlylean lines: "The literature which groups itself around a hero exhibits not only an [sic] unity with itself, but an acquaintance with the general course of the history of the country, and with preceding and succeeding kings."[47] As the epic belonged not only to literature but to life, it was important to establish its credentials as *history*, a record of the ancient past that presaged the future triumph of aristocratic values.[48] Claims to history, however, had to draw on available archives, and the scattered manuscripts and dilapidated ruins of the Irish past presented anything but an age of glory. For this reason, it was all the more important to draw on the epic to reinstate order: "And thus, regarding the whole from a point of view sufficiently remote, a certain epic completeness and harmony characterizes that vast panoramic succession of ages and races."[49]

It was with this in mind that O'Grady published his three-volume project: *History of Ireland: The Heroic Period* (1878); *History of Ireland: Cuculain and His Contemporaries* (1880); and *History of Ireland: Critical and Philosophical* (1881). Aiming for "a complete escape from positive history and unyielding despotic fact" (*HI*, 57), facts at most provided the raw material of history, which was not the most promising base to start from in Ireland. Unlike "more favored and gifted nations," there was in Ireland no "strong undivided current in the history of a nation moving forward between its firm shores, freighted with the destiny of a single people achieving its fate."[50] Instead, there was an inchoate "nation still unborn": "resultless movements full of hope leading no whither, flashing glories ever dimmed and blasted, travail and labor unceasing, expectation and resolution ever baffled" (*HI*, 145). Such "rubble" called for narrative transformations as complete as any shape-shifting among characters in the sagas, and it is not until facts are elevated in heroic action that history becomes epic: "Romance, epic, drama, and artistic representation are at all times the points to which history continually aspires—there only its final development and efflorescence. Archaeology culminates in history, history culminates in art" (*HI*, 56–57). Comparing the condition of Ireland to the spells or "great enchantment" that immobilized heroes of old in the sagas, he writes: "I had always thought such tales to be more exercises of the imagination, but it is not so. . . . The political understanding of Ireland to-day is under a spell and its will paralysed."[51]

Crucial to a "revival" (a term he coined for his project) was a process of refinement to bring epic into line with contemporary taste: "We may expect to see the vast mass of imaginative conceptions gradually reduced to order and teased and tortured in every way to bring them into harmony, not only with themselves, but with the tone of thought and feeling prevailing at the time of the last redaction."[52] To facilitate this harmony, coarseness and affronts to modern sensibilities had to be removed—"No confusion now, no dissolving scenes or aught that shocks and disturbs, no conflicting events and incredible re-appearances" (*HI*, 45)—but what

O'Grady did not envisage was a modern epic, in the form of *Ulysses*, that reintroduced these elements and that promised to undo Anglo-Irish leadership of the Revival. It was as if all that was discarded by O'Grady was readmitted by Joyce, and O'Grady's condemnation of the contemporary mode could have been written with *Ulysses* in mind: "some uncouth epic begun by a true poet, continued by a newspaper man, and ended by a buffoon: heroic verse, followed by prose, and closed in a disgusting farce."[53]

In straining to bring the unified world of the sagas into contact with the present, O'Grady overlooked the reverse possibility, exploited by Joyce, that the heterogeneity and banality of contemporary life might be re-imported back into the form, laying the grounds for "the fragmentary and ragged succession of events in time" (*HI*, 42) that were to be purged from the epic. Even Cuculain had to come face-to-face with the age of the commodity, as is clear from an anachronistic scene in O'Grady's *Cuculain and His Contemporaries* in which the young warrior visits Dublin ("Ath-a-Cliah") after his heroic exertions in defeating the forces of Queen Maeve:

> Cuculain and [his charioteer] Laeg wandered through the city of Ath-a-Cliah, wondering at the many strange things there, for there was much traffic, and many persons passing through and fro, and a roar of wheels and of hurrying feet. Moreover, along the streets, behind windows of bright glass, were exposed many curious goods of the merchants, and tempting wares of all kinds.... Cuculain and Laeg wandered on from window to gay window, for in some were choice swords, and spear-heads, and body-armour, and in others were chariots, some strong and low-wheeled and scythéd for war, but others also for pleasure.... [In some windows, there] were rolls and leaves of parchment in which men's thoughts were inscribed; and Cuculain wondered at this, for timber and stone only were used among his people for that purpose, and the form of the letters too was different. (*CC*, 290–91)[54]

Laeg buys a toy wooden chariot as a souvenir of the visit, but Cuculain, standing on the pavements gray, is already aware of paralysis in the city: "Cuculain was dejected when he looked upon the people, so small were they, and so pale and ignoble, both in appearance and behavior; and also when he saw the extreme poverty of the poor, and the hurrying eager crowds seeking what he knew not" (*CC*, 291–92). By contrast, the spectacle of two larger-than-life warriors lording it through the streets evokes a response that would not be out of place in a corner of Barney Kiernan's pub in "Cyclops":

[The inhabitants] were astonished at the heroes, the greatness of their stature, the majesty of their bearing, and their tranquility; also, at the richness and brightness of their apparel, the whiteness of their skin, and their long hair, parted in the middle and rolling over their shoulders. For, among the citizens of Ath-a-Cliah, they seemed like scions of some mighty and divine race long since passed away. (CC, 292)

For O'Grady, the imperative of order was such that narrative episodes, "being grouped around and integrally related within a single vital theme, would form a complete whole, and arrest and detain that attention which was dissipated by the *multiplicity of details* not interesting in this context, and by the *various disquisitions and unrelated stories* comprised in those volumes."[55] In *Ulysses*, by contrast, the "multiplicity of details" and "various disquisitions and unrelated stories" add a centrifugal force to the action, exploiting gaps, incongruities, and exaggerations that, for Thomas Kinsella, the leading contemporary translator of *The Táin*, constituted the actual condition of the ancient epics: "There is no unifying narrative tone: the story is told in places with a neutral realism, in places with an air of folk or fantasy."[56] T. S. Eliot famously looked to *Ulysses* to redeem the fallen world of mass society through the coherence of myth—a project, noted above, fraught with political risks—but failed to see that the tradition Joyce drew on in Ireland bore no semblance to the unity of the classical epic.[57] "Survivals" in these circumstances, as Walter Benjamin noted, testified less to continuity than to history working against the grain, owing "not only their existence but their transmission to a constant effort of society—an effort, moreover, by which these riches are greatly altered."[58] In the remnants of Irish sagas, catalogs and lists, heroic striving, shape-shifting, psychological transgressions, and enchanted landscapes have "come down to us [as] the rough-shaped material of an epic [rather] than a completed design."[59] As Maria Tymoczko has noted, "alternate narrative modes" in the later chapters of *Ulysses* deploying lateral, paratactic, and non-hierarchical arrangements of action are "typical of medieval literature as a whole and that Joyce's use of these narrative strategies is therefore consonant with his medievalism ... signals his definite break with the initial, signature, or establishing style of *Ulysses*."[60]

From Romantic to Modern Epic

Ireland was not alone in its reinvention of the epic. The destruction of ancien régimes and the unleashing of violence on an unprecedented scale in Europe in the early twentieth century was registered in fiction, as Michael Bell has noted, by the breakup of the novel form: "If the history of European fiction was the slow emergence of the novel from romance and ultimately from epic, the early twentieth century saw a conscious return of the novel to the bosom of epic."[61] When the quest for narratives of the nation is cited in *Ulysses*, it is associated not with Standish O'Grady but the more pronounced modern temperament of George Sigerson: "Our national epic has yet to be written, Dr Sigerson says" (*U*, 9.309).[62] Unlike O'Grady, Sigerson saw the epic's connection with the Gaelic past as foreshadowing the loss of coherence in contemporary life. As well as conducting a professional career as a neuroscientist and translator of Charcot, noted above, Sigerson was a linguist and literary scholar, acting as president of the National Literary Society from 1893 to 1925. In the second edition of his anthology *Bards of the Gael and Gall* (1907), the charge that ancient Irish sagas fall short of their more coherent, "rimed" Greek and Roman counterparts is answered: "Perhaps I may be allowed to say that the reason the Celts did not compose rimed epics was because of their extreme mental modernity."[63] A modern epic, in these terms, possesses many of the digressive qualities of the ancient form—asides, excessive detail, encyclopedic inclusiveness—but without an ordered cosmos to account for it. Bardic scribes for Sigerson acted not so much as "wordsmiths but as word-jewellers," and the "activity and restlessness of our own days were in their blood in all known time": "It is vain to blame them for outrunning their age. They were in truth the Moderns of the Past— perhaps they are also fated to be the Moderns of the Future."[64] That Sigerson never missed an opportunity to show Gaelic culture outrunning its age is picked up in references to *Bards of the Gael and Gall* in *Finnegans Wake*. "A gael galled by scheme of scorn? [. . .] It sounds an isochronism" (*FW*, 515.7, 11) prompts queries whether the reconstructions of modern epics— *Finnegans Wake* ("these funeral games") and *Ulysses* ("homer's kerryer pidgeons")—conform more to cyclical time ("rally round took place"):

> I want you, witness of this epic struggle, as yours so mine, to reconstruct for us, as briefly as you can, inexactly the same as a mind's eye view, how these funeral games, which have been poring over us through homer's kerryer pidgeons, massacreedoed as the holiname rally round took place. (*FW*, 515.21–26)

In the course of *Bards of the Gael and Gall*, Sigerson points out (perhaps tongue-in-cheek) how modern products such as the diving suit (later de rigueur for surrealists and Flann O'Brien), metal ships, and developments such as women's rights were anticipated in ancient Irish literature, not to mention "the earliest example of blank verse—which is supposed to be a modern invention."[65] His account of the love triangle between Cúchulainn, Emer, and Fanad led a contemporary reviewer to remark: "Here is in a nutshell, in an ancient Gaelic story, the plot of a novel of the type called ultra-modern published the other day in London. To the credit of Irish morality be it added that this Gaelic 'problem-story' belongs to pre-Christian times."[66] This is also the episode, shorn of "conventional sentimentality," that led Patrick Pearse to extol the essential modernity of much of the Irish literary past: "Alike in the Táin and in the fugitive love songs of the manuscripts and of the countrysides we come upon profound intuitions or flashes of imagination which reveal more than many modern novels and much modern poetry." For Pearse, this ranges from the story of Gráinne ("the Hedda Gabler of Irish Literature") to Thomas MacDonagh's verdict on the early dramatic lyric: "only modernly, he thinks, has the dramatic lyric had the intense human thrill of individual subtle character."[67] In MacDonagh's own account, "the long deferred appearance of the epic in [Irish] written literature" is "thwarted and frustrate[d] in many forms": it is as if experience does not lend itself to narrative but to the lyric, "the lyric form of a full literature, though to us a literature in fragments."[68] Citing the scholar Kuno Meyer, early nature poetry is considered by MacDonagh in terms that resemble the modernist techniques of the Imagist movement: "It is characteristic of these poems that in none of them do we get an elaborate or sustained description, but rather a succession of impressionistic pictures and images. The half-said thing to them is dearest: they avoid the obvious and the commonplace" (*LI*, 128). If a "great new literature" was to be made "in the tradition of this old world of Early Irish Literature," it might come, in words anticipating Joyce, "in a new manifestation. It is at its best and highest a new epiphany" (*LI*, 112).

That the shocks against sentiment and propriety delivered by modernity were preempted by medieval Irish texts was the reason Robert Atkinson—professor of Sanskrit and comparative philology at Trinity College, Dublin—sought to exclude the Irish language from the intermediate education curriculum: "I would say it would be difficult to find a book in ancient Irish in which there was not some passage so silly or indecent as to give you a shock from which you would never recover for the rest of your life."[69] Atkinson appears in *Finnegans Wake*, transferred as "my trinity scholar, out of eure sanscreed and into oure eryan" (*FW*, 215.26–27), that is, his Aryan becoming to his dismay the modern Éireann. The impropriety of Irish epic points to the difference in tone between, for example, the solemnity of Alfred Lord Tennyson's "Ulysses" (1842) and the parodies of Joyce's *Ulysses*, but it is not that the latter, as Franco Moretti would have it, is concerned "to put epic universalism into practice—but without taking it seriously." Without taking it at face value might be more accurate, as Moretti qualifies his remark by noting that this element of play does not detract from its epic scale: "The irony that renders its meaning unstable compels us for that very reason to take it seriously."[70] For Joyce, the modern epic is not only in the business of nation making but also empire breaking, so that "he would wipe alley english spooker, multaphoniaksically spuking, off the face of the erse" (*FW*, 178.6).[71]

In a pointed, critically astute exchange at the beginning of the Revival, John Eglinton took issue with the modern recourse to myth and legend on the grounds that while epic was suitable for bygone eras, a contemporary national literature should arise out of, and address, its own age: "The [present-day epic] poet looks too much away from himself, and from his own age, does not feel the facts of life enough, but seeks in art an escape from them."[72] Eglinton entered a caveat, however, for while archaic subject matter may be out of place, the *form* of the epic could still be pressed into service in the modern world. In an uncanny presentiment of *Ulysses* (and of his own presence in the chapter discussing the epic), he advises W. B. Yeats and other "dreamers who walk with their heads in a cloud of vision" to apply their creative faculties to "the mechanical triumphs of modern life":

> The epics of the present are the steam-engine and the dynamo, its lyrics the kinematograph, phonograph, etc., and these bear with them the hearts of men as the Iliad and Odyssey of former times uplifted the youth of antiquity.[73]

Prefiguring Picasso's collages, or indeed Joyce's appropriation of real life, Eglinton called for a new "concrete type of poetry" that brings an end to representation, and in which objects themselves acquire aesthetic form: "The kinematograph, the bicycle, electric tramcars, labour-saving contrivances, etc, are not susceptible of poetic treatment, but are, in fact, themselves the poetry, not without a kind of suggestiveness, of a scientific age."[74] Writing on *Ulysses* in the 1930s, Ernst Bloch reiterated a vision of modern epic that extends to actuality and things, "constitutive as montage which jointly builds real series of streets": "Montage can now do a lot, previously only thoughts lived easily alongside each other, now things do too, at least on the flood area, in the fantastic primeval forest of the void."[75] In antiquity, myth invested external reality with a purpose, but introducing montage wrests objects and events from the spurious myths of commodity culture, treating products themselves as ready-mades awaiting new modes of refashioning: "an invasion of fragments of empirical reality... accompanied by the attempt by works of art to reach out towards an extra-aesthetic reality."[76]

This is also the driving force of epic theater as conceived by Bertolt Brecht, leading the editors of a recent essay collection, *Patrick Pearse and the Theatre*, to suggest "it is also possible (though admittedly anachronistic) to think of the Easter Rising in terms derived from Bertolt Brecht's formulation of 'epic theatre.'"[77] The writer's block experienced by Brecht in exile forced him into new forms of creative activity, (re)assembling ready-made images, writings, and found pieces of journalism into arresting montages in an *Arbeitsjournal* (working journal) — a diary of the work one does not write, as Michel Foucault describes it.[78] Disruptive narrative structures, improvisation, and absence of the "I" produce a makeshift modernism that recapitulates Eglinton's view forty years earlier. As summarized by Georges Didi-Huberman (citing Brecht in the last sentence):

> The epic form for Brecht... takes position in the history of forms insofar as it explicitly articulates an ancient tradition with the most recent techniques of cinematographic, radiophonic and theatrical montage. It is a question first and foremost of "making use of the elements of reality in experimental rearrangements."[79]

As Didi-Huberman notes, Joyce was primarily responsible for Brecht's discovery of the importance of montage for epic theater, discerning "a fundamental domain of modern literature, beginning with James Joyce's *Ulysses*, which he recognized as having 'modified the situation of the novel [to the point] of creating a collection of different methods of observation' arranged in a heterogeneous or multiplying way."[80]

The radical rearranging of "elements of reality" in modern epic describes revolution itself, reactivating sedimented histories in the present. "Like nature," Moretti states, "literature does not make jumps,"[81] but montage operates on breaks and discontinuities in history, bringing times out of joint into contact with each other: for Brecht, "The jump is constantly being made from the particular to the general. From the individual to the typical, from the new to yesterday and tomorrow.... These days, science allows that the passage from one era to another occurs by leaps."[82] The spell cast by the "Return to Camelot" and the Gothic Revival in nineteenth-century Britain evoked not so much a vanished age as assurances of continuity: the queen was still in her castle, notwithstanding the factory at her gate. In Ireland, by contrast, the epic spoke for centuries of conquest and dispossession and if, as Standish O'Grady observed, the heroes were on the road, the past itself was on the move. In "*technical and cultural* montage," Bloch points out, "the *context of the old is decomposed*, a new one is formed. It can be formed as a new one because the old context reveals itself to be illusory, brittle, as one of surface."[83] Rather than reinforcing tradition, the thrust of epic form in Ireland was to reconstitute modernity: as John Wilson Foster wrote of Pearse's Brechtian moment in the Easter Rising, Eglinton "could not have foreseen that in 1916 Pearse proved that poetry and idealism could fatally rupture reality and without reality's permission."[84]

Always writing with an eye to the future, Standish O'Grady, as reported by Yeats, prophesized in 1899: "We have now a literary movement, it is not very important; it will be followed by a political movement that will not be very important; then must come a military movement, that will be important indeed."[85] The modern epic infused literary, political, and military movements in Ireland in the coming decades, but not always as conceived by O'Grady.[86] This has not prevented commentators from attributing the epic gesture of the Easter Rising to O'Grady's anti-democratic influence, most notably on the thought of Patrick Pearse as interpreted by Fr. Francis Shaw, S.J.: "It would seem that Pearse got many of his romantic ideas about early Ireland from the pages of Standish O'Grady. From this infected source he drank deeply; and he was much more of the 'Celtic Twilight' school that he was of the new realism of [Eoin] MacNeill."[87] As a visitor to St. Enda's, O'Grady was well known to Pearse, and his story "The Coming of Fionn" was adapted for the stage at a performance in the school in 1909, attended by O'Grady, Eoin MacNeill, and Yeats, among others. As Philip O'Leary points out, however, Fr. Shaw's characterization of Pearse as relying on epic romances in translation "is both disingenuous and misleading." Unlike O'Grady, who lacked competence in Irish, Pearse had a comprehensive knowledge of Irish manuscript literature and was able "to move well beyond the distortions of O'Grady."[88] For this reason, he had no compunction about reinserting rebarbative elements, making it clear, in his own words, that "the tales when presented to modern readers should not be shorn of their barbarism, or of their grotesqueness, and in fact the barbaric and grotesque element belongs essentially to them."[89] The Victorian Gael as fabricated by O'Grady was in no position to inspire a Rising dedicated (on his terms) to "a pauper Republic," but the extension of montage to the theater of revolt was more likely, as Brecht proposed, to bring about a transformation of society: "Its main function is not to illustrate or advance the action but on the contrary to interrupt it.... It is the retarding quality due of these interruptions and the episodic quality of this framing of action which allows gestural theatre to become epic theatre."[90]

Considered in this light, Wilson Foster's characterization of the impact of medieval Irish epics on Joyce could also apply to the cultural impulses of the Easter Rising: "The Medieval, eschatological cast of mind survived stubbornly among the Irish and has taken patterned forms of expression. That cast of mind coincided felicitously with the priorities of Modernism in this century."[91] It was this combination of forms produced by accelerated social change that forced the colonial state to devise new modes of governance representing an advanced modernity, in effect turning Ireland, as the historian W. L. Burn observed, into "a social laboratory": "The most conventional of Englishmen were willing to experiment in Ireland on lines which they were not prepared to contemplate or tolerate at home."[92] The disposition to experiment in the margins sets the stage for the modern epic outlined by Moretti as "prone to digressions: full of episodes flanking the basic Action": "The textual periphery functions as a kind of protected space, where an innovation has time to develop, and consolidate its own peculiarities."[93] By virtue of its capacity for transforming the national into a modern epic, however, Moretti concludes that the national or local never mattered in the first place: "The geographical frame of reference is no longer the nation-state" and for this reason, "*Ulysses* is not Irish."[94] In marked contrast to this, familiarity with Irish antiquity and the Revival shows that many components of the modern epic were already in place in Ireland, and while grounded in local conditions, had far-reaching, worldwide reverberations in both literature and society. Instead of canceling each other, the clash of old and new in resurgent cultures precipitates radical change: for Bloch, "the beat of the machines let in the African drum," adding "the spirit of Joyce is almost beginning to spook in here."[95] Revolutionaries in Ireland had no reason to believe they could not change the course of history, any more than their counterparts on the European mainland during and after of the Great War, and the vehemence of government responses to revolutionary outbreaks showed that the prospect was real. It is not just that a political vanguard coincided on many points with a literary avantgarde but that, in Wilson Foster's words, "the very shortcomings of the sagas as fiction"[96] broke the barrier that sealed art from reality, transforming the "shot off a shovel" (*U*, 12.1918) at the end of "Cyclops" into a shot that rang throughout the world.

✷ 3 ✷
"A World That Ran Through Things"

ULYSSES, THE EASTER RISING, AND SPATIAL FORM

> In regard to a general plan for the Rising in Easter Week, I heard Pearse say, "Plans were concealed in the form of a novel."
>
> DESMOND RYAN[1]

When F. Scott Fitzgerald in 1923 described *Ulysses* "as the great novel of the future," he did not envisage other less sympathetic critics taking exception to the lack of prophetic powers in a novel set in Dublin in June 1904.[2] Speaking at the Congress of Soviet Writers in 1934, Karl Radek criticized *Ulysses* for its failure to respond to the Easter Rising, which took place in Dublin in April 1916. It is not just that socialist realism, among its many progressive qualities, was expected to see into the future: Radek mistakenly understood Joyce's book to have been "laid in Ireland in 1916," and it would indeed have been strange if Leopold Bloom failed to notice the destruction of landmark buildings mentioned in the novel, such as the DBC (Dublin Bakery Company) on O'Connell Street, while walking in the city center. *Ulysses* purports to be comprehensive and impartial in its "clinical observation" of life, according to Radek, but in its emphasis on trivia and minutiae, it misses the bigger picture: "there is nothing big in life—no big events, no big people, no big ideas":

> For him [Joyce], the national revolutionary movement of the Irish petty bourgeoisie does not exist.... But even if one might conceive for a moment that the Joyce method is a suitable one for describing petty, insignificant, trivial people, their actions, thoughts and feelings... tomorrow these people may be participants in great deeds.... Socialist realism means not only knowing reality as it is, but knowing whither it is moving.[3]

Contrary to Radek, Joyce's method lies precisely in knowing whither a society is moving and discerning this in the most trivial actions: "I have often thought since on looking back over that strange time that it was that small act, trivial in itself, that striking of that match, that determined the whole aftercourse of both our lives" (*U*, 7.763–65). Radek proceeds to berate *Ulysses* for its endless digressions: "if the thought leads off at a tangent, the author hastens to follow it up." What this stricture fails to grasp is that revolution itself breaks off at a tangent, interrupting the imperious march of history "towards one great goal," as extolled by Mr. Deasy in "Nestor" (*U*, 2.380–81). In a perceptive contemporary review of *Ulysses*, Alfred Döblin noted: "It is not a question of combining grand, final ideas, whether internal or external. The connection between the individual, noticeable elements and moments establishes the association."[4] This cinematic eye for detail, and the ability to seize the most unprepossessing moments, brings epic in *Ulysses* down to the "shout in the street" with which Stephen counters Mr. Deasy's investment in grand narratives (*U*, 2.386). "Ideas manifest themselves rather in by-ways, in unobtrusive facts," wrote Siegfried Kracauer of the camera's eye for the incidental: "it may well happen that a close scrutiny of some minor event of the kind favoured on the screen allows one secretly to watch history's moving forces in full action."[5]

Though charting with meticulous accuracy a single day in the life of Dublin, June 16, 1904, *Ulysses* constantly bears witness to its own time of writing, leading to what Enda Duffy has termed the "double-timing" of narration.[6] Joyce began the novel in 1914, but did not complete versions of the first three chapters until late in 1917, by which time the horrors of the "European conflagration" (*U*, 2.327) and the brutal suppression of the Easter Rising had brought about dramatic changes in public opinion in Ireland, leading to successive validations of the Sinn Féin movement in a number of by-elections. Some of the characters in Joyce's fiction (or rather, their real-life counterparts) participated in the Irish revolution, including many in Joyce's inner circle of friends. Joyce's closest friend in Dublin, Constantine P. Curran (1883–1972)—"Curran, ten guineas" (*U*, 2.256), as he appears among Stephen's debtors in *Ulysses*—worked in the court service that would see him appointed as High Court Registrar in 1921 but, under the cover name "Michael Gahan," wrote influential reports on the escalating conflict in Ireland from 1917 to 1922 for the left-liberal British periodical *The Nation*, exposing British misrule and Black and Tan atrocities, and providing an important pro–Sinn Féin voice in Britain.[7] Another close friend of Joyce's, John Francis Byrne (1880–1960)—Cranly in *Portrait* and onetime real-life resident at the Bloom's home at 7 Eccles Street—returned to Ireland in February 1916 from the United States in advance of what he felt was an imminent Rising (itself testimony to his ability to read between the lines of what was already subject to war censorship). Despite Eoin MacNeill's personal assurances that a rebellion would not take place under his stewardship of the Irish Volunteers, a meeting with James Connolly, Seán Mac Diarmada, and Joseph Mary Plunkett in Liberty Hall persuaded Byrne otherwise. He was involved clandestinely in carrying to the *New York Times* correspondent in London copies of the leaked (and probably embellished) "Castle Document," which purported to relay plans of preemptive police raids on houses of sedition in Dublin, including (a hint that the text might indeed have been doctored) the Archbishop's Palace in Drumcondra.[8] The document was sourced from a close mutual friend of both Byrne and Joyce, Francis Sheehy Skeffington (1878–1916), the genial model for McCann in *Portrait*, who had served time in prison for pacifist opposition to recruitment in the Great War and was murdered by British forces in Portobello barracks during the Easter Rising while attempting to calm the urban chaos caused by looting and bombardment. The barracks is the port of call for the pugnacious Private Carr in "Cyclops": "PRIVATE CARR: (*to the navvy.*) Portobello barracks canteen. You ask for Carr. Just Carr" (*U* 12.620). George Clancy (1881–1921) was another close friend of Joyce's while at university, featuring as Madden in *Stephen Hero* and as Davin in *Portrait*. Clancy was briefly arrested after the Easter rebellion but his subsequent rise in nationalist ranks led to his election as Sinn Féin mayor of Limerick in 1921, during which time he was shot dead during a raid on his home by the Black and Tans.

As if in keeping with the "double-timing" of *Ulysses*, Dublin already had two temporal frames, Greenwich mean time (the Meridian), and Dublin time twenty minutes behind (as measured by Dunsink Observatory),[9] but in Joyce's hands, this is stretched to raise questions about time itself, just as its absolute nature was being called into question by the philosophy of Henri Bergson and Henri Poincaré, and the new physics of Einstein. Joyce was amused to hear stories from Wyndham Lewis that "I was a crazy fellow who always carried four watches and rarely spoke except to ask my neighbour what o'clock it was" (*JJ*, 510). Tabulating the past in isolated terms of cause and effect, facts and documentation, often belies the extent to which the historical record is structured by latent narratives, not always evident at the time of their occurrence but apparent later when events have ran their course. *Ulysses*, of course, was set in 1904 but its faithful picture of Dublin is also alert to portents of things to come, demystifying the stasis often implicit in claims to tell the past exactly as it was. In keeping with the telescoping of time in a revolution, the mandate of the Easter Rising was drawn from the future and the past, rather than a political present represented by John Redmond's Irish Parliamentary Party. "Just say [the] name to yourself. Redmond!" the republican *Irish Freedom* protested in 1914, following Redmond's support of the British war effort: "In twenty years there will no Redmonds left in Ireland for the name is disgraced and all decent folk will hide it."[10] For Seán Mac Diarmada, the Rising was necessary "to preserve the Irish national spirit and hand it down to future generations": "Posterity will judge us aright from the effects of our actions."[11] As will be shown below, the 1916 leader Thomas MacDonagh viewed the political vanguard in terms of literary avant-gardism, eschewing a politics of representation in the present for vistas that looked to the future: "We do not profess to represent the mass of the people of Ireland . . . the inert mass, drugged and degenerate by ages of servitude, must, in a distant day of resurrection, render homage and servitude" to the rebels, who will receive "in return the vivifying impress of a free people."[12]

In Joyce's *Portrait*, "The past is consumed in the present and the present is living only because it brings forth the future" (*P*, 273). Conventional autobiographies tend to recount (in retrospect) a life already lived, in which the meaning and selection of events benefit from the wisdom of hindsight. By contrast, in *Portrait* narration gives the impression of conveying life as it happens, catching events in transit and partly constituting them in the process. As Wyndham Lewis acutely observed of Joyce's backward (or forward) look:

> Proust returned to [times past]. Joyce never left them. He discharged it as freely as though the time he wrote about were still present, because it was *his* present. It is rolled out with all the aplomb and vivacity of a contemporary experience. . . . The *man* has not moved since his early days in Dublin. He is on that side a young man embalmed.[13]

In an early version of *Portrait*, the young Joyce had already given expression to this idea: "The past assuredly implies a fluid succession of presents, the development of an entity of which our actual present is a phase only."[14] This is carried over in *Ulysses* to embrace the future: "The past and present are collapsed, but the curious result is that futurity is gestured in."[15] Though adhering assiduously at one level to the present moment, examples abound in the novel of intrusions from the future. In "Wandering Rocks," the flash of the sun on a car windscreen prevents a clear view of Ned Lambert (or his brother) across the street, though the windscreen was only invented that year ("Is that Ned Lambert's brother over the way,

Sam? What? Yes. He's as like it as damn it. No. The windscreen of that motorcar in the sun there. Just a flash like that" [*U*, 10.757–59]). It could be, of course, that Dublin was to the forefront in acquiring such innovations: certainly this is the case when Professor MacHugh produces "a reel of dental floss" (*U*, 7.371) to clean his unwashed teeth, one of the earliest mentions of this advance in dental hygiene. In the National Library chapter, Shakespeare is credited by John Eglinton with putting anachronisms to good use by placing words of Aristotle in the hero Ulysses's mouth, and it is in this chapter that Joyce extends the time frame of *Ulysses* most notably beyond June 1904. The disputants in the debate on Shakespeare are familiar with "Herr Bleibtreu" (*U*, 9.1073), whose *The Solution of the Shakespeare Question: A New Theory* was not published until 1907. Likewise, in a more famous and much discussed example, the theory of "professor Pokorny of Vienna" (*U*, 10.1078) that Hell does not exist in ancient Irish literature is mentioned, though Pokorny was a seventeen-year-old student at the time: his later views on pre-Christian elements in the Celtic past may have been picked up by Joyce on his last visit to Ireland in 1912, or in Zurich while he was composing *Ulysses*.[16]

That the times are out of joint in Pokorny's Vienna is also clear from Stephen's reference to psychoanalysis, to "the new Viennese school Mr Magee [i.e., John Eglinton] spoke of" (*U*, 9.780). Freud's writings had barely made their way into the Anglophone world by 1904, let alone Ireland, though the term "Viennese School" in relation to Freud was used in a lecture by Dr. Cecil Smyly on "Some Aspects of Psychoanalysis" in Dublin, November 1920.[17] Joyce became acquainted with Freud's theories in Trieste, purchasing *The Psychopathology of Everyday Life* and discussing its attribution of meaning to "slips of the tongue"—accidents, throwaway details—with his student Paolo Cuzzi. Psychoanalysis may not be unrelated to the dual-time frame of *Ulysses*, moreover, for one of Freud's more controversial theories addressed the distinctly modern phenomenon of "belatedness" or *Nachträglichkeit*. This concerns the manner in which an experience, particularly of a traumatic kind, is not fully registered at the time of its occurrence but has to await a later occasion, or a fraught version of modern memory, for its realization (not just its recall) in the future. It is not so much that a time lag intervenes but that, to a considerable degree, the past itself is incomplete until it is represented. Freud had developed an early version of *Nachträglichkeit* in the 1890s in his contentious abandonment of "the seduction theory"— the idea, to which he initially subscribed, that hysteria or neurosis was caused by an event in the past that blocked memory, or lacked an outlet. In challenging this notion of an event set in a fixed past, Freud came to the conclusion that it was often memory itself, the transmission of the event as it comes down to the present, that caused the problem. Though Freud courted controversy in suggesting that "events are not the starting point of the analysis, but are deduced from their effects," it does not follow that events are spirited away and reduced to their representations.[18] Rather there is a dual focus: past and present do not displace but mutually define each other. When Freud returned to a more fully worked-out version of belatedness in his treatment of the "Wolf Man" between 1910 and 1918 (a case history familiar to Joyce),[19] the patient's neurosis was attributed not to an original childhood trauma but to a juxtaposition of past and present in which the primal scene coexists "side by side" with moments of its recall. Comparing the layers of time in the Wolf Man's psychic history to the sedimentation of the past in ancient Egypt, Freud wrote:

> So it was that his mental life impressed one in much the same way as the religion of ancient Egypt, which is so unintelligible to us because *it preserves the earlier stages of its development side by side with the end products, retains the most ancient gods and their attributes along with the most modern ones,* and thus, as it were, spreads out upon a two dimensional surface what other instances of evolution show us in the solid.[20]

Instead of unfolding in a linear sequence, a solid past dissolves into spatial contiguity along the lines of *Ulysses*: the past is set off against the present, taking shape in what might be seen as multiple temporalities. The detective work of narration—or therapy—does not lead back to an original, pristine event providing a key to the code: rather, each event generates a tangential narrative in its own right, not always pointing in the same direction. In Peter Brooks's formulation, one story is "juxtaposed to the other, indeed one superimposed upon the other as a kind of palimpsest, a layered text that offers different versions of the same story.... [A]ll tales may lead back not so much to events as to other tales."[21] It is thus that Joyce reintroduces the "various disquisitions and unrelated stories" purged by Standish O'Grady in his romances of the past to furnish the diffuse components of a distinctively modern epic.

Rising Time

Joyce possessed one of the earliest book-length accounts of the Easter Rising, John F. Boyle's *The Irish Rebellion of 1916: A Brief History of the Revolt and Its Suppression* (1916), and premonitions (or echoes) of events in Dublin recur in the pages of *Ulysses*, often in passages open to other interpretations.²² To cite the most obvious example, the reference in "Cyclops" to "lieutenantcolonel Tomkin-Maxwell ffrenchmullan Tomlinson" (*U*, 12.669–70) yokes together General Maxwell, who ordered the execution of the rebels, and the Irish Citizen Army officer Madeleine ffrench-Mullan, who served at the Royal College of Surgeons garrison.²³ In "Circe," the interpolation *"Time's livid final flame leaps and, in the following darkness, ruin of all space, shattered glass and toppling masonry"* (*U*, 15.4244–45) recapitulates earlier lines in "Proteus" referring to the Fenian Clerkenwell explosions of 1867, but their repetition in the later chapter in close proximity to the city center presages the ruin of downtown Dublin during Easter 1916.²⁴ This is more overtly the case in the response to the "Armed heroes" that appear in "Circe":

DISTANT VOICES

Dublin's burning! Dublin's burning! On fire, on fire!

(*Brimstone fires spring up. Dense clouds roll past. Heavy Gatling guns boom. Pandemonium. Troops deploy. Gallop of hoofs. Artillery. Hoarse commands. [...] Pikes clash on cuirasses. Thieves rob the slain. [...] Factory lasses with fancy clothes toss redhot Yorkshire barrabombs. [...] It rains dragons' teeth. Armed heroes spring up from furrows. [...]*) (*U*, 15.4661–81)

As Paul K. Saint-Amour comments, the sheer heterogeneity of references in this passage—including factory girls, perhaps alluding to James Connolly's socialist leanings, and the dragons' teeth of Cadmus (linked to the mythic Phoenician origins of the Irish)—opens the Rising to a vertiginous set of associations. Easter Week introduces the final section, book IV, of *Finnegans Wake*, and indeed is identified with the names of one of its "heroes" Earwicker: "Array! Surrection. Eireweeker to the wohld bludyn world. O rally, O rally, O rally! Phlenxty, O rally" (*FW*, 593.2–4).²⁵

The second paragraph of "Aeolus" begins with a description of the General Post Office (GPO) in the center of Dublin, noting at its side "His Majesty's vermilion mailcars, bearing on their sides the royal initials, E. R. [...]" (*U*, 7.16–17). The banner headline to the section "THE WEARER OF THE CROWN" reinforces links with monarchy but it is difficult not to suspect that in the shadow of the GPO, the initials might have another meaning: the Easter Rising. "Edward Rex," or at least his name, had spelled trouble for Joyce on previous occasions for, as he was preparing *Dubliners* for the printers in 1911, his publishers Maunsel & Company asked him to withdraw derogatory references to Edward the Seventh and "his bloody old bitch of a mother" in the story "Ivy Day in the Committee Room." Joyce, uncharacteristically, changed the words to the less offensive "old mother," but the damage was done. George Roberts, at Maunsel, did not accept the changes and had no difficulty finding other potentially libelous references in the stories to refuse publication of the entire collection. There is a certain poetic justice that Maunsel's premises on Middle Abbey Street were subsequently destroyed during the Easter Rising, for when Edward the Seventh pops up in "Circe" to referee a boxing match between Stephen and Private Carr, it is on account of Stephen insulting the king: ("PRIVATE CARR: 'I'll wring the neck of any fucking bastard says a word against my bleeding fucking king'" [*U*, 15.4644–45]). Edward asks for "peace" before the fight but as has already been made clear, "Edward the peacemaker" is a figure of fun: "—Tell that to a fool, says the citizen. There's a bloody sight more pox than pax about that boyo. Edward Guelph-Wettin!" (*U*, 12.1400–1401). Given the version of peace associated with Edward, it is not surprising to find him *"levitat[ing] over heaps of slain"* bodies, *"the English dogs / That hanged our Irish leaders"* (*U*, 15.4476, 4530): *"The dead of Dublin from Prospect and Mount Jerome in white sheepskin overcoats and black goatfell cloaks arise and appear to many"* (*U*, 15.4670–72)—an apparition that acts as a cue for duels between nationalist figures, including (from the vantage point of 1904) future conflicts between Sinn Féin and the Irish Parliamentary Party: *"Arthur Griffith against John Redmond"* (*U*, 15.4685). When John Wyse Nolan is reported in "Cyclops" as "saying it was Bloom gave the ideas for Sinn Fein to Griffith to put in his paper" (*U*, 12.1573–74), this clearly has more significance in the aftermath of the so-called "Sinn Féin" rebellion of 1916 than it would have possessed in 1904.[26] Sinn Féin, it seems, is ahead of its time and embraces even Great War massacres: "Sonne feine, somme feehn avaunt!" (*FW*, 593.8–9). The numerous mentions of Sinn Féin in *Ulysses*, one year before the movement was founded in 1905, raise questions as to the extent of the term's general circulation, but Wyse Nolan's comment is, in any case, a throwaway remark: out of such trivia, contra Radek, grow unforeseen events.[27]

"Fabled by the daughters of memory. And yet it was in some way if not as memory fabled it" (*U*, 2.7–8). In the classroom in "Nestor," Stephen recounts to his pupils the pyrrhic victory of the Battle of Asculum— *"Another victory like that and we are done for"* (*U*, 2.14)—in a manner that exposes the violence of the Great War or the destruction of Dublin as well as the distant past: "That phrase the world had remembered. A dull ease of the mind. From a hill above a corpsestrewn plain a general speaking to his officers, leaned upon his spear. Any general to any officers. They lend ear" (*U*, 2.15–18). The painful reality of events is all too clear, but what is not so evident is the rationale behind their occurrence, the means whereby mere succession in time assumes narrative coherence or retrospective necessity. The actuality of an event does not establish it had to take place, or that there was only one possible future:

> Had Pyrrhus not fallen by a beldam's hand in Argos or Julius Caesar not been knifed to death. They are not to be thought away. Time has branded them and fettered they are lodged in the room of the infinite possibilities they have ousted. But can those have been possible seeing that they never were? Or was that only possible which came to pass? Weave, weaver of the wind. (*U*, 2.48–53)[28]

Later in *Ulysses*, the theme is picked up again in the context of self-fashioning, our former selves constantly adjusting themselves to patterns woven in the present: "As we [...] weave and unweave our bodies, Stephen said, from day to day [...] so does the artist weave and unweave his image. [...] [T]hat which I was is that which I am and that which in possibility I may come to be. So in the future, the sister of the past, I may see myself as I sit here now but by reflection from that which then I shall be" (*U*, 9.376–85). Actuality is not necessity: as the historian Hugh Trevor-Roper famously observed, "History is not merely what happened, it is what happened in the context of what might have happened."[29]

It is not surprising, given these associations, that many contemporaries, particularly British writers, saw Joyce as a fellow-traveler of the Irish revolution, notwithstanding his pose of studied indifference toward events in Ireland. In his early review of *Portrait*, Ezra Pound noted in passing that Joyce's work illuminated the conditions that led to the Easter Rising of 1916: "If more people had read *A Portrait* and certain stories in Mr Joyce's *Dubliners* there might have been less recent trouble in Ireland. A clear diagnosis is never without value."[30] For Pound, Joyce's anatomy of culture diagnosed not only symptoms of revolt but was akin to those "medical facts" that "like flashes of lightning of the past storm ... reveal for an instant the whole landscape of their time and work and suffering."[31] For others, however, Joyce himself was a symptom of the ills besetting Ireland. According to H. G. Wells, if there is unifying principle in *Portrait*, "it is the fact that everyone in this Dublin story, every human being, accepts as a matter of course, as a thing in nature like the sky and the sea, that the English are to be hated." There are no hints of moderation or Home Rule, "an absolute absence of the idea of a discussed settlement": "It is just hate, a cant cultivated to the pitch of monomania, an ungenerous violent direction of the mind. That is the political atmosphere in which Stephen Dedalus grows up, and in which his essentially responsive mind orients itself." Wells sees *Portrait* as, in effect, a literary proclamation of an Irish Republic in that it removes all common ground between Irish and British culture: "These bright-green young people across the Channel are something quite different from the liberal English in training and tradition, and absolutely set against helping them. No single book has ever shown how different they are, as completely as this most memorable novel."[32] In a later letter to Joyce, Wells spelled out these differences more emphatically: "You and I are set on absolutely different courses. Your training has been Catholic, Irish, insurrectionary; mine, such as it was, was scientific, constructive, and, I suppose, English."[33] As Arthur Power recounts, Wells found *Ulysses* even more alarming than *Portrait*, for in it revolution itself was carried out in the name of affection and not just destruction:

> It is said that when H. G. Wells put down the loosely bound first edition [of *Ulysses*], with pages falling all over the place, he felt he had suppressed a revolution; but I knew that one had been launched. Taking for his subject his native city, which once he had evidently hated, but which now he had re-found to cherish, Joyce had created a new realism, in an atmosphere that was at the same time half-factual and half dream.[34]

Both Pound's and Wells's responses to Joyce have to be placed in the immediate contexts in which they were writing. Pound had been the prime mover in advancing Joyce's claims for a British Civil List pension in 1916, a series of representations that led to direct contact with the office of H. H. Asquith, the prime minister at the time of the Rising. It is hardly likely that Joyce's early pro–Sinn Féin or Fenian sympathies, or Pound's linking Joyce elsewhere to Thomas MacDonagh, one of the executed leaders of the Rising, would have endeared him to the British establishment.[35] On being contacted by Asquith's office to give his opinion of Joyce, George Moore replied: "Of his political views I know nothing. He was not in Ireland during the sowing of the Sinn Fein seed and I hope he is not even a home ruler" (*JJ*, 418). By contrast, Wells was to the forefront of a literary patriotism that led to his participation, with John Galsworthy and Arnold Bennett, in a cultural mission to the United States in 1917 to counteract the effects of the Easter Rising and, specifically, to curtail anti-British and possibly pro-German sentiments among Irish-Americans following the executions.[36]

Pound's observation that "the recent troubles in Ireland" might have been averted had people read Joyce's *Portrait* was hardly intended to be taken seriously by intelligence services at Dublin Castle, but if it meant that Joyce's work provided pointers to the forces that were gathering to foment revolution, it was timely advice. Not least of the "structures of feeling" (in Raymond William's term) in Joyce's work were reimaginings of the national "story" that made allowance for events whose disruptive force threw into question the very coherence of narrative, at least as understood in conventional fiction.[37] If rationales for the Easter Rising saw it as administering a shock to a comatose political system, the problem for narrative was how to address a decisive break in an unfolding story, a discontinuity that rips apart any semblance of order in everyday life. Even when not explicitly plotted (as in fictive dramas or novels), narrative structures govern human action and history, rendering events intelligible in sequential order and establishing discernible patterns of behavior: as proposed by Alasdair MacIntyre, "Narrative is not the work of poets, dramatists and novelists reflecting upon events which had no narrative order before one was imposed in one by the singer or writer" but is constitutive of life itself—with the crucial proviso that it does not *dictate* events but at most structures experience, fashioning the stories people tell of themselves.[38] Narrative requires an ability not only to view events in retrospect as in the usual understanding of history, but also—and perhaps more important for those intent on making radical interventions—techniques of obliquity, foreshadowing, and shaping the future. Without narrative connections between past, present, and future, history would be a mere chronicle, "one damn thing after another," rather than forming patterns that unfold in different ways over time. In a fictional story, the introduction of an entirely inexplicable event with no advance signposting amounts to a deus ex machina, a failure in plotting rather than a genuinely motivated narrative transition. In actual life, however, though existing narratives confer coherence on life, they are in no position to prevent events happening "out of the blue" without advance warning: "events do not occur because of any logical or historical necessity," writes Michael André Bernstein. "Even the laws of probability are regularly transgressed by the course of events, and the unlikely outcome can take place as often as the more likely one."[39]

As the reference to probability indicates, the problem with foreshadowing lies in conceptions of narrative itself, insofar as they adhere to tenets of realism or plausibility. Historians may aspire to write history blind, but for this to take effect in accounts of the years preceding 1916, for example, any possibility of a rising, although feasible in the republican margins, would have to be ruled out in advance, just as it was for contemporaries.[40] Writing in 1906, two years after the putative date of *Ulysses*, Moritz Bonn observed, as if with the Great War in mind: "The danger of an organized Irish revolution which is to take place at a moment when England is involved in political complications may, however, be estimated as very slight."[41] On the outbreak of war, this had not changed: "In my wildest dreams," Sir Augustine Birrell, the cabinet member with responsibility for Ireland, confessed after the Rising, "I never contemplated the possibility of what actually happened."[42] Major General Friend, general commanding officer in Ireland, concurred: "This unexpected rising which took place without any warning, so far as I could see was quite unforeseen by anyone."[43] A historical account that adhered strictly to recording facts as they appeared at the time would concern itself mainly with narratives of Home Rule and its discontents, but these did not account for everything: by writing history blind to the future, historical accounts themselves may end up in a blind alley.[44] Portents of the coming crisis were taking place in the shadows, but to allow for them, narrative methods would have had to be exhaustive and to deploy endless "sideshadowing," noting tangential or marginal incidents that attracted little or no interest at the time.[45] "Noting" is perhaps too strong a term here, for that already presupposes certain items are pressing for attention: what is required are narrative structures that address the *overlooked* as well as the noticed, including details at odds with the linear development of the story and which preempt foregone conclusions.

Such a method, mapping the contingencies of a city "on the borders of insurrection" (to use Joyce's phrase in relation to Parnell), was already taking shape at the time of the Easter Rising in the form of *Ulysses*.[46] Joyce's style is graphic or, as noted above, photographic/cinematographic, in that unlike conventional narratives, the camera puts everything in the picture, regardless of whether it is noticed or not. This technique is akin to what Seymour Chatman terms *naming* or "mentioning in passing," as against the more characteristic verbal means of *asserting*, or signaling, in a description.[47] In an image, an item can be shown without being stated: in an equivalent sentence, it has to be mentioned, but in such a way as if it did not matter—featuring in *Ulysses* as seemingly fleeting glimpses, chance encounters, desultory scene-setting, the inclusion of an item because it took place on June 16, 1904, or, in general, a proliferation of details with no guarantee as to their importance.[48] Much of the confusion experienced by the reader on first encountering the novel derives from narrative excess, leading Joseph Frank to comment on the endless digressions and asides that seem to cut across the story (such as it is):

Joyce assumes—what is obviously not true—that all his readers are Dubliners, intimately acquainted with Dublin life and the personal history of his characters. This allows him to refrain from giving any direct information about his characters, and thus betraying the presence of an omniscient author. What Joyce does instead is to present the elements of his narrative . . . in fragments, as they are thrown out unexplained in the course of casual conversation. . . . The same is true of all the allusions to Dublin life and history and to the external events of the twenty-four hours during which the novel takes place.[49]

Frank sees these fragments as constituting the basis of *spatial form*, descriptive elements spreading out spatially or laterally (as in Freud's description of the sedimentation of the Egyptian past above) to disrupt the temporal flow of the action: hence "the increasing liberation of description from its subordination to *narrative*."[50] This tends to portray spatial form in visual terms as eluding narrative entirely, without allowing for the possibility that spatial digressions may generate *counter-narratives*, resisting integration into the main story, but also preventing the "unity" that Frank considers integral to spatial form.[51]

While Joyce eschewed omniscient narration, other agencies, not least the police and the state apparatus of surveillance, were less willing to forgo "direct information" and were determined to integrate all data—even the most throwaway details—into coherent intelligence systems. The pervasive presence of Castle officials, touts, informers, and police hangers-on in *Ulysses* is in keeping with an all-accommodating narrative that records everything, but at the risk of losing sight of the woods for the trees ("Woods his name is. Wonder what he does" [*U*, 4.148–49]). As Greg Winston notes, "To a great extent, Joyce's fictional urban geography concerns itself with portraying the architectural and spatial realities of a Dublin dominated by military presence. Both *Dubliners* and *Ulysses* frequently orient themselves around key landmarks of British occupation or Irish insurrection, most notably those related to the period preceding and including the Easter Rising."[52] Dublin Castle had access to a considerable store of information, but not necessarily the narratives to make sense of it.[53] In Dublin Metropolitan Police intelligence reports of the period, accounts of notable occurrences—a visit by "Professor John McNeill" to the shop of "T. J. Clarke, 75 Parnell Street"—compete for attention with the most pedestrian accounts of individuals, Bloom fashion, going through their paces, meeting individuals, visiting houses, and always noted with a punctilious attentiveness to time:

J. J. Walsh left 37 Haddington Road at 11.30 a.m. and proceeded to McArthurs, House Agents, 79 Talbot Street, where he remained for twenty minutes. He afterwards inspected a vacant shop at 20 Blessington Street and after some delay returned to his lodgings which he entered at 3.20 p.m. At 4.30 he again left and walked to Sackville Street where he met F. B. Dineen with whom he conversed for a few minutes. He then continued his journey to Croke Park where he called on L. J. O'Toole. He returned to his lodgings at 7.20 p.m., and an hour later was seen to leave accompanied by Michael McCartan. Both visited the Coliseum where they remained until 11 p.m. when they returned to 37 Haddington Road.[54]

In a manner akin to such tedium, Stephen Dedalus at the end of *Portrait* notes an encounter with his nationalist friend Davin (based on George Clancy, as noted above, arrested following the Rising for his nationalist sympathies) at a tobacconist shop on Rutland Square North:

3 *April*. Met Davin at the cigar shop opposite Findlater's church. He was in a black sweater and had a hurley stick. Asked me was it true I was going away and why. Told him the shortest way to Tara was *via* Holyhead. Just then my father came up. Introduction. Father polite and observant. Asked Davin if he might offer him some refreshment. Davin could not, was going to meeting. (*P*, 273)

The cigar shop in question, "An Stad," as noted below (chapter 7), was owned by Cathal McGarvey and features as Cooney's in *Stephen Hero*: the subversive backroom visited by Dedalus/Joyce also hosted leading nationalists such as John MacBride, Arthur Griffith, and Michael Cusack, and was under constant police surveillance.[55] In a case of unwarranted foreshadowing, some commentators, following Chester G. Anderson, have taken the cigar shop opposite Findlater's to be the tobacconist owned by one of the future leaders of the Easter Rising, Tom ("T.J.") Clarke, that also became a clandestine meeting place for advanced republicans before the rebellion.[56] That Clarke did not return from the United States until 1907 to open his shop need not deter a prophetic reading since, as Greg Winston notes, "By the time *Portrait* was published in 1916, the reference to a tobacco shop opposite Findlater's church for many Dublin readers would have immediately suggested Clarke and other masterminds of the Rising."[57]

The "Wandering Rocks" chapter in *Ulysses*, in which various characters go about their business throughout the city with punctilious attention paid to the clock, might be seen as a parody of the type of police report above in which J. J. Walsh's comings and goings jostle with the activities of other individuals. As in the case of *Ulysses*, it was difficult at the time to determine which encounters carry weight, or what connections exist between the figures and, as noted above, Dublin Castle missed cues or was unable to join the dots even when intelligence reports had all but provided them with the final plans. (It is worth noting that Joyce evolved a narrative style based on dots, ellipses, and other seeming non sequiturs from the opening story, "The Sisters" [1904/1914], in *Dubliners*.) Ironically, the intelligence report recording Walsh's movements also notes an inspection of the Volunteers' magazine *Ná Bac Leis* ("Don't bother with it"). The Castle unwittingly seemed to take the magazine's exhortation to heart, at least in relation to details that might have uncovered a republican plot. It is no coincidence that the two most prominent secret service documents brought to bear on events surrounding the Rising, the so-called "Castle Document" and Roger Casement's "Black Diaries," have both drawn charges of forgery, their basic meaning and authorship contested from the outset.[58]

Frank Budgen's well-known account of Joyce writing "Wandering Rocks" with a stopwatch in one hand, and a large map of Dublin spread out before him, testifies not so much to an all-seeing eye but to what is required *in the absence* of such a bird's-eye view.[59] In this, precision in timing of police intelligence was matched by the Irish Volunteers themselves in their preparations for the Rising (though again, with the important proviso it was not clear to all Volunteers, any more than it was to Dublin Castle, that an insurrection was in the offing). As Frank Henderson writes of his role as captain in the Volunteers, operating from Windsor Villas, Fairview, around the corner from Joyce's onetime home on Windsor Avenue, punctuality took on an almost-spectral form, as if bodies materialized out of the air. Describing the training methods of the battalion leader Thomas MacDonagh, Henderson recounts:

> One of the things that he often said regarding punctuality was that the Volunteers when told to mobilise at a certain place at a certain time should arrive on parade as if they had come out of the ground, so that if a stranger was on the spot two or three minutes before the appointed hour there would be nothing unusual to be seen. The Volunteers were to appear as if out of nowhere. That was very important training, and it was a feature of the Volunteers, even the pre-1916 Volunteers. They saw the importance of it and took various measures to ensure punctuality such as correct timing of watches, knowing the time necessary to walk to and from different points in the city, etc.[60]

In *Ulysses*, this becomes a leitmotif, as characters continually appear out of the blue, or cross paths on their way to somewhere else: the flash of the "well heeled" woman's ankle outside the Grosvenor hotel; the glimpse of Boylan coming out of the Red Bank restaurant; Boylan cropping up again at the National Museum; Bloom hiding behind statues in the museum, and later passing, almost imperceptibly, between Stephen and Buck Mulligan as they leave the National Library—all of these compete with fleeting glimpses of the evangelical handout proclaiming "Elijah is coming," a one-legged sailor, the "matutinal" cloud, or "turfbarge" on the Royal Canal, that pop up in different chapters. The mysterious "man in the macintosh" who attends Paddy Dignam's funeral is the exemplar of this trope—"Where the deuce did he pop out of? He wasn't in the chapel, that I'll swear" (*U*, 6.826–27)—but as Frank Kermode points out, the enigma here may have as much to do with the limits of narrative coherence, as in the endless search by Joyce scholars to make sense of the characters' recurrent apparitions.[61] Hence Robert M. Adams's conclusion that there may indeed be dead ends in the novel, and that "the meaningless is interwoven with the meaningful."[62] The challenge is not unlike that faced by police intelligence attempting to weigh up chance encounters, or seemingly nondescript individuals walking the streets, in over-detailed reports: most may prove inconsequential but the difficulty is in knowing which. As if with this in mind, Joyce took it upon himself, following the initial serialization of fourteen episodes of *Ulysses* in *The Little Review* and *The Egoist* magazines, to substantially revise and rewrite the novel, as it were, backward, inserting innumerable seemingly innocuous pointers and signposts to what was coming down the line(s) of subsequent chapters, and multiplying thematic connections between them.[63] Through this proleptic memory, as John Rickard describes it, "forces outside the character or subject" tilt action in new directions in keeping with the narrative sweep of an epic, "break through the impasse of the present moment and move the character dynamically into the future."[64]

In its emphasis on both dispersal and simultaneity of action, the cartography of "Wandering Rocks" looks like a map of the Easter Rising, and it may have been these aspects, as well as subtexts of Fenian secrecy, that led British censorship, as reported by Ezra Pound, to suspect early versions of *Ulysses* of being written in a hermetic spy code. While this was stretching its direct subversive potential, perceiving affinities between its encrypted precision and the language of the outlaw were not wide off the mark.[65] Writing in retrospect, one of the most prominent military leaders in the Anglo-Irish War, Ernie O'Malley, noted that coded communications between republicans in British custody found it necessary to prefigure not only *Ulysses* but also the willful obscurity of *Finnegans Wake*.[66] While held in the guardroom of Dublin Castle, O'Malley managed to keep his identity as one of the most wanted IRA leaders secret from the authorities, and on recognizing another prisoner from joint maneuvers previously in Roscommon, impressed upon him the need to speak in cipher:

> We carried on many a strange conversation in the guardroom as cabbalistic as any magic ritual being made up of place names, personal names, nicknames and the hidden life and history of North Roscommon as I had seen and gathered into my web. An enigmatic remark would be instantly interpreted, or it would take some time to work out and so a kind of local 'Finnegans Wake' was formed before us. Double and treble allusions, hair trigger jokes at which we would find it hard to keep straight faces yet we would not pretend to a shared intimacy.[67]

On his appointment as solicitor of the US Post Office during the war, William H. Lamar's brief included prosecution of *The Little Review* that commenced publication of *Ulysses* in March 1918. Lamar considered himself well equipped for the task as dealing with mysterious words was simply a matter of "reading between the lines": "I am after three things and only three things—pro germanism, pacifism, and high browism."[68] What is of note here, according to Enda Duffy, is a use of language, akin to modernist difficulty, that relates shock tactics in writing to both Joyce and the "pro-Germanism" of events such as the 1916 rebellion:

> One may note that the shock tactics of modernist writing, which undermine a single point of view . . . allow for new representations of guerilla action. . . . [B]oth guerilla tactics in warfare and new levels of obscurity in prose are each symptomatic of a new willingness to transgress the apparently partitioned spaces occupied by the modern subject (for example, public versus private, or individual versus collective spheres).[69]

It is true that the kind of overt prefiguring used in realist narratives to render plausible unexpected shifts in a story mitigate the full force of "a big event," in Radek's terms, but this is not the only means of making sense of the unexpected. In keeping with modernist difficulty, significance may be grasped by those in the know, as against the detached spectator or third-party narrator of realism (akin to the stranger turning up at the Volunteers' training ground who sees nothing).[70] "It is in this precise sense," writes Slavoj Žižek, "that an Event involves subjectivity: the engaged 'subjective perspective' on the Event is part of the Event itself."[71] Hence the manner in which engaged Volunteers second-guessed the silence of the organizers concerning an imminent Rising, whereas Dublin Castle was left in the dark. "The 1916 revolutionaries were, before the event, comparative nonentities who would scarcely have rippled the surface of Irish history had they somehow vanished in 1916," writes Patrick O'Farrell, which accounts for "the astonishment when confronted with the 1916 rebellion. Outside its narrow circle of revolutionary cultists, it was totally unexpected, and thus initially seemed insane, a tragic farce."[72]

Shifting Ground: Spatial Form and the Urban Sublime

> ... the incessant turning of the ground under our feet that is the indispensable preparation for the radical overturning of the ground that we are under.
>
> FRED MOTEN, *The Universal Machine* (2018)[73]

The tendency of characters to pop up out of nowhere is reworked as a narrative device in *Ulysses* in sequences in which a body, if not quite teleported, appears to be *de-ported* (in Fritz Senn's term) to somewhere else, as in Denis J. Maginni's apparent surfacing in Father Conmee's field of vision at the opening of "Wandering Rocks," though he is several blocks or streets away (*U*, 10.56–60).[74] This interlocation may be put down to an editing technique, an unannounced crosscut shifting the action to another location that becomes a signature of the entire chapter, complicating the matter by shifts in time as well. In the phantasmagoria of "Circe," the body's capacity not only to see but also to pass through walls is introduced when Bloom is placed in a courtroom dock over his messianic pretensions and is asked to perform a miracle to back up his claims. In response, Bloom turns his attention to O'Connell Street, Dublin: "*Bloom walks on a net, covers his left eye with his left ear, passes through several walls, climbs Nelson's Pillar . . .*" (*U*, 15.1841–42). Prior to this, "the new Bloomusalem" (*U*, 15.1544) is proclaimed:

> ([. . .] *In the course of its extension several buildings and monuments are demolished.* [. . .] *Numerous houses are razed to the ground.* [. . .] *A part of the walls of Dublin, crowded with loyal sightseers, collapses.*) [. . .] (*A man in a brown macintosh springs up through a trapdoor. He points an elongated finger at Bloom.*) (*U* 15.1550–59)

Walking through walls on O'Connell Street, Bloom recapitulates the urban strategy of tunneling through houses used to strategic effect in the Easter Rising, "sideways" narratives or movements in space at a tangent or parallel to main thoroughfares. In his analysis of spatial form in the novel, Joseph Frank allows for lateral or horizontal movement cutting across the forward trajectory of a story but conceives of this as stasis and simultaneity, a suspension of time, leading to a final convergence: in Stanley Fish's summary, "The final and desired apprehension is one in which the temporal medium has been transcended and the network of internal references and cross-references can be grasped in a single moment of unified vision."[75] This partly conforms to a feature of photography described above where an incidental detail (or an item mentioned in passing) steps aside from the main narrative, but in Joyce such lateral movements are not purely spatial, stepping outside time. Rather, they secrete *alternative narratives*, running parallel or at odds with the main story, and certainly resisting integration into an overall spatially unified vision. In this sideshadowing, as outlined by Gary Morson,

> along with the event [main narrative], we see its alternatives: with each present, another possible present. Sideshadows conjure the ghostly presence of might-have-beens or might-bes.... In sideshadowing, two or more alternative presents, the actual and the possible are made simultaneously visible. This is a simultaneity not *in* time but *of* times.[76]

In Joyce, the throwaway detail is out in the open, but its immediate significance is not there for all to see: "The same facts might possess other vectors." Morson continues, "The products of different pasts, they might be directed to a different set of futures."[77] Dislocated narratives in *Ulysses* that set out at angles from different points to arrive at unexpected destinations resemble the multi-tracking of Volunteer movements through the city in the street warfare tactics of the Rising. The concentration of military shelling on the GPO and its surroundings forced the rebels to escape through adjoining side streets and alleyways, but also to move laterally into buildings where they proceeded to bore through walls in irregular zigzag patterns to prevent pursuers from finding clear targets. In "The Irish Grievance" (1917), one of the better-informed early accounts of the Rising written by Joyce's friend John Francis Byrne, an article in James Connolly's *Workers' Republic* in November 1915 is quoted in relation to house fighting, already flagging that "if the roofs cannot be used, openings must be made with crowbars, from one house to the next in the uppermost story."[78] The occupancy of Kelly's Guns and Ammunition shop ("Kelly's Fort") on O'Connell Bridge at the corner of Sackville Street and Bachelor's Walk led to the opening of passages through walls of houses all the way to Abbey Street close to the GPO, the crowbar and pick being as essential as the rifle in clearing ground.[79] These were the tactics Connolly had in mind when he stated in lectures to the Irish Citizen Army just before the Rising that "he would fight the way he wanted, not the way the enemy wanted. It would be a new way and soldiers had not been trained to deal with it."[80] For this reason, it is not surprising that a Bolshevik delegation, led by Ivan Maisky and Platon Kerzhentsev, made a secret visit to Dublin in the aftermath of the Rising to study Connolly's handiwork, seeing for themselves the fallout from modern urban warfare.[81] These clandestine tactics were emblematic of Ernie O'Malley's view of the Rising itself: "a new spirit was working slowly, half afraid, yet determined. . . . Without guidance or direction, moving as if to clarify itself, nebulous, forming, reforming. . . . It was as if the inarticulate attempted to express themselves in any way or by any method."[82] The crisis in representation that introduced shards of reality into modernist collages (as well as into the fictional worlds of Joyce and others) also worked in reverse, extending montage effects to the streets as though, in Fredric Jameson's words, "the very episodes themselves merged back into space" through the improvised methods of urban revolt.[83]

More than any contemporary British writer, Wyndham Lewis engaged in a sustained critique of Joyce's revolution in literature, considering his stylistic experiments an act of defiance against the spatial and visual coordinates of his own hard-edged modernism. For Lewis, the solidity of objects takes pride of place over movement or relations between things.[84] Writing of the dissolution of inert matter in the "time-philosophy" of Henri Bergson, A. N. Whitehead, and—his main target—James Joyce, Lewis protested that it reduced concreteness itself to the permeable condition of music: "a piece of music moves through you as it were . . . when you are half-way through the piece of music or it is half way through you," there "is no concrete shape existing altogether, once and for all, or *spatially*."[85] Lewis provides a glimpse into what happens when concrete literally gives way in a passage in his novel *The Apes of God* (1930), describing a vision of the Irish rebellion by one of the characters, Dan Boleyn, an Irish poet:

> It was something like a glancing landscape, like the dream that was there— he had had that as a schoolboy in Ireland, when the Rebellion was, the night before the arrest of his father, when he had seen through the pavement (as he had dreamed he was walking) scenery beneath his feet. There was a world that ran through things, like pictures in water or in glassy surfaces, where a mob of persons were engaged in hunting to kill other men, in a battle park. . . . At both ends there were groves of spikes. A withered

world altogether—spike planted parks it looked like. A needle pricked the skin and there was blood.[86]

When concrete ceases to matter, or ceases to *be* matter, the ground opens up to reveal anarchy and violence underneath, and the fear at the end of the novel is that the Irish rebellion will spread to London in the form of the General Strike (*AG*, 663). Though Lewis concedes that Joyce personally cannot be associated with the Easter Rising, his modernism, like that of Yeats, is consistent with the destructive bent of the rebellion: "Joyce and Yeats are the prose and poetry respectively of the Ireland that culminated in the rebellion. . . . Joyce is neither of the militant 'patriot' type, nor yet a historical romancer. In spite of that he is very 'Irish.' He is ready enough, as a literary artist, to stand for Ireland, and has wrapped himself in a gigantic cocoon of local colour in *Ulysses*."[87]

In *The Apes of God*, the shadows of certain characters have a mysterious power to pass through doors, not least the shadow cast by Horace Zagreus, a "satiric target" for aspects of *Ulysses*.[88] The protean Zagreus mentors Dan, the Irish poet and witness of the 1916 rebellion: "Dan was there like a shadow too, on and before the door. Were they inside the door as well, in further projections of still less substance?" Like Simon Magus, Zagreus is said to have a capacity to walk through walls.[89] Just as the Englishman's home is his castle, the nation as room in *The Apes of God* becomes a bastion against invasion, not only from foreign threats but the Celtic periphery within, and in particular Ireland.[90] In keeping with the Irish revolution, Joyce, in Lewis's eyes, is to the fore of a dissolute modernism, liquidating the hard objectivity of Victorian science: "Scientific naturalism . . . deal[s] with things from the outside" and "so achieves a very different effect—one of hardness, not of softness. But the method of *Ulysses* imposes a softness, flabbiness and vagueness everywhere in its Bergsonian fluidity." For Joyce, everything is relational and contextual: "the *things themselves* by which he is surrounded lose . . . their importance, or even meaning. Their *position* absorbs all the attention of his mind." Joyce thus produces the paradox of a *dynamic* still-life, a "torrent of matter, of *nature-morte*."[91] Lewis is taking issue here (though he would recoil from the technical language) with the process of "dereification," which, according to Jameson, is an organizing principle of *Ulysses*, the tendency to release objects and individuals from the petrified forms they assume in commodity culture.[92]

It was not only British artillery that "ran through things": the strategic urban warfare also operated to make a torrent of matter, to invert distinctions between inside and outside, public and private, mobility and the fixity of space. This, according to Joyce Wexler, is the signature style of

Ulysses: "Digressions and extraneous details frustrate the reader's search for causes and explanations. Exaggerated correlations between public events and individual lives domesticated the former and aggrandize the latter. Terrible events are described comically and everyday matters are treated as portents."[93] It is easy to see why aspects of the 1916 Rising were linked to Joyce in Lewis's imagination: in a discordant urban sublime, streets took on the trappings of domestic interiors, with tables, dressers, chairs, and bedstead piled up on each other to make road barricades: at the same time, bricks and masonry separating private rooms in buildings became passageways as insurgents tunneled through city walls. But the architectonics of the Rising was more than a matter of buildings, bricks, and mortar: as in *Ulysses*, time and space were recast themselves as the city opened itself up, in Gilles Deleuze's terms, to transverse pathways, relating disparate spaces through "connections that intensify differences," rather than iron them out.[94]

Writing of the Paris Commune as a harbinger of modernism, Kristin Ross observed that its shock tactics lay in its distribution of space "*not* as a static reality but as active, generative, to experience space as created by an interaction, as something that our bodies reactivate, and that through this reactivation, in turn modifies and transforms us."[95] The strategy of occupying buildings, shooting from hidden positions at open targets on the street, was part of this, but it also incorporated mobility, drawing on the revolutionary Louis Auguste Blanqui's advocacy of "piercing the houses," particularly in the lateral fashion adopted by General Gustave Cluseret during the Commune, "immediately break[ing] through the wall to the adjoining house and so on and so forth as far as possible." In this operation, insurgents move between buildings as if streets, in the Arcades fashion described by Walter Benjamin, were interiors: "It depends on changing houses into passageways—reversing or suspending the division between public and private space."[96] By contrast, main streets (primary narratives, as it were) that were barricaded disrupted the visible flow of traffic, displacing it on to imperceptible movements within seemingly static buildings. Public streets, in effect, became warrens or dead ends, unless countered by local knowledge of the kind highlighted in John F. Boyle's *The Irish Rebellion of 1916* (which Joyce, as noted above, possessed): "The narrow lanes and alleys [of Dublin], the tumble down houses, the opportunities for those who knew the locality of utilizing back-ways, and even of getting from house to house by means of roofs—all these circumstances made the neighbourhood a truly ideal one for the adventurous and enterprising sniper."[97] General Cluseret, one of the military leaders of the Paris Commune, was no stranger to Irish politics and had agreed to become commander of a planned Fenian insurrection in the 1860s that never materialized. His legacy stayed with James Connolly, the architect of street warfare in the Rising, who wrote in "Labour in Irish History": "The circumstances that the general chosen by Stephens [leader of the Fenians] to be the Commander-in-Chief of the Irish Republican army was no less a character than General Cluseret, afterwards Commander-in-chief of the Federals during the Commune of Paris, says more for the principles of the men who were the brains of the Fenian movement than any testimony of subordinates."[98] Connolly had come into personal contact with another veteran of the Commune, Leo Meillet, and with Prosper-Olivier Lissagaray's classic *History of the Commune of 1871* on his bookshelf, the Paris uprising was a key inspiration for his ideas on urban warfare. If these tactics sought to conceal insurgents in city surroundings, making use of local knowledge to appear and disappear from view as circumstances demanded, Joyce's *Ulysses* also elaborates a distinctive narrative style juxtaposing person and place, character and location. The action of walking the city prompts shifts not only in public interactions but also in intimate spaces and inner lives. Peter Hart's description of the Easter Rising as an event that took place to a considerable extent in the minds of its inhabitants also applies to Joyce's Dublin.[99] Ordinary life itself is out of the ordinary, riven with anxieties, exclusions, betrayals, and homelessness that images of "normality" gloss over. In this lies much of the irony in *Ulysses*: Dubliners reside in the city but it is not their own, as the pompous viceregal cavalcade through the heart of the city serves to remind them. It is thus, as Enda Duffy contends, that "the collage of the shocks ... used to represent the cityscape in *Ulysses* bear similarities to the representational impetus of nationalism itself," as the city itself was recast in the revolutionary imagination.[100]

C. Desmond Greaves, no doubt, overstated the case in depicting Dublin "as the most revolutionary centre in the world" in 1916,[101] but insofar as it possessed one of the few national movements that organized a rebellion against an imperial war, the description has some substance.[102] It was a long way from the back streets of Dublin to the far corners of empire, but for James Connolly "the 'far-flung battle line' of England is weakest at the point nearest its heart, [so] that Ireland is in that position of tactical advantage, that a defeat of England in India, Egypt, the Balkans or Flanders would not be so dangerous to the British Empire as any conflict of armed forces in Ireland."[103] Insofar as the stability and solidity of English ground relied on empire, it faced dissolution by the breaching of national boundaries, and it is difficult not to suspect that Wyndham Lewis's defense of the solidity and impregnability of objects arises from this sense of national integrity.[104] "For the Germans," Modris Eksteins noted, "this was a war to change the world; for the British this was a war to preserve a world."[105] The metaphor of passing through walls was construed by Alfred Döblin in Germany as a new aesthetic, "the new objectivity," which, however close to objects, did not leave them as they are: "The truly productive artist, however, must do two things: he must get up close to reality, to its objectivity, its blood, its smell, and then he has *to break through the object*, that is his specific task." This was the achievement of James Joyce's *Ulysses* in Döblin's eyes, "neither a novel nor a poem, but a blow to their foundations."[106] As Winston Churchill reflected, in a not entirely different context, on the impact of the Easter Rising and the War of Independence: "How is that the great English parties are shaken to their foundations and even shattered, almost every generation, by contact with Irish affairs."[107]

✻ 4 ✻
The Easter Rising as Modern Event

MEDIA, TECHNOLOGY, AND TERROR

"What do you think of the Irish Question?"
"It requires too much thought."
CHARLIE CHAPLIN, replying to an interviewer, 1921[1]

Accounts of the Easter Rising in 1916 are frequently offset by the comic bathos of looting on Dublin streets, the upstaging of the heroic ideals of the leaders by the tawdry appeal of commodity culture, and the harshness of life in the tenements. "Probably never in the world's history," wrote an onlooker (not without a little hyperbole), "had there been such a strange combination of pathos and humor, and it will haunt everyone who saw it to their dying day: and if mere passive spectators felt the clash of divergent emotions how much more must these [the leaders], for all their idealism must have appeared to them as crashing down with the first touch of reality."[2] But the clash of emotions can also release other energies: that of montage effects, bringing the Rising within the sphere of the modern and the new medium of cinema. Certainly, some of the looters added a touch that would not have been out of place in Hollywood genres such as the Western or slapstick comedies. Ernie O'Malley noted how looted toy shops added to the cinematic mise-en-scène: "Ragged boys wearing old boots, brown and black, tramped up and down with air-rifles on their shoulders or played cowboys and Indians, armed with black pistols supplied with long rows of paper caps."[3] In this spirit, another contemporary witness observed "a youngster go up to the very steps of the Provisional Government House of the New Republic of Ireland [the GPO] and amuse the armed rebels with impersonations of Charlie Chaplin."[4]

These sideshows draw attention to an aspect of the Easter Rising often lost in Celtic Revival narratives: its essential modernity and integration into the world of media technologies, transport, mass culture, and urban

FIG. 4.1 "A New Form of the Chaplin Craze" from *Film Fun* (January 1916). Charlie Chaplin impersonators line up in Dublin. Photograph: Private collection.

warfare. As Denis Condon has shown, Chaplin was general all over Dublin in the lead-up to the Rising, impersonation competitions already proving crowd pleasers at the Masterpiece Theatre on Talbot Street and at the Rotunda.[5] The major National Museum 2016 centenary exhibition in Collins Barracks, "Proclaiming a Republic: The 1916 Rising," opened with a slideshow highlighting the screening of Chaplin films at the Bohemian Picture Theatre, in Phibsboro, and Chaplin's fame was such that as early as 1915, John Redmond, leader of the Irish Parliamentary Party who committed the National Volunteers to fighting in the Great War, was cast in a political cartoon as a figure of fun in the image of the comedian. "Chaplin has won the hearts of *many* nations; he performs the miracle of which kings are no longer capable," wrote Siegfried Kracauer, "bringing the parties to a ceasefire."[6] Chaplin himself paid an oblique homage to the Easter Rising in his film *The Vagabond*, shot in 1916. The form of a shamrock birthmark on the arm of the heroine Edna attracts the attention of the traveling artist who paints her portrait, and which wins first prize at an exhibition, "paying tribute," as Wes D. Gehring suggests, "to one of America's largest immigrant populations," but in the immediate circumstances of the time, also "acknowledging the attempted 'Easter Rebellion of 1916,' the failed attempt to establish an Irish Republic—which occurred shortly before production started on *The Vagabond*."[7]

The incongruity of Chaplin on the streets or in public life can be seen as a spin-off of modernism, for one of the functions of montage, in Walter Benjamin's estimation, was to close the gap between image and event. Montage was not only a filmic or aesthetic principle: it also took shape in the material culture of the city, "a form which, if already visible in the early arcades, in the kaleidoscopic fortuitous juxtaposition of shop signs and window displays was raised by technology during the course of the century to the level of a conscious principle of construction."[8] Considered in this light, it was not only heroic ideals that came up against reality in the mayhem of looting: with the smashing of shop windows, the dream potential of the commodity also crashed to earth. If the shocks of montage acquired material form in the debris of the Easter Rising, their political effects were to break up existing narratives of the nation that brought Ireland, not always seamlessly, under the dominion of empire. As Alasdair MacIntyre has written, "stories are lived before they are told," and to the extent that history weighs on the minds of the living, it does so through its narrative appeal and hold on memory.[9] The breakdown of conventional narration in Joyce foregrounds and disrupts this process, thus generating, as Laura O'Connor remarks, "opportunities to bring alternative and supplemental stories (and histories) to the fore": "the insurrectionists who imagined, planned, and conducted the Easter Rising did so with a view to making it pivotal to the 'Story of Ireland' and also how it would be remembered and narrated in the future."[10]

That the "story of Ireland" in this period lacked closure or preordained outcomes is clear from the epic film *Ireland a Nation* (dir. Walter MacNamara), begun in 1914 but interrupted by the real-life events of the Rising and the War of Independence.[11] The original film—showcasing derring-do and authentic locations in dramatic reconstructions of the 1798 rebellion, Robert Emmet's insurrection, and Daniel O'Connell—was upstaged by history in the making, as the film sought to catch up with events taking place in Ireland during its production. Actuality footage took over from dramatic reconstructions, sequences seemingly unfolding at random—a Home Rule meeting, Éamon de Valera's visit to the United States, extensive scenes from the funerals of Terence MacSwiney and Michael Fitzgerald following their deaths in hunger strike in 1920, Black and Tans being reviewed by the British prime minister David Lloyd George, and an intertitle toward the end announcing "Ireland Today," featuring a jump cut to the Statue of Liberty in New York—all brought to a close by the artifice of "The Story Told," showing a grandfather telling the story to young children.[12] The only resolution to the narrative is the right to tell one's story, and in this sense, as Roy Foster notes, "it would be Joyce who would in the end subvert the idea of the novel as the story of nations," replacing it with the montage of the modern epic.[13]

The images of Ireland projected by the Easter Rising belong to a world illuminated by electric light as much as the Celtic Twilight. Taking place in a city availing of recent innovations in transport, lighting, and commercial life, as well as new media technologies of photography, film, advertising, and the wireless, the rebellion had more in common with the world of *Ulysses* than a rearguard insular nationalism. New communication technologies cut across the action in *Ulysses* as when, in "Aeolus," the journalist Ignatius Gallaher explains how he wired instant news of the Phoenix Park assassinations in 1882 to New York, including spatial maps in a nonvisual medium; in a reverse movement, news of the General Slocum boat disaster in New York on June 15, 1904, is hot off the press the following day in *Ulysses*, by virtue of advances in wireless telegraphy. One of the first planned actions of the Easter Rising was the seizure of the transatlantic wireless station on Valentia Island, County Kerry, and though Volunteers died in a drowning accident on the mission, a cryptic message was sent on Easter Monday: "Kathleen was successfully operated on today at 12 o'clock." In Dublin, the Irish School of Wireless opposite the GPO was occupied and reactivated to transmit news of the Rising to ocean liners, thus establishing its (disputed) claim, in Marshall McLuhan's *Understanding Media* (1964), to be the world's "first radio *broadcast*."[14] Media technologies are shaped by transformations in society but also act on them, recasting familiar tropes—in this case, heroism, romance, republicanism, even effects of space and time—in their own image. Marx noted that to legitimize revolution, radical innovations often clothed themselves in raiments of the past, and though the 1916 Rising was at first variously perceived as a German plot, a Larkinite socialist revolt, or a Sinn Féin rebellion, the language of Christian martyrdom in propaganda organs such as the *Catholic Bulletin* soon gained currency in popular narratives. But these were by no means the only images available in popular culture, and just as Marx cited the example of the French Revolution draping itself in Roman garb, so also the French Revolution acted as an avatar of events in Ireland, not least in the adoption of the tricolor as the new flag of the Republic.

Screen Memories

With the disenchantment of modernity, "aura," according to Walter Benjamin, passes out of myth and ritual to be replaced by mass media, but it is not clear that the two are incompatible, all the more so in situations where the modern heroic basked in the reflected glory of the star system in theater and cinema.[15] In received images of the Easter Rising, myths of sacrifice are attributed conventionally to Catholic cults of bloodshed and Christlike (rather than Chaplin) impersonations. If we look at the political doctrines in whose name the Rising was staged, it is clear that notwithstanding spiritual graftings, civic republican codes of honor, virtue, and upholding the public interest were also formative principles. The Proclamation of the Rising dedicated itself to "saving the honor" of the nation, but honor, in this sense, is republican virtue, placing the public good before narrow private interests, or even one's life. Sacrifice is only mentioned in the Proclamation in the context of the common good, and in the run-up to the Rising, the IRB's newspaper, *Irish Freedom*, looked to Socrates and Cicero as models of self-sacrifice, in keeping with the tenets of classical republicanism. Socrates is cited on the notion of duty to the Athenian republic (and for which Socrates famously gave up his own life): "[A]re you so wise as not to know that one's country is more honorable, venerable, and sacred and more highly prized.... [I]f it sends one out to battle there to be wounded or slain, this must be done, for justice so requires; and one must not give way or retreat or leave one's post.... [O]ne must do what one's city and country enjoins." Cicero is also quoted to this end: "No man could be called good who would hesitate to die for his country."[16]

These were the motives that informed the republicanism of the United Irishmen at the end of the eighteenth century and, more particularly, Robert Emmet, whose selfless vision owed little to Catholic teaching, messianic or otherwise, and who was a ghostly presence in the grounds of Patrick Pearse's school, St. Enda's, at Rathfarnham. Emmet's mind "was so imbued" with "the oratory and poetry of Greece and Rome," according to his biographer R. R. Madden, that he seemed "to have lived in the past": "The poets of antiquity were his companions, its patriots his models, and its republics his admiration."[17] In the 1840s, Thomas Davis recreated Ireland's claim to be "A Nation Once Again" in the image of the "ancient freemen" of Greece and Rome. At his trial for treason in Dublin in 1848, John Mitchel explicitly invoked republican ideals of self-sacrifice: "The Roman, who saw his hand burning to ashes before the tyrant, promised that three hundred would follow his enterprise. Can I not promise for one, for two, for three, aye for hundreds?"[18] The point of these allusions, as W. B. Stanford notes, was not a display of classical erudition but instead to show a common touch: the assumption was that these are "familiar and emotive emblems and exemplars," and listeners would be expected to know them.[19] In the case of Thomas MacDonagh, one of the leaders of the Rising, "the historical figures that appealed to him were the Gracchi.... Most prophetic of all was his mental dramatization of the end of Tiberius Gracchus. At last he, too, had ascendency over the crowd."[20] That Pearse was also conscious of this republican legacy is clear from his homage to Thomas Davis: "The Romans had a noble word which summed up all the moral beauty and civic valour: the word virtus. If English had as noble a word as that it would be the word to apply to the thing which made Thomas Davis so great a man."[21]

The Irish public, moreover, did not have to read Socrates or Cicero in the original (though the classics were integral to education), for much of the currency of these ideals derived from the popular literature of the French Revolution. Familiarity with the classics, Edith Hall and Henry Stead point out, was to be found "even among the lower orders in Ireland" and "aggravated the British fear of Irish insurgency, since ancient history was associated with the Republican ideology of French revolutionaries."[22] In Eimar O'Duffy's autobiographical novel *The Wasted Island* (1919), a key text in understanding the formation of political sensibilities in Ireland at the turn of the twentieth century, a "History of France came into the hands" of the young protagonist Bernard Lascelles, "and the tale of the French Revolution made him at eleven years of age a red republican": notwithstanding his loyalist Catholic upbringing, republicanism provides a "creed" and a passion for "the general revolution."[23] In the young boy's newly politicized imagination, the ideal "state became a republic of extraordinary virtue in desperate contention with the villain state, now a bigoted upholder of the ancien régime."[24] It was perhaps through the extraordinary fame of Charles Dickens's *A Tale of Two Cities* (1859) that the association of the French Revolution with virtue and self-sacrifice took hold in the popular imagination. As the insuperable odds facing the rebels during the Easter Rising become clear in *The Wasted Island*, one insurgent, Moore, announces, "'I'm going to my death so I salute you. Goodbye all,'" to which his friend, Hektor (itself a nod to antiquity), responds, "'I thought that kind of character didn't exist outside novels. . . . Who says Sidney [*sic*] Carton's improbable now?'"[25] In Lennox Robinson's *The Lost Leader* (1918), a play (in every sense) on the possibility of Parnell's return from the grave, the journalist who "discovers" that Parnell is still alive initially proposes "Recalled to Life" as the headline for his scoop, the title coming from the first book of *A Tale of Two Cities*.[26] Dickens was staple reading in the Pearse household: Willie Pearse, according to Desmond Ryan, was "a devout student of Dickens, he told me once that nothing delighted him so much in all the volumes of that writer than David Copperfield slapping Uriah Heep in the face."[27] As founding members of the Leinster Stage Society, both Willie and Mary Brigid Pearse staged dramatizations of Dickens's works, and Willie adapted several of Dickens's works to celebrate the centenary of the writer's birth in February 1912.[28] Nor were the Pearse family strangers to the modern cult of the celebrity: they subscribed to the George Newnes series *Celebrities of the Stage*, twelve issues of which remain in the Pearse Museum at St. Enda's, Dublin.[29]

Sydney Carton's words on the scaffold in *A Tale of Two Cities*—"It is a far, far better thing that I do, than I have ever done; it is a far, far better rest that I go to than I have ever known"—passed into popular culture to such an extent that they exemplified the set piece pilloried by Gustave Flaubert in his encyclopedia of clichés or "Accepted Ideas": "SCAFFOLD. When mounting it, be sure to utter several eloquent phrases before dying."[30] In Ireland, Carton's iconic status was given additional currency on account of the highly successful dramatization, *The Only Way* (1899), co-written by the Rev. Freeman Wills, son of historian and philosopher, Rev. James Wills, a close friend of the Wilde family in Castlerea, County Roscommon (one of Oscar's middle names, Wills, derived from their neighbors). *The Only Way* opened in Dublin at the Theatre Royal in 1899, showcasing one of the first stars of the modern stage, John Martin-Harvey, whose fame had spread to Ireland: "Harvey was by 1904 one of Dublin's favorite actors, especially in his portrayal of Sydney Carton."[31] Among Martin-Harvey's admirers, we learn in *Ulysses*, was Gerty MacDowell, who uses "matinée idol" (*U*, 13.417) in one of the first mentions of the term to evoke his modern aura, but the starstruck Milly and Molly Bloom were also among his avid fans. Milly was so carried away by his performance, Molly recalls,

> she clapped when the curtain came down because he looked so handsome then we had Martin Harvey for breakfast dinner and supper I thought to myself afterwards it must be real love if a man gives up his life for her that way for nothing I suppose there are a few men like that left its hard to believe in it though unless it really happened to me the majority of them with not a particle of love in their natures to find two people like that nowadays full up of each other that would feel the same way as you do theyre usually a bit foolish in the head. (*U*, 18.1054–61)

It is not just his looks, à la Gerty MacDowell, that stays with Molly but the heroic gesture of giving up one's life for another, a combination of romance and political sacrifice in the case of Carton and Lucie Manette that also surrounded the story of Robert Emmet and Sarah Curran. The cult of Martin-Harvey found a ready audience in the Dickens Fellowship of Ireland, founded in 1907, whose members made a pilgrimage to "the residence of Mr and Mrs Martin Harvey" in October of that year.[32] Martin-Harvey's appeal embraced high as well as popular culture, the celebrity taking up invitations to lecture on the art of acting at Trinity College (he was involved with Gordon Craig in setting up a School for the Art of Theatre),[33] and also lunching with literati such as Edward Dowden, W. B. Yeats, Lady Gregory, J. M. Synge, and political radicals such as Maud Gonne and Countess Markievicz. Yeats was greatly taken by his playing of *Hamlet*, praising it in terms that would not have been out of place in perceptions of the Easter Rising: "A performance of *Hamlet* is always to me

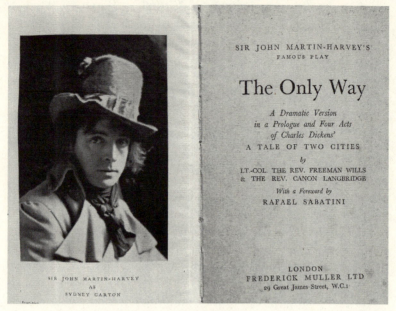

FIG. 4.2 *The Only Way* (1899; 1942). Title page with frontispiece of matinee idol, John Martin-Harvey. Photograph: Private collection.

what High Mass is to a good Catholic. It is my supreme religious event, I see in it a soul jarred & broken away from the life of the world.... I feel that the play should seem to one, not so much deep as full of lyrical loftiness & I feel this all the more because I am getting tired of our modern delight in the Abyss."[34] Martin-Harvey's charisma even extended to the outskirts of the Pale, leading, as Stephen Watt notes, "one resident at Maynooth to request that a special train be assigned to leave Dublin at 11.30 P.M. so that playgoers living in outlying suburbs could see Harvey when he visited Dublin and still manage to find their way home that night."[35]

The reference to Maynooth may not be entirely unrelated to Martin-Harvey's appeal in Ireland, for while the first part of Dickens's hero's name has been traced to the English republican martyr Algernon Sidney, the link of the surname Carton to another republican figure, at least where Irish readers and audiences were concerned, has received less comment.[36] Lord Edward Fitzgerald (1763–1798), one of the leaders of the 1798 rebellion, was born into Carton House, outside Maynooth, and Fitzgerald's escapades in France and Ireland, and his French wife Pamela de Genlis, almost vied with Emmet and Sarah Curran in the Irish national imagination. Dickens published material relating to the 1798 rebellion in his periodicals: "The Last Howley of Killowen," dealing with the execution at the gallows of an innocent man, young Howley, was published in *Household Words* in 1854, and the later "Old Stories Retold: The Battle of Vinegar Hill," featured in *All the Year Round* in 1867.[37] Dickens began work on *A Tale of Two Cities* following his reading tour of Ireland and Scotland in 1858, and Ireland was close to his heart in another way: his secret relationship had begun with the young actor Ellen Lawless Ternan, daughter of the Irish actor-manager Thomas Lawless Ternan and actor Frances Jarman. Lucie Manette's name in *A Tale of Two Cities* was drawn from the character played by Ellen in the stage performance of Wilkie Collins's *The Frozen Deep*, the occasion of her meeting Dickens in 1857, and the resemblance of Lucie's physical appearance to herself can hardly have escaped Ellen's notice when reading proofs of Dickens's novel while it was being prepared for publication.[38]

The issue is not so much Dickens's overt intentions as what Irish audiences brought to readings, or to performances, of the story from their own interpretative communities. That popular memory of the 1798 rebellion, and particularly of Lord Edward Fitzgerald, was part of the substratum of consciousness in Joyce's Dublin is clear, as noted above, in Tom Kernan's unwitting invocation of "The Memory of the Dead" in relation to Lord Edward on his walk by Thomas Street in "Wandering Rocks," and its recurrence in other chapters. In "Araby" in *Dubliners*, "the nasal chanting of street-singers, who sang a *come-all-you* about O'Donovan Rossa, or a ballad about the troubles in our native land . . . converged in a single sensation of life" (*D*, 23) for the young boy, and, mingling with his affections for a young girl, Mangan's sister, take on the force of musical sensations so that his "body was like a harp and her words and gestures were like fingers running upon the wires" (*D*, 23). This theme is picked up in the story "Two Gallants" when, on their mission to exploit a vulnerable "slavey" or servant girl, Corley and Lenehan pass by the Kildare Street club where they encounter a forlorn harpist:

> Not far from the porch of the club a harpist stood in the roadway, playing to a little ring of listeners. He plucked at the wires heedlessly, glancing quickly from time to time at the face of each new-comer and from time to time, wearily also, at the sky. His harp too, heedless that her coverings had fallen about her knees, seemed weary alike of the eyes of strangers and of her master's hands. One hand played in the bass the melody of *Silent, O Moyle*, while the other careered in the treble after each group of notes. (*D* 48)

The compromised condition of the harp, with "her" body exposed pitilessly to the public gaze, links it to the servant girl in the story, but also to the abject condition of Ireland and its ignominious political servitude.[39]

The harp in question, with its display of a bare female torso, recalls the symbol of the United Irishmen, and rather than raising itself to the level of consciousness, this association, with its "mournful music," percolates physically through Lenehan's body. When Corley leaves on his tryst with the servant girl, Lenehan walks down one side of Merrion Square, his involuntary actions recalling the forlorn harpist:

> Now that he was alone his face looked older. His gaiety seemed to forsake him and, as he came by the railings of the Duke's Lawn, he allowed his hand to run along them. The air which the harpist had played began to control his movements. His softly padded feet played the melody while his fingers swept a scale of variations idly along the railings after each group of notes. (*D*, 50).

The Duke's Lawn is that of Leinster House, the Dublin residence of the family of Lord Edward Fitzgerald, and it is as if, in keeping with the boy in "Araby," Lenehan's insensate body has become an Aeolian harp, strummed not so much by his own fingers as by a historically charged physical environment at the turn of the twentieth century. In this capacity, Walter Benjamin cites Ferdinand Leon's description of how the montage of historical time in the modern city, formally exploited by cinema, infiltrates the mind of even the most casual passerby: "The most heterogeneous temporal elements thus coexist in the city.... Whoever sets foot in the city feels caught up as in a web of dreams, where the most remote part is linked to the events of today.... Things which find no expression in political events, or find only minimal expression, unfold in the cities: they are a superfine instrument, responsive as an Aeolian harp—despite their specific gravity—to the living vibrations of the air."[40]

In this reading, the resonances of "Carton" in Ireland would have fallen on receptive ears, just as buried memories of "Sidney" would have stirred radical sentiments in English audiences. It did not take long for *A Tale of Two Cities* to find its way onto the cinema screen. Though adapted as early as 1907, the first major film, citing *The Only Way* in its intertitles and starring the Irish-American actor Maurice Costello, was made for the Vitagraph company in 1911 and was screened in 1913 at the Camden Theatre in Dublin. On a visit to Long Island, New York, it caught the eye of an Irish admirer, the future film director Rex Ingram, who found that the theatrical version was still hard to emulate:

> I did not go to the picture with an open mind, for I had seen the stage version, *The Only Way*, at the Theatre Royal in Dublin with Martin Harvey

as the star. It was the first play I had seen and was still my favorite. But after the Vitagraph version got underway I found myself liking Costello in spite of my prejudice.[41]

Impersonation was a theme in Dickens's novel, and it is not surprising it had its own doubles in Irish popular fiction, not least Annie M. P. Smithson's best-selling *The Walk of a Queen* (1922), which ends with a prison escape in which a morally compromised IRA Volunteer saves his more heroic twin brother facing execution in a last-minute substitution.[42] The plotline led Eimar O'Duffy in his tart review of the novel to note: "Whenever Doubles or Twins (as in this case) appear in a tale in times of terror, with executions looming in the background, I always know what to expect":

> May I suggest to Miss Smithson that no Black-and-Tan would allow a prisoner to talk with a visitor in Irish, or turn his back to allow them to change coats? And that nobody who has read *The* [sic] *Tale of Two Cities* (as Desmond [the errant brother] must surely have done), would have the slightest doubt that the substitution must mean death to the rescuer. Dickens' arrangement of the episode was improbable enough; Miss Smithson's plagiarism is impossible.[43]

The popularity of Dickens suggests that much of his fame derived from versions on stage and screen, as well as abridged versions of his novels. By 1886, up to sixty plays had been staged based on his work. By the same token, in addition to the cult of Lord Edward, over forty plays were written about Robert Emmet, including Dion Boucicault's melodrama *Robert Emmet* (1884), as well as two operas and innumerable novels. It is not surprising, as Kevin Rockett has shown, that the story of Emmet dominated the first Irish political films, featuring as the subject of a silent film as early as 1911 proclaiming "the pathetic love story of Emmet and Sarah Curran is a page of history that will never be forgotten by their countrymen."[44] Emmet, as noted above, took center stage in the first national epic film, *Ireland a Nation*, and as W. J. McCormack has suggested, Emmet's story may also be backlit by Dickens's version of the French Revolution:

> Suffice to say . . . that the influence of Charles Dickens can be assumed in the household of James Pearse, and that of *A Tale of Two Cities* (1859) discerned in the tangled political rhetoric of Patrick, his son. Juxtaposition of "the republic" and "resurrection" gradually converges in the death of Sydney Carton, whose demeanour surely contributes to Pearse's imagined Robert Emmet.[45]

McCormack is right to focus on tangled rhetoric and an aesthetic of juxtaposition, for republicanism is being mediated through the jarring techniques of modern cinema. The heroic may have less to do with Romantic Ireland and more with the spell of the matinee idol, or indeed the comic montage of a Chaplin impersonation in front of the GPO.

It was in fact the narrative techniques of Dickens, according to Sergei Eisenstein, that prepared the ground for the disjunctive methods of narration in early cinema, the disruptions of time and space occasioned by close-ups, crosscutting, flashbacks, panning and tracking shots that early commentators discerned in the films of D. W. Griffith and others. "This is why I dig more and more deeply into the film-indications of Dickens," Eisenstein wrote. "So I must be excused, in leafing through Dickens, for having found in him even—a 'dissolve.' How else could this passage be defined—the opening of the last chapter of *A Tale of Two Cities*":

> Along the Paris streets, the death-carts rumble, hollow and harsh. Six tumbrils carry the day's wine to La Guillotine.... Six tumbrils roll along the streets. Change these back again to what they were, thou powerful enchanter, Time, and they shall be seen to be the carriages of absolute monarchs, the equipages of feudal nobles, the toilettes of flaring Jezebels, the churches that are not my father's house but dens of thieves, the huts of millions of starving peasants![46]

It is striking that a "dissolve" is used in *A Tale of Two Cities* to bring "the most heterogeneous temporal elements [that] thus coexist in the city," as described by Benjamin above, into contact, for similar juxtapositions between past and present—between the French Revolution, the 1798 rebellion, and 1916—are also found in the staging of the Easter Rising. "Have they a flag?" a character asks, looking at the GPO, in Michael Farrell's bildungsroman *Thy Tears Might Cease* (1963): "Those colours come from '98 and the French Revolution. It's like the Republican tricolour." "Bloody playboys—doing the Robert Emmet!" another responds.[47] Raising the tricolour was a significant gesture in this context, for affinities with French republicanism offset tendencies that might have settled for German monarchical rule in the event of an Axis victory in the Great War: as Ronan McGreevy remarks, "French republicanism was much mistrusted in Ireland especially by the Catholic Church, and France's status as republic with a president at its head was an anomaly in Europe at the time."[48] *Thy Tears Might Cease* recounts how the succession of past revolts invoked in the Proclamation makes a deep impression on Martin, the main protagonist of the story: "In the name of the dead generations.... The people of

Ireland. . . . Six times in the last one hundred years they have asserted it in arms. Again asserting it in arms."[49] As Roisín Higgins notes, "The Easter Rising was itself a commemorative event," and each commemoration "carries echoes of previous demonstrations and anniversaries so that they can be understood better as palimpsest than replica."[50]

Time Transfixed

Viewing the Rising through the lens of media technologies familiar to Dubliners at the turn of the twentieth century is in keeping with its own reconfigurations of time and space, outlined above in chapter 3. One of the recurrent features in the background of photographs of the Rising is the amount of billboard advertising, as in recruitment campaigns for the British army, posters of which already catch Bloom's attention in the post office in Westland Row (U, 5.56–75) but which became particularly graphic and arresting during the Great War. A detail in a photograph of a military checkpoint at Mount Street Bridge, the scene of the heaviest fighting during the rebellion, shows another set of posters, including a billboard display with an advertisement for the Coliseum Theatre on Henry Street (fig. 4.3). In this, we see the photograph's own intervention in time, not only the frozen moment but the cancellation of the future. The coming attractions on the poster never took place, for the Rising diverted the course of events; in a sense, the Rising as originally envisaged did not take place either, due to the last-minute countermanding order by Eoin McNeill on Easter Sunday, 1916, which ensured that, in unforeseen circumstances, the leaders had to look to immediate alternative futures for its realization. In a photograph taken after the Rising, it becomes clear why the future attraction at the Coliseum never materialized: the new theater is in ruins, barely identified by its canopy (fig. 4.5). Other images show the rubble and tangled girders of the shattered auditorium where Volunteers (as noted above) had tunneled through and holed up to escape the shelling of the GPO.

According to Max Caulfield, life in the center of Dublin came to a standstill during the Rising: "There was no theatre, no cinema. There was no time indeed, indeed; for every public clock in the city had stopped—in need of rewinding."[51] The famous image of the stopped clock in the GPO did not need a revolution to arrest time, however, for the photograph, as Eugene Cadava notes, does not so much step outside time as *redirect* it:

> [The photograph] interrupts history and opens up another possibility of history, one that spaces time and temporalizes space. A force of arrest, the image translates an aspect of time into something like a certain space,

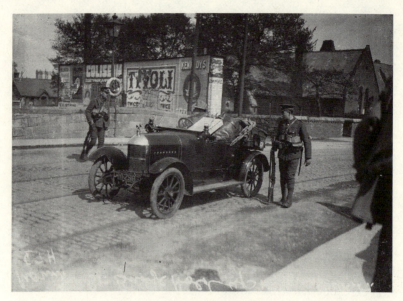

FIG. 4.3 Military checkpoint, Mount Street Bridge (1916). A poster for the Coliseum Theatre is in the background on the left. Photograph: Courtesy of the National Library of Ireland.

FIG. 4.4 Henry Street (1916). The ruins of the Coliseum Theatre. Photograph: © National Museum of Ireland.

camera. The myth that Michael Collins escaped capture because Dublin Castle had no photograph of him has been questioned, but the story is not entirely without foundation. Several accounts survive of Volunteers meting out rough justice to photographers suspected of working for the state. Patrick Kelly noted how he with a number of others were ordered "to intercept a camera man who had taken photographs of Mick Collins," but who eluded them:

> Some time later we carried out a raid on a photographer who had taken pictures of a review by Lord French. [We] waylaid him on his way to the Castle at the junction of Cork Hill and Dame St. He struggled to retain his camera but finally relinquished it. We passed it to [Tom] O'Reilly who was on a bicycle in Parliament St. He rode away with it and dumped it in the Liffey.[54]

In a well-known photograph of prisoners on a landing in Stafford jail after the Rising, the "X" marking Collins in the background is so insistent as to seem part of the original scene: this is a marked man. Collins himself was not averse to the use of the camera, particularly for propaganda purposes. Following the example set by the Jeremiah O'Donovan Rossa funeral in 1915, he arranged for the filming of Thomas Ashe's funeral in 1917, at which he gave the graveside oration. Five years later, at the height of the Civil War, it was the turn of his former friend Harry Boland to die at the hands of the state, except this time Collins was in power: cameras were confiscated at the entrance to Glasnevin Cemetery, and the only visual record of the event is an evocative painting by Jack B. Yeats.

Photography, therefore, did not only represent but was part of the struggle. When Tom Kernan in "Grace" in *Dubliners* states he is willing to make his peace with the Catholic Church apart from "the magic-lantern business" (*D*, 171), he could have been referring to republican activism as well. During the Queen Victoria Jubilee celebrations in Dublin, Maud Gonne used a magic lantern to project images of recent eviction scenes on a large screen in Rutland (now Parnell) Square, Dublin.[55] To ensure a darkened setting, James Connolly arranged for workers in the corporation to cut electric wires to black out city center electric displays in shop windows and streets celebrating the jubilee. As Catherine Morris has shown, magic lantern shows of Irish scenery and history were central to Alice Milligan's state-of-the-art Celtic Revival activities, the still image finding its charged dramatic equivalent in the "living pictures" of tableaux vivants.[56] For all his interest in photography, Pearse was camera-shy for sensitive, personal reasons: a slight cast in his eye which he concealed by

FIG. 4.5 Count Plunkett speech, Loopline Bridge, with Cabman's shelter vis[ible in] the crowd (1917). Photograph: Courtesy of the National Library of Ireland.

and does so without stopping time, or without preventing it from b[eing] time. . . . [It] opens a space for time itself, dispersing it from its con[tin]uous present.[52]

Holding on to the here and now, the suspension of the prevailing flo[w of] time opens up the present to both unresolved pasts and narratives wh[ose] time has yet to come. In a photograph of the newly elected Count Pl[un]kett, father of one of the executed leaders of the Rising, addressing a cro[wd] at the Loopline Bridge, a cabman's shelter is visible in the background, [the] late-night rendezvous memorialized in the "Eumaeus" chapter of *Ulys[ses]* as the haunt of the notorious jarvey, James Fitzharris ("Skin-the-Goat[")] who drove the decoy cab following the assassination of Thomas Hen[ry] Burke and Lord Frederick Cavendish in the Phoenix Park in 1882 by t[he] Invincibles.

It is not surprising that in times of crisis, the camera was considered [a] threat by the authorities, leading to an official ban on troop photograph[y] in the Great War, and on suspicious uses of the camera or photographi[c] displays in Ireland (under the Defence of the Realm Act). Given the por[-]tability of the new "Soldier's Kodak," as noted by Orla Fitzpatrick, it wa[s] not too difficult for soldiers or civilians to evade the ban and to take sur[-]reptitiously many of the photos that have now passed into the visual ar[-]chive.[53] The power of the image showed that those with something to hide, or who had good reason themselves to hide, were justifiably wary of the looking away from the camera or by cultivating a profile. Ironically, it was this pose—head "worthy of a Roman coin" in Yeats's description of John O'Leary[57]—that contributed to the nobility and idealism that retrospectively surrounded the image of Pearse, the profile suggesting, in Roland Barthes's terms, that while one eye was on the real world, the other was on eternity.[58] Like Cúchulainn, the camera seemed to be a member of the staff at St. Enda's, resulting in an enormous visual archive of photographs of sporting teams, pageants, and pictures of individual pupils. In the promotional literature for *The Boy Deeds of Cuchulain at St Enda's*, the casting of a pupil, Frank Dowling, as Setanta is imbued with the look of the modern photogenic face consistent with Pearse's self-conscious approach to photography. As Elaine Sisson has noted, the promotional literature for the school included photographic postcards publicizing its achievements, "images of the boys dressed in the clothes of ancient Ireland—as warriors, saints, and heroes—... were a visual shorthand to suggest that the current pupils and heroes of ancient Ireland existed within the same narrative":

> How better to isolate a single moment and present it as a visual link between past and present than to produce a fixed image which can also be mass produced? Photographic images produced at St Enda's of Cúchulainn as a boy illustrate how the photograph is a powerful way to demonstrate the collision of history and temporality.[59]

As a young man, Pearse followed Milligan's lead and overcame his natural shyness in public speaking by lecturing with the help of magic lantern slides: among the images in the Pearse family's collection were slides showing a military display by the French army in Versailles in 1889 to commemorate the centenary of the first meeting of the Estates-General in Versailles in 1789, and another depicting the iconic Eiffel Tower, which was the centerpiece of the Exposition Universelle, held to mark the centenary of the French Revolution.

In the tableaux vivant favored by the magic lantern, still and moving image, photography and film, come together. But the charged figure of the tableau has another peculiarity: its moment of transformation lies not in the present but in the future. The exemplary scene denotes the point of "peripeteia" in an action, "that pregnant moment in the narrative in which the past can be seen to give way to the future."[60] In paintings such as Jacques-Louis David's *Oath of the Horatii* (1784) and Henry Fuseli's *Oath of the Three Confederates on the Rutli* (1780), the warrior sons are not so much engaging in heroic action as pledging themselves to *a future* of honor and *virtú*. The countenance of a profile may suggest, as we have seen, that one eye is focused on higher things, but in John Hassall's famous poster for *The Only Way*, two eyes are uplifted to the future, a stance given further popular currency in postcards of John Martin-Harvey (fig. 4.6). That this became a set piece is clear from other dramatizations, such as the denouement of James W. Harkin's American version of Dickens's novel, *Sydney Carton: A Tale of Two Cities* (1900):

> GUARD. Hello! hello! here's a saint with upturned eyes, but they are fixed on eternity. What is it, O great and honored saint, that you see so far away? (bows mockingly)
>
> CARTON. I see long ranks of this new oppression—leaders, judges, spies, and all mounting the same steps that we'll ascend and leading to the guillotine.[61]

This redemptive vision may be abbreviated to the point of caricature, but it is consistent with Dickens's view in the original novel that seemingly futile or destructive actions in the present, such as revolutionary events, may await their vindication in the future. Though hardly a Republican sympathizer, Dickens's treatment of the French Revolution carries certain pro-Jacobin sentiments, not least in its justification of the fall of the Bastille and revolt against the brutality and corruption of the ancien régime (as in the dissolve, noted by Eisenstein above, to "absolute monarchs, the equipages of feudal nobles, the toilettes of flaring Jezebels, the churches that are not my father's house but dens of thieves").[62] Though Dickens drew much of his knowledge of events in Paris from Thomas Carlyle's monumental history of the Revolution, it is clear, as Gareth Stedman Jones notes, that he did not share Carlyle's contempt for the starving populace ("the mob"): "Dickens's language for the description of crowds and of the violence of the French Revolution was not that of Burke or Carlyle, or later of Hippolyte Taine, but of the radicals of the 1790s, Paine and Wollstonecraft."[63] *A Tale of Two Cities* issued a warning to the complacency of unpopular, autocratic regimes, and Sydney Carton's lesser-known words envisioning the future on ascending the scaffold would not have been out of place in the Dublin of the Easter Rising: "If the Republic really does good to the poor, and they come to be less hungry, and in all ways to suffer less" due to revolutionary violence, then it may be possible to envisage "a beautiful city and a brilliant people rising from this abyss, and in their struggles to be truly free, in their triumphs and defeats, through long years to come, I see the evil of this time and at the previous time of which this is the natural birth, gradually making expiation for itself and wearing out."[64]

In naturalistic tableaux or history painting, the frozen moment is part

FIG. 4.6 John Martin-Harvey as Sydney Carton on scaffold (1907). Publicity postcard for *The Only Way*. Photograph: Private collection.

of a narrative unfolding toward the future but with montage, temporal flows are themselves diverted, precipitating other possible futures."[65] It is for this reason, Hayden White maintains, that the dissolution of narrative is itself bound up with revolution or traumatic social upheavals: "This is why it seems to me that the kinds of antinarrative nonstories produced by literary modernism offer the only prospect for adequate representation of the kind of 'unnatural' events—including the Holocaust—that mark out an era and distinguish it absolutely from all of history that has come before it."[66] In *Mise Éire* (1959), the first major documentary film of the 1916 period, the director George Morrison, in Steve Coleman's words, "wove fragmentary archival footage of events surrounding the Easter Rising of 1916 into a national narrative," as much through the resonant soundtrack of Seán Ó Riada's music as through editing, and the use of nature imagery. It is notable, however, that the film is still composed of *fragments*: "An admirer of Eisenstein, Morrison collaged together fragmentary newsreel footage to recreate the story of the 1916 Dublin insurrection and the birth of the Irish State."[67] It is not that incongruous film techniques were being imposed on reality in this instance: rather, as Benjamin suggests, "The first stage in this undertaking will be to carry over the principle of montage into history."[68] Modern media technologies were not just in the business of reporting the Rising: in their reconfigurations of time and space—past, present, and future; national and international—they were bringing out the global dimensions of the Rising. "To assemble large-scale constructions out of the smallest and most precisely cut components," continues Benjamin, is to break "with vulgar historical naturalism": it is "indeed, to discover in the analysis of the small individual moment the crystal of the total event."[69] It is perhaps at such stray moments that Chaplin, like montage, steps off the screen. Describing a raid on an income tax office and an RIC (Royal Irish Constabulary) barracks in Cork during the Anglo-Irish War in 1920, Sean Healy, an IRA captain, recalled: "I remember that my disguise was made up of heavy goggles and a small moustache. When I was about to enter the barracks, a youth remarked to his companion: 'Charlie Chaplin is going into the barracks.'"[70] Nor was Chaplin himself entirely above the fray: when the Irish socialist leader and supporter of the Rising James Larkin was sentenced to five years in Sing-Sing Prison in New York for sedition in 1920, one of his visitors was Chaplin, who was so moved by his predicament, imprisoned and exiled thousands of miles from his family, that he arranged to send a package of gifts to his wife and children back in Dublin.[71]

✳ 5 ✳
"Paving Over the Abyss":

IRELAND, WAR, AND LITERARY MODERNISM

> Joyce linked the rebellion against realism with a rebellion against discursive language.... One need only note how impossible it would be for someone who participated in the war to tell stories about it the way people used to tell stories about their adventures.
>
> T. W. ADORNO, "The Position of the Narrator in the Contemporary Novel"[1]

In a well-known vignette of the scene in the GPO during the Easter Rising, Michael Collins noted that from the outset, events bore all the ominous signs of a death foretold: "They died nobly at the hands of the firing squads, so much I grant. But I do not think the Rising week was an appropriate time for the issue of memoranda couched in poetic phrases, nor of actions worked out in a similar fashion. Looking at it from the inside (I was in the G.P.O.) it had the air of a Greek tragedy about it."[2] Collins's eye for detail picked up on the literary ambience of the scene, but that the dramatic gesture was a decidedly *modern* take on Greek antiquity escaped his notice. As Irish politics took an increasingly conservative turn in the post-revolutionary era, however, it was not surprising the doomed, mythic version should move center stage, with Romantic idealism and Catholic messianism added to complete the stage effects. An image of the Rising consigned to Romantic nostalgia (or regret) acted as a useful foil to the new modernizing Ireland of the 1960s, as the Irish economy opened to international investment, commodity culture, and growing European integration, and as the Catholic Church ceded its role as arbiter of public opinion to the mass media and consumer lifestyles. It has to be remembered, however, that half a century earlier, everyday life in *Ulysses*, though steeped in ideologies of both empire and Catholicism, was also integrated, as noted above, into the worlds of merchandise, new media technologies, electrification, transport, and the advanced bureaucracy of the colonial state. Instead of lagging behind mainland Europe, or acting as a distraction from the Great War, the Easter Rising was a catalyst in the long process of decolonization that was to play out globally over the twentieth century. As Lenin observed, "A struggle capable of going to the length of insurrection and street fighting" in Europe, "breaking down the iron discipline and the army and martial law" during the Great War, presaged the possibility of revolution in other colonized societies.[3] Though hardly a kindred spirit, Edward Carson shared a similar view while addressing the British government: "If you tell your empire in India, in Egypt, and all over the world that you have not got the men, the money, the pluck, the inclination, and the backing to restore law and order in a country within 20 miles of your own shore, you may as well begin to abandon the attempt to make British rule prevail throughout the empire at all."[4] Field Marshal Sir Henry Wilson was more succinct on the part of the British administration: "If we lose Ireland we have lost the Empire."[5]

Recasting the Rising as a modern event is a measure of its contemporary impact, displacing complacent narratives of Home Rule and empire that presided over the early twentieth century. Playing on the ordinariness of the foot soldiers who answered the call to revolution, Raymond Queneau's surrealist fantasy *We Always Treat Women Too Well* (1947) enlists characters from *Ulysses*—Larry O'Rourke, Cissy Caffrey (who turns out to be male), Mat Dillon, Corny Kelleher (an unlikely rebel, as he is a Castle tout in *Ulysses*)—in the staging of the 1916 rebellion.[6] The main female character, the loyalist Gertie Girdle, finds herself locked in the ladies' toilet during the seizure of the building and, in the course of her captivity, seduces a number of the rebels, two of whom are executed at the end for dishonoring "her legitimate modesty."[7] Queneau's novel presents the Rising as the forerunner of decolonization, with Larry O'Rourke ridiculing a portrait of the king before Gertie, in the spirit of "Circe" in *Ulysses*: "that mediocre personage is the symbol of the oppression of hundreds of millions of human beings by a few tens of millions of Britons, but the oppressed no longer swoon in ecstasy at the sight of that insipid face, and you see here and now [in the Rising], Miss Girdle, the first consequences of this critical judgment."[8] The code word—and more general salutation—for revolution in the novel is "Finnegans wake," no doubt depending on inscrutability to prevent deciphering by police intelligence, and when Gertie describes herself as an "agnostic" under interrogation, it is taken as a play on "acrostic": "'Well well,' said Caffrey, 'we're certainly learning new words today. Anyone can see we're in the land of James Joyce.'"[9]

Mythic interpretations of the Easter Rising number the patriot poets

(Patrick Pearse, Joseph Mary Plunkett, Thomas MacDonagh) with Yeats among the "last romantics," an appellation that may also apply, as Jay Winter has observed, to the persistence of the past in much early consolatory verse and commemorative rituals of the Great War in British poetry.[10] But as Paul Fussell, Samuel Hynes, and others argue, the enormity of the violence and mass destruction unleashed by the war placed both romanticism and realism at odds with jarring experiences that looked instead to discordant modernist forms for expression.[11] Though found at their most catastrophic in the experience of war, the shocks of modernity at the onset of the twentieth century had already brought an end to art as illusion, signaling, as Georges Didi-Huberman has noted, the "kind of crisis of representation already at work in painting with Picasso, in cinema with Eisenstein, and in literature with James Joyce."[12] This process was already underway before the war. The alienation of the factory worker diagnosed by Marx had spread from the factory floor to estrangement in social life, calling for distancing or "de-familiarizing" effects in art, "whether popular (Chaplin) or arduous (Joyce), whether formally elaborate (Cézanne) or presented as a documentary, whether geometric (Russian suprematism) or erotic (French surrealism)." It was with this in mind that Brecht pointed to the following:

> (*Distancing effects in Chaplin*): Eating a boot (with table manners, by removing the nails like chicken bone, with the little finger raised).... [*Distancing effects in other arts:*] Joyce uses the distancing effect in *Ulysses*. He distances as much by his way of presenting things (above all by the fact that he frequently and rapidly changes this), as the processes themselves.[13]

The intensification of the rifts that opened between experience and expression in the Great War made it seem as if trenches were cut deep into language itself. As Fussell notes, the derring-do of battle and the clichés of patriotism—blighty, plucky, staunch, valor, enemy foe, baptism of fire—were blown to pieces with the shrapnel of mechanized warfare, and those on the receiving end of unimaginable terror were lost for words, cut off in a sensory no-man's-land.[14] Outdated, precious styles of poetry, more used to evading than confronting experience, were at first pressed into service to make sense of the horror, but these forms eventually came to grief:

> Finding the war "indescribable" in any but the available language of traditional literature, those who recalled it had to do so in known literary terms. Joyce, Eliot, Lawrence, Pound, Yeats were not present at the front to induct them into new idioms which might have done the job better.... It would

take still another war, and an even worse one, before such language would force itself up from below.[15]

The stilted Georgian diction of early war verse maintained its popular appeal, but even before hostilities ceased, the enormity of the catastrophe was looking to the kind of disjointed forms that found their found their iconic expression in "The Waste Land" and *Ulysses*. As Samuel Hynes describes it: "['The Waste Land'] is a poem that takes fragmentation as its formal principle, as though the visual reality of the Western Front had imposed itself on language. This is a perception the war poets never came to, and it makes Eliot's poem an expression of the war's impact on consciousness in a way that theirs wasn't, and makes it modern."[16]

The tension between available and emergent forms of diction was evident in many diaries, journals, and letters from the front, whose outworn language and pro forma sentiments prompted Fussell to conclude provocatively that "any historian would err badly who relied on letters for factual testimony about the war. . . . It is only the *ex post facto view* of an action that generates coherence or makes irony possible."[17] This is an important corrective to historical approaches that limit the record strictly to contemporary perceptions: while experiences seared both mind and body, the forms to give them expression had not caught up with the unprecedented scale of suffering. For many with firsthand experience of the Great War, the present had yet to sink all the way down, and proved as elusive as any unforeseeable future. In Ireland, the rhetoric of faith and fatherland, redemptive suffering, and Romantic nationalism were drawn upon in a manner akin to Georgian diction to give expression, however ineffectually, to what had in fact "changed utterly," in W. B. Yeats's memorable phrase. These available repertoires were in no position to do justice to the complexities of a revolution that were, as the modernist poet and critic Thomas MacGreevy observed, "still too obscure to have become completely articulate in art," but which lent themselves to distinctive innovations in modernism such as—the case MacGreevy had in mind— the late work of the painter Jack B. Yeats.[18]

There is a risk, however, that in placing breakthroughs in style solely in the literary avant-garde, they are completely removed from contemporaneity or immediate experience, for it was the exigencies of the present that called for experimental forms beyond the genres of realism or romance. As early as August 1914, according to Geert Buelens, letters written by the German poet August Stramm "described how the war placed everything in a new light: relations, emotions, experiences. . . . [N]othing was as it had been. This was even true of his [Stramm's] use of language. His sentences flowed one into the next like experimental prose that James Joyce was just then inventing."[19] Stramm's faltering, yet apt, prose bears this out:

> War. Everything is behind me. Hope friendship and love. I love you but you are behind me far far do not be angry but another knew you another not I. [...] Oh power is glorious power Now we are waiting for the enemy waiting waiting he will come he must come that's what we want nothing more in the world 250 rifles my rifle will come before them.[20]

Stramm's language is not straining for aesthetic effect (though Stramm was referred to as the "Ezra Pound of Germany"), but is contained in a personal letter to his publisher Herwarth Walden and his wife, Nell.[21] The extent to which narrative and syntax were breaking down under the pressures of modern life was already evident in the language of Baudelaire, whom Benjamin designated as the first fully attuned surveyor of the contemporary scene. For Baudelaire, the inundation of the senses, the collisions and shocks induced by crowds and traffic, induced a mechanical effect in walking the streets: "Pedestrians act as if they had adapted themselves to the machine and could express themselves only automatically. Their behaviour is a reaction to shocks."[22] As the shocks of modernity were converted into the explosive violence of modern war, consciousness and language appeared to collapse in tandem with the buildings falling around them. As Buelens describes the effects on Stramm's correspondence:

> In this volley of words, a fragment like "life has no value" could run directly into a passage that seemed to suggest the opposite ("Dear friends how are you") only to relapse into an anxious delirium ("only one fear he might not come not come go back") followed by a command ("Enemy come!") and the thought that he, Stramm, might not be able to write again, but that they should take courage.... By writing these words in a letter for others to read, Stramm may have persuaded himself to take courage as well.[23]

Such disconnected writing did not spring fully formed from daily life and was mediated by the innovations noted by Benjamin, and more recent avant-garde movements including futurism, symbolism, cubism, fauvism, and related innovations in literary style. On being called to military service, Filippo Marinetti, the leader of Italian futurism, "filled his notebook with page after page of drawings, typographical experiments, and onomatopoeic words, trying to capture the sounds, color and tumult of war."[24] Even before the war, Wyndham Lewis published the first issue of *Blast*, listing James Joyce in its dubious pantheon of heroes though the first reviews of *Dubliners* had hardly begun to appear. An early review of *Dubliners*, published the same day as *Blast* (June 29, 1914), commended Joyce's stories but noted the discomfiting tone, encouraging the author "to enlarge his outlook and eliminate such scenes and details as can only shock, without in any useful way impressing or elevating, the reader" (*JJCH*, 1:62). A self-styled "dyspeptic" review in the *Freeman's Journal* relates the shock effect directly to the war front, writing of the bleakness of Joyce's description of the tea table at home: "Had it been a description of the desolation of No Man's Land on the Somme or the Yser, the horror could hardly have been laid on more thickly."[25] The one work comparable to *Ulysses* in epic scale and startling innovations, Karl Kraus's *The Last Days of Mankind*, a montage of theater and journalistic effects featuring over five hundred characters and taking ten nights to perform, was written (or assembled) during the war, and published in partial form in 1918, but only received final publication (constituting almost six hundred pages in translation) in 1922, though it was never fully staged during Kraus's lifetime.[26]

These modernist overtures underline the relationship between revolutionary ferment and cultural experiments, as if old certainties, whether as content or form, were no longer adequate to the social and political upheavals at hand. As Elaine Sisson has noted of Irish drama, "If, by the 1920s, Europe experienced existential displacement, then Ireland experienced both social dislocation and the giddy responsibility of political freedom: theatre was more important than ever as an expression of the possible."[27] In the turbulence of the period, fears of survival in extreme conditions augmented the need to tell the tale as language itself was breaking down. Experiments in modern epic or montage—dismantling linear narratives, relaying discordant voices, using ellipses, gaps, omissions, non sequiturs—were not introduced for innovation's sake but to disrupt the flow of an unbearable present, reaching beyond or below surface realities. Experience is not so much evaded as decomposed and reassembled, finding refuge from the existing order or oppressive regimes in what Ernst Bloch called the "despised corners" of society.[28] Certainly, for many contemporaries (and, in some cases, later acquaintances) of James Joyce who took part in the Irish revolution, language itself required new registers, and in the hands of writers as diverse as Kathleen Coyle, Frank Gallagher, Joseph Campbell, and Francis Stuart, the inadequacy of words became palpable under harsh regimes of imprisonment, threats of summary execution, or the imminence of death by hunger strike. In the confines of prison, the senses are placed under considerable strain so that language, at times, takes on a life of its own: "Words," Constance Markievicz wrote from Aylesbury prison in 1916 about her own attempts at poetry, "suddenly become alive and mean all sorts of things on their own and not what you meant at all. And they simply run away with me and I can't manage them at all."[29] Markievicz mentions one reason why words cannot say directly what they mean, at least for political prisoners—the prison censor: "If one had more paper and a less obvious Censor, one might have been tempted to be indiscreet.... It's awful to think that even Art is conquered by militarism" (January 30, 1919).[30] Language takes refuge in abbreviation and "a great hurry" in these circumstances:

> The modern curt style is, to me, often telegraphic. We rather like adjectives and symbolic things over here. . . . I know it was a common sneer in England at one time that we could not talk of Ireland in Plain English. It was always 'Kathleen ni Houlihan' or some unpronounceable name, and her 'four green fields' gave offence too. Now I like that . . . when I read a book I just like to get facts and ideas in a great hurry and only disliked the style if it was too obscure and long-winded.[31]

Prison experience at its most extreme took a distinctive form of protest in the hunger strike, a twentieth-century weapon of the weak.[32] The death of Terence MacSwiney in Brixton Prison on October 25, 1920, following seventy-four days on hunger strike, took place in a world far removed from the literary avant-garde, but touched a nerve in modernist sensibilities as befits, perhaps, an experience at the limits of human endurance. One of the more unlikely figures moved by MacSwiney's death was Marcel Proust, who brushed aside a query by a visitor about the latest volume in his masterwork *Le Côté de Guermantes* (The Guermantes Way), with the suggestion they might speak instead "about the Lord Mayor of Cork, that will be more interesting."[33] As MacSwiney's funeral wound its way through London, Virginia Woolf wrote in her diary: "[I]t's life itself, I think sometimes, for us in our generation [that is] so tragic—no newspaper placard without its shriek of agony from someone. McSwiney [*sic*] this afternoon and violence in Ireland; or it'll be the strike. Unhappiness is everywhere; just beyond the door; or stupidity, which is worse." She considered that getting back to her work might be restorative, except for these forces: "To write *Jacob's Room* again will revive my fibres. . . . If it weren't for my feeling that it's a strip of pavement over an abyss."[34]

The idea that modernist writing is akin to paving over an abyss, that the ground may open up under one's feet, ran also through Wyndham Lewis's mind, as noted in the previous chapter above, and MacSwiney's funeral raised questions over Irish claims to political independence given, as far as he could see, there were no obvious visible differences between the Irish and English people watching the cortege as it moved through the streets:

> During the martyrdom of the Lord Mayor of Cork I had several opportunities of seeing considerable numbers of irish people [Lewis refused to capitalize adjectives referring to nationality] demonstrating among the London crowds. I was never able to distinguish which were irish and which were english, however. They looked to me exactly the same. With the best will in the world to discriminate the orderly groups of demonstrators from the orderly groups of spectators, and to satisfy the romantic proprieties on such an occasion, my eyes refused to effect the necessary separation, that the principle of 'celtism' demanded, into chalk and cheese. I should have supposed that they were a lot of romantic english-people pretending to be irish people, and demonstrating with the assistance of a few priests and pipers, if it had not been that they all looked extremely depressed, and english-people when they are giving romance the rein are always very elated.[35]

There is a mote in Lewis's eye since visible markers, contrary to the imperial gaze, are not the only criteria of racial discrimination, and the physiognomy of politics is apparent in hunger striking itself, as the body becomes a site of protest. MacSwiney's emaciated figure, imaginatively rendered in an illustration with an accompanying friar on the cover of the French *Le Petit Journal* during his protest, lay in state for public viewing in the days before his massive funeral. Lewis may have been indifferent to MacSwiney's death, but its impact on the Irish public was such that even James Joyce broke his silence during the War of Independence, penning a scurrilous squib against the English authorities. The Cork MacSwineys were relations of the Joyce family through their connection with "my cousin" (as Joyce called him) Peter Paul MacSwiney, twice lord mayor of Dublin and benefactor of Joyce's father, John Stanislaus Joyce.[36] In response to the death of MacSwiney, Joyce penned "The Right Heart in the Wrong Place" in October 1920, which he sent on a postcard to his brother Stanislaus. The lines are notable for their acuity as much as petulance, given that spite is directed at a British official, Sir Horace Rumbold, who had made life difficult for Joyce in Zurich:

THE RIGHT HEART IN THE WRONG PLACE

> Of spinach and gammon
> Bull's full to the crupper
> White lice and black famine
> Are the Mayor of Cork's supper
> But the pride of old Ireland.
> Must be damnably humbled
> If a Joyce is found cleaning
> The boots of a Rumbold. (*JJ*, 547)

Joyce considers MacSwiney's death through starvation in terms of England's larder being full at the expense of the Famine in Ireland, a theme also picked up in *Finnegans Wake* in relating Partition after the Anglo-Irish Treaty to "the split hour of blight" (*FW*, 519.35–36). But the hunger strike is also a refusal, on the part of both MacSwiney and Joyce, to collude in one's own humiliation. Though exemplifying at one level complicity in self-destruction to the point of abjection, MacSwiney's protest also presented the opposite extreme of an indomitable will, an assertion of solidarity and collective purpose: the hunger strike in Brixton was in support of a similar group protest in Cork Men's Gaol that led to the death of two other Volunteers, Michael Fitzgerald and Joseph Murphy (covered in the film *Ireland a Nation*, noted above). The refusal to yield to pressure also linked Joyce to MacSwiney in Ezra Pound's imagination in late October 1920, on account of Joyce's unwillingness to accede to prudent edits on the suppression of *Ulysses'* chapters in the publication *The Little Review*: "I think Joyce has the same mania for martyrdom that Pierce [sic] had, that MacSwiney had, it is the Christian attitude, they want to drive an idea into people by getting crucified.... I think Joyce has got this quirk for being the noble victim."[37] Pound rightly brings Joyce within the ambit of MacSwiney but fails to see that for all "the Christian attitude," Joyce is challenging dominant mythic forces, in keeping with other "noble victims," as will be shown below, who had recourse to modernist forms in response to extreme situations.

Frank Gallagher: Days of Fear

As conflict intensified in Ireland, signature modernist devices such as interior monologue, free indirect discourse, and cinematic techniques began to disrupt conventional styles of fiction and memoir writing. In some cases, authors were familiar with Joyce's works, at least with *Portrait*, and kept abreast of modernist publications such as *Poetry* magazine, but extremes of experience also forced the writer's hand. The fragmentation of narrative is seen to telling effect in prison diaries and memoirs, particularly when, faced with slow starvation, an attempt is made to capture the pitiless fate of the hunger-striker. At Easter 1920, the British administration, expecting a reenactment of the 1916 Rising, conducted mass arrests all over Dublin and placed the city under virtual lockdown. Instead of an uprising, the influx of prisoners to Mountjoy Prison led to an organized hunger strike on Easter Monday, April 5, initiated by thirty-six inmates demanding the right to be treated as political prisoners, and predating MacSwiney's more famous protest.[38] One of the hunger-strikers was Frank Gallagher (1893–1962), a key figure in Sinn Féin's Publicity Department and coeditor of its highly successful propaganda publication, the *Irish Bulletin*. Gallagher's diary, *Days of Fear*, was written in a telegraphic, abbreviated style during the hunger strike but was not published until 1928, raising the question whether, having possibly gained access to *Ulysses* in the meantime, the amputated phrasing and extended interior monologue had acquired a new legitimacy in his eyes.[39] Certainly its unorthodox form posed problems for prospective publishers and, as Declan Jackson, relates, Gallagher found "efforts to publish his hunger strike diary extremely frustrating. The difficulty in securing a publisher could have been due to the stream of consciousness style of writing employed throughout the text. It was extremely unconventional and as such would have been challenging to market in large numbers."[40] Some of the initial reviews seized on this, the *Irish Independent* lamenting that the author "relies, perhaps, too much on the staccato and sentence to get dramatic effect, but his confession bears the mark of candor."[41] But others, such as Lady Augusta Gregory, saw things differently, exerting her influence through well-placed reviews of the book and heralding it in almost Joycean terms: "'Days of Fear' will be one of the great books of the world."[42]

"Staccato" refers to the use of interior monologue technique to capture the discontinuous flow of thought when the body and physical movement are hemmed in, leaving the mind only to roam at will, but literary montage is perhaps a better term to describe what Bloch calls an "already involuntary experimental" stylistic departure.[43] Notwithstanding the apparent retreat into subjectivity, the technique for Bloch involves the dismantling of the "ego . . . the bourgeois context of subjects" in a "flood" rather than a stream of consciousness. Noting "it does not even have the ego as witness" and that the "whispering of leitmotifs lives at a crooked angle to the surface of the text," Bloch continues in his account of these words from the abyss: "Bubbles of steam from the unconscious rise up too: they create the crazy word-structures, fill the deep spaces, the masterless treasure-chambers, the abyss beneath the claptrap of these run-of-the-mill people, compose themselves at best in that architecture . . . in which for the first time multi-story ways of talking were in a single one."[44] When forced into montage, language is at the mercy of circumstances, uniquely tied to its historic moment, but yet is "blasted out of the continuum of historical succession" by the disruption of narrative, as words and images break free of their surroundings, even time.[45] Montage gives voice to isolation and breakdown, the effect of which, in the case of Gallagher's hunger strike, was to maintain social solidarity with others on the protest ("If any go, all go"): "Not only the actors now, these tight-skinned, clammy bodies on the prison pallets. . . . The whole Nation has crowded into the cast. . . . It is the world which has become the audience."[46] In Gallagher's hands, the technique reconnects with the external world, as every fragment from outside—newspapers, street sounds, bells, noise of crowds, traffic (even airplanes)—makes its way into consciousness. As the General Strike in April 1920 in support of the protest demonstrated, contact between inside and outside worlds proved the prisoner's strongest weapon in the end.

Diary entries at the outset of the strike are written in a standard discursive style, with third-person narration clearly demarcated from passages of dialogue, and though disorientation is setting in, there is still a firm resolve: "Must have raved all night. . . . But even an uncontrolled imagination darting in and out among dark thoughts, searching the closets of the mind, tearing up the very floorboards of the soul, could not find the idea of compromise—that gives me great strength" (*DF*, 39). As the days on strike take their toll, the syntax breaks up, and past tense slips into present tense: "Now for that poem . . . Hallo! . . . What's up? . . . Three warders running . . . The doctor . . . The cell door they are opening is on this side" (*DF*, 50). The doctor is then addressed in absentia, or at least without recording his speech: "'Oh! Quite well, Doctor, thanks, how are the others?' He has stopped smiling, the doctor. Why should he be afraid?" (*DF*, 59). Switching to the present tense underlines the physical act of writing, giving the impression that words are caught up in the events themselves. As in Molly Bloom's responding to a far-off train in her soliloquy in *Ulysses*, Gallagher imagines his father's literal train of thought on the rail journey to visit him from Cork, recalling the death of his brother two years earlier: "The six hours, during every minute of which the rhythm of the train sang the one thing he wished to forget. . . . The telegram . . . the time of the year . . . the associations . . . the uncertainty . . . the overcrowding sorrow of that former journey" (*DF*, 61). At times, the style is close to delirium and, as in Molly Bloom hearing church bells from nearby Hardwicke Place ("wait theres Georges church bells wait 3 quarters the hour 1 wait 2 oclock well thats a nice hour of the night for him to be coming home at" [*U*, 18.1231–33])—the reverie of the half-dozing sleeper in Mountjoy is invaded by external sounds, imagined or otherwise:

> The clocks again, thank God!... One... Two... Three... Fo... Fo... Ah! I missed it... But there's the Rathmines Town Hall... How long after the chime it strikes!... Ah!... One... Two... Three... Fo... F... *Three* O'Clock!... Oh, God... God. I will take all the suffering of a generation on me tomorrow if I sleep now...
>
> Perhaps by thinking of drowsy things... bees... sunlight... tall soft grass [...] they are only a shadow... a... shadow... softly... deepening... a shad... ow... a...
>
> "HALT! WHO GOES THERE?"
>
> "Friend." [...]
>
> Wonder how the others are. What if some of them be already dead? Am I responsible? Men joined the strike voluntarily... (*DF*, 37–38)

Vagaries of time are a recurrent theme, and psychic drift is frequently arrested by a sudden intrusion from the outside world, bringing the mind back to its physical surroundings: "The clocks... Half past something... Ssh!... somebody coming.... Hear the pad of rubber boots... The man with the lantern... On the upper landing... He'll be here in a minute... That's Neill shouting at him... 'What the hell do you think you are doing shining that thing into our eyes for? Do you think we are going to climb out of the ventilators?' [...] 'What's the time?' 'Two o'clock.' Must have slept about half an hour... It is quite a good poem... What a fight this has become!" (*DF*, 54).

If losing track of time releases the grip of the present, it also helps to connect with more troubled legacies of the past, and others who have engaged in the fight for freedom. "The present was going out but not only the future but the past was flowing in," Gallagher wrote in his later history of the period, *The Four Glorious Years*, invoking the republican legacy of Wolfe Tone, Thomas Davis, and John Mitchel.[47] Noting the backward look in Irish prison writings at the time, Michael Biggs comments that while starvation as protest "stirred 'memories' of past atrocities... [o]ne might expect explicit reference to the great famine, but I have not seen this."[48] In fact, as Joyce's squib on Terence MacSwiney indicates, memories of the Famine do surface, and they recur in Gallagher's grim roll call of memory, not only on account of hunger and disease but also the state-sanctioned violence of evictions and scorched-earth policies: "The by-gone generation seems to be standing beside this generation . . . [who] felt this presence of the past; of the Croppies in their mass graves, the Famine dead under tumbled roofs . . . the gaunt parents who from the woods saw their ripe corn burning under [Sir George] Carew's torches and pressed their famished children to their sides?"[49] In *Days of Fear*, Gallagher wonders if death by hunger strike is the equivalent of the sacrifice of lives in a revolution that might have saved greater numbers in Famine days: "Perhaps for the greatness of Ireland it were better that we died. It may be that if we die now, thousands, who would have to die later, can live. . . . As in the famine days . . . a revolution, the willful giving of hundreds of lives, might have saved hundreds of thousands" (*DF*, 59).

In *The Four Glorious Years*, a later revisiting of events recounted in his prison diary, Gallagher writes that only the expressly modernist style of an artist such as the Irish painter Cecil Ffrench Salkeld (1904–1969) could capture visually the moment of release from Mountjoy:

> If an artist had only beheld it then: if even young Salkeld were there whom they sent out when they learned he was no more than fifteen, what a canvas it would be: the greyness of the darkening prison; the groups of men, their hands on one another's shoulders; with transparent faces raised to the glass roof through which that cheering [of the crowds outside] came. It would have been a grotesque of caged and famished men entitled "Victory."[50]

Salkeld, though only sixteen years of age, had been arrested in the Easter weekend roundups in 1920 and was taken to Mountjoy Prison at the onset of the hunger strike, vehemently protesting against his treatment: he was released after a few days, perhaps, as Gallagher suggests, on account of his age.[51] A prodigy in art—at fifteen, he was admitted to the Metropolitan School of Art in Dublin—Salkeld traveled to Germany in 1921 to study at Kunstschule Kassel under Ewald Dülberg, where he came into contact with the New Objectivity (alternatively "magic realism") school, exhibiting with the Young Rhineland Circle of Painters associated with Otto Dix, Jankel Adler, and others.[52] It is not difficult to see how Salkeld's style, drawing on an avant-garde in Germany infused by rage against empire and the brutality of the Great War, might lend itself to the "grotesque" of the hunger strike in Mountjoy, for Gallagher's style, as Joseph Lennon notes, could be read in similar terms: "When Gallagher's somewhat edited diary appeared in 1928 as *Days of Fear*, it read almost as an experimental modernist text."[53]

Kathleen Coyle, A Flock of Birds *(1930)*

In one of the last entries in a notebook before her untimely death in the Grosvenor Sanatorium, Kent, 1943, the French philosopher and activist Simone Weil (1909–1943) reflected on a novel she had read with a bearing on her own severe state of malnutrition at the time. In an act of extreme empathy, Weil had chosen to subsist on the bare necessities of food akin to what she imagined was the sparse diet of her compatriots in Nazi-occupied France and, due to her emaciated state, was in no position to fight the tuberculosis that brought about her death.[54] In the story that drew her attention, the mother (Weil remembers her as "the sister") of a young man about to be executed returns home and, numbed by shock, sets to work making jam from strawberries piled in dishes in her kitchen. In so doing, the story relates, she knows she would never eat strawberries again.

The story is not annotated in the translation of Weil's notebooks, but it refers to *A Flock of Birds* (1930) by the Derry-born author and former revolutionary, Kathleen Coyle (1886–1952), set during the Great War and Anglo-Irish War. The French translation of the novel, published in 1932, was undertaken by Louisette Gillet, daughter of Joyce's close friend Louis Gillet, and it may have been through this connection that Coyle became a visitor to the Joyces' apartment in Paris.[55] In Weil's summary, the slight imprecision in detail suggests Weil may have been writing from memory but the passage struck a deep chord in her thinking:

IRISH STORY—STRAWBERRY JAM

> The Irish story ('A flock of birds'?) in which the sister of a young man who has been executed returns home and, in an upsurge of vitality, to throw off the effect of his death, devours a whole pot of jam—and for the rest of her life she cannot bear even to hear strawberry jam mentioned.
>
> If a romantic adolescent fabricated a tragedy out of some imaginary great love, it could not modify his or her attitude to strawberry jam.
>
> transference   It is only real feelings that possess this power of transferring themselves into inert matter.[56]

"In a curious way," writes Weil's translator Richard Rees, "this last page of her book sums up and illustrates the whole extraordinary range of her mind."[57]

In *A Flock of Birds*, a mother, Catherine Munster, returns home having just heard the sentence of death by hanging pronounced on her son, Christy, for his part in a republican raid during the Irish War of Independence in which a fatal shot was fired. She does not "devour" jam but it sinks into her body as if it had been eaten. It is noted she does not often make straight for the kitchen on entering the house, but this time, as if acting from "some instinct," heads there and relieves her servant Brigid of the task of making jam:

> "I'll make it," she [Catherine] answered, and sent for an apron. She was grateful for the occupation. But by the time her labor was done she knew she would never eat strawberries again. They had ceased to be food for her and had become an exercise in distraction. She would have a new dream now—strawberries. Strawberries fresh, boiling, potted, labeled—strawberry 1919.[58]

Catherine goes in search of her daughter Kathleen, home from Paris, expecting to find her writing but instead discovers her taking a dress apart with scissors: "Fresh from her experience with the strawberries, Catherine saw at once beyond the denial that she was saving her writing for the future" (*FB*, 14). Kathleen's comment on James Joyce prompts Catherine to think of other worlds and different times:

> "You know, mother, James Joyce says that we have a country that is like a sow that eats her own farrow." She was silent again. She did not live in Kathleen's world. She thought of Paris, where Kathleen lived . . . a place where Christy had never gone. No, Christy stayed in the mountains. And now he was in prison. She thought of lions in cages, of the Einstein theory. . . . In another world these three: Valentine [her other son] and Kathleen and Christy had been her children. Centuries ago. (*FB*, 15–16)

Kathleen considers Joyce's remark (in *Portrait*) to be directed at Mother Ireland's demand of sacrifice from her sons, but in this case the mother does not eat her offspring, or even eat preserves. Weil's idea of sacrifice was bound up with a "bel[ief] in the value of suffering, so long as one makes every (legitimate) effort to escape it"[59]—yet suffering concentrated the mind and was far from being null and void. It forced individuals in on themselves, stripping away surface concerns and moving beyond "finite time" to consider "perpetual duration."[60] In *A Flock of Birds*, the mind moves from the present into deeper historical time, as residues of the past—in keeping with the "Einstein theory"—indicate alternative futures, or at least ways of responding to what could have been otherwise.

One of the riddles of the story is precisely the indeterminacy of time and place, dates and locations: as Catherine meets Christy for the last time in his condemned cell, "[t]ime and place were unsteadied in her."⁶¹ "Strawberry 1919" is on the label of the jam made by Catherine, but when "Russell" is named as a possible signatory of a petition organized for Christy, it is pointed out: "He is full of the trouble in the Belfast shipyards"— troubles that began in summer 1920.⁶² The first execution by hanging—of the IRA Volunteer Kevin Barry—did not occur until November 1, 1920, and Barry may have provided the model for Christy: his young age and death sentence due to participation in a raid in which fatal shots were fired are shared by both. Barry's execution took place only days after the death by hunger strike of Terence MacSwiney, lord mayor of Cork, and this is also cited in relation to Joyce's dictum on sacrifice: "She heard herself saying [of Christy]: 'History was his strong point. He was always good on history.' All the heroes in turn—from William Tell to the Lord Mayor of Cork. Kathleen had said that somebody had said: a sow that eats her own farrow" (*FB*, 56).⁶³

The paralysis that virtually anesthetizes Catherine over the impending death of her son is mitigated by declensions of time that allow her to escape the present. The story takes a Borgesian turn when it transpires that attempts to organize a petition to plead with the Home Office for a last-minute pardon are twisted into the suggestion that a pardon would prove Christy, by virtue of his Anglo-Irish background, was a British spy—thus exchanging death for a dishonor that (citing Dostoevsky) "may lead to a greater sacrifice" (*FB*, 155). Dostoevsky is not the only outrider of intensity to feature in the text: Catherine's thoughts also turn to Nietzsche. With "Nietzsche vague in her mind" (*FB*, 33), the idea prevails that death has more to do with *timing* than time: "'Die at the right moment' Nietzsche said, as though youth were full of God-like certainties" (*FB*, 30). In a paradoxical manner, dying for the cause (as in the legacy of Kevin Barry) preserves rather than vanquishes life: "Die at the right moment. Even if he did not know it, the truth was infallible. Felon! Felon! Someone had called him a felon" (*FB*, 198). The numbness deflected earlier onto the making of preserves, strawberry jam, is reclaimed from silence: "It would pass. She would take up her writing again. She had preserved it from memories— not like the strawberry jam. It was different" (*FB*, 85). There is no redemption through sacrifice in the novel, however, which may explain its appeal to Weil, but suffering is retrieved from paralysis, if only by means of the indirection that remains the preserve of art.

As in Joyce's *Portrait*, images of birds recur, flight opening up the future: at an impasse, Catherine reflects: "There was neither flight nor future. She would live by going backwards."⁶⁴ But the title of the novel presents other possibilities, recalling a scene in which Christy as "a tiny boy of four" once asked his sister Kathy (Kathleen) "[W]hat is that black cloud in the sky? And Kathy said: it isn't a cloud, it is a flock of birds" (*FB*, 12). For Weil, death is never willed, even when it appears so through self-starvation: "death is not a suicide. One must *be killed*, to experience the heaviness, the weight of the world."[65] As if lifting that weight, the upward flight of birds scatters clouds, bringing Joyce once again to mind: "Kathleen lived in Paris and mixed with queer people. She found it difficult to value Joyce.... Joyce had begun so differently—in another climate, among heavenly wings, layers and layers of ecstasy" (*FB*, 26). In a play on words that would not be out of place in Joyce, the stultifying effects of making strawberry jam ("preserves") is transformed into a means of preserving Christy's memory, reorienting the past toward flight and the future: "Yes. She would preserve him. She would surround him with wings that would shut out terror. Her flight would be his, his hers" (*FB*, 167). As Anne Fogarty suggests, the conventional association of sacrifice in republicanism with Catholic messianism is transvalued so that "Christy is less a Christ-like figure than a potentially transfigured Zarathustra."[66] If this is the case, Catherine is also less a Pietà figure than an embodiment of Weil's resolute ethos of suffering: "The strength came right enough, but the love and glory were absent. Women hated sacrifice as they hated childbirth but they had to face it" (*FB*, 13). In the hours before execution, Catherine is the last family member to visit her son and tells him of her plans, Stephen Dedalus fashion, to leave Ireland: "out of the country, away.... There is a place in Provence, desolate and high" (*FB*, 254). As she makes her way through the banners and the crowd on its knees outside the jail with her remaining son Valentine, she raises her eyes to "the dark clouded chimera of the sky, the flying clouds of the night that had yet to come." At which point, Valentine observes: "'It is going to rain.' A smile widened her mouth, and she gave him back madness: 'It is only a flock of birds.'"[67]

It is unlikely Kathleen Coyle knew of Simone Weil, though the philosopher Gabriel Marcel, who wrote an introduction to a volume of Weil's writings, was a personal friend of Coyle's in Paris (James Joyce also attended a lecture in Paris organized by Marcel in 1937).[68] Critics, not inaccurately, have drawn comparisons between Coyle and Virginia Woolf, "the short, clipped sentences, with their focusing on seemingly grotesque details ... recall[ing] Clarissa Dalloway's tremulous probings of her menacing past."[69] Coyle was friends with Rebecca West—whose *The Return of the Soldier* (1918) was one of the first novels to confront the psychological damage of the Great War and who wrote the introduction for Coyle's most successful novel, *Liv* (1929)—and she encouraged Coyle's experiments in style. Coyle had met West upon moving to London in 1909 to work in journalism, but Coyle returned to Dublin in 1911, where she befriended Desmond Ryan (later Patrick Pearse's secretary, of which more in chapter 9) and the Westmeath-born socialist activist Charles O'Meagher, whom she married in 1915. Like Thomas Pugh, she joined the Socialist Party of Ireland (SPI), which sought to uphold James Connolly's socialist republicanism after the Easter Rising, and contributed a column on Irish affairs, under the name Selma Sigerson, to the weekly *Socialist*, the organ of the radical SLP (Socialist Labour Party) in Britain. With O'Meagher, she was part of a breakaway group from the SPI, the Revolutionary Socialist Party of Ireland (RSPI), founded in Belfast in May 1919 to pursue a more militant Bolshevik line inspired by the major Belfast engineering strike. Imprisoned for "unlawful assembly" in 1919, O'Meagher went on a hunger and thirst strike that led eventually to his release—a prison experience that perhaps haunts *A Flock of Birds*. Coyle's more sustained but equally uncompromising position was outlined early in 1919 in her pamphlet *Sinn Féin and Socialism*, the most concise presentation of the case for what, following Connolly, has been termed "Hiberno-Marxism," relating revolution to vernacular traditions of collective resistance in Ireland dating back to the Middle Ages. On her first meeting with Lucia Joyce, the writer's daughter, Coyle expressed puzzlement that she was drawing illustrations at her father's behest of early Irish medieval illuminations "to which there was no beginning, and no ending"—a suitable description of Joyce's narratives as well as her own troubled fiction.[70]

Joseph Campbell: Modernism under Duress

The poet Joseph Campbell (1879–1944), born and educated in Belfast, brought vernacular Irish culture into contact with international modernism as a founder in 1909–10—with T. E. Hulme, F. S. Flint, Florence Farr, and others in London—of what later became known the Imagist movement, described by T. S. Eliot as "the starting point of modern poetry."[71] Campbell was joined by his fellow Irishman Desmond FitzGerald and, with Farr, they attracted Ezra Pound to the group, the American arriviste being so taken by Campbell's sonorous voice in reading poetry that he began to affect an Irish accent.[72] The principles of the Imagist movement, as outlined by Pound some years later, placed an emphasis on the "hard and clear" image, crystallized in an instant outside a story or plot structure, thus rescuing moments, in Hugh Kenner's formulation, "from the flux of time, [which] will render them static, hence pictorial."[73] Returning to Ireland, Campbell joined ranks with figures such as Thomas MacDonagh, whose championing of the new "Irish mode" in verse free from the Celticism of the Revival looked to, as Alex Davis points out, those "Irish poets of his generation most deeply involved with the pre-War London avant-garde": "The militant nationalist politics embraced by MacDonagh and Campbell which would lead to execution and internment, respectively, find a correspondence in the politics of the avant-garde, at a time Mac-Donagh saw as 'a period of disturbance and change.'"[74]

Another current, however, developed by Hulme, drew on Walt Whitman's free verse and Henri Bergson's philosophy, and looked to temporal succession, outside linear progression but not necessarily narrative itself, to convey a succession of "momentary phases in the poet's mind."[75] To this, Campbell added an Irish note of musical rhythm, influenced by Yeats's collaboration with Florence Farr in setting poetry to musical or chanting scores.[76] Campbell saw his poetry, pared down to the simplicity of ancient Gaelic verse and lore, as subscribing to these tenets but, in contrast to the introspective turn in its metropolitan variant,[77] was inclined to animate the still image through stirrings of history and tradition. The implication of movement suggests, as Helen Carr notes, that many of the clear observations recorded in his poetry come from "a wanderer, someone on the move,"[78] not unlike Campbell himself, who struggled for employment and financial security all his life.[79] A sense of movement animates his frequently anthologized poem, "I Am the Mountainy Singer": "I am the mountainy singer— / The voice of the peasant's dream, / The cry of the wind on the wooded hill, / The leap of the fish in the stream... Travail and pain I sing— / The bride on the childing bed, / The dark man laboring at his rhymes, / The ewe in the lambing shed."[80] These may have been the lines James Joyce had in mind when, stinging under the rejection of *Dubliners* by Maunsel & Company—who had published *The Mountainy Singer* (1909) and Campbell's play *Judgment* (1912)—he wrote in "Gas from a Burner" (impersonating the voice of George Roberts, his nemesis at Maunsel's):

> To show you for strictures I don't care a button
> I printed the poems of Mountainy Mutton
> And a play he wrote (you've read it I'm sure)
> Where they talk of "bastard," "bugger" and "whore."[81]

Campbell's wife, for one, did not take offense: it was Nancy Maude, at Pound's behest, who brought the first copy of *Portrait* "to the Emerald Isle" to place it in the hands of reviewers.[82]

Following the Rising, Campbell worked as an intelligence officer for the republican movement, prompting repeated raids on his Wicklow home by the British military. Taking a more public stand, he wrote in *New Ireland*, in September 1917, condemning Standish O'Grady's (and G. K. Chesterton's) endorsement of military conscription for the Great War, and was subsequently elected on a republican platform as acting chair of Wicklow County Council. His republican politics led to his opposition to the Anglo-Irish Treaty and to a long period of imprisonment during the Civil War. In prison, his literary interests warded off despair, and he befriended Frank Gallagher in Mountjoy as well as the much younger writer Francis Stuart (1902–2000) at the Curragh. He kept in touch with international literary developments as best he could, helped by magazines such as the *New York Times Book Review* and the *New York Freeman* (sent by his brother John, an artist living in New York), *Poetry* magazine, and the *Times Literary Supplement*.

A shift in tenses and rapid transitions in thought are notable in his prison diary of this period, published only in recent years, as reporting is tied to the physical ordeal of writing—the arduous conditions in which the text is produced, hidden during searches, or smuggled out as contraband: "May try & get out a selection of MSS tomorrow."[83] An entry one morning comes to a momentary halt to register shivering from the cold:

> Hut filthy—dust, ashes, papers, sputum everywhere.—Got up—made bed in military fashion—washed in workhouse, Nobody about, a city of the dead. Fine, but cold. Doherty (pale, fat, furtive) gives me a look as he passes—I am the only one about—B-r-r-r-r—grating of gears—I looked out & saw grey Red Cross ambulance drive up past Black House & towards hospital. (*JCPD*, 99)

The range of authors coloring Campbell's literary style is apparent from the names that crop up in the diary—Gogol, Tolstoy, Herman Melville, George Meredith, Katherine Mansfield, John Middleton Murry—but responses to international current affairs also recur, some with evident distaste. Looking at the *New York Times* and other American papers, he notes: "Mussolini at an anniversary march of the Fascisti in Rome—looks like Napoleon—thrust out lips—rather fancies himself as a dictator" (*JCPD*, 117). The commentary then switches to the kind of sensational photos in American newspapers that grab attention, much like the denizens of Barney Kiernan's pub in "Cyclops" looking at American magazines: "Prisoners (with light from blazing fires on paper & faces, or backs of heads & shoulders—some are sitting with their backs towards me, where I write on my bed) looking at N.Y. Times pictures (They *love* pictures)"

(*JCPD*, 117). Authors that Campbell did not appreciate previously take on new meaning in a prison setting: "[O]h, like Job, I curse the day I was born! I understand books like 'Job,' 'Timon of Athens,' 'Lear,' 'De Profundis,'—'The Inferno,' Dostoevsky's novels, as I never understood before. They have sprung out of a terrible personal suffering" (*JCPD*, 78). Dostoevsky is seen as a precursor of Joyce in an exchange with Francis ("Frank") Stuart:

> Talked with Fr. Stuart. I thought Gogol's *Dead Souls* old-fashioned. But it was published in 1842. No literary form becomes more quickly passé than the novel. "Dostoevsky," said Frank, "is as modern in his method as James Joyce." *War and Peace* is not as old fashioned as *Anna Karenina* or *Resurrection*. I'm slogging away at W&P. There's lot of reading in it. No hope of release. "We'll be the last to go," I said. "The young men who carried the guns will be let out: the old young men with the ideas will be kept in." (*JCPD*, 84)

The succession of images in Campbell's prison diary is akin to a stream-of-consciousness technique, particularly when, as in the case of Frank Gallagher's *Days of Fear*, the writer's mind is disoriented during the abortive mass hunger strike on which over five thousand republican prisoners embarked during October–November 1923.[84] An entry for November 22, 1923, begins in a graphic style: "Frost, post outside. All taps in warehouse frozen—for first time. Over to sandbank opposite Black House to get grease & carbon deposit off utensils. Foggy sentry (*always* the sentry): frozen gulls, frozen cakes of sand; frost white on barbed wire—like frost on thorny sprays of a country hedge" (*JCPD*, 109). Noting that the new Irish government refused to hand over the body of Denis Barry, who had died on hunger strike, the diary then imagines political discussions between prisoners of "Garibaldi & Roman Republic of 1849, & subsequent movement," which turns into a list of topics and writers that is redolent of the lists of "Cyclops" ("Prisoners moving about like figures in a Cyclops' forge" [*JCPD*, 41–42]), with Jack Keogh as the counterpart of the citizen holding forth: "Old Jack Keogh at stove (back to cold-door) on history of Catholic Church in Ireland. Strongbow's time—Sir Felim O'Neill 1641—Rinucinni—Owen Roe only leader that ever led an Irish army—Sarsfield—Pepys' references to Irish Catholiques. George III and America. Rip Van Winkle. 'Farmer George' of Windsor (Thackeray). Dean Swift. Only a foreigner could lead an Irish army etc." (*JCPD*, 110). At this point, the train of thought veers off abruptly in a self-conscious direction, as words seem to disintegrate:

> (As I wrote this insects eating me—close to forms with prisoners talking around stove (revolvers—"Ballina"—"armoured car"—snatches of talk—arm of western prisoner, gesticulating, jostles me—the "sh" sound of western speech—"g's" at ends of words—"ing" pronounced carefully.) [...] Letters in. One handed to me by Sean Mooney—"Here, Joseph!"—from N. dated Sunday 18/Nov/23 (quote) [...] Lemon drink between P. Cahill T. D. & Billy Walsh frozen into sold block of ice. This will give you an idea of the temperature in the hut. (*JCPD*, 110)

The (self-)directive to write up a fuller account—to "quote" from the letter received from "N" (his wife, Nancy)—is offset by the physical contact, snatches of sound, and the sudden direct address to the reader at the end of the passage—"This will give *you* an idea" (emphasis added).

In her insightful introduction to the published edition of Campbell's prison diary, Eiléan Ní Chuilleanáin notes that Campbell was inspired by prison writing in the past, among them Ezekiel in the Old Testament (the source of the title "As I Was among the Captives"), Sir Walter Raleigh, John Bunyan, and Leigh Hunt. But as it was style, not just subject matter, that concerned him, the modernist turns echo Joyce's and Proust's experiments in form:

> Perhaps more importantly, for a writer who had many contacts with modernist as well as traditional writing, he compares himself to Joyce, who recorded the minutest details of his own and others' lives, and to Proust, who had chronicled his society shut away by illness as the prisoners were by barbed wire.[85]

Ní Chuilleanáin cautions that "the Joycean tone of some of the observations may be fortuitous; he may be simply reminding himself to write up at a later stage something he has just spotted" (*JCPD*, 7), but such a disconnected, abbreviated style, as also in Gallagher's diary, is particularly suited to the captive mind.[86] Not surprisingly, the desire to escape through the walls of buildings—those of the cell, the fortress-like walls of the prison, or the perimeter of the camp itself—preoccupied prisoners, and both Campbell and Francis Stuart (and other memoirists of the time) elaborated on the intricate systems of tunnels dug beneath both Mountjoy and the Curragh camp ("under the direction of an engineer from the Arigna coalmines").[87] While keeping watch for the tunnel-makers at the Curragh, H, the protagonist of Stuart's autobiographical novel, *Black List, Section H* (1971), gazed "intently out between the bars until he imagined the hazily illuminated door had opened and shadows were thronging out," and he "reflected on what becoming a writer meant. He believed it was being able to exteriorize in fiction or poetry the intense but cloudy and otherwise inexpressible intimations and insights that obsessed him." The extent to which suffering itself had been relegated to the underground made the writer more determined to explore the abyss: "It struck H that away from the card table or the intense atmosphere of the prison, they had little to talk of. What they shared were instincts and, perhaps, an outlook too subterranean to discuss except in rare moments."[88] If trauma was, in effect, the piercing of the walls of the psyche from the outside, such freedom as could be attained took the form of exteriorizing the wound in tangible, aesthetic form, tunneling through the dark corners of both self and society to where, in Samuel Beckett's words, "there might have been, mathematically at least, a door."[89]

* 6 *

"Through the Eyes of Another Race"

ULYSSES, ROGER CASEMENT, AND
THE POLITICS OF HUMANITARIANISM

> The Irishman called O'Neill, O'Brien, O'Donnell, steps out of a past well-nigh co-eval with the heroisms and tragedies that uplifted Greece and laid Troy in ashes, and swept the Mediterranean with an Odyssey of romance that still gives its name to each chief island, cape, and promontory of the mother sea of Europe....
>
> ROGER CASEMENT, "The Romance of Irish History" (1914)[1]

For all his skepticism of the excesses of the Celtic Revival, James Joyce's eye for arcane scholarship did not fail him when it came to controversies on the ancestry of the Celts, not least General Charles Vallancey's (1725–1812) eighteenth-century theories on the Phoenician/North African origins of the Irish language. In his lecture "Ireland: Island of Saints and Sages," Joyce spoke of Gaelic to his Trieste audience, informing them:

> This language is eastern in origin and has been identified by many philologists with the ancient language of the Phoenicians, the discoverers, according to historians, of commerce and navigation. With their monopoly over the sea, this adventurous people established a civilization in Ireland which was in decline and had almost disappeared before the first Greek historian took up his quill.... The language that the comic dramatist Plautus puts in the mouth of Phoenicians in his comedy *Poenula* is virtually the same language, according to the critic Vallancey, as that which Irish peasants now speak. The religion and civilization of that ancient people, later known as Druidism, were Egyptian.[2]

Why did Joyce feel compelled to invoke the contentious scholarship of Vallancey and his followers to support an Atlantic genealogy of the Celtic past, as against the prevailing consensus of an exclusively central European

Hallstatt or La Tène origin?[3] Part of the answer may be that it allowed him, even as early as 1907, to make a series of intricate connections between Ireland and the Mediterranean Sea, as if in preparation for a modern reworking of Homer's *Odyssey*, but also, via a more circuitous route, for the later appearance of Roger Casement's name in relation to abuses of human rights in Africa in the "Cyclops" chapter of *Ulysses*.[4] Joyce drew on a range of Irish Gaelic scholarship, some of it highly inventive, that linked Ireland with ancient Carthage and Phoenicia in the Levant and North Africa, in the process allowing him to reclaim the much-maligned Cyclops figure in Greek mythology as Ireland's own. The early antiquarian researches of Roderick O'Flaherty (1629–1718), living on the western seaboard in Connemara, identified Ireland with Ogygia, the original of Calypso's isle at the edge of the Atlantic Ocean, and through this and subsequent historical speculation, Joyce was in a position to fasten the connection between Homer's imaginative geography and Ireland.[5] The Gaelic past was aligned not only with the glory that was Homer's Greece, but also, by means of Phoenicia and Carthage, with the ruin and desolation brought about by Rome's early forays into colonialism. Reinserting the Hebraic and Levantine contribution to classical antiquity—as in "Jewgreek is greekjew" (*U*, 15.2097–98)—was central to this project, and one of the reasons Joyce was drawn to Victor Bérard's revisionist remapping of the geography of Homer's *Odyssey* in *Les Phénicians et l'Odyssée* (Paris, 1902–3) was its portrayal of Ulysses as a Phoenician adventurer, setting in place connections between Ireland and the Oriental origins of *The Odyssey*: "the gran Phenician rover. By the smell of her kelp they made the pigeonhouse" (*FW*, 197.32–34), that is, the Pigeon House power station newly opened at the mouth of the Liffey on Dublin Bay.[6] Joyce wrote to Louis Gillet in 1938: "A strange parallel occurred with Victor Bérard's Ulysses. His Homeric study confirmed my theory of Semitism in the *Odyssey* when I had already written three quarters of the book," but as has been pointed out, awareness of Bérard's work was far from an afterthought and is a structuring presence throughout *Ulysses*.[7]

The connections with Troy and Carthage are flagged in the opening line of "Cyclops": "I was just passing the time of day with old Troy of the D.M.P." (*U*, 12.1).[8] Cross-colonial connections were not only in the eyes of Irish beholders but informed British perceptions, with *The Graphic* ridiculing Heinrich Schliemann's pioneering excavations in the early 1880s that laid claim to the discovery of ancient Troy (as much because they questioned British ownership of the classical past, as anything else) on the grounds that the "so-called Scaean Gate, and Priam's Palace" resembled "rather a jumble of Irish hovels than a royal abode," and might be better renamed "the palace of Priam's pig."[9] In decentering the classical past, Joyce was, in effect, establishing the coordinates of an anti-colonial modernism, one that countered empire on several fronts, not least from "the edge of the continent": "Is the Celtic spirit, like the Slavic one (which it resembles in many respects), destined in the future to enrich the consciousness of civilization with new discoveries, and institutions?" (*OCPW*, 124). For Roger Casement, it was vital that Irish nationalists make common cause with oppressed peoples in other outposts of empire. "The claim of the Congo people must appeal to every sincere and genuine Irish national: the more we love our land and wish to help our people the more keenly we feel we cannot turn a deaf ear to suffering and injustice in any part of the world."[10] In the heyday of the Irish Parliamentary Party in Westminster, Casement advocated giving eight Irish seats to India, and four to Egypt in North Africa, and later he described his aptly named essay "The Elsewhere Empire" (1914) as "reverting to '48 and '98—when Irishmen preached not freedom for themselves alone, but freedom for all others."[11] Joyce shared Casement's aversion to the nationalism of John Redmond and an Irish Parliamentary Party that did not question the basis of empire, only Ireland's lowly position within white global expansion.[12] As in Derek Walcott's later *Omeros* (a work indebted to *Ulysses*), Joyce's "reorienting" of Homer realigned the epic genre from the closed, monological form of the classical epic, and its romantic variant in the work of Standish O'Grady, to the heterogeneity of the modern novel: "Its roots are not in Europe or Africa, but necessarily in both Europe and Africa; consequently it is not epic or novel, but only epic and novel."[13]

The figure of the brutish Cyclops hovers in the background of colonial images of the Irish, for it was their savage and cannibalistic tendencies, inherited from their putative origins in the nomadic Scythian tribes of Asia and spread through central "barbarian" Europe, that early apologists for colonial rule such as Edmund Spenser seized upon to justify extermination policies against the Irish. Nationalist histories, understandably, sought to furnish the Irish with a more civilized pedigree, leading in the eighteenth and nineteenth centuries to a Phoenician or Carthaginian ancestry for ancient Irish civilization. As Joep Leerssen observes:

> In the opposition between civility and barbarism, the Anglocentric view saw the Irish as savages and the English presence as a force of civility; the Phoenician hypothesis turned the tables, and predicated civility upon the native Gaels while bracketing the English presence with the Viking spoliations, seeing them as violent disruptions. This implicit valorization was subliminally reinforced by the fact that the link between Phoenicia and

Ireland was usually traced by way of Carthage, and that a similar pattern was detected in Carthaginian-Roman relations as in Irish-English ones.[14]

Not least of ancient Phoenicia's claim to distinction was the invention by Cadmus of letters, or written script, which in *Finnegans Wake* is brought to Dublin (and its suburb Santry) by Ireland's founding sons: "These sons called themselves Caddy and Primas. Primas was a santryman and drilled all decent people. Caddy went to Winehouse and wrote o peace a farce. Blotty words for Dublin" (*FW*, 14.12–15). Hence, as noted above in Joyce's 1907 essay, the Phoenicians were on their way to Ireland "before the first Greek historian took up his quill" (*OCPW*, 110). General Vallancey established to his own satisfaction that ancient Punic and Irish were cognate languages, and Joyce went a stage further in *Finnegans Wake*, endowing the Phoenix Park—"our own sphoenix spark" (*FW*, 473.18)— with a Phoenician/Egyptian ancestry, and Tyre, the Phoenician birthplace of Cadmus and Queen Dido, with the mythical Irish land of youth, "Tyre-nan-Og" (*FW*, 91.25–26), as well as County Tyrone in Scottish-Irish planted Ulster: "the brutherscutch or puir tyron" (*FW*, 163.8–9).[15] In *Ulysses*, Queen Dido's offer of help to the Trojan Aeneas who lands as a refugee on her shores—"*haud ignarus malorum miseris succurrere disco etcetera* as the Latin poet remarks" (*U*, 16.175–76) ["not at all unacquainted with misfortune, I have learned to help the wretched"]—cites a classical source for an ethics of solidarity based on a shared moral history which was to feature prominently in Casement's indictment of colonialism.

Given these figures of descent, it is not surprising that the Phoenician model came under sustained pressure in the 1790s as sectarian and political divisions intensified in the run-up to the 1798 rebellion, and Protestant antiquarians such as Edward Ledwich and Thomas Campbell launched polemical counter-offensives against the very idea of an ancient Irish civilization. The defeat of the rebellion all but extinguished its faltering credibility, but like its mythical namesake, the Phoenician model rose again from the ashes in the 1820s with the revival of the Catholic fortunes under the leadership of Daniel O'Connell. This time around, Vallancey's subaltern orientalism was given additional ballast by the antiquarian endeavors of Sir William Betham, the propagandizing zeal of Thomas Moore, and— fatefully—the tragicomic speculations of Henry O'Brien (1808–1835), the Chatterton of Irish antiquarianism.[16] O'Brien's unsurpassed ingenuity, and his ability to conscript even the most recalcitrant facts into a Phoenician ancestry, is evident in his "translation" of an arcane treatise, *Phœnician Ireland*, by the learned Spanish scholar, Dr. Joachimo Villanueva, in 1833 (fig. 6.1). In this work, O'Brien's own scholarly apparatus and footnotes conduct a kind of semiotic guerrilla warfare with the original text, not least when he attempts to rescue the benighted figure of the Cyclops, and his ignominious connection with primitive Ireland, from the condescension of antiquity.[17] The contention of the Greek historian Strabo that the ancient Irish "used to seek refuge from the cold in caverns"—an observation, incidentally, that led to the hibernation of winter being designated by the cognate of Iberia, "Hibernia," as the name of the island— led to an early association between the Cyclops and the Irish. The reiteration of this in the account of Gildas (c. 500–c. 570), the sixth-century British historian, that "from their little caves crept forth the Irish like so many swarthy, sooty little worms," is taken up by Dr. Villanueva to refer to none other than the "original Erii," or Irish, whose name "in the singular number, means a giant, abbreviated from Cau ur, 'a cave man,' such as Cacus and the Cyclops are reported to have been."[18] Aware of the obloquy cast on such an unfortunate genealogy for the Irish, O'Brien leaps to the defense of the much-maligned Cyclops in a footnote, pointing out that so far from being savages, they were in reality ahead of their time, working as miners underground:

> The Cyclops are represented to have but one eye in the middle of their forehead, the origin of their name, from Kuklos, a circle, and Ops, an eye; but in reality were so called from their custom of wearing small steel bucklers over their faces, having but a single aperture in the middle, which corresponded exactly with the form of an eye. This practice they had recourse to in their capacity of miners, or in their profession of archery, as we find a Scythian nation, too, who excelled in the same art, who called themselves Arimaspi, from Arima, one, and spia, an eye, in allusion to the habit of closing one eye to take the better aim, by collecting the visual rays to one focus.[19]

It is not clear if Joyce was familiar with O'Brien's/Villanueva's *Phœnician Ireland*, but he had in his library another source linking the Cyclops with Ireland, the Abbé Cesarotti's Italian translation of *Ossian* (1763), which associates the wildness of the Cyclops as described by Vico with the landscape of Ireland:

> In the rude wildness of this man, Vico would see with pleasure those primitive descendants of Polyphemus, who, according to Plato, were heads of families in a savage state, and who lived in their dens, shunning all intercourse with society.... He detests everything that is not his own, and considers himself as the centre of nature. In the morning he has no other care

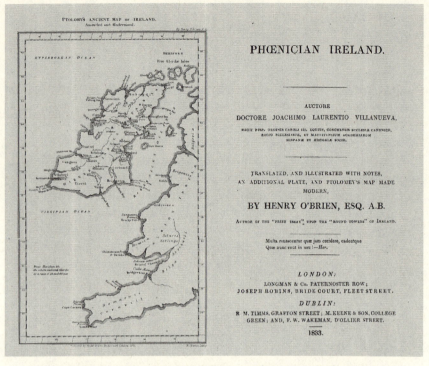

FIG. 6.1 Doctore Joachimo Laurentio Villaneuva, *Phœnician Ireland*, translated and illustrated by Henry O'Brien (1833). Title page, facing Ptolemy's map of Ireland. Photograph: Private collection.

but that of keeping up his fierceness. The east belongs to him. If the sun arose on the side of Ireland, he would abhor it as his enemy. The selfishness of this great Cyclopic character, and the uncouthness which proceeds from it, are painted with astonishing force.[20]

There are echoes of this in the Phoenix Park/Phoenician passages of *Finnegans Wake*—"the phaynix rose a sun before Erebia sank his smother! [...] The west shall shake the east awake" (*FW*, 473.16, 22)—but the main interest here lies not so much in fabled mineralogy or wild speculation (the only wildness evident), as in the determination to rehabilitate the wild man against all odds under the Phoenician model.

Though the association of Celtic round towers with Carthaginians was dealt a hammer blow, so to speak, by George Petrie's *The Ecclesiastical Architecture of Ireland* in 1845, which established the Christian origins of the towers attributed by O'Brien to the Orient, the North African genealogy continued to exert influence throughout the nineteenth century and, due to its anti-colonial agenda, passed from history into literature and into new ways of imagining Ireland's strategic location in the British empire.[21] The recourse to Carthaginian ancestry was motivated originally by a desire to buttress Ireland's claim to a distant pre-colonial past, but the chronology of this pre-colonial civilization was shifted to the Dark Ages after the fall of Rome, when Ireland's reputation as an island of "saints and sages" disseminated learning throughout Europe. It is this which accounts for its reemergence in the writings of Joyce, who, as Norman Vance suggests, tended only to be "residually Catholic and nationalist when confronted with Protestant Unionism."[22] By bringing both Phoenician and medieval strands together in his Italian lecture (and noting, in the process, that the ultimate roots of the Irish language were Indo-European in the oriental sense), Joyce was in effect amalgamating the Gaelic past in both its ancient and medieval lineages to counter the "Calvinist and Lutheran fanatics from across the water" who subjected Ireland to new forms of "British tyranny" (*OCPW*, 115). But having rid Ireland of the imputation of cultural inferiority, Joyce was careful not to relapse into nationalist nostalgia that idealized the past as a consolation for a fallen present: "If it were valid to appeal to the past in this fashion, the fellahins of Cairo would have every right in the world proudly to refuse to act as porters for English tourists. Just as ancient Egypt is dead, so is ancient Ireland.... It is high time Ireland finished for once and for all with failures. If it is truly capable of resurgence, then let it do so.... [A] revolution is not made from human breath, and Ireland has already had enough of compromises" (*OCPW*, 125–26).

Joyce made little secret of the fact that the physical features and rhetorical powers of the citizen/monster in "Cyclops" were based on the real-life figure of Michael Cusack (1847–1906), but the more insular values expressed are closer to those of Oliver St. John Gogarty and Arthur Griffith, particularly in relation to insular nationalism and anti-Semitism. As Colum Kenny has clarified, Griffith's views on Judaism do not conform to caricatures of anti-Semitic bigotry, as he welcomed strands that embraced nationalism, such as Zionism, and opposed what he considered threats from cosmopolitanism and usury to a revitalized national economy from whatever source, however stereotyped (the "gombeen man" or moneylender, for example, was already a native bogeyman in Irish society).[23] But Griffith's newspaper, the *United Irishman*, did intervene with anti-Semitic sentiments in the Limerick Boycott against Jews early in 1904, the backdrop against which attitudes toward Jews in *Ulysses* set in June of that year is best viewed.[24] By contrast, Cusack, the founding figure of the Gaelic Athletic Association (GAA) in 1884, did not promote sectarian versions of nationalism, prompting Gerald Goldberg, onetime Jewish lord mayor of Cork, to conclude: "Those who regard Michael Cusack as the prototype of the character [of the citizen] travel a road that leads to nowhere. 'The citizen' is a composite reconstruction by Joyce of thoughts and sentiments expressed from time to time by Griffith and Gogarty, through their respective writings. The voice may be the voice of Cusack, but the hands and the heads and the thoughts are those of Griffith and Gogarty."[25]

That Joyce's knowledge of Cusack was far from superficial is clear from several throwaway details in his portrayal of the citizen. At one point, the citizen and the barflies in his company in Barney Kiernan's pub challenge Bloom's claims to Irishness:

—What is your nation if I may ask? says the citizen.
—Ireland, says Bloom. I was born here. Ireland.
The citizen said nothing only cleared the spit out of his gullet and, gob, he spat a Red bank oyster out of him right in the corner. (*U*,12.1430–33)

One of Cusack's earliest friends in Dublin was Joe Hynes, owner of the Red Bank Oyster bar, and it is likely that the oyster expelled from his gullet came from Carranroo Bay, a short distance from Cusack's birthplace in the parish of Carron on the Burren, County Clare, which was owned by the Red Bank restaurant.[26] Cusack taught at Lough Cutra School, Gort, from 1867 to 1871, and this may lie behind the offhand remark of the nameless narrator of the chapter in an exchange with Joe Hynes when he leaves the pub to relieve himself in the backyard:

—Mind, Joe, says I. Show us the entrance out.
—There you are, says Terry.
Goodbye Ireland I'm going to Gort. (*U*, 12.1559–61)

One of the reasons Cusack lent himself to the comic potential of the chapter was, no doubt, his prowess as a sportsman in the shot put, making him eminently suitable for a parody of the scene in the original *Odyssey* in which the Cyclops hurls a massive boulder at the fleeing Ulysses and his companions.[27] As Cusack's biographer Marcus de Búrca suggests, Joyce may have deleted Cusack's name from the final published version in *Ulysses* because the caricature had departed so much from the original.[28] Notwithstanding Cusack's irascible temperament and vitriolic pen, there is no evidence of racism or anti-Semitism in his writings: he kept his most sarcastic invective for those with whom he disagreed in the Gaelic Athletic Association, and for prominent nationalist figures such as E. Dwyer Gray, editor of the *Freeman's Journal*. So far from being an out-and-out reactionary, Cusack was "an ardent egalitarian, and even socialist in outlook."[29] His early friendship with Michael Davitt and his admiration for the radical reformer Henry George led to strong sympathies for trade unions, cooperative societies, and the international Labour movement: "American Labour Notes" shared the pages of his newspaper, the *Celtic Times*, with "Appeal[s] to the Toilers of Great Britain," and articles on the importance of Irish women's industries.[30] Cusack's anticipation of Arthur Griffith's Sinn Féin economic policy took the form of advocating the development of Irish industry and, as his biographer de Búrca remarks, some of his accounts of native industries such as flour milling, iron galvanizing, paper manufacture, printing, and photographic processes "are so detailed that they required considerable research, mostly in Dublin and also elsewhere, and they reveal his skill as an investigative reporter."[31] More to the point, they were shared by Joyce himself in his support of Arthur Griffith's program for economic development, which, he wrote to his brother Stanislaus, "at least tries to inaugurate some commercial life for Ireland.... You may remember that on my arrival in Trieste I actually 'took some steps' to secure an agency for Foxford tweeds there."[32] The citizen's protests over the destruction of Irish economic life echo Joyce's views while in Trieste: "Ireland is poor because English laws destroyed the industries of the country, notably the woollen one; because, in the years in which the potato crop failed, the negligence of the British government left the flower of the people to die of hunger" (*OCPW*, 119).[33]

To introduce these qualifications into simplistic accounts of the "Cyclops" chapter is not to absolve the citizen of racism but to pose a different question: Where do such views come from, and how are they inflected in their (re)circulation? One of the subtexts of the "Cyclops" chapter is how, notwithstanding the rhetoric of de-anglicization and cultural purity, Irish Revivalism as exemplified by Standish O'Grady and others ventriloquized imperial sentiments, not least where discourses of militarism, manliness, and whiteness were concerned.[34] The Celt, racially conceived, mirrors the culture of the pantomime or the British music hall: "Is it you is going to write that pantomime about Finn MacCool or Brian Boru, isn't it?" asks a character in one of the early drafts of "Cyclops": "'What about it? says O'Madden Burke. Haven't we enough of those English importations with (flash) musichall songs and flash girl in tights.'"[35] This Victorian Celt is the object of Joyce's satire throughout *Ulysses* and may be seen as a cultural expression of "the Liberal tactic," which, according to his essay "The Home Rule Comet," aims at "deliberately and secretly undermining Nationalist feelings, while... it creates a new greedy dependent social class that is free from any dangerous enthusiasms" (*OCPW*, 158). This "elastic" liberalism, as Joyce went on to describe it in "The Shade of Parnell" (1912), is characterized by the "high-sounding sentences, Homeric studies and speeches on Artemis or marmalade" of Gladstone, who "in the case of other nations, maintained (as far as he could) a sincere admiration for liberty" (*OCPW*, 194–95), but was not so adept at recognizing it closer to home. It is not surprising that elevated attitudes to Homer are questioned here, for it was precisely the task of releasing the epic from the high seriousness of Victorian Hellenism—"masked with Matthew Arnold's face" (*U*, 1.173)—that Joyce set himself in *Ulysses*, rewriting it for a post-colonial world.

Cries from Roger Casement

The determination to connect anti-colonial struggles both at home and abroad was a feature linking figures in Joyce's circle in Ireland, among them Francis Sheehy Skeffington and Frederick Ryan, with prominent figures in the Congo Reform movement such as Roger Casement and Alice Stopford Green. A forthcoming publication of Ryan's is mentioned by John Eglinton in an exchange in "Scylla and Charybdis," in all probability the essay "Empire and Liberty" in the periodical *Dana*, which vehemently attacked those who found fault with Irish nationalism while ignoring British nationalism at home and throughout the empire. Taking his adversary "Ossorian" to task, Ryan writes that he "seems to be singularly blind to such iniquities. He has an eye for the supposed inconsistency of Mr. Thomas O'Donnell, M.P. . . . but he has no eye for the Jameson Raid, the Transvaal War, the age-long tragedy of India, prevented from developing along her own lines and taxed to famine point by English officialism, and the age-long tragedy of Ireland, kept in a state of perpetual smouldering civil war and bleeding to the point of extinction."[36] The one-sided view targeted by Ryan would seem to be close to the type of Cyclopean vision excoriated by Joyce in *Ulysses*. According to Constantine Curran, "Fred Ryan [was] a socialist and nationalist of the same temper as Frank Skeffington and in his outlook not very far removed from Joyce himself."[37] Ryan left Ireland in 1907 for Cairo to assume editorship of the anti-imperialist *Egyptian Standard*, which led Arthur Griffith to complain bitterly that "the suffering Egyptian had not less claim on him than his own countrymen."[38] It is this stand-alone nationalism, projected on to the citizen, that lies at the basis of the chauvinism directed at Bloom in "Cyclops," and which is opposed by the international outlooks associated with Ryan and Casement, a counter-narrative ironically introduced by the citizen himself.[39]

When Bloom proclaims in Barney Kiernan's bar that "love" is the answer to hatred and violence, this provides a cue for the citizen to pour scorn on the evangelical zeal and atrocities committed in the name of love: "What about sanctimonious Cromwell and his ironsides that put the women and children of Drogheda to the sword with the bible text *God is love* pasted round the mouth of his cannon? The bible! Did you read that skit in the *United Irishman* today about that Zulu chief that's visiting England?" (*U*, 12.1507–10). Taking up his copy of Griffith's paper, the *United Irishman*, the citizen then reads out a sarcastic skit on a trade mission to Britain in June 1904 by the Nigerian chief, the Alake of Abeokuta:

—A delegation of the chief cotton magnates of Manchester was presented yesterday to His Majesty the Alaki of Abeakuta by Gold Stick in Waiting, Lord Walkup of Walkup on Eggs, to tender to His Majesty the heartfelt thanks of British traders for the facilities afforded them in his dominions. The delegation partook of luncheon at the conclusion of which the dusky potentate, in the course of a happy speech, freely translated by the British chaplain, the reverend Ananias Praisegod Barebones, tendered his best thanks to Massa Walkup and emphasised the cordial relations existing between Abeakuta and the British empire, stating that he treasured as one of his dearest possessions an illuminated bible, the volume of the word of God and the secret of England's greatness, graciously presented to him by the white chief woman, the great squaw Victoria, with a personal dedication from the august hand of the Royal Donor. [...]
—Widow woman, says Ned. I wouldn't doubt her. Wonder did he put that bible to the same use as I would.
—Same only more so, says Lenehan. And thereafter in that fruitful land the broadleaved mango flourished exceedingly.
—Is that by Griffith? says John Wyse.
—No, says the citizen. It's not signed Shanganagh. It's only initialled: P.
—And a very good initial too, says Joe.
—That's how it worked, says the citizen. Trade follows the flag.
(*U*, 12.1514–26, 1534–41)

The question of tone is vital here as some commentators have interpreted the citizen—and by extension the author of the skit—as mocking the African chief, not his colonial masters.[40] The citizen, writes M. Keith Booker, "describes the visit of a 'Zulu chief' to England in 1904 in terms that make clear his recognition of British imperial activities in black Africa while treating the African leader as a figure of fun and derision."[41] There is an element of truth in this, to the extent that it ridicules the obsequiousness of elites among colonized peoples, voicing sentiments in keeping with Joyce's own comments on the "gratefully oppressed" (*D*, 35). On this basis,

Booker argues that Irish hostility to empire was couched entirely in white terms, expressing solidarity only with other whites such as the Boers: "The Irish were able to sympathize with the Boers only because the Boers were white and of European descent and were unable or unwilling to recognize that the people of Ireland had much in common with black Africans as well."[42] The skit on the Alake is attributed in *Ulysses* to the *United Irishman* but it was, as John Nash has shown, the London *Times* that carried the initial journalistic account: the more absurd honorific titles, moreover, are not primitive caricatures but genuine designations of the British monarchy, as in "the Captain and Gold Stick of His Majesty's Body Guard of the Honourable Corps of Gentlemen-at-Arms."[43] The sentiments informing the parody echo those of the citizen in his condemnation of Cromwell and, as Emer Nolan points out, "the document which the citizen reads is a *protest* against the African's subjection to the protocols of British manners, and the pretended equivalence between languages, customs and culture, the illusion of 'free translation' when the question of power is disregarded."[44] The image of colonialism as operating with love and the Bible, on the one hand, and military force, on the other, was used by Joyce in his Trieste lecture on Irish history, "Ireland: Island of Saints and Sages," citing the example of Cromwell in Ireland: "the great Protector of civil rights . . . a savage animal who came to Ireland to propagate his faith by fire and sword" (*OCPW*, 121).

In his Trieste lecture, Joyce proceeds to question the wisdom of attacking English rule in Ireland without relating it to a wider critique of imperialism, since "what England did in Ireland over the centuries is no different from what the Belgians are doing today in the Congo Free State."[45] This is taken up in "Cyclops" following the parody of the African chief's visit in a manner that demonstrates, contrary to Booker's statement above, that Irish anti-imperial solidarity was not confined to white people but extended to the brutal treatment of Black populations under colonialism. Ned Lambert's quip on what the Alake should have done with "the secret of England's greatness"—"Wonder did he put that bible to the same use as I would" (*U*, 12.1534–35)—shows which side his sympathies are on, and following the citizen's comment that British trade follows the flag, the conversation picks up as if on cue from Joyce's Trieste lecture:

—Well, says J. J., if they're any worse than those Belgians in the Congo Free State they must be bad. Did you read that report by a man what's this his name is?

—Casement, says the citizen. He's an Irishman.

—Yes, that's the man, says J.J. Raping the women and girls and flogging the natives on the belly to squeeze all the red rubber they can out of them. (*U*, 12.1542–47)

"Red rubber" meant rubber stained with blood, and Casement's evidence of brutalities in the Congo Free State formed a central part of E. D. Morel's *Red Rubber*, published in 1906, two years after the imaginary scene in Barney Kiernan's.[46] There seems little doubt where the sympathies of the exchange lie, and that the castigation of empire is not confined to Britain but extends to Belgian atrocities as well. The reference to Casement has also been foreshadowed in the graphic scene describing the "poor bugger's tool" (*U*, 12.457) with hanging, and the association of the hangman with Pentonville Prison, where Casement was executed for treason in 1916.[47]

That this wider perspective informs the "Cyclops" sequence is clear from the actual circumstances that surrounded the visit of the Alake of Abeokuta to Britain in June 1904, and its underlying connections with both Casement and radical currents in Irish nationalism. According to Philip F. Herring, Joyce probably chose to misspell the Alake's name to "Alaki"—"a lackey"—because of the visiting chief's seeming obsequious behavior: "To Joyce the Alake seemed fair game because he conspired with colonialism at a time when Roger Casement's reports of Belgian atrocities in the Congo were receiving wide publicity."[48] This is not the full story, however, for during his visit, the Alake was hosted not only by royalty and colonial interests such as the British Cotton Growing Association, but also by Casement's friend, the Irish nationalist and leading anti-imperialist Alice Stopford Green, who arranged for him to meet a number of prominent liberals at her house.[49] According to her biographer R. B. McDowell, Stopford Green was "quick to see parallels between Irish and African conditions" with the result that her "comments on British colonial policy and British colonial administration were often extremely harsh, Irish nationalist feeling putting an edge to her criticism."[50] In common with Joyce, Stopford Green expressed exasperation at the deference shown by native colonial elites to their European rulers, and hence was particularly impressed by the Alake's determination to stick to his native language and dress, and to conduct himself with dignity. Shortly before her meeting with the Alake, Stopford Green was one of the first to join the Congo Reform Association, established at the behest of Casement by her close friend E. D. Morel. Morel traveled to Ireland to meet Casement, writing: "it was ... on that Irish soil ... fertilized by so many human tears, that Casement and I conspired further ... and drew up a rough plan of campaign."[51]

In the spring of 1904, when the association was taking shape, Casement wrote a fifteen-page letter to Stopford Green, "without reflecting but straight from my heart." Noting how they both had in common a love of Ireland, Casement declared that had he not been "an avowed believer in the nationality and rights of Ireland," he would have observed the Congo horrors with "a cold and reserved heart."[52] Casement's purpose in writing was to encourage Stopford Green to use her influence to prevent the constitutional Home Rule party under John Redmond from supporting King Leopold—the kind of Irish nationalism that Joyce or the "bigots" in Barney Kiernan's pub conspicuously did not share. In an article written ten years later, Casement quotes a letter from Eoin MacNeill to Stopford Green in which he asserts, in relation to Irish people, that "the remarkable absence of insular exclusiveness, notwithstanding their geographical position, serves to bring their nationality in higher relief." This provides a cue for Casement to record that the Irish first enter recorded history through their resistance to Roman invasion: "The first external record we possess thus makes it clear that when the Irish went forth to carry war abroad, it was not to impose their yoke on other peoples, or to found an empire, but to battle against the Empire of the World in the threatened cause they held so dear at home." Hence, he notes, "Agricola's advice to the empire-builders of his day was that Rome should 'war down and take possession of Ireland, so that freedom might be put out of sight.'"[53] It is in this light, Emer Nolan suggests, that the "citizens" of Barney Kiernan's are best viewed, since "in their more global interests in imperialism and in politics they actually transcend the narrow focus of the novel itself on the Irish situation."[54] This counters the narrow Irish-Ireland program of many leading figures of the Celtic Revival and is threaded through "Cyclops," not only in its many references to imperialism elsewhere, and to Casement, but also the citizen's own allusion to Tacitus's account of Agricola: Irish wool, he contends, "was sold in Rome in the time of Juvenal. . . . Read Tacitus and Ptolemy" (*U*, 12.1241–43, 1250–51). This is the point of the indictment in "Cyclops" of colonial policies suppressing trade, particularly the cattle trade, leading Richard Ellmann to observe that the manner in which the citizen "windily discusses the plight of cattle in terms of Irish glories and English injustices, is an aspect of Joyce's mind as well as the butt of his satire" (*JJ*, 285). It is not clear if the citizen has actually read Tacitus's *Agricola*, but one of his (or perhaps Joyce's) sources for the peroration on the vitality of Irish trade before its strangulation by British colonial policy may have been Stopford Green's dismantling of the myth of Irish insularity in her article "The Trade Routes of Ireland":

In the time of the Roman Empire therefore Irish trade with Europe was already well established. Tacitus (A.D. 98) tells us that its ports and harbours were well known to merchants; and in the second century the geographer Ptolemy of Alexandria gave a list, very surprising for the time, of the rivermouths, mountains, and port towns of Ireland, and its sea-coast tribes.[55]

The mention of Tacitus evokes one of the turning points in perceptions of the civilizing mission of imperialism in its early forms, as recounted in Calgacus's much-cited speech to the assembled Britons. Exposing the inner logic of Roman expansionism, he exclaims: "To robbery, butchery, and rapine, they give the lying name of 'government,' they create a desolation and call it peace."[56] Colonial civility, on this reading, is equivalent to the "faultless morning dress" (*U*, 12.592–93) the hangman Rumbold wears before disemboweling Irish patriots, or to the refined sensibility of "the stern provostmarshal, lieutenantcolonel Tomkin-Maxwell ffrenchmullan Tomlinson" (with its echoes of the 1916 Rising, as noted above), who shed a tender tear when he "had blown a considerable number of sepoys from the cannonmouth without flinching" (*U*, 12.669–72). As Patrick Mullen notes, moreover, Joyce's inscriptions of Casement's homosexuality in the grim sequence noting the effects of hanging on the male body—"the poor bugger's tool"—suggests that Casement's indictment of empire may be based on a double sense of oppression.[57] An earlier reference to the role of the Bible in establishing an empire on which "the sun never sets" (*U*, 2.248) may allude also to Casement, who wrote that for imperialists, "the British Bible was the Bible that counted. It was the Bible upon which the sun never sets, the Bible that had blown Indian mutineers from its muzzle in the 'fifties . . . the unctuous rectitude that converts the word of God into wadding for a gun is certainly a formidable opponent, as Cromwell showed." And yet Casement added, neither the Bible nor the navy is the secret of England's greatness: "The British Empire is founded not upon the British Bible or the British dreadnought but upon Ireland. The empire than began upon an island, ravished, sacked and plundered shall end on an island."[58]

In one of the earliest uses of the concept of "crimes against humanity," Casement wrote in October 1910 of the "hellish crimes" committed by colonial overlords against Indigenous peoples: "These men have never been punished for the most awful *offences against humanity*. Not one" (emphasis added). Returning to the topic a short while later, Casement expressed dismay that though the crimes were committed openly, English observers turned a blind eye to the proceedings:

An Englishman educated at an English university should be able to smell right and wrong in a case of this kind. This thing we find here is carrion—a pestilence—*a crime against humanity*, and the man who defends it is, consciously or unconsciously, putting himself on the side of the lowest scale of humanity, and propagating a moral disease that religion and conscience and all that is upright should uncompromisingly denounce.[59]

Casement's invocation of "religion and conscience and all that is upright" recalls the image of Cromwell with the Bible in one hand and the sword in another, and his work in the Putumayo region of the Amazon built on the previous campaigns of the Congo Reform Association (CRA), which can be regarded, as Sharon Sliwinski notes, "as a forerunner to the work of present-day humanitarian groups such as Human Rights Watch and Amnesty International."[60] The extent to which popular movements against gross injustices such as slavery were driven by different principles—whether Christian concepts of philanthropy and social justice, universal commitments to human rights, or political radicalism—is still a matter of debate, but condemnations of modern slavery in the Congo and the Putumayo drew not only on religious or humanitarian concerns but also on wider political critiques of imperialism. Rosa Luxemburg was at the forefront of the latter, seeing in the Putumayo an instructive example of capitalist modernity's dependence on the "pre-modern" or non-Western societies—in essence, the logic of imperialism—to sustain accumulation in the metropolitan center. Contrasting concern for "Little Belgium" in the Great War with the destruction of Indigenous peoples by European powers, Luxemburg protested:

A cry of horror went up through the world when Belgium, that priceless little jewel of European culture, when the venerable monuments of art in northern France, fell into fragments before the onslaughts of a blind and destructive force. The "civilized world" that has stood calmly by when this same imperialism doomed thousands of Hereros to destruction . . . when in Putumayo, within ten years forty thousand human beings were tortured to death by a band of European industrial rubber-barons, and the remnant of a whole people were beaten into cripples.[61]

James Connolly's "Belgium's Rubber and Belgian Neutrality" (1914) preceded Luxemburg's critique and, citing Casement, pointed out how in the newly found concern for Belgium in the Great War, British memories had forgotten crimes exposed only ten years before: "Why was the exposure of these outrages suddenly stopped; why did the British and

French Governments suddenly exert themselves to choke off all further revelations, and to re-establish cordial relations with the Belgian Court?"[62] Though appealing to universal standards, the designation of crimes against humanity is mediated through contingencies of political power and grounded in particular cultural capacities to perceive them as such, as was noted by the *Irish War News* on April 25, 1916, the first republican bulletin issued in the Easter Rising. Noting sardonically how "agitation for English intervention in the Congo" was stirred up "as the only hope of saving the heads and the hands of the natives being cut off," defenders of "Little Belgium" cannot "be unmindful of the campaign . . . 'to save humanity from Belgium barbarities'" and which "incidentally, of course, handed over the Congo to the British Rubber monopolists."[63] The rapidity with which humanitarian concerns, based on a shared, universal human nature, changed according to political alignments, showed that spectacles of suffering did not appeal to an "esperanto of the eye," speaking all languages and transcending cultural boundaries.

This is made clear in "Cyclops" through the cultural inflections of responses to Thomas Jones Barker's painting *The Secret of England's Greatness* (1863), silently quoted to underline the irony of the gift presented to the Alake of Abeokuta: "he treasured as one of his dearest possessions an illuminated bible, the volume of the word of God and the secret of England's greatness, graciously presented to him by the white chief woman, the great squaw Victoria, with a personal dedication from the august hand of the Royal Donor" (*U*, 12.1522–27). Jones Barker's painting, according to Antony Taylor, "remains central to our understanding of the Victorian mind-set," conveying in emblematic form "a set of precise meanings about the relationship between the Crown, state and empire in the nineteenth century."[64] The painting went on tour all over Britain, in Dublin and in Belfast, but in Ulster Unionist circles it became a badge of identity, finding lasting expression on the banners of several Orange Lodges. This veneration of the image contrasts strongly with the contempt shown for it by the citizen and his friends, but, contrary to the art connoisseurs in Barney Kiernan's, other historians have discerned in the noble rendering of the African chief a possible note of dissent from empire, suggesting it "contains an unintentional acknowledgment of the potential for independent colonial growth, and perhaps ultimately foreshadows the eventual separation of the colonies from the motherland"[65] — an intimation of the sympathies underlying the irony of the passage in "Cyclops," and an indication of the cultural codings of responses to seemingly universally legible images.

Casement's courageous stand on crimes against humanity was interpreted by the London *Times* as evidence of Britain's civilizing influence

FIG. 6.2 Thomas Jones Barker, *The Secret of England's Greatness* (1863). Photograph: National Portrait Gallery, London.

(the report was prepared for the British Foreign Office), in contrast to other barbaric imperial regimes: "No one who reads Sir Roger Casement's Report can fail to wish it the means and power to extend its civilizing influence. The existing system cries aloud to Heaven."[66] But as Rosa Luxemburg suggested, the civilizing influence of the existing system, driven by British imperialism at its apex, was the problem, not aberrations from it. Perpetrators of atrocities "maintained they were only doing in the Amazon what European powers had been doing for centuries worldwide: subduing local populations, often by force, and deriving great commercial benefit therefrom."[67] Casement's exposure of atrocities in the Congo was welcomed in British circles because it impugned Belgian imperialism (though, as noted above, the Anglo-Belgian India Rubber Company was involved): the problem with the Putumayo region was that English commercial interests were directly implicated, and even though the Foreign Office commissioned the report, they had not fully grasped the moral sensibility Casement, as an Irish republican and outlier in the diplomatic corps, would bring to the proceedings.

It is characteristic of the nuances of the "Cyclops" chapter that the first words uttered by the citizen on mentioning Casement's name, notwithstanding his status as a British diplomat, is "He's an Irishman"

(*U*, 12.1545).⁶⁸ Writing to the *Times* three years before the Easter Rising, Casement explained:

> Whatever of good I have been the means of doing in other countries was due ... to the guiding light I carried from my own country, Ireland, and to the very intimate knowledge I possessed not only of her present day conditions, but of the historical causes that led up to them. With a mind thus illumined, I was not ill-equipped for comprehending that human suffering elsewhere originated in conceptions of human exploitation that are both very old and very widespread.⁶⁹

Casement's awareness of Britain's supremacy in the imperial system concentrated his mind not only on humanitarian intervention but also on colonized cultures emancipating themselves from their condition. As Samuel Moyn has shown, demands for universal human rights were originally conceived in collective terms and were inextricably bound up with rights of national self-determination, particularly in the worldwide decolonizing period following World War Two.⁷⁰ To assert human rights at a collective, political level in the early twentieth century required a national situation strategically placed to exploit a stress point in the "overpowering supremacy of Great Britain's influence in world affairs," and Ireland presented for Casement—as well as for James Connolly, Lenin, and indeed the British authorities—such a prospect.⁷¹ The historical research and indefatigable campaigning of Alice Stopford Green enabled Casement to place his increasing identification with the cause of Ireland in a wider imperial frame to which he had devoted his considerable humanitarian energies. Following Casement's organization, with a number of other leading Protestant and Anglo-Irish figures, of a meeting at Ballymoney, County Antrim, to prevent Ulster public opinion from following the Unionism of Edward Carson, the London *Times* dismissed him, in what it presumably considered a slur, as one who "combines citizenship of the world with an enthusiastic attachment to romantic nationalism." Casement accepted the put-down as a compliment—"Your correspondent is good enough to refer to me as one who combines citizenship of the world with an enthusiastic attachment to romantic nationalism," and continued: "It was doubtless an enthusiastic attachment to romantic humanitarianism that led my footsteps from Ulster up to the Congo and Amazon rivers, and probably without that quality I should have failed in the very practical investigations I was privileged to conduct alone, in both regions, and to bring to a not unsuccessful issue."⁷² Just as the romantic epic underwent radical transformation in the pages of *Ulysses*, so romantic nationalism was given a global expression through the exploitation of a geopolitical stress point in the modern world system:

> I knew the F[oreign] O[ffice] would not understand the thing—or that if they did they would take no action, for, I realized I was looking at this tragedy *with the eyes* of another race—of a people once hunted themselves, whose hearts were based on affection as the root principle of contact with their fellow men and whose estimate of life was not something eternally to be appraised at its "market price."[73]

As Hannah Arendt argued later of crimes against humanity, being human is not sufficient for the recognition of human rights, and the capacity to see injustice is only as good as the "moral history" (Joyce), or what she referred to (quoting Edmund Burke) as the "entailed inheritance" of a culture brought to bear on it.[74] Rights are not individual possessions, acquired in a pre-political state of nature, but are dependent on political worlds and mutual recognition to give them substance, "the right to have rights" (*OT*, 376–77), as Arendt famously described it. The paradox for Arendt, however, was that a society's eligibility for human rights depended on its attaining the stage of civilization of the society that was about to wipe it out: "If a tribal or other 'backward' community did not enjoy human rights, it was obviously because as a whole it has not reached that stage of civilization" (*OT*, 370). Though she identified the scramble for Africa "as the most fertile soil for the flowering of what was to become the Nazi elite ... and how one might put one's people into the position of a master race" (*OT*, 268), she did not focus on colonized peoples or their rights, but on the crimes of colonizers. The "entailed inheritance" Arendt had in mind in her citation of Burke was the "rights of an Englishman," but it was precisely this imperial gaze that was founding wanting in Casement's eyes, who turned his attention instead to the "tribal or other 'backward' community" of colonized peoples: too often, as suggested in *Finnegans Wake*, universal morality is informed by a categorical "empirative" (*FW*, 187.31).[75] When Wyndham Lewis seized on a phrase from W. E. B. Dubois's novel *Dark Princess*, "The Congo ... is flooding the Acropolis," to decry to extension of European civility to non-Western peoples, he could have had both Casement and Joyce in mind, for it is this African infusion of classical antiquity that presides over the "Cyclops" chapter in *Ulysses*.[76]

Casement makes no attempt to equate levels of suffering in contemporary Ireland with those of the Congo or Putumayo (though he shared with others, such as James Connolly and Maud Gonne, a concern that the specter of the Famine was ever present in the West of Ireland): what is common to both is subjugation within a new age of imperialism in which Ireland, at this juncture, constituted a weak link.[77] Britain's commanding position in the global order ensured its primacy in anti-imperialist struggles, as "Skin-the-Goat" (the former member of the underground Invincibles organization) forecasts in "Eumaeus" in relation to the coming war:[78]

> But a day of reckoning, he stated *crescendo* with no uncertain voice, thoroughly monopolising all the conversation, was in store for mighty England, despite her power of pelf on account of her crimes. There would be a fall and the greatest fall in history. The Germans and the Japs were going to have their little lookin, he affirmed. The Boers were the beginning of the end. Brummagem England was toppling already and her downfall would be Ireland, her Achilles heel. (*U*, 16.997–1003)[79]

Imperialism in the abstract, therefore, was not Casement's immediate concern, any more than humanity in the abstract governed his moral vision, but his outlook was no less universal for that. By the same token, Joyce's universalism did not rest on analogies or formal parallels between Homer's *Odyssey* and the Dublin of *Ulysses* but on historical and textual webs woven between Ireland, antiquity, and African civilizations: "This allegory would be mere jest," wrote Hermann Broch, "if it did not possess deeper spiritual significance ... an allegorical cosmogony in which, moreover, Ireland and its history are raised to the position of a world allegory, a cosmogony possessing such wealth of strata and such complexity" that could only be mapped by Joyce's "poly-historical" mind.[80] Broch had personal experience of the crises in the mid-twentieth century that heightened his awareness of universal human rights. On his arrest by the Nazis in 1938, Joyce sought to assist his escape from Austria by obtaining a French visa for him, pursuing the issue "with monomaniacal obsession": in the end, Joyce was able to assist Broch's securing an entry permit for England.[81] Broch traveled eventually to New York, where he was one of the instigators of the moves that the led to the UN Universal Declaration of Human Rights in 1948, and in his exchanges with Hannah Arendt, another key figure in the movement, he introduced an emphasis on human dignity or recognition by others, that is, a respect for *diversity* rather than uniformity as the basis for universalism.

According to Sharon Sliwinski, "Contemporary calls for human rights ... utilize atrocity photographs, demand intervention, and rely on transcendental notions of dignity and duty,"[82] but it is not transcendental rights that are at stake: crimes against humanity are committed against members of despised *groups*, and genocide is directed not at persons as isolated individuals but at their right to belong to certain collectives or societies. For this reason, as Arendt points out, "the only given condition for the establishment of human rights is the plurality of men": crimes against humanity are "an attack upon *human diversity* as such, that is, upon a characteristic of the 'human status' without which the very words 'mankind' or 'humanity' would be devoid of meaning."[83] Human rights extend beyond national sovereignty in that no nation-state is a law unto itself, but that is because the right to belong to a particular community is itself the most basic human right and cannot be denied by any other nation-state. In keeping with the right to national self-determination under decolonization, concerted efforts were made subsequently to extend rights to social and economic rights to development as a "prerequisite for any progress in terms of civil and political liberties," but this was curtailed in the 1980s with the rise of neoliberalism.[84] As Moyn points out, the decanting of human rights in the late twentieth century from a wider political conception to a liberal individualistic interpretation, often opposed to the nation-state, belied Arendt's fundamental insight that rights are anchored in political communities, even if, as noted above, Arendt did not follow the logic of her critique of imperialism by linking it to decolonizing rights of national self-determination and development.[85] The basis of Casement's critique of empire in his courtroom speech before his execution lies precisely in the need for diversity underlined by Arendt: "The liberty of Ireland and Irishmen is to be judged by the power of England. Yet for me, an Irish outlaw, there is a land of Ireland, a right of Ireland, and a charter for all Irishmen to appeal to, in the last resort, a charter that even the very statutes of England cannot deprive us of."[86] For Arendt, being stripped of her German citizenship under the Nazis did not elevate her to a transcendental ethical plane but instead reduced her to "nothing more than the abstract nakedness of being human" (*OT*, 577). To be deprived of one's moorings on this basis is to be cut adrift of all rights: "The concept of human rights can again be meaningful only if they are redefined as a right to the human condition itself, which depends upon belonging to some human community, the right never to be dependent upon some inborn human dignity which *de facto*, aside from its guarantee by fellow men ... does not exist" (*OT*, 630). In Raphael Lemkin's pioneering indictment of genocide, "an attack on one of them is an attack on them all," and the list of historical precedents drawn up by Lemkin for outlawing genocide (a term he devised) included under "Antiquity": "Celts, Carthage," and under "Modern Times": "3. Belgian Congo.... 17. Ireland."[87]

Rebecca Solnit has written perceptively of Casement that "he dangled between two worlds for most of his life, between two countries, two churches, two philosophies," a predicament that "seems built into his name, for a casement is a window, something that itself mediates between two realms and is contained by neither."[88] In his essay "The Elsewhere Empire," Casement wrote, "The Irish patriot was, in truth, a world voice—a summons to every audience wherever men gather in quest of freedom.... Substitute India for Ireland and the Grattan of 1780 becomes the India patriot of today."[89] In a related vein, Joyce wrote of the dual mode of address in French and Russian novelists, their ability to speak at once to their own nations but also to the world at large: "They were national first, and it was the intensity of their own nationalism which made them international in the end, as in the case of Turgenev.... For myself, I always write about Dublin because if I can get to the heart of Dublin I can get to the heart of all the cities of the world. In the particular is contained the universal" (*JJ*, 505). Joyce brought to world literature what Casement brought to international humanitarianism, the "doubling stutter" (*FW*, 197.5) of a modernism at once home and away. When Casement wrote of the "the Irishman" who "swept the Mediterranean with an Odyssey of romance that still gives its name to each chief island, cape, and promontory of the mother sea of Europe,"[90] he could have been referring, in a modern idiom, to Joyce as well as to his own humanitarian quests.

✵ 7 ✵

Transatlantic "Usable Pasts"

AMERICA, LITERARY MODERNISM,
AND THE IRISH REVOLUTION

> Ireland and America really are alike in that they inherit
> a dominant academic tradition, colonial in essence.
>
> VAN WYCK BROOKS, "The Critics and Young America" (1917)

On June 28, 1916, a public reading was held by a number of eminent writers in Central Park, New York, to protest against the executions of the "poet patriots" among the leaders of the Easter Rising in Dublin, April 1916.[1] The meeting was organized by the Enniskillen-born poet Eleanor Rogers Cox and featured readings by Edwin Markham, who presided over the event, as well as Joyce Kilmer, Louis Untermeyer, Margaret Widdemer, and others. Events in Dublin had featured on the front page of the *New York Times* throughout the rebellion, with over ten articles being devoted to it on certain days, in addition to opinion columns and editorials.[2] The émigré poet Padraic Colum, writing in the *Washington Post* while fighting was still in progress, was foremost in publicizing the literary aspect of insurrection, and this was given full-page treatment in Joyce Kilmer's article "Poets Marched in the Van of Irish Revolt," in the *New York Times*, on May 7, 1916. Kilmer had met the executed poet and 1916 leader Joseph Mary Plunkett in New York in 1915, and his elegy "Easter Week: In Memory of Joseph Mary Plunkett" was published in his *Main Street and Other Poems* in 1917, shortly before the American writer's death in action in France in 1918.

Though the United States in 1916 had not yet entered the Great War and had assumed a pose of neutrality, disloyalty to the Allies at this period was considered tantamount to treason, leading to Theodore Roosevelt's and Woodrow Wilson's attacks on "hyphenated Americans" ultimately being brought to bear on Irish-American and German-American disaffection. In the shrill terms of Wilson's rhetoric, "Any man who carries a hyphen about with him carries a dagger that he is ready to plunge into the vitals of this Republic whenever he gets ready."[3] This metaphor also came to mind when the Anglo-Irish author and diplomat Shane Leslie (1885–1971), based in Washington, DC, saw fit to denounce the rebellion as a threat to an already precarious balance of power in Anglo-American transatlantic relations: "It was the only important event in Ireland since the death of Parnell. It seemed as though Dublin had risen like a hysterical woman and stabbed a man in armor with a broken bodkin to avenge some far off unhappy thing, and was summarily suppressed."[4] Leslie, a first cousin of Winston Churchill, was working with the British embassy and, as a supporter of Home Rule, undertook an exercise in damage limitation on the effects of the Easter Rising on Irish-American opinion.

A convert to Catholicism, Leslie's activities were not confined to diplomatic channels but extended to friendship with Monsignor Sigourney Fay, headmaster of the Newman School in Hackensack, New Jersey, where the young F. Scott Fitzgerald (1896–1940), then a pupil there, came under his influence. Writing to his cousin Mars Richard Taylor ("Ceci") in 1917, Fitzgerald exclaimed:

> Had I met Shane Leslie when I last saw you? Well, I've seen a lot more of him—He's an author and a perfect knockout.... Every man I've met who's been to war—that is, this war—seems to have lost youth and faith in man unless they're wine-bibbers of patriotism which, of course, I think is the biggest rot in the world. Updike of Oxford or Harvard says "I die for England" or "I die for America"—not me. I'm too Irish for that—I may get killed for America—but I'm going to die for myself.... Do read *The End of a Chapter* and *The Celt and the World* by Shane Leslie—you'd enjoy them both immensely.[5]

Leslie recommended (and helped to prepare) Fitzgerald's first novel, *This Side of Paradise*, for publication by Scribner's in March 1920 and was the co-dedicatee of his second novel, *The Beautiful and Damned*.[6] While a student at Princeton in 1917, Fitzgerald published a review of Leslie's *The Celt and the World*, expressing sympathy for a constitutional nationalism that was disintegrating as he was writing: "To an Irishman the whole book is fascinating. It gives one an intense desire to see Ireland free at last to work out her own destiny under Home Rule." Yet Fitzgerald reserves judgment on the Celt's aptitude for political affairs, for Leslie's picture is "cultured with an unworldliness" of "the mystical core and legend of the island which 'can save others, but herself she cannot save.'" This gives the book a pessimistic turn, even if it is of an inspirational rather than a "dreary" north European kind in its account of the Easter Rising: "At the end of the book," writes Fitzgerald, "that no less passionate and mystical though unfortunate incident of Pearse, Plunkett and the Irish Republic is given sympathetic but just treatment."[7]

These sentiments are picked up early in *This Side of Paradise*, which recounts a conversation between the young Fitzgerald-like protagonist Amory Blaine and his mentor Monsignor Darcy, modeled closely on Monsignor Fay at the Newman College. Amory provocatively identifies with the underdogs or losers of history—Bonnie Prince Charlie, the Southern Confederacy—but holds back from the Irish cause: "He was rather sceptical about being an Irish patriot—he suspected that being Irish was being somewhat common—but Monsignor assured him that Ireland was a romantic lost cause and Irish people quite charming, and that it should, by all means, be one of his principal biases."[8] These biases shape Monsignor Darcy's view of his irresolute protégé in the novel to such an extent that he eventually re-creates Amory in the image of one of Patrick Pearse's student warriors at St. Enda's School, modeled on the boy-hero of Irish legend, Cúchulainn. On Amory's joining the army, Darcy sends him a lugubrious poem conforming to the "keen"/elegy genre in Gaelic literature, "A Lament for a Foster Son, and He going to the War Against the King of Foreign":

Ochone

He is gone from me the son of my mind
    And he in his golden youth like Angus Oge
Angus of the bright birds
    And his mind strong and subtle like the mind of Cuchulin on
        Muirtheme.... (*TSP*, 147)

Leslie conveyed his deep misgivings to Fitzgerald over the letters penned by "Monsignor Darcy" in *This Side of Paradise*, not least because they were based on transcripts of actual letters written by Fay to the young Fitzgerald.[9] Fay invited Fitzgerald to accompany him as private secretary on a diplomatic mission to Rome in 1917 in which Fay acted, in Fitzgerald's words, as "Cardinal Gibbons' representative to discuss the war with the Pope (American Catholic point of view—which is most loyal—barring the Sinn Fein ...)."[10] That Fay's attitudes were moving from Home Rule toward the more radical Sinn Féin is clear from his letter to Leslie from the Irish College in Rome, evoking a scene that could also have come from St. Enda's (apart from the alcohol): "Naturally the College is a hotbed of SinnFein [*sic*]. [...] The boys sang Gaelic songs to me after dinner. I must say they are a splendid lot of young fellows. [...] After dinner and a bottle of Irish whisky [*sic*] we all got confidential."[11] Fitzgerald himself imbibed his "first whissky [*sic*]" with Fay while a pupil at the Newman College, and in his letter to his fellow university student Edmund Wilson recounting Fay's invitation to travel to Rome, he signs off somewhat whimsically as "Gaelically yours" (using "Celtically" on another occasion).[12]

Traces of these issues surface in *This Side of Paradise* when Amory reflects on the nature of prodigies, whether in the literary or political world, following a visit to his friend Mrs. Lawrence in uptown Manhattan:

> "Monsignor was here just last week," said Mrs. Lawrence regretfully. "He was very anxious to see you, but he'd left your address at home."
> "Did he think I'd plunged into Bolshevism?" asked Amory, interested.
> "Oh, he's having a frightful time."
> "Why?"
> "About the Irish Republic. He thinks it lacks dignity."
> "So?"
> "He went to Boston when the Irish President arrived and he was greatly distressed because the receiving committee, when they rode in an automobile, *would* put their arms around the President."
> "I don't blame him." (*TSP*, 193)

The shadow of Bolshevism may be as much responsible for the "common" nature of Irish republicanism in the Monsignor's eyes as the lack of social graces shown by the welcoming committee upon Éamon de Valera's visit to the United States, but on leaving the house, Amory parts company with the ethereal Celtic Twilight that was itself being overtaken by events in Ireland:

> When he left her house he walked down Riverside Drive with a feeling of satisfaction. It was amusing to discuss again such subjects as this young poet, Stephen Vincent Benet, or the Irish Republic. Between the rancid accusations of Edward Carson and Justice Cohalan he had completely tired of the Irish question; yet there had been a time when his own Celtic traits were pillars of his personal philosophy. (*TSP*, 194)

Glossing these exchanges, Patrick O'Donnell notes that "for the 'revolutionary' Amory, this upheaval [the Irish Troubles], along with the Bolshevist Revolution, represent the most compelling progressive historical movements of the day."[13] In these heady circumstances, it is not surprising that on its publication, Leslie saw *Ulysses* itself as an emissary of the anarchy that was let loose upon the world: "We shall not be far wrong if we describe Mr. Joyce's work as literary Bolshevism. It is experimental, anti-conventional, anti-Christian, chaotic, totally unmoral."[14]

It is striking that Leslie's pronouncements on the Easter Rising in the *New York Tribune* in May 1916 were also partially responsible for turning the thoughts of the American modernist poet Marianne Moore (1887–1972) toward Ireland, as a means of reclaiming her own dissident poetic voice.[15] Writing from New York in 1956 on hearing Moore's reading of her poetry, the Irish artist and critic Brian O'Doherty noted how she spoke "in that practical voice of hers" of "poetry, of her Irish roots, which she felt important": "'one must not forget one's roots' she said again and again."[16] Her major poem "Sojourn in the Whale," originally entitled "Ireland," was prompted by the poet's experience of being somewhat at sea on a sojourn in New York in late 1915 and early 1916, a visit that coincided with news from Ireland of the Easter Rising. In the poem, the feminization of Ireland by its colonial detractors is turned on its head by seeing in the stereotype a means of fighting back, transforming femininity into an active force. The poem begins with upended images—"planting shade trees upside down"—and is addressed to Ireland, which is imagined as being "swallowed by the opaqueness of one whom the seas / love better than they love you, Ireland."[17] Britain indeed ruled the waves, and Napoleon had famously described the British navy as a whale: in later working-class caricatures, the Prince of Wales was depicted as the "Prince of Whales," the only proviso being that sharks were perhaps more appropriate for royalty.[18] In keeping with the notion of the impractical Celt, Ireland has "lived and lived on every kind of shortage" due to its own alleged female incompetence:

> ... [you] have heard men say: "There
>   is a feminine
> temperament in direct contrast to
>
> ours which makes her do these things. Circumscribed by a
>   heritage of blindness and native
>   incompetence, she will become wise and will be forced
>   to give
> in. Compelled by experience, she
>
> will turn back; water seeks its own level."

Passivity and constraint are evident here, but the pressure to "turn back" can be read in different ways, including the possibility of turning back on oppressive forces. Playing on the word "rise," the poem shifts register and, as if to turn adversity against itself, proposes that obstacles can generate new turbulent energies that belie any notion of surface calm:

> ... and you
>   have smiled. "Water in motion is far
>   from level." You have seen it when obstacles happened
>   to bar
> the path — rise automatically.[19]

Leslie wrote of the deceptive calm of transatlantic relations in similar terms, citing the words of J. F. Maguire, MP: "It may subside, so may the sea. But like the sea the first breath will set it in motion, while a storm would lash it into fury."[20] According to Laura O'Connor, "Sojourn in the Whale" was a "vocational Rubicon" for Moore, due to "the boldness of conflating her own destiny as a poet with Ireland's destiny." When asked imperiously by Ezra Pound in 1919 to position herself in ethnic or racial terms, Moore famously replied: "I am Irish by descent, possibly Scotch also, but purely Celtic."[21] Celticism is perhaps invoked to reconcile Irish and Scottish family histories, but it also lays claim to diversity and openness in the New World, threatened by nativist attacks on hyphenated Americans: the most welcome feature of American culture, Moore wrote with Henry James in mind, is that it is "incapable of the shut door in any direction."[22]

Thomas MacDonagh: The Critical Idiom

Writing in 1918 of St. Enda's School at which he had spoken as a guest lecturer, Shane Leslie noted it had such "first class litterateurs as Thomas MacDonagh and Padraic Colum" on its staff, and that before the Ulster Crisis of 1913 in which Unionists reintroduced the gun into Irish politics, the "whole trend of the Gaelic movement was to save Ireland by books rather than the blunderbuss. By ballad and not by bullet would Mac-Donagh have preferred to train boys to free their land."[23] As it transpired, the poet and critic Thomas MacDonagh was the last of the leaders of the Easter Rising to be brought in on plans for the rebellion and, as late as January 1916, was still preparing his critical study *Literature in Ireland* for publication. He never saw the book into print. Following his execution on May 3, 1916, it was published posthumously, and as some reviews of the book coincided with the emerging reputation of James Joyce, Mac-Donagh's views on what he termed the "Irish mode" in literature helped to recast the Rising in a vernacular modernist idiom. Reviewing *Literature in Ireland* in the September issue of *Poetry* magazine, Ezra Pound lauded the challenge presented to Romantic Ireland by "a great novelist like James Joyce and so level and subtle a critic as Thomas MacDonagh." Pound noted that MacDonagh had already situated himself within the ambit of modernism by engaging with *Poetry* magazine in his book: "One of the finest tributes to the magazine is that he should have chosen to quote from it at some length, from an essay by A.C.H., who is probably the best critic now writing in America."[24] "A.C.H." was Alice Corbin Henderson (1881–1949), assistant editor of *Poetry*, and Pound's reference is to a long passage quoted by MacDonagh in which Corbin Henderson praised the poetry of adversity emanating from "the Irishman's love of Ireland, the celebration of Bengal by the great East Indian poet [i.e., Tagore], or the passionate spirit of the Roumanian folk songs" (*LI*, 15). The sense of striving, according to Corbin Henderson, was rooted in the personal but "becomes transmuted into something beyond the personal emotion" when grounded "in folk-songs and legends—always an enduring basis for subsequent poets and artists."[25] MacDonagh's reference was to Corbin Henderson's essay "Too Far from Paris," published in *Poetry*, in June 1914, and Pound, in a letter to Corbin Henderson on June 16, 1916, mentions this posthumous tribute to her: "MacDonagh has done you a fine compliment in quoting you at length in the introd. to his 'Literature in Ireland' (I have just sent a review of it to H[arriet] M[onroe]). It is your remarks on patriotism in the Poetry of a subject country. . . ."[26] In a later letter to John Quinn, Pound disagrees with Quinn's view that Roger Casement's "treason" did not merit execution, but he exempts MacDonagh from censure: "RE/Casement. I am afraid I cant sympathize. I was very sorry that MacDonagh [was] shot. Some of the men made a fine end."[27]

Alice Corbin Henderson came to prominence in literary circles in 1912 as co-founder, with Harriet Monroe, of the Chicago-based *Poetry* magazine, a showcase for the modernist revolution in poetry. In 1917, Corbin Henderson and Monroe edited a landmark anthology, *The New Poetry*, which, while drawing on the prewar canon, also brought Imagist poetry—by H.D. (Hilda Doolittle), Amy Lowell, F. S. Flint, Pound—and the experimental work of T. S. Eliot, Wallace Stevens, William Carlos Williams, and D. H. Lawrence to a wider public. Defending the stylistic turns and linguistic traits in the "New Poetry," Monroe and Corbin Henderson rejected the "stiffened" rhetoric and "over-appareled" diction of prewar verse, looking instead to "contemporary speech" and a focus on concrete objects, "whether these be beautiful or ugly," to widen the scope of art beyond the "shop-worn subjects of past history and legend." The informal rhythms introduced by Swinburne and others were central to this, as was the free verse of Whitman and Mallarmé. These disruptive challenges to the canon in the twentieth century were also found on the periphery, "among far away peoples who never heard of our special rules" of diction, meter, and rhyme:

> Perhaps the first of these disturbing influences from afar to be felt in modern English poetry was the Celtic renascence, the wonderful revival of interest in old Irish song, which became manifest in translations and adaptations of the ancient Gaelic lyrics and epics, made by W. B. Yeats, Lady Gregory, Douglas Hyde and others. This influence was most powerful because it came to us directly, not at second-hand, through the English work of two poets of genius, Synge and Yeats. . . . It is scarcely too much to say that "the new poetry"—if we may be allowed the phrase—began with these two great Irish masters.[28]

A related publication, *The New Poetry: A Study Outline*, was devoted to listing representative poems of, and bibliographical guides to, the New Poetry, under thematic headings that attested to the rapid shifts in sensibility in the postwar period. Pound provided the epigraph for the heading "Some Radicals," under which "Cubists, Futurists, and Vorticists" featured as a subentry. T. S. Eliot appeared under "New Poets," Wilfred Owen, Siegfried Sassoon, and Edward Thomas under "Poets of War and Peace," but Irish poetry featured under three headings: "The Great Three" (Yeats, Synge, Æ); "The Younger Poets," including Joseph Campbell, Padraic Colum, Seamus O'Sullivan, James Stephens, Francis Ledwidge, Winifred Letts, and Moira O'Neill; and, as a separate grouping, "The Revolutionary Brotherhood," made up of executed 1916 figures MacDonagh, Pearse, Plunkett, and Casement.

The vernacular turn in literary modernism, moreover, was not confined to creative writing but also extended to criticism. For Corbin Henderson, "nothing as good as Thomas MacDonagh's *Literature in Ireland* has yet been written of contemporary American poetry,"[29] and this critical reputation also underlies MacDonagh's selection in Ludwig Lewisohn's *A Modern Book of Criticism*, published in 1919.[30] Wilhelm Dilthey, Hugo Von Hoffmansthal. H. L. Mencken, Van Wyck Brooks, and Randolph Bourne were among the leading critics in the anthology, and MacDonagh was not the only Irish contributor: George Moore, George Bernard Shaw, and Kilkenny-born Francis Hackett, by then an established literary figure in the United States, also featured in its pages.[31] Lewisohn (1882–1955), a prominent Jewish intellectual, critic, and novelist, was to the fore in promoting a multi-ethnic America, contesting the "melting pot" idea of assimilation that sought to remove the hyphen from American experience. This call for cultural diversity received its most influential formulation in Bourne's "Trans-national America," published in *The Atlantic* in July 1916, which pointed out that while assimilation to Anglo-Saxon values was now expected of immigrants, the original purveyors of these values had no intention of assimilating to the Native American culture they found on arrival: "They did not come to adopt the culture of the American Indian."[32] For Lewisohn, the Irish Revival, rooted in realism and vernacular culture, showed how art was better served by democratic vistas than by an aloof aestheticism, and for this reason "liberal critics of America" needed to be reminded that "the chief creative minds of contemporary England and Ireland are fighting with them."[33] It was this democratic address that Padraic Colum chose to highlight in his *Seven Arts* essay titled "Youngest Ireland":

> The new Irish poetry is the most democratic that is being written—it is democratic not only because it deals with the folk of the country and the town, but because it attempts to give everyone a voice and because it is written out of a recognition of the fact that in every life there are moments of intensity and beauty. It may be that this feeling for spiritual democracy manifested and propagated by the poets and dramatists is preparing Ireland for a new crystallization of ideas—a crystallization that will have an effect on her social and economic life.[34]

The section chosen from MacDonagh in *A Modern Book of Criticism*, under the title "Ireland and the New Paths," was excerpted from *Literature in Ireland* and aligns literary innovation with wider transformations in intellectual and political life. In it, MacDonagh argues that just as the achievements of Elizabethan drama were an integral part of the Renaissance, so Romanticism was an offshoot of the French Revolution. Neither of these had a decisive impact on Irish culture—a partial explanation of how Irish medievalism extended into the modern period—and it is for this reason that an "Irish mode" introduces new accents into literary modernism. In a clear linking of the rationale for the Easter Rising with literary innovation, he notes that the risk facing any innovative movement is lack of immediate approval: the avant-garde does not so much defer to as *defer* its own public, creating the audience that will validate its work. "Hostile critics," according to MacDonagh, "use words and weapons so like those used against other work that survived attack [in the past] and afterwards became great and right and good": "Yet the new path of some pioneer to-day may prove the right turning for all. The path of glory in literature has not been, as many appear to think, the broad and easy way. . . . It is not the obvious path that leads from height to height." Impressionism, he goes on to say, did for the visual arts what Wagner effected in music, but to "anyone conversant with modern literature the same change of order is evident here."[35] The distinctive feature of this stylistic turn resides in indirection rather than overt content, since the "unknown transcends the known": "To us as to the ancient Irish poets the half-said thing is dearest. The rhythm made by an emotion informs the poem and so creates the emotion. . . . I am introducing a movement that is important to English literature because it is in part a revolt from it."[36] In a passage that may have inspired Corbin Henderson and Monroe's assessment of Irish contributions to the New Poetry, MacDonagh continues that the Irish mode enters "literature at a period, which seems to us who are of it as a period of disturbance":

> Its mode seems strange to the critics and to the prosodists of the old order. Its mode is not that of the Futurists or the writers of *vers libre*; but still, coming with the work of these, it stands as another element of disturbance, of revolution; it stands free from the old authority imposed by the Renaissance, while the other elements in this disturbance are rebelling against that authority.[37]

The modernist cast of MacDonagh's thinking set its face against realism, as in his welcoming the capacity of impressionism to transform rather than mirror reality. Commenting on this to his friend Dominick Hackett in 1911, MacDonagh wrote: "After having seen their pictures, which shock you with their wrongness, as you think, by depicting things you have never seen, or in a way you have never seen them, they make you see them over and over afterwards in the commonest things. . . . The whole thing is as unlike what a photograph might give as it can be." As a comic aside, he recounts Padraic Colum's rejoinder to an objector who complained they never met characters on the Abbey stage in real life: "'You'll probably meet them from this out,' said Colum."[38]

MacDonagh's criticism, and his role in the Rising, attracted the notice of H. L. Mencken (1880–1956), one of the leading figures in the American literary world. Developing a line of thought similar to that of *The New Poetry*—and perhaps ultimately indebted to MacDonagh—Mencken considered the Irish Revival not only in its own national terms but in light of its idiomatic energies, akin to the revolutions of the Elizabethan period: "It is something quite new under the sun. . . . No man who is genuinely an artist will ever write English hereafter without giving an ear to it, and borrowing from it, and owing inspiration to it." The ethereal aspects of the Celtic Twilight are brought down to earth in the capturing of actual speech, not "an exact rendering of Gaelic idioms in a foreign tongue, but an effort to set down and preserve the peasant's difficulties with and blunderings in that tongue. It is thus from the true Irish, the countryfolk of Ireland, that the new dialect derives."[39] The impact of Irish idioms on English is developed at length in Mencken's landmark *The American Language* (1919), an example being the Irish use of intensives to emphasize a point: "The Irishman is almost incapable of saying plain yes or no; he must always add some extra and gratuitous asseveration":

> Amusing examples are to be found in Dunlevy's Irish Catechism. To the question, "Is the Son God?" the answer is not simply "Yes," but "Yes, certainly he is." And to the question, "Will God reward the good and punish the wicked?" the answer is "Certainly; there is no doubt He will."[40]

This is picked up, according to Mencken, in American add-ons such as "Well, I guess," "No-siree," "Thank you kindly," and so on. Mencken's general point here is to show that rather than forming a seamless "native" language, American English is a patchwork of borrowings and importations from immigrant experience, the argot of hyphenated Americans.

For Mencken, the achievement of the Irish Revival lay not only in its creative output but also in its criticism: "On the dramatic side alone it has engendered three times as much criticism as drama."[41] Among the critical "talents of the highest consideration," Mencken distinguishes two for special mention: Ernest Boyd's *Ireland's Literary Renaissance* (1916) and MacDonagh's *Literature in Ireland*: "MacDonagh confines himself to a relatively narrow field. It is Irish verse that chiefly interests him, for he was a poet himself and a good one, and his execution was a heavy loss to Irish letters. To appreciate him to the full, perhaps, one must be an Irishman; his very criticism is full of a Celtic Twilight; he never proceeds by direct statement when he can proceed by allusion." Mencken points to tensions in the Revival between strands based on the acceptance of English ("while not forgetting their debt to Gaelic"), and "intransigeants [sic] . . . much prospered by the rebellion of last Easter,"[42] who look to the restoration of the Irish language (which was not, in fact, a stated aim of the rebellion). "But this antagonism, after all, is more academic than real" for "the same man [MacDonagh] has belonged to both camps": he attended to "the unforgettable phrases of Maurya in *Riders to the Sea*" and "discusses its genesis at great length, and shows its dependence on the idioms of Gaelic."[43] It was through Ernest Boyd (1887–1946), however, that Mencken developed his closest relationship to Irish letters, Boyd sending Mencken two of Joyce's stories, "The Boarding House" and "A Little Cloud," that appeared in *The Smart Set*, in July 1915, the first to be published in the United States, to Joyce's considerable satisfaction. Boyd befriended Mencken on his emigration to the United States in 1920 and was published in Mencken's second magazine, the *American Mercury*. Boyd co-founded the *Mercury*'s successor, the *American Spectator*, and published a short critical biography of Mencken in 1925, highlighting his achievement as the first American publisher of James Joyce, and defending Mencken against what he caustically referred to as the "Ku Klux Kriticism" of Puritan America.[44]

The most sustained engagement with the literature of the Rising is in the criticism of Van Wyck Brooks (1886–1963)—with Mencken, the most prominent exponent of the demand for a distinctive American criticism, indebted to but not encumbered by British and mainland European traditions. To counter these influences, Brooks devised the principle of a "usable past" in American experience, applying to history elements of the pragmatism that informed the philosophy of William James and John Dewey:

> The present is a void, and the American writer floats in that void because the past that survives in the common mind of the present is a past without living value. But is this the only possible past? If we need another past so badly, is it inconceivable that we might discover one, that we might even invent one?[45]

The rationale behind this was to provide for alternative pasts to Manifest Destiny, the belief that the only preordained path from the past to the future was that of the Puritan Anglocentric tradition, establishing commerce rather than culture as a civic ideal. Brooks's thinking is often presented solely in American terms, as if it emerged fully formed in an internal debate with nativism or the classicism of the New Humanists (Irving Babbitt, Paul Elmer More), but it also looked to other models of usable pasts, not least those furnished by elements of the Irish Revival that crystalized in the Easter Rising. The cultural renaissance in Ireland set an example of how to challenge an overpowering British heritage, and with this in mind, Tara Stubbs notes, "American writers actively sought a tradition to 'make use' of—and one that allowed them . . . to declare 'aesthetic independence' from England."[46] In a lengthy review of the rush of publications on Ireland following the Rising, Brooks observed that the "dozen or so books . . . suggest that Ireland this Autumn has become a sort of obsession with American publishers."[47] Part of the reason for this, he surmises, is a fascination with the influence literature could exert on the affairs of a nation, as against its decorative role in American society. Discussing Padraic Colum's highlighting of the poets' Rising and Boyd's *Ireland's Literary Renaissance*, he notes (not without exaggeration):

> [Never] before probably has it occurred that virtually all the leaders of a revolutionary movement were poets; and the fact, in a way, both confirms and sanctifies the extraordinary part played by literature in the development of Ireland's national consciousness. [Even] the agricultural and educational movements that are making Ireland into a new country have sprung so largely from poet's brains that her social life seems more an expression of literature than vice versa.[48]

Crucial to this development was independence not only from London publishing houses but also, as MacDonagh argued, the principles of criticism in which literature was received: "The fact is, as Thomas MacDonagh suggests in his wonderfully interesting testament he has left behind him,—'Literature in Ireland,'—that the new movement has already suffered too much from criticism of the wrong kind and that its materials have not yet reached a sufficient degree of coherence for the right kind of criticism to emerge."[49] This criticism of the wrong kind, referring "by implication to the late Professor Dowden and the pundits of Trinity College," exalts monuments of the great traditions in English and French literature not to enable other literatures to speak, but to cower them. "Ireland," in MacDonagh's own words, "is not the only country that suffers so to-day. America also has a fully grown criticism and a baby literature. Something of the same relation exists between the two there as in Ireland" (*LI*, 142).

Brooks elaborates on this in his manifesto-type essay "The Critics and Young America" (1917), once again citing MacDonagh's claim that a "naissant literature" is ill-judged by ordinances from elsewhere: when such criticism "does get a clear view of its object," writes MacDonagh (cited by Brooks), "it misses the shapes and forms it saw in other lands and expresses its disappointment" (*LI*, 141). To which Brooks adds:

> Of our own criticism, of our own critics, one could hardly have a better description than that. For Ireland and America really are alike in that they inherit a dominant academic tradition colonial in essence, having its home in centers of civilization remote from the springs of a national life, which has only of late come into its own national consciousness.[50]

Literature and criticism are not sealed off from national culture, formed solely by the canon: they also need "to meet the exigencies of our life, to seize and fertilize its roots."[51] MacDonagh's identification of competing strands in Irish literary history prefigures Brooks's pursuit of usable pasts in the United States to counter a canon that not only marginalized writers like Whitman, Melville, and Dickinson but also those outside the dominant Anglocentric culture. Brooks's early enthusiasm for things Irish was cultivated at Harvard and by his friendship with the émigré artist John Butler Yeats, who painted his portrait and whose introduction of Brooks to the émigré writer Mary Colum gave the critic's romance with Ireland a decidedly personal cast. As in the case of Ezra Pound, Brooks pairs MacDonagh with Joyce's *Portrait,* discerning in his analysis of Hiberno-English the basis of the linguistic innovations that Joyce uses to startling effect:

> Emotionally the book [*Portrait*] is direct, spare, and true to its flight as hardly any Anglo-Saxon books are, and its style bears out Thomas MacDonagh's assertion that the English tongue possesses in Ireland an uncodified suggestiveness, a rich concreteness, that it has largely lost in its own country.

"It is a living society that Mr Joyce pictures, one that conforms to the twentieth century in its worldly apparel," but which still, in keeping with MacDonagh's study, "reveals in its table-talk and its more intimate educational recesses a medievalism utterly untouched by that industrial experience which has made the rest of the world kin, for good or ill."[52] With the exception of the urban concentrations in Ulster, Ireland lacked heavy industry but was no less modern for that: as MacDonagh stated, "We cannot pray to old Gods.... We are of a different day. A different light shines upon us. History is between us and our heroes" (*LI*, 112). The different light is seen to amusing effect in Padraic Colum's account of an Irish theater audience's reflexive response to high-flown sentiments in a production of the legendary tale of Diarmuid and Gráinne, "in which one of the characters was made to say at a tragical moment 'I have heard the laughter of the gods.' Instantly, the sixpenny gallery—'the gods,' became vociferous, 'ha, ha, ha.' It was an extraordinary responsive audience."[53]

Joyce's innovations in narrative form also help to make sense of the fragmented legacy of the past outlined in MacDonagh's *Literature in Ireland*. As Tara Stubbs notes, the "myth" and "authenticity" of the Irish Revival appealed to American writers in a new world lacking a sense of antiquity, notwithstanding the irony that, as modernists, the qualities "they were seeking in Irish culture—permanence, coherence, continuity—were the same qualities that they were prepared to break with in their understanding of nations and national literatures."[54] However, Stubbs continues, "some of these breakages [also] found their models in the activities of the Irish writers themselves,"[55] and in this, MacDonagh's recurrent emphasis on the broken nature of Irish tradition(s) is salutary. "English had to be broken and re-made" (*LI*, 39) to serve Irish experience: "It is possible that here we may resume a broken tradition and make a literature in consonance with our past" (*LI*, 137). Tradition is not fixed and has to be true to its own time, as well as its pasts: "A part of the old world lives in us," but "we are true to the best of the old literature when we are true to that part of it which we inherit now in the twentieth century . . . something that has remained by *the changing standards and measures*" (*LI*, 113; emphasis added). Whereas the European Renaissance revitalized a relatively discrete body of classical texts in Greek and Roman antiquity, no similar intact archive was furnished by the Irish past, "a literature, as far as poetry is concerned, of fragments" (*LI*, 106): "The Gaelic Renaissance means to us not only the revival of interest in this old Irish literature . . . but added to these, the study of modern Irish as a language capable of literature, the interest in the fragments and traditions that have survived" (*LI*, 107).

In view of this, the Irish elements in F. Scott Fitzgerald's *This Side of Paradise* may lie not in overt discussions of Celticism or Cúchulainn but at the level of form, in the breakages of its narrative structure. As critics have noted, the disjointed assemblage of voices and points of view in the novel are indebted to Joyce's *Portrait*, which, indeed, figures in Amory's reading: "He read enormously. He was puzzled and depressed by 'A Portrait of the Artist as a Young Man.'"[56] These fissures have also been detected in Fitzgerald's Irish affiliations, with critics observing that "he reconceptualizes Irishness as a collection of abstract personality traits," thereby "divest[ing] the terms (and its traits) of any historical, cultural, or geographical punctuation."[57] But this lack of coherence and continuity may be precisely what Fitzgerald's displaced Irishness consists in, bearing witness to a past that is continually remade, and in which narrative unity itself is given a new critical valance in Brooks's concept of a "usable past."

Race and Transnational Solidarity

> Harlem has the same role to play for the New Negro as Dublin had for the New Ireland.
>
> ALAIN LOCKE, "The New Negro" (1925)[58]

Louis Untermeyer's poem "To England (Upon the Executions of the Three Irish Poets—Pearse, MacDonagh and Plunkett—After the Uprising in Dublin)," most likely read at the Central Park protest in June 1916, was first published in the left-wing review *The Masses* and subsequently reprinted in W. E. B. Du Bois's (1888–1963) *The Crisis*, the periodical of the National Association for the Advancement of Colored People (NAACP).[59] As early as August 1916, Du Bois declared, "Few colored people know or realize what Ireland has suffered at the hand of England" and went on to explain why: the "bitter industrial competition" that followed free Black labor moving north after the Civil War induced racial hostility among the Irish that "has given the Irish cause little or no sympathy so far as Negroes are concerned." The Easter Rising, however, has changed all that:

> But all this is past. Today we must remember that the white slums of Dublin represent more bitter depths of human degradation than the black slums of Charleston and New Orleans, and where human oppression exists there the sympathy of all black hearts must go. The recent Irish revolt may have been foolish, but would to God some of us had sense enough to be fools.[60]

The September issue followed up with a commentary, "Sir Roger Casement—Patriot, Martyr," deploring the execution of a "worthless rebel" in English eyes, but who in his own country emerges as "a heroic saint... from a felon's grave." Casement's exposure of atrocities in "Angola and the cocoa islands of San Thomé and Principe, the Congo," in the Putumayo in South America, and his subsequent turning "to his dear native land, Ireland, still bleeding and languishing in the hands of her historic oppressor," belie the charges of treason leveled against him: "This was the time for English expediency rather than the bleak upholding of laws and customs. Someone has blundered."[61] Within a year, a radical Black organization, the African Blood Brotherhood (alluding to the underground Irish Republican Brotherhood [IRB]/Fenian movement that organized the Easter Rising), was founded by the communist Cyril Briggs (1888–1966), who also edited its organ, *The Crusader*. The Brotherhood called for armed resistance against lynchings and for separate Black trade unions, and under headlines such as "Heroic Ireland" and "The Irish Fight for Liberty the Greatest Epic of Modern Times and a Sight to Inspire to Emulation All Oppressed Groups," developed into a fully-fledged supporter of Irish independence.[62] The Jamaican writer Claude McKay (1889–1948) published his most famous poem, "If We Must Die," in *The Crusader*, and it is in McKay's writing that the most nuanced expressions of Black cross-cultural solidarity with Ireland emerge, linking literature and culture to wider political and economic struggles.

As has been noted by several scholars, even before the Harlem Renaissance Black writers drew parallels with the Irish Renaissance, particularly the use of dialect and demotic language to challenge, rather than to imitate, metropolitan models. The poet Paul Laurence Dunbar (1872–1906) switched between African American and Irish patois in his verse, displaying a versatility that undercut purist forms of authenticity.[63] The implications of this were not confined to language, as is clear from conservative critics such as Paul Elmer More—the target of Van Wyck Brooks's most vehement criticism—who saw linguistic standards as the barrier against "the mongrel sort to be expected from a miscegenation of the gutter."[64] McKay was among the pioneers of vernacular modernism before he arrived in New York, and while dialect ran the risk of folkish or (in its Irish variant) "Kiltartanese" stereotypes, Lee Jenkins is correct to argue that McKay's practice is closer to that of Thomas MacDonagh:

> If we consider McKay's dialect poems with MacDonagh's theories in mind, however, the placing of Jamaican dialect with standard poetic forms has a greater affinity with the dissonant Irish mode than with the more decorative Celtic Note practiced by certain Revivalists in that both MacDonagh and McKay roughen the texture of poetry.... Both thus produce a poetics the hybridity of which is the conscious result of strategy and not the inevitable fate of the writer who has experienced the fractured colonial condition.[65]

In keeping with the tendency of New Americans (Bourne, Mencken, Brooks) and expatriates like Colum to link culture to material politics, McKay took issue with economistic conceptions of class that avoided questions of race and nation, and turned a blind eye to imperialism. Writing in *The Masses* in July 1916, the Irish Labour leader James Larkin had to go to considerable lengths to clear international socialism from the taint of a bourgeois "Sinn Féin" Rising, but by 1920 McKay could speak of participating with "Sinn Fein communists and regular Sinn Feiners" at a demonstration in support of Terence MacSwiney's hunger strike at Trafalgar Square, London.[66] This shift had important consequences for McKay's critique of the English Left, which in his eyes, by continuing to equate the Irish revolution solely with the bourgeoisie, advanced imperial interests in opposing Irish independence: they feel "they must back the red flag against the green."[67] McKay had no illusions about cross-racial solidarity of the part of the Irish in the United States, noting that "the social and economic boycott against Negroes was begun by the Irish in the North during the Civil War and has, in the main, been fostered by them ever since."[68] To this extent, the Irish "are, indeed, like Anglo-Saxons," but then, drawing on Revivalist parlance, he identifies countercurrents in Irish experience deriving from colonial subjugation:

> However, I react more to the emotions of the Irish than to those of any other whites; they are so passionately primitive in their loves and hates. They are quite free of the disease which is known in bourgeois phraseology as Anglo-Saxon hypocrisy. I suffer with the Irish. I think I understand the Irish. My belonging to a subject race entitles me to some understanding of them. And then I was born and reared a peasant; the peasant's passion for the soil possesses me, and it is one of the strongest passions of the Irish revolution.[69]

Denouncing the "Return to the Primitive" elsewhere,[70] it here signifies resistance to colonial versions of "primitivism," becoming a shorthand for energy and the political equivalent of dialect in language, rejecting what McKay termed "the dead weight of formal respectability."[71] "We blacks are all somewhat impatient of discipline," he wrote in *Constab Ballads* (1912), to which was added in his case, "a fierce hatred of injustice": "I had not in me the stuff that goes to the making of a good constable; for I am so constituted that imagination outruns discretion, and it is my misfortune to have a most improper sympathy with wrongdoers."[72] This sympathy was carried over into his views of rural protest, showing that his use of "peasant" invokes not so much romantic pastoral as the kind of agrarian insurgency found in the Irish Land War, which stood in stark contrast to the cultural conformity of English rural wage labor—"the psychology and possibilities of a quick witted and insubordinate peasantry as distinguished from those of a population of disciplined and depressed Anglo-Saxon agricultural labourers."[73] Such "disciplined and depressed" standards also constrain the English working class in McKay's eyes, and by relating Jamaica and Ireland to their own cultural codings of revolution, he took significant steps in reclaiming non-Western aspects of oppressed people's experience for dissenting peripheral modernities. McKay concedes that "there is no other way of upward struggle for colored peoples, but the way of the working class movement, ugly and harsh though some of its phases may be," but class in colonial circumstances takes on different complexions to revitalize the metropolitan center: "[The Irish] are imbibing the atmosphere and learning the art of revolution. I heard from an Irish communist in London that some Indian students had been in Dublin to study that art where it is in practical operation. It is impossible not to feel that the Irish revolution—nationalistic though it may be—is an entering wedge directed straight to the heart of British capitalism."[74] Whereas Van Wyck Brooks and likeminded critics in the United States saw Anglophilia as a residue of a bygone colonial era, writers from Ireland or Jamaica (such as McKay and Marcus Garvey) were still living under British rule, in conditions where colonialism had yet to become history.

When Rudyard Kipling warned his friend Brander Matthews "that non-Anglo writers were degrading American literature,"[75] he bore witness to stylistic shifts in Irish and American literature aiming to challenge the imperium of the English language, an Anglocentrism that received a new lease of life due to pressure to enlist American intervention in the Great War. Given Irish-American opposition to such participation, it is not surprising that "the right to self-determination" proclaimed by President Woodrow Wilson at the Versailles Peace Conference was withheld from the Irish, on the grounds, as the US Secretary of State Robert Lansing asserted, that it would open the door for decolonization the world over:

> Why, since we are so solicitous about oppressed nations, do we not take a definite stand for the independence of Ireland, Egypt, India, and South Africa.... From the standpoint of domestic politics it would be a very unwise policy.... We would be, I think, embarrassed in no small degree at the peace table by having admitted beforehand the subject races of the Central Powers and Turkey and by having ignored the claims of the Irish and others under the sovereignty of the Entente Powers.[76]

Though intended primarily to protect the British empire, this clearly applied to all subject races seeking to rise above their station. Mencken, Brooks, and others may have exaggerated the strength of colonial ties and attitudes persisting between the United States and Britain, but American inability to act against British interests on the Irish question reinforced this perception: "America," the Irish republican Liam Mellows asserted, "by its silence on the question of Irish independence, has been and still is ... tacitly acquiescing in England's domination."[77] On the other hand, it was the link between Ireland and other subject peoples seeking to throw off the shackles of racism and colonialism that attracted the support of Black organizations such as Marcus Garvey's Universal Negro Improvement Association (UNIA) for Irish independence, leading Garvey to proclaim:

> They speak about the almighty might of Great Britain, but all political scientists can foresee the doom coming; can foresee the wreck that threatens imperial England. Why, they will not give Ireland freedom because

they calculate "if we give freedom to Ireland . . . India will want freedom, Egypt will want freedom; and why not? Therefore only little England will be left." . . . She is afraid if she gives freedom to Ireland, all her other dominions will cry out "We want ours."[78]

Responses to the Easter Rising in the United States coincided with a number of critical flashpoints in American national culture. One was externally directed, manifested in increased hostility toward immigrants and exacerbated by the rhetoric of "hyphenated Americans" during the Great War. The other had internal sources, directed at territorial dispossession and subjugation of Native Americans, and deriving from racial discrimination against African Americans in the Jim Crow era, intensified by reigns of terror conducted by white supremacists. Both of these were underpinned not just by an abstract "whiteness" but by particular assertions of Anglo-Saxonism: the point of jeremiads such as Madison Grant's *The Passing of the Great Race* (1916) and Lothrop Stoddard's *The Rising Tide of Color against White World Supremacy* (1920) was that while whiteness came in different colors, only the Anglo-Saxon breed represented the true master race. "Have you read *The Rise of the Colored Empires* by this man Goddard?" Tom Buchanan asks in *The Great Gatsby*: "Well, it's a fine book, and everybody ought to read it. The idea is if we don't look out the white race will be—will be utterly submerged. It's all scientific stuff; it's been proved."[79] In the literary domain, this found expression in the belief that American literature "can only come from pure English racial stock uncontaminated by alien European races—from those 'thoroughbred' Americans who are indistinguishable in taste, manners, and speech from cultivated Englishmen."[80] As late as 1922, British government propaganda sought to disabuse American public opinion of any possibility that Irish Celts were compatible with the United States' racial identity: "All history, both recent and remote," C. J. C. Street (based in Dublin Castle) warned, "shows that the Irish appeal to America is based upon self-seeking and not at all upon racial affinity."[81] It was perhaps the persistence of such sentiments that enabled F. Scott Fitzgerald, even in his rejection of Celticism, to evince "a vantage point of contempt for 'Teuton' material success which he never lost" and which, in his fiction, attained "the sharpest cultural form it ever found."[82] As Joe Cleary observes, citing Edmund Wilson's view it was Fitzgerald's "partly Irish" sensibility that brought "both to life and to fiction certain qualities that are not Anglo-Saxon," it is through these qualities that "the polo-playing Tom's WASP anxieties about the collapse of the white race betray an upper-class crudity that is not more refined."[83] In

Claude McKay's *Banjo* (1929), an appeal is made to "educated Negroes" to stop deferring to a white culture "living solid on its imperial conquests" as models of civility, and to look elsewhere instead: "If you were sincere in your feeling about racial advancement, you would turn for example to whites of a different type. You would study the Irish cultural and social movement.... You would be interested in native African dialects and, though you don't understand, be humble before their simple beauty instead of despising them."[84]

In 1929 the travels of the Irish revolutionary Ernie O'Malley (1897–1957) in the United States brought him to Taos, New Mexico, where he settled down in the artists' colony founded by Mabel Dodge Luhan that hosted, at various times, D. H. Lawrence, Hart Crane, Georgia O'Keeffe, Paul Strand, and Edward Weston. For O'Malley, artistic life in Taos and Santa Fe also promised a new start as he set to work on his memoirs of the Anglo-Irish War and the Civil War in Ireland, immersing himself in the study of Native American culture, modernism, and Irish literature: "I got on very well with the Indians. I am their amigo now. We talk Spanish. An additional relish to them as their carpenter does not understand. They drop into Indian when there are things I should not hear in Spanish."[85] O'Malley went on to draw parallels between Irish and Native American history: "This is of course an Indian country though it has been mostly ruled by whites and mestizos; it's the problem of mixing Gaelic and Anglo-Irish and solving the problem of both."[86] In a sense, O'Malley was returning to the issues of hybridity and cross-cultural transfers discussed in Thomas MacDonagh's *Literature in Ireland*, and it was these connections that drew the attention of Alice Corbin Henderson at a series of lectures he delivered on James Joyce and Irish literature in Santa Fe in 1930. O'Malley recalled their meeting in letter to Harriet Monroe in 1935 when *Poetry* magazine accepted some of his own poems for publication:

> In the Southwest I first met Alice Corbin Henderson after a lecture of mine on the continuity of Gaelic thought in Irish poetry. She was, I found, the A.C.H. whom Tom MacDonagh, executed after the Easter Rising of 1916, had referred to in his book on Irish literature. She knew the work of the Anglo-Irish school and we spent many pleasant evenings together.[87]

Having first taken up arms himself in 1916, O'Malley's pairing of MacDonagh with Corbin Henderson recalls the many cultural spaces and "usable pasts" shared by national and international political movements, and, in early modernism, by Irish and American literary worlds.

※ 8 ※

On Another Man's Text

ERNIE O'MALLEY, POLITICS, AND IRISH MODERNISM

> The war with its drain on circumstances and destruction made casual inconsequence, which was a surrealist virtue, an ordinary event. Destruction brought him back to ... architectural fragments, which with their disjointed edges and cavernous interiors in telescoped time, made him avoid his feeling for nostalgic decay.
>
> ERNIE O'MALLEY (1947)[1]

In August 1930, the *Santa Fe New Mexican* newspaper carried a report of a series of lectures on the unlikely topic—at least for the American Southwest in that period—of Irish literature. "General Ernest O'Malley," the report noted, gave "a complete outline of the genesis and history of Irish poetry, from the ancient Gaelic" to the new Irish poetry:

> Reading translations from the earliest poems [he showed] how these furnished, not the material, but the root soil and spiritual source and strength of the younger Irish writers—particularly that group whose lives were sacrificed in the cause of Irish freedom in 1916—Padraic Pearse, Joseph Plunkett, Thomas McDonagh [sic], Francis Ledwidge [sic], a costly sacrifice not only for Ireland, but for poetry. Among other writers, most of them still living, whose poems Mr. O'Malley read were James Stephens, Joseph Campbell, Eva Gore-Booth, Moira O'Neill, Dora Sigerson, Austin Clark [sic], James Joyce and Padraic Colum.

The report makes it clear that by placing the younger school in the context of 1916, there is an attempt to distance Irish poetry from the first phase of the Revival led by W. B. Yeats, Æ (George Russell), J. M. Synge, and others. The engaged nature of "the modern Irish poetic movement" is further spelled out: "Mr. O'Malley pointed out that with certain exceptions, the work of these men is not 'literary'; not, that is, of the schools or universities, but of life; and he also stressed the fact that it was the Gaelic League of Ireland, started by Douglas Hyde, which really instigated the *modern* Irish poetic movement."[2] O'Malley's linking of "Gaelic" to the "modern" was not an isolated event, and it was indeed to modernism, and the distinctive literary innovations of James Joyce, that he turned his attention a few months later.

In late November 1930, the newspaper reported on another series of lectures on Irish literature that culminated in an introduction to Joyce, and which were delivered in climatic conditions that would not have been out of place in Joyce's story "The Dead": "Last week's talks by Ernest O'Malley at the house of Mr. and Mrs. Raymond Otis on the subject of Irish poetry, was attended by a number of interested listeners, in spite of the blizzard."[3] O'Malley's first lecture covered the transition from Gaelic literature to modern writing described above, but the second talk, an introduction to Joyce, proved so successful that another lecture, on *Ulysses*, was arranged for the following week:

> At the talk by Ernest O'Malley at the Raymond Otis house last Tuesday evening, so great was the interest of the audience in the subject of James Joyce that they demanded a continuation of the same subject for another evening.... Mr. O'Malley read many scenes from The Portrait of an Artist as a young man [*sic*], to the great delight of his listeners, and from other early work of Joyce, with a discussion of his writing based on much critical reading and a personal acquaintance with Joyce.[4]

We can assume the suggestion of "personal acquaintance" with Joyce means firsthand experience of Joyce's daunting texts as against secondary criticism, and the final lecture "on the great Ulysses" was delivered the following Tuesday.[5] This received more extended treatment in the *Santa Fe New Mexican*, which noted in passing O'Malley's military background ("the general"):

> Though still reluctant to break away from what may be called professorial decorum, the general in a too-limited time covered his study of Ulysses convincingly. Certainly this was the best of his lectures. He became fluent and assuring. Beginning with an image of Joyce as a "dark Napoleon," Mr. O'Malley began to reveal the powers of his countryman.[6]

In the course of his talk, O'Malley took issue with the overemphasis on the Homeric parallels in the novel, preferring the *Ulysses* that "needs move forward fulfilling its own destiny which is the tracing out with rhythmic psychological imagination the huge mind-pattern of Mr. Bloom." "Character relationship" and the hauntings of the past drove the novel, not just literary parallels, linking

> Bloom and Mrs. Bloom together to Stephen who wandering through the timeless day haunted by the phantom of his dead mother has commiserated "Ulysses" whose ghost is sometimes twofold—both the lover and his (Bloom's) dead baby son; and finally that of Mrs. Bloom to her (in the closing page) more assertive husband:—these connections were all emphasized. And O'Malley read in direct quotation some of the burlesquerie, the flamboyant adjectivism, the characterology, the disssonnances [sic] and the guttlanguage of the stream-of-consciousness catalogue.[7]

The detailed nature of O'Malley's talk is clear from references to his adhering too closely to his notes, which unfortunately have not come down to us: "Well in a year O'Malley will probably speak extemporaneously on Joyce in a way that would not surprise him to hear. Credit, much credit is due to him and it is particularly gratifying to know that he has stimulated interest in the modernist literature. It is a pity more people have not been to hear him especially on Joyce who is influencing American literature."[8] The writer of the first reports of O'Malley's talks in the *Santa Fe New Mexican* was Alice Corbin Henderson, onetime assistant editor, as noted above, to Harriet Monroe at *Poetry* magazine in Chicago, and it was in fact Corbin Henderson who encouraged O'Malley to make contact with Monroe, an introduction that led to the publication of some of his own poems in *Poetry*.[9] That O'Malley was not just speaking from notes in his lectures but from experience is indicated by his own hauntings at the time: sympathizing with Dorothy Brett earlier in the year on the death of D. H. Lawrence, he wrote that he was no stranger to ghosts himself:

> I have seen so many of my comrades die that death seems as much part of life as life itself. Yet I know there were some deaths I never recovered from. They left a strange void which has always remained, a gap, yet a communion as well for I can feel the dead, nor would I be surprised to find someday that they walked in to resume an interrupted conversation.[10]

O'Malley's hauntings and the title of "General" refer to his guerrilla activities during the Irish War for Independence and the Civil War, in which he established a legendary reputation as an IRA leader and gunfighter. As a nineteen-year-old medical student, he participated in a minor role in the

Easter Rising of 1916, but his military expertise and leadership qualities soon became evident with the outbreak of hostilities in 1919, his role as an IRA organizer and strategist bringing him to fourteen counties in Ireland. Wounded five times in action, he was captured and tortured in 1920 but made a dramatic escape from Kilmainham jail in February 1921. His rejection of the Anglo-Irish Treaty of December 1921 led to his appointment as assistant chief of staff of the republican anti-Treaty forces, and he was the commander of the garrison at the end of the republican occupation of the Four Courts, June 1922, managing to escape once again in the roundup afterward. He was captured some months later in a near-fatal shoot-out at Ailesbury Road, Ballsbridge, receiving seven bullet wounds that affected him for the rest of his life. While in prison in 1923, he was elected to the Dáil as an abstentionist Teachta Dála (TD), and his health was further impaired by a forty-one-day hunger strike. Along with Seán Russell, he was the last republican prisoner to be released from the Curragh Camp in July 1924—a backhanded acknowledgment of the threat he presented to the new Free State.

O'Malley spent 1925–26 traveling and mountaineering in Europe and North Africa to recover his health, but not cut off entirely from politics: his time in the Pyrenees may even have been used to assist in the Catalan struggle for independence. Throughout this period, he visited art galleries and museums extensively to enhance an already keen interest in the visual arts. He returned to Ireland to resume his medical studies but in 1928 was asked by Éamon de Valera to accompany Frank Aiken on a tour of the United States to raise funds for the proposed *Irish Press* newspaper, a visit that turned into a seven-year stay in California, New Mexico, Mexico, Peru, and the East Coast of the United States. During this period, he immersed himself in the study of literature, theater, painting, and Indigenous cultures, and met the sculptor Helen Hooker, whom he married in 1935, the same year he returned to Ireland. It was in these settings he commenced work on his two landmark memoirs of the War of Independence and the Civil War, *On Another Man's Wound* (1936) and *The Singing Flame* (published posthumously in 1977), both of which, given his Joycean proclivities, might be seen as portraits of the artist as a gunman.[11] It was perhaps with this in mind that Yeats responded to a proposal to elect O'Malley, on the strength of the first volume of his memoirs, to the Irish Academy of Letters: "What do you two rascals mean by trying to fill my academy with gunmen?"[12] It was, in fact, the literary integrity of the memoirs that yielded "imaginative truth," in John McGahern's telling phrase, with O'Malley's uncompromising eye placing the Irish revolution in the wider frame of international war literature, on a par with the classic memoirs of T. E. Lawrence, Siegfried Sassoon, Robert Graves, Vera Brittain, and Victor Serge.[13]

O'Malley's three-year stay in California, New Mexico, Mexico, and Peru (1929–32) brought him into contact with many visual artists and writers, among them Sergei Eisenstein, Georgia O'Keeffe, Robinson Jeffers, the photographers Edward Weston and Paul Strand (who became a lifelong friend), and many Irish and English expatriates, among them the émigré nationalist and mystic Ella Young and D. H. Lawrence's close companion Dorothy Brett. He struck a particularly close friendship with the modernist poet Hart Crane, a writer struggling with his own troubles. In a letter to Malcolm Cowley in 1931, Hart Crane wrote:

> I have my most pleasant literary moments with an Irish revolutionary, red haired friend of Liam O'Flaherty, shot (and not missed) seventeen times in one conflict and another; the most quietly sincere and appreciative person, in many ways, I've ever met. It's a big regret he's Dublin bound again after three years from home, in a few weeks. Ernest O'Malley by name. And we drink a lot together—look at frescoes—and agree![14]

On his return to Ireland in 1935, O'Malley befriended writers and artists such as Peadar O'Donnell, Louis MacNeice, Seán Ó Faoláin, Frank O'Connor, Samuel Beckett, Patrick Kavanagh, Jack B. Yeats, Evie Hone, and Louis le Brocquy, and established his reputation as a critic, curator, and important collector in the Irish art world. He was elected to the Irish Academy of Letters and appointed book review editor of *The Bell* magazine in the immediate post–World War Two period, and spent the last decade of his life on an immense archival oral history project, gathering and collating firsthand accounts of over 450 activists in the counties he helped to organize during the revolutionary period.

O'Malley's immersion in Joyce's writings is already evident in his Santa Fe talks, of which he wrote to the photographer Edward Weston in February 1931: "[I] gave lectures, even on James Joyce, leaving a group behind me who were able to read *Ulysses* aloud!"[15] A shared interest in Joyce proved a valuable asset in other circles, such as his friendship with Gerald Sykes and Harold Clurman (of the famous Group Theatre in New York): "We talked of Joyce and that in itself was a bond."[16] In early 1935, O'Malley recalled these talks in a letter to Harriet Monroe, placing Joyce once again in the Irish as well as the international canon: "In the Southwest I lectured on Gaelic and Anglo-Irish literature from our first poet to James Joyce."[17] It was not until the post–World War Two period that O'Malley took up the study of Joyce again in earnest. In late 1947 he wrote to

John V. Kelleher, an Irish-American pioneer in Irish approaches to Joyce, to send on recent American books, building on the substantial number of critical studies he had already acquired.[18] By the early 1950s, he was also in correspondence with John J. Slocum, the first major bibliographer of Joyce, seeking to procure more Joyce material, and as late as 1953 was still studying Joyce while renewing work on the articles that comprised his book *Raids and Rallies* (posthumously published in 1982) and his memoir of the Civil War, *The Singing Flame*.

How are we to account for this sustained engagement with the work of Joyce and relate it to O'Malley's own formidable military reputation and his lifelong commitment to Irish republicanism? O'Malley's early interest in Joyce may have been stimulated by his friendship with Denis Devlin, Roger McHugh, William Fay, and others in the UCD Dramatic Society, which he helped to found on his brief return to university to resume his medical studies in 1926–28. O'Malley's growing interest in Joyce coincided with the first systematic publication of *Work in Progress* in *transition* magazine, edited by Eugene Jolas and Elliot Paul, and on the day of O'Malley's arrival in New York, in October 1928, on the mission to raise funds for the *Irish Press* newspaper, he found his way to the newly opened Gotham Book Mart that sold the publication.[19] The magazine carried Stuart Gilbert's pathbreaking exposition of the "Aeolus" chapter in *Ulysses* (masterminded by Joyce himself), and other landmark essays on Joyce by Eugene Jolas, Elliot Paul, and Ernst Robert Curtius, all of which feature in O'Malley's notebooks. By 1928 Joyce's *Pomes Penyeach* (1927) is included in lists of O'Malley's reading, and in 1929 another list included *Anna Livia Plurabelle* (1928), *Tales Told of Shem and Shaun* (1929), *Exiles* (1918), and *A Portrait of the Artist as a Young Man* (1916).[20] While visiting New Mexico in 1929, O'Malley recalled his futile attempts to renew his medical studies at UCD while his mind drifted elsewhere, noting ruefully in his journal:

> I heard Professor McLoughlin, old E.P. say "Now, Mr O'M.[alley] will you please place the bone in position. What age would you say it is? Now are you quite sure?" . . . Oh shades of medical examination. Dear old Cecilia Street with its "stiffs" and dissections, sitting on the College steps in the sun discussing everything from middle Irish poetry to James Joyce. Will I ever sit on the steps again with a notebook and a Material Medica discussing everything but medicine?[21]

At a time when Joyce's status as a modernist icon was increasingly emphasized at the expense of his Irishness, O'Malley's reading of Joyce was informed by the starker, hard-edged approaches of the later Revival. In his powers of concentration, fascination with maps and lists, and assiduous eye for detail, O'Malley deployed in his military activities qualities not unlike those Joyce brought to bear on *Ulysses,* and the same eye for detail informed his reading of Joyce's work—but with one notable difference. Not only did he never publish, but his written lectures have also disappeared, so that his studies of Joyce, as he said of his own vision of the Irish Republic, have "not been realized except in the mind."[22] As in the case of Walter Benjamin's monumental *Arcades Project,* which survived only in the quotations and glosses assembled for a magnum opus never completed, O'Malley's notes, devoted mainly to *Ulysses* and a wide range of critical responses to the work, are all that is left of his intensive forays into Joyce's revolution of the word.[23] The five main notebooks contain several hundred pages of notes, consisting primarily of key passages from Joyce's works, glosses and summaries, indices (of people, places, themes, etc.), and notes on his extensive reading of the already imposing body of Joycean criticism. In this, they resemble Benjamin's dream of a work consisting entirely of quotations, their juxtaposition with each other bearing witness to a highly selective intelligence over and above the designs of the original authors of the passages. As Hannah Arendt writes of this aspect of Benjamin's method:

> Like the later notebooks, this collection was not an accumulation of excerpts intended to facilitate the writing of the [subsequent] study but constituted the main work, with the writing as something secondary. The main work consisted in tearing fragments out of their context and arranging them afresh in such a way that they illustrated each other and were able to prove their *raison d'être* in a free floating state, as it were.[24]

It would be imputing too much to O'Malley's notes to consider them a self-conscious exercise in montage along Benjamin's lines; yet in his lists, taxonomies, and cross-referencing of motifs, persons, places, and names in *Ulysses,* he engages precisely in the process of "tearing fragments out of their context" and reassembling them to create new meanings. It is only when the notes are compared with the original published texts that the eclectic and even idiosyncratic nature of O'Malley's own reading becomes apparent.[25] The transcription of a passage does not, of course, mean that O'Malley agrees with it, still less that it can pass as his own voice, but if certain patterns manifest themselves across widely disparate sets of notes, it can at least be assumed that they are of interest to him. Not surprisingly, the Irish allusions and references to Irish history predominate in the homemade concordances designed to facilitate his own rereading and cross-referencing of *Ulysses*, but the extensive notes transcribed from Joycean criticism constantly set Irish aspects in the context of universal or mythic themes, rather than emphasizing one at the expense of the other.

Notes from the Underground

Two early notebooks from the period of his Santa Fe lectures testify to the background reading and concerns that informed O'Malley's talks. One of the notebooks is devoted primarily to *Ulysses* and *Work in Progress*, and opens with a chapter-by-chapter outline of *Ulysses* but in a schematic manner that highlights seemingly marginal Irish political aspects alongside Homeric parallels. The scheme of "Aeolus" is given as "Rhetoric 111–143 News Paper Office: Cave of the Winds. Skin the Goat," and "Eumaeus" as "573–622 Skin the Goat Eumaeus more of mood than of mind."[26] That James Fitzharris ("Skin-the-Goat"), one of the Rosencrantzs or Guildensterns of the Parnellite period, should assume center stage is in keeping with Joyce's own fascination with the cast-offs of history.[27] The notes on "Aeolus"—or "Cave of the Winds"—are introduced by one of the newspaper headlines in the chapter, followed by a succinct gloss of the location: "The Wearing of the Crown: E.R. under the G.P.O." (*U*, 7.16–17): it is difficult to imagine O'Malley missing the irony of "E.R.," as noted above, given the subsequent history of the General Post Office. The numerous plays by Joyce on the themes of "the wind" are picked out, and Mulligan's reference to the death of Stephen's mother is followed somewhat abruptly in his notes by a mention of the Invincibles:

> In mourning for Sallust, Mulligan says. Whose mother is beastly dead.
>   the invincibles ... Where Skin-the Goat drove the car.
>   —Skin-the-Goat, O'M Burke said. Fitzharris. He has that cabman's shelter, they say, down there at Butt bridge. (*U*, 7.583–84, 632, 640–42)

The exchanges on famous orators are noted, particularly John F. Taylor's speech at the College Historical Society, picking up again of the various associations with wind.

In his notes on the opening "Telemachus" chapter, the focus on the death of Stephen's mother and her ghoulish reappearance to him in a dream is followed by the description of the "poor old woman," Mother Ireland or "silk of the kine," who brings milk to the tower, and who signals the theme of betrayal in *Ulysses*: "names given her in old times. A wandering crone, lowly form of an immortal serving her conqueror and her gay betrayer, their common cuckquean, a messenger from the secret morning"

(*U* 1.403–6). Stephen's remorse is highlighted in what becomes a recurring preoccupation of O'Malley's, "Agenbite of inwit" (*U*, 1.481), as is his defiance of the twin sources of power in Ireland: "I am a servant of two masters, an English and an Italian [...] The imperial British state... and the holy Roman catholic and apostolic church" (*U*, 1.638–44). In the notes on "Nestor," the "fabled by the daughters of memory" (*U*, 2.7) sequence is transcribed and scored at the side, ending with a passage in *Ulysses* that may point proleptically, as noted above, to the destruction of Dublin in 1916: "I hear the ruin of all space, shattered glass and toppling masonry, and time one livid final flame. What's left us then?" (*U*, 2.9–10). Another quotation is underlined further down the page: "History, S., is a nightmare from which I am trying to awake" (*U*, 2.377), followed a few lines later by a comment in parentheses: "(Deasy anti semite)?" In the pages on "Proteus," the exiled Fenian in Paris Kevin Egan is noted, followed by "(43 obscure)"—referring to page 43 of *Ulysses*, which evokes the Clerkenwell explosion, Maud Gonne in Paris, and other tangled memories. The "ghostwoman with ashes on her breath" (*U*, 3.46–47) also recurs, followed immediately by Stephen's musing, as he stands by the sea, on "The whitemaned seahorses, champing, brightwindbridled, the steeds of Mananaan" (*U*, 3.56–57)—a reference to the ancient Celtic sea god, of which more below, with personal resonances for O'Malley.

O'Malley's most extensive engagement is with the "Cyclops" chapter, which is prefaced by an unattributed quotation: "Parody reduces serious matters to a lower plane or makes emotions amenable to common existence."[28] Notwithstanding O'Malley's seriousness, the leveling element in parody, its capacity to imbue gravitas with an everyday, common leavening, appealed to him, as in the excesses of the high-flown description of the citizen sitting at the counter of Barney Kiernan's, or the comic exchange between Joe Hynes and Alf Bergan over Paddy Dignam's funeral. The black humor evident in the purple prose evoking the gallows scene at Kilmainham is noted, and it is not surprising, given O'Malley's own close calls with execution in the prison, that the grotesquerie of both the hangman Rumbold and his "sensitive" audience during a hanging, should attract attention. The mockery of Queen Victoria and the royal family—"the Prooshians and the Hanoverians" (*U*, 12.1390) on the throne—is recorded, as are the tirades on English "syphilisation," which the citizen excludes from "[t]he European family" (notwithstanding the German background of the monarchy): "They're not European, says the citizen. I was in Europe with Kevin Egan of Paris. You wouldn't see a trace of them or their language anywhere in Europe except in a *cabinet d'aisance*" (*U*, 12.1203–5). The throwaway reference to the Fenian Kevin Egan as a guide to European culture is acknowledged, but interestingly the famous exchanges about the definition of a nation pass without comment. The only passage recorded is Bloom's pacifist response to the violent invective at the bar: "But it's no use, says he. Force, hatred, history, all that. That's not life for men and women, insult and hatred. And everybody knows that it's the very opposite of that that is really life. . . . Love" (*U*, 12.1481–85).

Picking up on his earlier notes, O'Malley notes how "Aeolus" is a showcase for oratory and rhetorical effects, in keeping with the "King of Winds" that blows through the original episode in Homer's *Odyssey*. Stuart Gilbert's observation that the modern press is a palace of the winds is of more than passing interest to O'Malley as he notes how the circulation of newspapers guides the caprice of public opinion: "Cities are taken by the ears."[29] It was this "illicit union, of aspiration and compromise, of literature and opportunism," that informed O'Malley's account, in *The Singing Flame*, of how pro–Free State journalism molded popular opinion to accept the Treaty he vehemently opposed during the Civil War (*SF*, 42).[30] It was indeed the lack of an oppositional republican voice that prompted de Valera to found the *Irish Press*, sending O'Malley, with Frank Aiken, on the fundraising drive for the proposed newspaper to the United States. In contrast to the ill winds of the modern press, O'Malley concentrates on another theme in "Aeolus," that of *akasic* memory, the theosophical belief in the indestructibility of the records of the past (once again an ironic reflection on his own life, given his presence in the Four Courts when the archives of the Irish past were blown up during government shelling in the Civil War).[31]

It is Gilbert's discussion of a seemingly incidental passage in the "Aeolus" chapter that catches O'Malley's eye above all else: Bloom's suggestion to use a design of two crossed keys, reminiscent of the "House of Keys" of the Manx Parliament, to illustrate the advertisement he is seeking to place for Alexander Keyes in the *Freeman's Journal*.[32] As Gilbert points out (and O'Malley notes), this links the motif "with one of the magical themes of *Ulysses*, the legend of Mananaan MacLir, the founder of the Manx nation." Stephen Dedalus's description in "Proteus" of sea waves as "the steeds of Mananaan" (*U* 3.56–57) is noted, as is the connection drawn later between *King Lear* and the lines from Æ's play *Deirdre* (1902): "Flow over them with your waves and with your waters, Mananaan . . ." (*U* 9.190–91). Gilbert's citing of Mananaan's appearance in "Circe" is also taken down by O'Malley: "The bearded figure of Mananaun MacLir broods . . ." (*U*, 15.2262), as is Gilbert's suggestion that the ancient sea god also maintains a mystical link to *akasis* and the god of creation:

This linking up of the vulgar with the esoteric, as here in this sequence: Alexander Keyes' "ad"—Keys—Isle of Man—Mananaan—AUM—Brahmátma's secret Word, is characteristic of the Joycean method and it is appropriate that several items in the series should be named in the Aeolus episode, for Mananaan MacLir... is own brother to Poseidon's son, ruler of the fog-girt isle of Aeolia.[33]

It is not surprising that this digression on Mananaan should be of more than passing interest, for the O'Malley clan was associated, through their territory around Clew Bay in County Mayo, with the great sea god in Irish legend: in Irish genealogical tradition, "the O'Malleys are celebrated in several poems as expert seamen. They are called the Mananaans, or sea-gods, of the western ocean."[34] O'Malley took great pride in living at Burrishoole on Clew Bay, a seat of the O'Malley clan, and O'Malley's wife, the sculptor Helen Hooker O'Malley, was so impressed with a maquette of a sculpture of Mananaan MacLir executed by Peter Grant for the New York World's Fair of 1939, that she bought the exhibit and commissioned an enlarged version of the work.[35] It is this figure that forms the basis of the bronze monument to Ernie O'Malley, donated by his family, on the Mall in his native Castlebar.[36]

The extent to which the sea, and the related trope of the drowned body, exerts a continual fascination for O'Malley is clear from the manner in which these themes recur in his notes on Ernst R. Curtius's essay "Technique and Thematic Development in Joyce." Curtius wrote this critical commentary as a follow-up to his introduction to the first German translation of *Ulysses* in 1929, which was translated by Eugene Jolas in *transition*, in July 1929.[37] Counting Samuel Beckett among its admirers, the essay quickly established itself, with Gilbert's writings, as a classic in the rapidly expanding field of Joyce criticism. The theme of the drowned body is examined in detail by Curtius, and O'Malley transcribes the summary of Joyce's fusion of realism with symbolic/mythic allusions: "These examples might illustrate how a motif, offered conjointly with the reality of external events and mirrored in poetic form (Milton, Shakespeare), is enlarged in the case of Stephen to a symbol of his problems of life: death, misery, sorrow, repentance."[38] The immediate cause of Stephen's sorrow and repentance reverts to the navel cord and the maternal, prompted by his guilt over his inability to save his mother at the hour of her death: "She is drowning. Agenbite.... Agenbite of inwit. Misery! Misery!" (*U*, 11.875, 879, 880). O'Malley's reading of Curtius is in a separate notebook from his earlier notes on the sea and Mananaan MacLir in "Aeolus," but when

Curtius notes Stephen's struggles with remorse, and that the "reality of external events" is "enlarged... to a symbol of his problems of life: death, misery, sorrow, repentance," it is difficult not to imagine O'Malley reflecting once more on the violence and suffering of his own past in both the Anglo-Irish War and the Civil War as he wrote the words down.

In his notes on the "Scylla and Charybdis" chapter, these issues surface again. Æ's contributions to the debate in the National Library are prominent in the notes, including his pronouncement: "The movements which work revolutions in the world are born out of the dreams and visions in a peasant's heart on the hillside... the desirable life is revealed only to the poor of heart, the life of Homer's Phaeacians" (*U*, 9.103–10). The librarian Richard Best's insistence on the close relationship of Hamlet to Shakespeare's personal life is emphasized, and O'Malley again underlines the moral soul-searching of Stephen, as in the repetition of notes on "Agenbite of inwit": "Agenbite of inwit: remorse of conscience. [...] Hurrying to her squalid deathlair from gay Paris on the quayside I touched his hand" (*U* 9.809–10, 825–26). The attentiveness to "Agenbite" or "conscience" in *Ulysses* is of interest given the repeated view, promulgated first by Seán Ó Faoláin, that O'Malley was a man without pity or remorse.[39] This is qualified by the frequency with which O'Malley reflects precisely on the emotional or moral cost of violence, most notably in his suggestion that in a war such as the Irish revolution without the official backing of a state to absolve the individual of direct responsibility, conscience weighs more heavily, notwithstanding the justice of the cause: "Action grew out of personal responsibility and individual effort rather than as an organized service of authority and a symbol which relieved the individuals of personal responsibility."[40] Joyce's use of the term "agenbite" diagnoses precisely this particular crisis in conscience, in which regret is felt even for actions that were right at the time: justice is not sufficient to appease the ghost and regret is to be distinguished from remorse, which would entail the action was wrong. The meaning of remorse is originally connected with "morsel," with biting and eating, and it is as if, having passed the conscious or mental test of conscience, a residue of conflicting claims to justice still remains in the body. Hence the "gnawing" of remorse, or "pangs" (akin to those of hunger) of conscience, somatic responses that have to do with sensitivity and humane feelings not fully resolved by acting on principle, or the justness of one's conduct. These can be self-destructive but may also initiate "reparative efforts that tend to reduce self-torment by restoring some positive self-esteem"[41] through the acknowledgment of damage—not only to others but to oneself, as in the psychic injuries of trauma. As noted above, the shock that passes out of the mind into the body, or that lodges in the body and does not make it to the mind at all, was diagnosed as shell shock or, with the officer class, neurasthenia, and it is not surprising this was diagnosed as O'Malley's medical condition, over and above the severe physical wounds that scarred his body.[42] Stephen's anguish in *Ulysses* over his mother's death is a clear case of conscience in crisis, as his principled refusal to grant her dying wish, that he make his peace with the Catholic Church, condemns her to an agonizing death. In O'Malley's notes on "Wandering Rocks," this is related to the theme of drowning (already noted in "Proteus") and once more to "Agenbite" (underlined by O'Malley), and he notes the imperial narrative of the lord lieutenant's viceregal cavalcade unifying the chapter: "[The Lord lieu connects them all up]." So far from sleeping easily on another man's wound, as the old Irish proverb that informs the title of his memoir declares, O'Malley notes in a harrowing account of the execution of British hostages in his memoir that, having been tortured and having faced death himself, "It seemed easier to face one's own execution than to have to shoot others."[43]

In his summary of Stuart Gilbert's essay "An Irish *Ulysses*: 'Hades' Episode," O'Malley notes Gilbert's opening comment on *Ulysses*: "Much of the work seems a merely meticulous study of the commonplace, and its clues seem buried beneath a rubble of detail."[44] Gilbert's discussion of the funeral/graveyard episode in "Hades" addresses issues of burial and rebirth, and how meaning can (re)emerge from a "rubble of detail." The rubble of 1916 may not have been far from O'Malley's mind as he reflected on Paddy Dignam's funeral passing by the national icons of the O'Connell and Parnell statues ("the shades of Heracles and Agamemnon") on O'Connell Street, and Gilbert's emphasis on the affinities between the ambiguous prophecy of Tiresias and Robert Emmet's "Speech from the Dock," stipulating the birth of the nation as the condition for his own epitaph, is also duly noted by O'Malley. The downward movement or experience of descent that constitutes the "mortuary atmosphere" of the chapter is noted, akin to the Royal Canal "dropping down, lock by lock," but this "downward pressure"—"interpreting a long postponement of Ireland's freedom" in O'Malley's notes—is nevertheless counteracted by the prospect of rebirth at the end. While O'Malley had no illusions about the overwhelming defeat of the Civil War, there is no succumbing to despair or disowning of the cause; in words that could apply to much of his life, he wrote to Paul Strand: "This last year I went through several kinds of hell, and it was only last month I realized I was above defeat. That may sound presumptuous but it's true. I touched bottom and found that at any rate."[45]

"Telescoped Time"

Time jumped a gap with us.

ERNIE O'MALLEY (*SF*, 275)

Maurice Murphy's essay "James Joyce and Ireland," published in *The Nation* (1929), opens with a paragraph that must have given O'Malley pause for thought: "James Joyce has done more for Ireland than any other man of letters. It is not at all inconsistent with Irish character that he is looked on as a kind of pariah, not only of the peasantry but by many otherwise intelligent people."[46] This could have been an image of O'Malley himself, or other republican activists, cast as pariahs in the bitter aftermath of the Civil War. Joyce's modernism touched on another aspect of radical republicanism as it drew closer to the daily rounds of everyday life in Dublin: the very attempt to articulate popular consciousness as it is lived may lead to rejection by the people whose lives are represented for the first time. O'Malley wrote of the challenge presented by the more radical images of the Revival to a complacent, popular consciousness:

> It was difficult for a people not accustomed to creative work to see themselves in print or on the stage. The sudden realization was not at first accepted, as the absence of a steadying influence of a printed creative tradition had made people glorify themselves or explain away their faults, and had made them less amenable to the writer's intuition and understanding.[47]

O'Malley welcomed disillusionment if by that is meant tearing away romantic illusions that provide a futile escape from harsh realities, while yet emphasizing the equal need to challenge the conformity and passivity (Joyce's "paralysis") that accepts such harsh realities as fate.[48] O'Malley notes Cyril Connolly's view that "each of his [Joyce's] books reveals a growing fear of beauty; not because life is not beautiful, but because there is something exceedingly false and luxurious in the 'Celtic Twilight' approach to it."[49] For all Joyce's aloofness, it is his willingness to deal with the base metal of everyday life that constitutes his true democratic achievement for Connolly, acquiring form in "the smithy of my soul" (*P*, 276):

> What Baudelaire and Laforgue did for Paris, or T.S. Eliot for modern London, Joyce has done for Dublin and at a time when Yeats and Synge had monopolized the Gaelic side of the Irish, he was able to create a language of the demotic commercial speech of the anglicized burghers of Dublin

itself.... Joyce in *Ulysses* set out to revive it [literary English] by introducing the popular colloquial idiom of his own city...."[50]

What O'Malley wrote of a people finding its voice was equally applicable to the language of *Ulysses* (making allowance for its primary urban focus): "Flowing intonations of those who had read well, the sturdy speech of the soilsman, Gaelic from the Gaeltacht, Gaelic idiom in English, the slang of cities, especially that of Dublin with its tongue stuttering against the palate" (*SF*, 276).

Joyce's demotic style echoes O'Malley's own politics, particularly the republican conviction that the restoration of the voice of the people, whether among the reading public or at the ballot box, may not initially meet with popular approval. Revolution by definition is ahead of its time, and like the avant-garde, its justification lies in the shock of recognition, the shattering of inertia that, in Joyce's terms, paralyzes a people. This was the rationale of the Easter Rising of 1916, which had less of a democratic mandate than opposition to the Treaty in the Civil War, as an anti-Treaty handbill pointed out in 1922: "Will of the people. If you had answered the will of the people in August, 1914, you would all have gone to Flanders. If you had acted on the will of the people in Easter Week you would have lynched Padraig Pearse."[51] In linking revolution with the vanguard thinking of modernism, it is striking that O'Malley uses Joyce's image of forging the conscience of the race to describe his own revolutionary awareness: "We were being hammered red-hot in the furnace of the spirit and a spark was bound to fly and disclose us to each other, with a word, a look, a chance remark."[52] O'Malley was sent down the country by IRA General Headquarters to light the spark nationwide. Though acting in the name of the nation, it was clear that many of the people he encountered as an IRA organizer were not always on his side, except in a vague way: "I was on the outside. I felt it in many ways by a diffidence, by an extra courtesy, by a silence. Some were hostile in their minds; others in speech; often the mother would think I was leading her sons astray or the father would not approve of what the boys were doing" (*OAMW*, 143). In a description that seems once more to be indebted to Joyce's conception of the artist in *Portrait*, he continues:

> I felt that I should be able to *fuse with my material*, the people, so that I could make better use of it, yet look at them dispassionately, as if from a distance. My approach to teaching and training the men was impersonal.... This often meant a cold quality creeping in, but few could mingle with them without gaining warmth. (*OAMW*, 143)

It is for this reason, as Richard English points out, that imagination is ineluctably bound up with political freedom in O'Malley's mind, as democracy without the cultural conditions of self-determination is empty: "O'Malley conceived of freedom as involving both formal political and lasting cultural emancipation. National freedom and individual, intellectual freedom were interlinked."[53] Following the classical democratic tenet that people cannot consent to their own slavery, O'Malley wrote that "it was an urge difficult to interpret: the right of a people to their own soil so long as that people would not accept domination" (*SF*, 286). Remaining in the British empire under the sovereignty of a foreign monarch was still subjection in the eyes of those who opposed the Treaty. Writing from Kilmainham jail following the collapse of the mass hunger strike in November 1923, O'Malley took issue with those among his own ranks who refused to face difficult truths, and who persisted in wresting victory from centuries of the "slave mind":

> I have pointed out that our traditions are wrong and that we foster them knowingly or without thought. We are and have been slaves and so have the slave mind. The open fighting of 1920–1921 and some of the fighting of 1922–1923 has helped somewhat to eradicate slavish defects. . . . Even though there are such outstanding deeds the mass cannot rise to them save in a certain form of enthusiasm.[54]

The appeal of the modernist turn in art toward formal innovation was that while rejecting passive or mimetic representation, the "slavish" reproduction of reality in politics as well as art, it acted *on* history, refusing to accept an oppressive past as given.

For O'Malley, it was the avant-garde gesture of the Easter Rising, and the coercion of loyalty in the threat of conscription, that awoke a population from its imperial slumbers in the election of 1918, having voted "democratically" against their own interests for decades: "There was a tradition of armed resistance, dimly felt; it would flare up when we carried out some small successful raid or made a capture"—all the more so if it provoked and drew disproportionate State reprisals.[55] Rather than retreating into elitism as in the case of right-wing modernism, the experimental techniques of writers like Joyce—and those inspired by him such as Bertolt Brecht, Alfred Döblin, and Hermann Broch on the continental mainland—drew closer to the demotic and everyday life, seeking to retrieve the world of newspapers, mass politics, and new media technologies from the sedation of the culture industries.[56] "Only hard-headed Irishmen and cosmopolitan Jews are as sophisticated as he [Joyce]," wrote Frank Swinnerton, in a passage transcribed by O'Malley:

> They know the argot of every language, the drinks and bywords of every medium.... [T]hey are without reverence, hard as stone, proud of their knowingness and exhibitioning of it, but at heart worried to death because they are without illusions.... [Joyce] rarely soars above the base, but the base is known to him without mercy.[57]

The point of disrupting prevailing attitudes and power relations through the jarring aesthetic devices of modernism was to break up habits of authority, enabling a cowered population to reclaim their own voice and culture in the process. Joyce's radicalism is closer to what Peter Bürger has termed "the historical avant-garde," aligned to political as well as cultural radicalism. Though initially in advance of society, the avant-garde sought to induce transformations that would eventually intervene in, and percolate through, the comatose state of everyday life that led to widespread acceptance of the Great War.[58] *Finnegans Wake* was both acclaimed and berated for its assault on the English language, and its bewildering attempts to mingle scores of tongues, but for all its opacity, O'Malley was still drawn to accounts that discerned an Irish accent in the universal babble. In his reading of Benjamin Gilbert Brooks's "Shem the Penman" (1941), he noted Brooks's extended discussion of Joyce's "Irish stew" of language, and its plays on the slapstick of Charlie Chaplin and the automation of the machine age:

> A farce of words, a farce even in the fundamental culinary sense, imposes its spontaneous pattern and flings actuality into the rippling stuttering world of Irish talk. Here we have what remained unexpressed in his earlier work.... Besides the hurrying and tripping of the native brogue there is a more deliberate, over fashioned early 19th century pomposity which gives some feeling of the foreign slowness of English. Joyce has learned from modern entertainers like Hulbert and Chaplin the degree to which meaning can be conveyed convincingly by the purest mechanical qualities of speech, those tricks of rhythm and emphasis which, more than the presence of known words, often make things understandable in actual life.[59]

The unexpected jolts in Joyce's use of montage is found in formal and stylistic shifts in O'Malley's own writing, most notably in the sudden juxtaposition of myth and realism in a key passage in his Civil War memoir,

The Singing Flame.[60] Hiding in a secret room on Ailesbury Road, Ballsbridge, in Dublin, O'Malley recounts how he awoke one morning in November 1922 to find the house completely surrounded by Free State soldiers. Resolving to shoot his way out, he describes in slow-motion cinematic detail how he dressed, gathered his gun and hand grenade, and listened in the darkness: "I shielded a match with my hand for I did not want a light to show at the back of the house through the sepia blind" (*SF*, 180). At this point, the great Irish saga, the *Táin Bó Cúailnge*, flashes up in his mind, the inflated diction of the epic, recounting Ferdia's battle dress on the last day of his fight with Cúchulainn, posing an ironic contrast to his own humdrum preparations:

> Outside of his brown-leathern, well-sewed kilt he put a huge goodly flagstone, the size of a millstone.... On his left side he hung his curved battlesword, which would cut a hair against the stream with its keenness and sharpness. On the arch-slope of his back he hung his massive, fine buffalo shield whereon were fifty bosses.... (*SF*, 181)[61]

This mythic outtake continues at some length until it is brought back to earth by the clamor of soldiers ascending the stairs and imminent capture or death: "There was nothing very splendid about a Smith and Wesson, but I was fond of it as a good piece of mechanism, and my one grenade was not very warlike to look at" (*SF*, 181). The abrupt narrative transitions raise questions about the role of myth in supplying reserves of courage, questions that surface again when, in detention at the Curragh camp, he encounters the legends that had grown around his own exploits: "I was told stories of myself, what I had said or done in different places. I could not recognize myself for the legend. That was a difficulty. The confusion between the legendary and the real self. Time jumped a gap with us. People saw us as a myth which bore little relation to ourselves; and our real selves, where could we find them?" (*SF*, 274–75).

Contesting Yeats's image of the romantic hero summoning Cúchulainn to his side, O'Malley sees myth as a poor consolation for the sundering of the Irish past: "Ours was the country of broken tradition, a story of economic, social and political oppression, propped up by a mythological introduction innocent of archaeological or historical interpretation" (*SF*, 278). In his reading of Joseph Warren Beach's account of Joyce, his attention is drawn to the non-directive method of *Ulysses*, noting "the unwillingness of the author to show us the way, even to indicate the point and plausibility of the hiatus and ellipsis."[62] The very nature of stream of consciousness precluded the imposition of order on the psyche as the quickening of inner life brought submerged or clandestine thoughts to the surface, akin to the sudden shift in consciousness that followed the Easter Rising: "The people as a whole had not changed; but the new spirit was working slowly, half afraid, yet determined . . . later would come organization and cool-headed reason. Now was the lyrical stage" (*OAMW*, 51). In *The Singing Flame*, this is carried over into the mindset that prevailed during the Civil War: "There was no background into which men could imperceptibly fit. We were particles in suspension waiting for further tests of our properties. There was a recasting, a reshaping of values" (*SF*, 276).

John McGahern has written perceptively of traces of the Revival and Romantic Ireland in O'Malley's writing but also notes an urgency in which "observation is usually close and excitingly accurate, especially when action is linked to landscape. . . . He learnt to judge men by a look, bearing, intensity or deliberateness of speech. Often, his own life and the lives of his men were dependent on these judgments."[63] It is perhaps this willingness to "fling . . . actuality into the rippling stuttering world of Irish talk" (in Benjamin Gilbert Brooks's terms above) that constitutes the Joycean elements in his outlook on life. As preparations began for a new military offensive in the immediate wake of the Rising, O'Malley, while still a student, perceived that an intimate knowledge of the city would be vital for success:

> We expected to fight in the city, when we did not know. . . . We walked around the lanes and backalleys of the North side. We selected observation and sniping positions, or checked up on the food supplies in shops in given areas. We climbed to the tops of buildings to get panoramic views of the city or to study roof tops, and we learned to know by sight the bigfooted men of the G division.[64]

Joyce's recall of the city he grew up in was uncanny and, as noted in chapter 1, visitors from Dublin to his Paris apartment were invited to accompany him on imaginary walks through the streets of their native city as he named all the shopfronts, pubs, and other buildings along the way. There is a related intensity of place in O'Malley as he crossed the Irish countryside, his eye for landscape and knowledge of local communities bound up with his own quest for identity. Writing of Patrick Moran, his confidant in Kilmainham prison during "the Tan War," he mentions how his experience of Moran's home place while organizing Volunteer action allowed them to draw closer: "It was easy to begin an acquaintance when

I could talk of a county I had liked. The men carried their home places in their minds.... When you knew a man's district well and could talk about its personal geography, you became, for a time, closer than a blood relation":

> Moran knew the lonely shores of Lough Allen, the bare recession of hills towards Leitrim and the smells of ferny undergrowth of woods near the lakes of Skean and Meelagh.... To test his memory, and to take him out of gaol, I would ask him to walk down the right bank of the Shannon from Lough Allen to Carrick and come back on the opposite side. Next day we would add further details. (*OAMW*, 58)

The planning behind O'Malley's dramatic escape from Kilmainham aimed to spring Moran as well, who was facing execution on charges arising from the Mount Street shootings of the British Intelligence "Cairo Gang" on the morning of Bloody Sunday. At the last moment, Moran refused to go, believing his cast-iron alibi would lead to his acquittal, but his optimism proved unfounded: he was found guilty on framed evidence and hanged a month later.[65]

A sensibility scored by tragedy and defeat such as O'Malley's after the Civil War could hardly be accused of optimism, but perhaps Joyce's home truths aided his own subsequent negotiations of the Irish social and cultural landscape after the Civil War. In *Finnegans Wake*, Shem "cutely foretold" the burning of the Four Courts—"the dynamatisation of colleagues, the reducing of records to ashes, the levelling of all customs by blazes" (*FW*, 189.35–36), and, as Nicholas Allen has shown, disparate jottings from the *Irish Times* that reported O'Malley's arrest on Ailesbury Road were seemingly threaded into the text. "Aylesburg" (*FW*, 387.9) is invaded by mercenaries, "scotobrit sash and his parapilagian gallowglasses" (*FW*, 387.4–5) followed by the jailing of Roger Casement ("official landing of Lady Jales Casemate" [*FW*, 387.22–23]), and the foreshadowing of a later showdown "with a twohangled warpon and it was between Williamstown and the Mairrion Ailesbury" (*FW*, 615.18–19). In the end, though, "[o]f all the green heroes everwore coton breiches, the whitemost, the goldenest," it was not rebels but the "anterevolitionary, the churchman" (*FW*, 234.8–11) who "shall reside with our obeisant servants among Burke's mobility at La Roseraie, Ailesbury Road" (*FW* 235.12–13). It is difficult to know whether these are Joyce's cryptic meditations on another man's wound ("never get stuck on another man's pfife" [*FW*, 411.10–11]), but there is little doubt that for O'Malley himself, Joyce's own unflinching art helped to cauterize the past he carried around in his battle-scarred body.[66] In *Finnegans Wake*, the renouncement of happy endings, "Noo err historyend goody" (*FW* 332.1), is followed, as Adaline Glasheen points out, by a play on the formulaic ending of fairy tales in relation to the marriage of HCE and ALP in the novel, as recounted in O'Malley's *On Another Man's Wound*: "for he put off the ketyl and they made three (for fie!) and if hec dont love alpy then lad you annoy me" (*FW*, 332.3–5), alluding to O'Malley's recall of his nurse inducting him into the world of Irish folktales as a child, with which he also ends his own book: "Put on the kettle now and make the tay, and if they weren't happy, that you may."[67] Rather than masking over grim realities, it may be that the yoking together of the epic and ordinary in Joyce's work helped to rescue the new Ireland from the retrenchment into which it had sunk, in his disenchanted eyes, under the new conservative Free State. Dispelling illusions, disillusionment was empowering rather than disempowering, modernist formal energies holding out for new futures that draw on unresolved pasts.

✸ 9 ✸
Beyond Disillusionment

DESMOND RYAN, *ULYSSES*,
AND THE IRISH REVOLUTION

> One-sided and distorted too is the mighty and mournful epic
> of *Ulysses*.... It alone could explain the Irish revolution.
>
> DESMOND RYAN, *Remembering Sion*[1]

In 1936, the Irish republican Ernie O'Malley wrote to Desmond Ryan, a combatant in the GPO during the Easter Rising, to compliment him on his memoir, *Remembering Sion*, published two years earlier: "I read *Remembering Sion* and liked it very much. Your approach was a very interesting way to telescope or capture memory."[2] While living in New York, O'Malley heard that Ryan sought to make contact with him, but his informant must also have mentioned O'Malley's reputation as a gunman during the Irish revolution: "I don't mind being called a gunman," he wrote to Ryan, "we were, I suppose, though we didn't use that term ourselves. And as you are a pacifist, and I respect you for your beliefs, I don't see why you shouldn't use the term."[3] Desmond Ryan had not always been a pacifist: in preparation for the Easter Rising, he had helped to make explosives and grenades under the guidance of the science master at Patrick Pearse's school, St. Enda's, and it was as Pearse's closest aide that he ended up in the GPO during Easter Week, 1916.[4] Such was Pearse's confidence in him that he appointed Ryan as his literary executor, also entrusting him, in his last instructions from Arbour Hill Military Detention Barracks before his execution, with the task of completing his history of St. Enda's School: "I should like my friend and pupil, Desmond Ryan, to add an additional chapter, describing the fortunes of St. Enda since then [1913], and the whole to be published as a book under his editorship."[5]

Ryan devoted his considerable energies to producing the first important histories of the revolution. In 1917 he published *The Story of a Success*, completing Pearse's account of St. Enda's, and followed this with a pioneering short biography, *The Man Called Pearse* (1919), and a five-volume edition of Pearse's works in 1924.⁶ As a socialist, Ryan was also devoted to the legacy of James Connolly, writing the first biography, *James Connolly*, in 1924, and later editing a three-volume collection of Connolly's writings.⁷ The title of Ryan's memoir, *Remembering Sion*, was borrowed from a passage in *Ulysses* recounting the dedication of émigrés to the cause of Ireland. In the "Proteus" chapter, Stephen recalls meeting Kevin Egan in Paris, one of the exiled Fenian "Wild Geese" based on a real-life figure, Joseph Casey (1846–c. 1907). Casey's political imprisonment in England in 1867 led to a disastrous attempt to spring him from Clerkenwell Prison by setting off an explosion that killed twelve people: "he prowled with colonel Richard Burke, tanist of his sept, under the walls of Clerkenwell and, crouching, saw a flame of vengeance hurl them upward in the fog. Shattered glass and toppling masonry" (*U*, 3.247–49). Joseph's brother Peter was an organizer of the rescue mission and eventually settled in Cabra, Dublin, where he befriended the Joyce family. Joseph Casey lived in exile in Paris following his release and remained as part of the Fenian underground, while working as a printer for the Paris edition of the *New York Herald*. It is the sequence of thoughts relating to this in *Ulysses* that provides the epigraph to Ryan's book:

Of Ireland, the Dalcassians, of hopes, conspiracies, of Arthur Griffith now [...] In gay Paree he hides, Egan of Paris, unsought by any save by me. [...] Weak wasting hand on mine. They have forgotten Kevin Egan, not he them. Remembering thee, O Sion. (*U*, 3.226–27, 249–50, 263–64)⁸

Acknowledging his indebtedness to *Ulysses*, much as Joyce had borrowed the passage from the Psalms, Ryan wrote that "in this quotation, Joyce sums up all the nostalgia of exile and suggests the whole movement of life and thought and history," shorn of romance or sentimentality.⁹ Given the formidable challenge that *Ulysses* presented to official pieties of both faith and fatherland in Ireland, it is noteworthy that radicals such as Ryan, O'Malley, and others did not consider it a betrayal of their political vision but welcomed the critical eye it cast on an Ireland they had tried to change through revolution. Answering accusations leveled against him of hero-worship of Patrick Pearse and Michael Collins, Ryan cited his equal respect for Joyce, only to find that did not work either: "hero-worship being the least sign of enthusiasm apparently for we heard too we had had been hero-worshippers of Joyce, a charge we had least expected."¹⁰ *Remembering Sion* contains one of the most acute early appraisals of *Ulysses* from an Irish perspective, and to understand how its acknowledgment of Joyce shaped the "telescoping" of memory, it is worth giving a brief account of Ryan's own intellectual development as an activist, writer, and journalist in both Ireland and Britain in the first half of the twentieth century.

Desmond Ryan was born in 1893 in Dulwich, London, where his father, W. P. Ryan, worked as a journalist and featured prominently in Irish nationalist and Labour circles, writing the first history of the early Irish literary movement, *The Irish Literary Revival* (1894). In 1905, W. P. Ryan returned to Ireland to edit the outspoken *Irish Peasant* in Navan, County Meath, a socially committed nationalist newspaper whose robust independence brought it into repeated conflict with the Catholic Church. The young Desmond moved to Ireland in 1906, and when Patrick Pearse opened St. Enda's in 1908, Ryan was among the first pupils to enroll. While studying later for his degree in Irish, English, and French at University College, Dublin, he returned to St. Enda's as a teacher, also acting as Pearse's secretary. In addition to his father's socialism, the left-leaning Irish language writer Pádraic Ó Conaire was a close family friend, and the young Desmond's interest in socialism and the Labour movement was intensified by the 1913 Lock-Out. Fighting alongside one of the leaders of the 1913 strike, James Connolly, in the GPO in 1916 gave expression to Ryan's distinctive socialist brand of republicanism. Following the Rising, he was interned at Stafford jail, Wormwood Scrubs, and Frongoch camp in Wales, where he wrote in an autograph book held by Thomas Pugh, later (as noted above) to befriend Joyce. On Ryan's release, he returned to resume his studies for a BA degree and to reorganize the Rathfarnham Company of the Volunteers. Based at Cullenswood House (the initial site of Pearse's St. Enda's), he came into regular contact with Michael Collins and developed the lasting admiration—"one of Collins's few socialist admirers"[11]—that formed the basis of his subsequent historical narrative, combining real with fictive characters, *The Invisible Army: A Story of Michael Collins* (1932).

By 1918, Ryan had gravitated toward journalism rather than active military service and took up a position as Irish correspondent of the Labour *Daily Herald* (on which his father had acted as assistant editor). In 1919, he joined the *Freeman's Journal* as part of a new group of younger pro–Sinn Féin journalists, working under the news editor Seán Lester (1888–1959), formerly a prominent Volunteer. The Treaty debates, however, produced a profound crisis of loyalties in Ryan, for though supporting Collins's pro-Treaty position, he was ill at ease with Partition and other aspects of the settlement.[12] His strong disapproval of the *Freeman's Journal*'s treatment of Éamon de Valera led to his resignation from the newspaper: "I never had such a disillusioning experience since then as I discovered two political groups had begun to hate each more than they had ever hated the Black and Tans" (*RS*, 279–80). Moving to London, he worked at the *Daily Worker* and the *Daily Herald*, and subsequently embarked on a literary career, sustained in the 1930s by the publishing house Arthur Barker. The Ryan household narrowly escaped destruction by bombing on the outbreak of World War Two, and on returning to Ireland, Ryan edited the Labour Party periodical *The Torch* during the war years. Over several decades, he published a wide range of studies of Irish history, following his semi-fictional account of Michael Collins with a major history of the Easter Rising based on his firsthand experience; critical biographies of de Valera, the IRA leader Seán Treacy, and the Fenian leaders James Stephens and John Devoy; studies of socialism in Ireland, Irish literary history, interventions in public affairs (with particular reference to Partition), as well as a fantasy novel, *Saint Eustace and the Albatross* (1935)—and, not least, his experimental memoir, *Remembering Sion*.

In a public lecture many decades later reflecting on the publication of *Remembering Sion* in 1934 and its critical reception, Ryan noted that while some readers took issue with its perceived politics or biases, others commented on its unusual style and composition. The book not only contained a chapter on James Joyce that seemed strangely out of place among reminiscences of Patrick Pearse and the Easter Rising, but its episodic and fragmented style was also indebted to Joyce, posing questions of tone and narrative voice not usually raised by journalistic or political memoirs. Ryan visited Joyce in Paris in 1936 and was candid about the risks taken by the experimental approach in the memoir, but remained "unmoved by remarks about style and journalism, knowing that the style adopted by us was the only one for what we had set out to do: to evoke all, or most of the sides of Irish life we had known, and as the sides were different, we changed the style to suit the side":

> In that, brazenly and openly and with deep gratitude, [we] took several leaves from the book of Mr James Joyce, who gave us a title and a chapter; in that used flowery journalism, swear words, slang, and threw all commas, semi-colons, colons, dashes and dots and grammar and sense and all dessicated [*sic*] word-polishing and mincing phraseology and restraint to the devil when it suited us. ("SRS," 245)

The assumption that experimental prose which sets out to voice spontaneity must be unrestrained and off the cuff is noticeable here, for part of the problem with Ryan's technique is that unlike Joyce's "scrupulous meanness," careful word-polishing and calibration of effects are not always present. At times, the effusive prose is more in keeping with Seán O'Casey's autobiographies, but yet in its eye for detail and mood, the originality and vivacity of *Remembering Sion* is compelling. For Ryan's contemporary and fellow-combatant in the GPO during the Rising, Desmond FitzGerald, the task of combining personal experience with objective history proved intractable in the end, as he confessed his inability to continue his memoir beyond the tumult of the Rising. Though FitzGerald's memoir is written in the first person, it was clear that "all the time he strove to avoid mention of himself in any but an objective way. The attempt to write an eye-witness account with minimum reference to the 'I' was one reason why he did not pursue his task with greater rapidity, for on other subjects he wrote easily and relatively quickly."[13] For Ryan, by contrast, modernist strategies are introduced at the level of form to render conflicts that crosscut both personal and national memory, complicating and even controverting any undue coherence in narratives of the self or the nation.

In the semi-fictional account of Michael Collins, *The Invisible Army*, Ryan used stylistic techniques—a novelistic plot structure, descriptive montage, improvised dialogue, a combination of fictive and real characters (as in *Ulysses*)—to "concentrate on reviving the atmosphere of that very abnormal time, and yet not distort the truth" ("SRS," 246). Stream-of-consciousness and montage effects proliferate: as Patrick Pearse enters the room, time is blurred in the mind of Harding (based on Ryan) between flashbacks, Roman antiquity, the French Revolution, Pearse's voice, and the crashing of gunfire:

> Harding's mind wandered back to the November night when he first heard Pearse speak in the Rotunda Rink at the launch of the Irish Volunteers, and in that speech had sounded the directness some historians of imperial Rome put in the mouth of ancient Britons flaunting a last defiance at Caesar's eagles ... A crash of gunfire, a rumble of falling houses, a rattle of rifles overhead ... Pearse's voice grew louder: Dublin would be forever an heroic city like the Paris of old ... The main positions were intact....[14]

At times, descriptions read like directions for a film script: "Up the stairs to a small, bedroom with the unconscious Condron.... Back to the main body, lying on the floor and staring at the irregular gaping holes in the tunneled walls of each room" (*IA*, 22). Cinematic techniques of the kind employed in *Ulysses* feature throughout Ryan's narrative, as if only montage effects could capture the mechanized violence of the rebellion, just as Samuel Beckett recommended for the romantic set pieces of the Revival: "the sense of confinement, the getaway, the vicissitudes of the road, the wan bliss on the rim. But a large degree of freedom may enter into the montage of these components, and it is very often in virtue of this, when the tics of mere form are in abeyance, that attributions are to be made."[15] The depiction of Collins using swear words and bad language drew opprobrium from conservative readers, but it was precisely this earthy heroic that attracted Ryan to Joyce's method in *Ulysses*: a willingness to incorporate frailties and imperfections of both character and place, as well as the everyday patois of the street. As against ivory-tower academicism, in which "professors enjoy themselves as they please in libraries, turning black into white, debunking, theorizing, praising, blaming, or even disguising a pamphlet in ten volumes," Ryan returned to Dublin and "sat again in Bewley's café and listened again to the speech of the Dubliners" ("SRS," 248):

> All the fascination and melody of the Irish speech slowly growing into more than a row of letters, unlocking its treasures to blows of dictionaries and groaning over grammars and hints from enthusiasts: fish sellers, beggar women, milkmen who knocked at the door and said something worth hearing or something one would never hear in London in twenty centuries.... As Dubliners refused to do justice to Dublin, we decided just to please ourselves and let the Dubliners keep talking. ("SRS," 250)

The language of the tribe also helped to throw light on dark places, "the ruin, the shams, the inertia, the Anglicization and the darker sides of Irish life": "I don't for a moment suggest that a picture of the past must be all painful or shocking—except for party politicians who live on half-truths and plaster saints who live on scruples" ("SRS," 250, 249). For all the control exercised by Catholicism over education, the Church never managed—as the revolutionary generation confirmed—to fully purge the dissent that offset the craving for respectability in the emergent bourgeois Ireland. Christian Brothers' schools (which Ryan has attended before St. Enda's) had to deal "with the material that Dublin had sent them, and in that material lurked all the violent contrasts of Ireland":

> Sometime an echo of the Rabelaisian vocabulary of the slums rose in playground or classroom, or in some sudden gleam a flash of that deep instinct of the Irish which sends them into revolutions or hermit's cells or wafts the towers of some cathedral above a nest of slums or crown's history's vigil with a glow of red and purple, a cross of aeroplanes above Dublin Bay and thundering cannon. (*RS* 68)

It was, however, images fostered by Romantic Ireland, the dream world of the Celt, that the young Ryan brought with him from London to the bleak vistas of a clerically dominated society. The first view of Navan in County Meath, the family's initial dwelling place, was far removed from the expectations that stirred his imagination on the boat crossing: "Perhaps it was because we had not lingered in Dublin that some melancholy is associated with this first glimpse of Navan, for to me Navan had to be my first real look at the Ireland I had weaved into such a pattern of history and memory on the boat. It rained. And rained. And rained. . . . The car drove across what seemed some bleak and very empty space to the centre of the town" (*RS*, 23). The petty skirmishing in the various factions of Irish-Ireland nationalist circles, and more bitter conflicts between the progressive outlook of the *Irish Peasant* and the rigid control of the Catholic Church under Cardinal Logue, ensured "a thin, dark and ugly thread had to be woven into my dream-pattern" (*RS*, 26–27). The recourse to a disjointed narrative style can be seen as an attempt to do justice to the clash of allegiances, and competing images of Ireland, that lacked resolution in his brain, finding expression in montage techniques akin to stream of consciousness but, more accurately, eddies and cross-currents in the psyche that registered the maelstrom of public life.

Narrating Self and Nation

The opening chapter of *Remembering Sion* relays through inner reverie the ferment in the young Ryan's imagination as he travels on his first boat crossing to Ireland. His mind is grounded in the immediate sense experience of the moment but is also at sea, in more ways than one, in the backwash of the past—the dreams and memories of Ireland conveyed by his father and grandfather, his uncle Thomas Boyd, and family friends such as the émigré Irish-language writer Pádraic Ó Conaire:

> Spray and waves over the steamer's side and a rush of many passengers below. I linger alone looking over the railings at the waves beating time with the howling engines. On across the seas never yet sailed before except on a heeling paddle-boat down the Thames, remembering my grandfather had been a sailor [. . .] excited at this voyage to green fields and dreams and an ageless battle in which the Irish had always lost and fought again and lost and wandered to Spain and France and America thereafter, to a magic land built up of the sad tales my grandfather had told me of the corpses he had seen on the roadside as he went to school as a boy, giving his lunch

to the starving people and escaping the famine fever which killed his own father, of the romantic tales I had read in Joyce's *Old Celtic Romances*, and the wilder tales Padraic O'Conaire had scattered when he came in to see my uncle [...] all that endless ebb and flow of the Irish tale I had read in the history books. (*RS* 11)

The experience of "waves beating time" at the outset commingles with the "ebb and flow" of the past in a manner facilitated by the interior monologue (or dialogue) that runs through the memoir. But the technique does not only allow for the free flow of thought: there are also "violent contrasts" between images of the Irish past, the "magic land" of *Old Celtic Romances* versus harrowing memories of the Great Famine, and the adversity that drove emigrants from Ireland in the first place. Though the backward look of the exile is prone to nostalgia, Ryan's memoir picks up repeatedly on "the dark threads" that run through the pattern—one of the dark threads being the hostility often directed at the émigré Irish by those who remained at home, espousing an unwelcome inward-looking nativism.

It is for this reason that Ryan takes issue with Daniel Corkery's insistence that "a normal literature is written within the confines of the country which names it. It is not dependent on expatriates."[16] Corkery had in mind cultural rather than mere physical displacement: Ibsen and Turgenev lived abroad, but they still wrote for audiences at home. By contrast, certain Irish expatriates, according to Corkery, draw on Irish subject matter but forgo an Irish point of view: the *form* or treatment of the material is "to a greater or lesser extent imposed on him by alien considerations."[17] For Ryan, by contrast, it is precisely through form that Irish writers have broken out of typecasting and reclaimed their own voice on the world stage. Corkery, he suggests, "is too great a mind to believe that only those who never leave Ireland know Ireland best": such are the curtailments on expression in Ireland that it is only by stepping back that the truth can be told—or even known—in the first place:

> The truth was that that some demon had turned Daniel Corkery the patriot into Daniel Corkery the provincialist. To leave Ireland often means to know Ireland better, and too few of those who should leave their country for their country's good have the sense to do so. The "expatriates"—only literary expatriates are included in the phrase of opprobrium for some strange reason—do for Ireland what Ireland too seldom does for herself. This is no great virtue on their parts—looking back over their shoulders they see the thing half seen before. (*RS*, 37)

Ryan recounts a story of the writer Brinsley MacNamara's in which soldiers return from the Great War to an Irish country town, only to find themselves lamenting: "'This is a bloody awful place!'" MacNamara himself received no thanks for telling the truth in his own fiction: "The author had to fly from his infuriated fellow-Midlanders for similar cameos of Midland life" (RS, 27).

The importance of an external perspective facilitates Joycean colloquies of the self, for stream of consciousness is marked not only by interior monologue but also interior *dialogue*, the interplay with, and traces of, other voices in one's life. Discussing narratives of the self, Peter Goldie distinguishes between a (Virginia) *Woolfian* view, in which the self is known from inside out, and a (Saint) *Augustinian* view, in which the self is known "from the inside, but as if from the outside": in the latter case "what is taking place is not an inner Woolfian *monologue* but an inner Augustinian *dialogue*."[18] As befits James (Augustine) Joyce's middle name, the latter is more in keeping with the stylistic experiments of *Ulysses*. In *Remembering Sion*, passages of inner speech are interspersed with external voices, not least echoes of *Ulysses* itself. On leaving—or being pressured to leave—Navan, Ryan's family moved to Sandymount, Dublin, and Ryan recalls the strand in front of their house:

> There is the Strand sweeping in its ridgy brownness towards the red fortress of the Pigeon House, past the wall where the sailor tried to teach me to swim, and I floated in a circle on one finger for all his pains, and Merrion Gates clanging to let the trains whistle by with white clouds over the sea-wall towards Blackrock [...] ... and the tide surging in, white-horsed and singing ... and a golden moon over all the roofs of Sandymount. (RS, 49–50)

Stephen Dedalus's musings on Sandymount in "Proteus" are recalled here: "They are coming, waves. The whitemaned seahorses, champing, bright-windbridled ..." (U, 3.55–56). Stephen's memories of meeting the old Fenian Kevin Egan in Paris (which, as noted above, are picked up by the title and epigraph of *Remembering Sion*) are also evoked by the next paragraph describing the old Fenian who lived beside them at Sandymount:

> Down from the Strand slopes the road to our house and the house next door, where the old Fenian and his son and his daughter-in-law live. [...] In his little drawing-room, he broods, hoping, stubborn old Henry Flood, remembering the day at Manchester when England's cities quaked and

howled at the Fenian name, revolvers spitting over the heads of encircling mobs. (*RS*, 50)

The incorporation of multiple vantage points, internal and external, does not signify—contrary to Corkery—a loss of voice but an opening up of inner life, both in personal and in cultural terms. On one occasion, Ryan distinguishes between what can be *thought* in private and *said* in public, as in the Catholic Church's exertion of its influence to crush his father's newspaper, the *Irish Peasant* (which moved to Dublin under a new name, the *Irish Nation*): "A great wave of caution comes from confessionals and pulpits and visiting clergymen dropping gentle hints and sweeps many Gaelic Leaguers off the subscription list of the *Irish Nation*.... It is unheard of to criticise the clergy so openly and flirt with theosophy and modernism.... Socialism too.... Think what you like but don't write it" (*RS*, 59). Elsewhere, the distinction is not so much between thought and writing as between modes of expression, vernacular speech as against the language of decorum and propriety. In London, he writes: "I go to Mooney's [pub] about twice a year to catch an Irish accent and the honest speech of Ireland which shocks Ireland on the platform in Ireland's virtuous and hypocritical moods but which is the speech of Ireland in private, and long may that be so" (*RS*, 39).

Echoes of *Ulysses* are one manifestation of how an external voice—or literary text—breaks into the first-person narration of *Remembering Sion*, but throughout the memoir, the merging of inner speech with dialogue is closer to the technique of *free indirect discourse* mastered by Joyce, the audible presence of another's speech in an utterance. The dual voice of free indirect discourse disrupts the purely subjective flow of a stream of consciousness, opening inner life to other voices and, at times, to dissonant views that cannot always be integrated into the narration.[19] When Ryan remembers other people, or incidents that concern others, their catch-phrases often make their presence felt, even in the case of incidental characters. Recalling a beggar woman who called to their house in Sandymount, he writes: "The beggar woman knocks, the loquacious one who gets so much tea from the kind Protestant lady round the corner and lives in a room where, saving your presence, the rats ate the back out of her best skirt" (*RS*, 52). In the case of more well-known figures, such as Arthur Griffith, descriptions also carry impersonations of their voice. Part of James Connolly's stature, he notes, was the respect in which he was held by his enemies: "Even Arthur Griffith, hostile to Larkin and the Strike, admits Connolly is a man of his word, nay, the one man with a head on his shoulders amongst these Internationals, Benevolists, Foreign Emissaries and riff-raff down in Liberty Hall" (RS, 179). The second part of the sentence is in Griffith's own idiom, but Ryan is distancing himself from these sentiments—in keeping with the irony permitted by free indirect discourse. At another point in the memoir—in a passage not without its relevance for the Dublin of Joyce's *Ulysses*—Ryan notes of his early education by the Christian Brothers that for all their zealotry, they "made no distinction in creed, for there were Jews on the Westland Row roll most courteously and scrupulously educated by the Brothers":

> During religious instruction or prayers, on a pleasant smile or nod from the Brother in charge, the Jews retired—objects of envy or curiosity to some of us, but strangely enough never of the keen wit of their class-mates. The Brothers were partly responsible for this as the strap had been known to go vigorously into action on the unhappy hands of the too-enquiring pupil who slyly examined a quiet little Jewish boy upon the plot and moral of *The Merchant of Venice*. (RS, 65)

Tolerance is found in unexpected places, but in an earlier sequence recalling his introduction to socialism, Ryan ventriloquizes the sentiments of a "wild-eyed" adversary of the Labour leader William O'Brien, whom he encounters at a socialist meeting:

> [O'Brien] talks to some one beside him about a tremendous row in progress between Connolly and Daniel de Leon. The last name is familiar to me on various pamphlets, which have fired the wild-eyed man to further protest: Englishmen are bad enough without bringing in a lot of New York Jew-men to corrupt the Catholic city of Dublin, a gang of toe-rags who want to destroy whatever industries the bloody English have left us and set up a World Republic with the help of the Grand Orient and every bowsie from James Street, Monto and the Coombe. (RS, 55–56)[20]

In another extended passage, the crusades of the Vigilance Committees are recalled and the practice of "upholding purity by plastering cinema-screens with eggs and the shop windows with bricks whenever film vamps gave too overpowering hints to the young persons of Dublin or Venus of Milo or some other shameless exhibition imperilled the chastity of Grafton Street and offended his very inflammable eyes" (RS, 78). The parodic tone continues in the description of "the whore-prowled streets" of the city's nightlife: "When Dublin became a free capital again she turned and swept her streets clean of mud and harlots, and youth was no longer darkened by that mournful, pox-eaten, howling army of harpies befouling all its dawning dreams. This army of night town was parasitic on the Army of Occupation" (*RS*, 79). Purple prose is used to send up the myth that prostitution was solely a colonial vice, "imperil[ing] the chastity of Grafton Street": "Again here James Joyce passed and looked and remembered and painted the truth a more prosperous and sleeker Dublin would like to forget" (*RS*, 79). One of the uncomfortable truths Joyce presented to his readers was that virtuous denizens of Catholic Dublin were no strangers to night town, and while crusaders sought to clear up the red light Monto and related districts following the establishment of the new state, the conditions of many of the slums from which it sprang were largely left intact.

The instabilities and shifts in narrative voices relating to the past attest not only to Joyce's stylistic innovations but also to upheavals in Ryan's own life, giving expression to uncertainties and crises induced by his own divided loyalties. Constantly divided against himself, the pacifism commented on by Ernie O'Malley surfaced in the midst of the conflagration in the GPO during the Rising: "I stood within it all, and a curious cloud fell over my mind and spirits, and a conflict sharpened in my mind. My old Socialist-pacifist hatred of war, my doubts about the jingoism and race-hatred of Sinn Fein and then the spell of Pearse" (*RS*, 199). Tensions between pacifism and violence, socialism and nationalism, republicanism and romanticism, ideals and realties, were brought to a head by the external shock of revolution: "Before Easter Week they crowded in upon me with an overwhelming insistence that almost proved too powerful for my mental balance. . . . Easter Week and its tragedies were terrible solutions, their personal shock must survive the last survivor of the tragedies."[21] In the case of the Civil War, however, the severity of the shock broke his resolve, forcing his departure from Ireland: "Then came the crisis which swept me over the seas from Sion and a minor nervous breakdown to round off the journey, or my memories of Sion would have been even grimmer at this stage than they were" (*RS*, 276). Or as he states in *The Invisible Army*: "Beneath the debris the spirit of the Irish Revolution was buried" (*IA*, 229). In this latter narrative, the character Harding (based, as we have seen, on Ryan) temporarily joins Free State forces but begins to question the price paid following the death of Collins and in light of acts committed in the name of the new state: the executions of previous comrades, Terence O'Donovan (based on Erskine Childers), and Sean Condron and Dermot Considine, out of "vengeance" (*IA*, 229); the shootings of unarmed Republican ("Irregular") prisoners—"'Shot while trying to escape.' Ancient and familiar excuse" (*IA*, 222)—and "the wild savagery which binds captured Irregulars to land mines and blows them to atoms" (*IA*, 223), alluding to the Ballyseedy massacre of Republicans by Free State soldiers in Kerry, in 1923.[22] Following Collins's death and the new state terror, Harding begins to lose heart and questions the price paid for it all: "One thought beat through his brain: NOTHING ON EARTH WAS WORTH IT. In spite of victory, in spite of Michael Collins, in spite of the tricolour waving over three of Ireland's four green fields. . . . Something was wrong with his brain. The arguments went round and round. Tomorrow away over the Bay to cool his thoughts" (*IA*, 228, 230).

As in Ernie O'Malley's drawing on the mock heroic of both Joyce and the heightened diction of ancient epics, "Michael Collins rose to haunt," summoning up the sea god Mananaan MacLir also recalled by Stephen Dedalus and O'Malley:

> Like a mocking refrain through his thoughts went the words of the old heroic tale: "An awesome Spectre, forbidding in looks, a Fearsome One, like a ferocious Devil-giant, Fionn saw, and he going through the gloomy and tangled wood . . . A Drab coat was wrapped around him with mud-beplastered skirts, his tremendous brogues thundering like mighty waves every pace he strode . . . But [. . .] lo!, the wind and the sun flamed before and behind, and they saw then 'twas MANANNAN MAC LIR, Fairy Phantom of Rathcroghan, who had come to save them in the dire strait in which they were." Wind and rain . . . dire strait. (*IA*, 225)

The cooling of Ryan's thoughts "away over the Bay" in exile in Britain led to subsequent forceful questioning of the Treaty and Partition as "a state of smothered war": "here indeed was no final Irish settlement."[23] Ryan became a founding member of the Anti-Partition of Ireland League established in Britain in 1938, castigating "Lord Craigavon and his Junta" in Northern Ireland as "the first totalitarians in Europe": a "system of government that would turn the stomachs of Hitler and Mussolini."[24] He condemned the IRA bombing campaign that, with the outbreak of war, brought a sudden end to the Anti-Partition League's activities, but he also took issue with those in the British Left who "can be very eloquent against the present Irish bombers" but ignore the fact that republican "idealists (or scallywags if it comes to that)" have been "maddened by the dictatorial regime in Northern Ireland which British Labour has condoned in the past."[25]

The rendering of conflicting pressures is brought to bear on Ryan's portraits of his mentor, Patrick Pearse. "It is doubtful," wrote Patrick Lynch, "if any colleague was more closely acquainted with Pearse; certainly none was better equipped to become Pearse's interpreter for posterity."[26] As Peter Goldie notes, the randomness of interior monologue/dialogue bears witness to "a multiplicity of occurrent thoughts, feelings, emotions, memories, that crude talk of personality tries to capture in a single word," as if Leopold or Molly Bloom could be reduced to any one of the kaleidoscopic thoughts that run through their heads. By the same token, the Pearse known to Ryan stands in stark contrast to the typecasting of either his hagiographers or detractors. To be sure, Pearse's single-mindedness lent itself to monologue in that he was not easily swayed by others: "He was a good listener, but when roused the conversation ended as a monologue which sounded very like one of speeches, although there was more humour" (*RS*, 162). Yet, as Ryan notes, Pearse had his own "borrowed accents" (*RS*, 123) to the extent that he wondered "whether there were not two Pearses, one grim and aloof, the second a jocund orator capable of kindling listening hosts at will. He declared in the end he is in doubt as to which Pearse was which" (*RS*, 126):

> There were strange contradictions in this great man, a man so great it goes against the grain to have to search for flaws in him. [...] Although his ideal was the sword, he could not cut a loaf to save his life or shave himself even with a safety razor, or for all his lyrics to smoking battlefields bear the sight of human suffering without squirming, but he would watch all night beside an ailing pupil, and on the eve of his surrender [in the GPO] he soothed a wounded British soldier to sleep with gentle words. (*RS*, 125)

As late as July 1914, Pearse was still an outsider to the revolutionary movement and was not directly involved in the Irish Volunteers' gun-landing at Howth; yet within two years, he led the insurrection brought about—at least in part—by those guns. These "strange contradictions" were also evident in the GPO when, as the building went up in flames, Pearse gave the lie to fanatical certitude when he approached Ryan in silence: "Then he suddenly turned and asked me, casually but with a certain abruptness: 'It was the right thing to do, wasn't it?'" (*RS*, 125, 201).

Pearse comes across as a combination of opposites in Ryan's portraits: a mystic averse to introspection; a shy, reclusive person with a flair for public speaking. The multifaceted images include the Pearse devastated in 1909 by the death through drowning of the woman he "loved," Eibhlín Nic Niocaill (Eveleen Nicolls) (*RS*, 97);[27] who discussed with Mary Hayden his intention to marry later in life;[28] who protested against the gender imbalance of proposing only one woman for the new Irish Universities Senate;[29] and who established St. Ita's School for girls—aspects that sit strangely alongside the Pearse denounced by the mob as a "pederast" and "scorner of Women" by characters in Bryan MacMahon's *A Pageant of*

Pearse (1979). The messianic Catholicism often imagined as summing up Pearse's personality is also hard to reconcile with his trenchant attacks on the Catholic hierarchy over its treatment of the Irish language, and the sanitizing of ancient Irish myths, just as his view that corporal punishment was "a stupid and purposeless folly" coexists with a perceived bloodlust for political violence.[30] Recollecting Pearse in her memoir *Life and the Dream* (1947), Mary Colum attributed the lack of self-absorption in Pearse and many of his generation to their dedication to public rather than private impulses, "the impression that they were obeying some call and personal choice had little to do with it." Identity turned on selflessness, as in classic republicanism, and this underpinned the notion of sacrifice: "There was something else that was in all of them: a desire for self-sacrifice, a devotion to cause, everyone was working for a cause, for practically everything was a cause."[31] The difficulty was that not all causes seemed immediately compatible with each other, and to this extent only commitments over which one was prepared to make a stand, perhaps even to give up one's life, were the ultimate test of personality (it is striking that Pearse was consoled at Eveleen Nicoll's death from the belief that she appeared "to have drowned in an attempt to save another girl").[32]

Notwithstanding coming under the "spell" of Pearse, and his own role in the making of his reputation, Ryan was critical of Pearse's early suspicion of the Labour movement and the militarism that led to a denigration of one of Ryan's own heroes, Tolstoy:

> His glorification of war expressed itself in a violent dislike of the writings of Tolstoy: he could find no merit in the Russian's short stories and novels, and refused even to consider their claims as literature. His worship of military discipline was fanatical to the point of absurdity. Until the 1913 Strike turned his mind to Connolly's writings, which left a deep mark on his thought, he feared the Irish Labour movement and the friendly relations with British Labour unions was a danger to Nationalism. His early desire to live in history was so intense as to be almost insane. And always in him there was a curious conflict between the dreamer and the doer. (*RS*, 123)

On hearing that Pearse's mother thought he was a "young god," Ryan reflected on how he was all too human, "for I had a vivid recollection of Pearse showing his weakest side to his mother" (*RS*, 129).[33] The "shadow" of the self thrown by Stephen Dedalus on Sandymount strand (*U*, 3.408–24) was also cast by Pearse: "There was a disconcerting side to Pearse, especially in his earlier years. No honest portrait can hide certain shadows"

(*RS*, 124)—but as with Joyce's attachment to Dublin, the dark side did not take from the affection shown toward the man: "The testimony of his friends is unanimous: they all loved him even when his faults stood out before their eyes" (*RS*, 124).

Beyond Disillusionment

Recalling his youthful romantic ideals, Ryan addressed an issue often faced by writers who, rejecting pressure to write propaganda or to promote positive images, depict hitherto unrepresented cultures with an unsparing realism: "Sometimes in Ireland a comfortable Civil Servant will come up smiling darkly or an Irishman of an older generation or a young girl wrapt in some dream-pattern like mine on the boat [on which he traveled from London], and ask smugly, ferociously or sadly: 'Why do our young writers all hold up their fellow-countryman's faults to foreign countries?' Sometimes the addendum follows, 'and for gain.' Or there is talk of 'playing to the English gallery' or 'the Sewer School'" (*RS*, 36). The "Sewer School" is code for James Joyce, disgust at the uninhibited depiction of bodily functions in his fiction leading to H. G. Wells's charge that he displayed "a cloacal obsession"—a theme in many early reviews.[34] Ryan does not disagree with this characterization but sees it as a case of blaming the messenger for the bad news relayed to unreceptive audiences:

> Ulysses is strong meat and takes long to digest. Yet when the initial nauseation over the ordure has gone and this work of genius and affection, never to be repeated and imitated literally only by fools, remains with its irony, wit, detail, and portrayal of an everlasting day, and those who therein passed and struggled and still live on. In vain the politician and professional Catholic (and what is as bad, the tame Protestant chameleon hobnobbing with the same) will continue to [...] howl that Joyce is the Father of the Sewer School, for Joyce has only described the sewer for which they are largely responsible. (*RS*, 46)

Rather than attacking the representation, Ryan as a socialist argues that it would be preferable to do something about the reality, transforming the lives of those with "few dreams to sweeten dry bread and rank tea and meatless boards" (*RS*, 79). Leading lights of the Revival, determined to counter primitivist stereotypes of the Irish as mired in dirt and filth, were likely to take offense at Joyce's "alimentary symbolism," as one study tactfully describes it, and look to myths of Mother Ireland and the Romantic past to raise national spirits.[35] Yet, for Joyce, it is precisely maternal love that is unconditional, embracing not only "young gods" (as in the case of Mrs. Pearse) but also squalor, imperfection, and death. In a condensed account of *Ulysses*, Ryan writes:

> Two stories link these characters and scenes: Stephen who has struggled starward from a sordid home to the freedom of negation, haunted by his mother's deathbed and his father's oaths and fecklessness and songs: Leopold Bloom, sex-racked, frustrated by his whorish wife, haunted by all the loss of his young son Rody [sic], the young boy who steps with a burst of poetry into the dream-clouds of the brothel as Leopold guides Stephen to the calm of the cabman's shelter.[36]

Stephen breaks into poetry at the end of the "Circe" chapter as lines from W. B. Yeats's poem "Who Goes with Fergus," which he had recited at his mother's deathbed, come back to haunt him as he lies semiconscious on the ground:

STEPHEN (*murmurs*)

>   ... shadows ... the woods
>   ... white breast ... dim sea. [...]

BLOOM (*communes with the night*)

> Face reminds me of his poor mother. In the shady wood. The deep white breast. (*U*, 15.4941–43, 4949–50)

Yeats's poem deals with loss of the mother but the mystery of maternal love—"love's bitter mystery"—is that, unlike romantic love, it does not turn on idealization but accepts realities, with all their bitter truths. In *Portrait*, Lynch asks Stephen, "What do you mean [...] by prating about beauty and the imagination in this miserable Godforsaken island?" (*P*, 233) but Stephen has already preempted the question by pointing to beauty in the most unlikely places: "*Can excrement or a child or a louse be a work of art? If not, why not?*" (*P*, 232; emphases in original). Speaking of a child in terms of excrement or a louse may fall short of Victorian ideals of childhood but as C. D. C. Reeve makes clear in *Love's Confusions*, primordial bonds in "the theatre of eros" are nurtured not in sentiment but in "dramas of eating and excreting, and the fantasies associated with them" in child care:

... Mommy, or some equivalent caregiver ... is the one who interprets what is happening and replaces pain with pleasure, if she interprets correctly. In the process, she provides her child with an embryonic model of loving relationships, a foundation for the concept of love he will have as an adult.[37]

Attention to bodily needs and physical contact satisfies not just hunger and creature comforts but the deepest desires for attachment and recognition. When Cranly reminds Stephen in *Portrait* that "whatever else in unsure in this stinking dunghill of a world a mother's love is not. Your mother brings you into the world, carries you first in her body. What do we know about what she feels? But whatever she feels, it, at least, must be real" (*P*, 263), Stephen contests the view that a mother's love and bodily functions are incompatible in the first place. At its most vulnerable or affectionate, love does not shy away from the discomforting but suspends embarrassment and disgust. As Reeve notes, areas of life out of bounds to strangers are disclosed to intimates, and this extends not only to the body but to knowledge, trust, and confidences: "To accomplish this, however, a key anxiety must be overcome, namely, that our friend or lover might feel disgust rather than love for what full disclosure on our part would reveal to her."[38] Revelations undergo the risk of leading not only to disgust but to hurt and humiliation, as when Gabriel discovers in "The Dead" that he was not the only (or even the deepest) love in Gretta's life. Judged by the intensity of Michael Furey's passion, he cuts a pitiful figure; yet in one of Joyce's earliest writings, he had already suggested that in love lies an ability to embrace truth beyond disenchantment: "As we stand on the mountains today, looking before and after, pining for what is not ... [t]he sooner we understand our true position, the better."[39]

If images of Romantic Ireland fostered by the Revival share many affinities with romantic love, a pursuit of perfection all the more desired because unattainable, then Joyce's embrace "of the sudden reality that smashes romanticism to a pulp," as he expressed it to Arthur Power, can be understood as an attempt to rescue love from its own "disappointed romanticism."[40] E. M. Forster's query in *Howard's End* is apposite as a coda to Joyce's work, and to its echoes in Desmond Ryan: "To have no illusions and yet to love—what stronger surety can a woman find?"[41] Dedication to truth in all its complexities and uncertainties is less an act of disaffection than an attempt to retrieve a culture, in Yeats's words, which "had fed the heart on fantasies."[42] Viewed in this light, Ryan's embrace of Joyce's "dear, dirty Dublin" amounts to a love beyond illusions, an attempt to bring readers into a close, intimate relation to the text, on the terms outlined by Reeve: "The truth in these anxious reflections on love is that sharing heart's secrets is a two-sided game—if for no other reason than that the anxieties of one-sided sharing are usually too great. When each confides, however, each has equal reason not to divulge to a third party."[43] Eager to pass judgment, the third party risks misunderstanding: hence the rapport between writer and reader that refuses third-person narration or "objective description" in both Joyce's and Ryan's texts, the narrative equivalent to denying access to the aloof outsider or detached observer.[44] If *Ulysses* opens up the inner life of a community as never before, allowing strangers and readers the world over to share a culture's most intimate conversations with itself, it is because it elicits the attentiveness to tone and detail required by aesthetic form. In one encounter, Ryan is on the receiving end of a tirade for his defense of the "Sewer School," which convinces him that the fear of many Irish people is that "our writers were telling too much": "when a man like Synge, a man in whose sad heart there glowed a true love of Ireland, one of the two or three men who have in our time made Ireland considerable in the eyes of the world, uses strange symbols which we do not understand, we cry out that he has blasphemed and we proceed to crucify him" (*RS*, 41). It is as if distance lends *dis*enchantment to the view, detachment or insensitivity misconstruing words against both speakers' and listeners' better judgments.

It is in this sense that Ryan, in his biographies of John Devoy and James Stephens, might be seen as adopting a Joycean sensibility: "He was to be the first historian," according to Patrick Lynch, "to establish the individual characteristics of the Fenian leaders, to show them as human beings rather than as legendary figures of fantasy. His candour and honesty spared neither people nor causes."[45] If demythologizing does not lead to debunking or the destruction of reputations, this is because commitment and attachment were not incompatible with truth in Ryan's eyes. Hence his determination to exonerate Joyce from charges of betrayal or apostasy for refusing to glorify Ireland: "Who loves the Jews less for Zangwill, the Welsh for Caradoc Evans, or the Irish for O'Casey?" (*RS*, 42). Though O'Casey's portrayals of 1916 received a hostile reception from nationalist audiences, Ryan was less critical, not least because he shared O'Casey's own reservations about bloodshed: "Thousands, too, have seen a sudden light on the agony of Ireland in the distorted mirror of *The Plough and the Stars*, where O'Casey in his rage against war and the agony of the common people mixed passages from Pearse in the dregs of bad porter" (*RS*, 42–43). Joyce's work too, illuminates the conditions of a society on the eve of insurrection:

One-sided and distorted, too, is the mighty and mournful epic of *Ulysses*; not all the laughter and light of our Dublin is here, but it is no mere distorted fresco formed of gold and slime. It alone would explain the Irish revolution, for it reveals Dublin as none other than an Irishman could reveal her, an Irishman who at heart loves Dublin, and writes with all the indignation of love, the very pulse of this remorseless and brutal protest. (*RS*, 43)

Ryan is wary of looking back in hindsight for signs of the upheavals that were to come in Ireland, yet he sees in Stephen's rebellion against both church and empire a premonition of what might have been. Though defiance is imbued with free-thinking from "gay Paree" and elsewhere, it has its own lineages of dissent in Gaelic culture (the subject of Ryan's study *The Sword of Light*): "In reality, Joyce is the heir of a great tradition. There is no need to call him the sad Rabelais of Liffeyside. Eoghan O'Rahilly, Brian Merriman and many a Gaelic bard has travelled the same road before him, not to mention the Fathers of the Church."[46] As Valéry Larbaud suggested, Joyce's Irishness consisted not in birthright or subject matter but genealogies of *form*, some of which led back to the Gaelic tradition that resurfaced in the fractured epics of *Ulysses* and *Finnegans Wake*. In marked contrast to Daniel Corkery's juxtaposition of the Gaelic "hidden Ireland" to the apostasy of émigré literature, internationalism is a two-way street for Ryan, as is clear from the vital contribution of exiled clerical scribes and scholars to maintaining Gaelic learning from outposts in continental Europe. In a reverse movement, Ryan was also among the first to grasp the importance of the internationalism of the Fenian movement, as in his pioneering article "When a Scepter Haunted Cork," tracing the relationship between Ireland and the First International of Marx and Engels.[47] Just as Joyce drew on sublimated traditions in his own culture to energize world literature, so also the Easter rebellion transcended local horizons and "was transformed into the world force it has since proved itself to be: from Ireland to Cyprus, to India, to Africa and in all the anticolonial struggles of today."[48]

Taking issue with Fr. C. C. Martindale's "penetrating" contention that Joyce is "at his best when he portrays collapse," conjuring up "the phantom word of the neuropath," Ryan insists that the hauntings of *Ulysses* derive not from pathology but from a truth beyond disillusionment, "the tangle of the Dublin of that day in the summer of 1904, a picture in large part true as all must feel whose minds are haunted by those hundreds of Dublin folk" (*RS*, 44) who pass through its pages: "a city emerges fixed for ever from its whirling in one amazing memory, a city one must grow to love even if one never has known it for all that is grotesque and twisted and scarred" (*RS*, 44). The unsparing realism of the novel brings the reader closer to both text and the city, backlit by home truths: "To read *Ulysses*," writes Ryan, "is to revisit Dublin, a Dublin not wholly gone. [. . .] The visit at first sight is a sordid one, and to many readers can never be more" (*RS*, 46).

Ryan's achievement in mixing memoir with montage is to transform the Rising from the faded aura of Romantic Ireland into a distinctively modernist idiom. Yeats's image of the "fanatic heart," the assumption that "hearts with one purpose alone" make revolutions, is thrown into question in Ryan's depiction of Pearse, in which the backstage figure, not just the front-stage political leader, accounts for the enigma of the hero. Lytton Strachey's *Eminent Victorians* (1918), in which great figures are taken down from their pedestals, is no doubt behind Ryan's approach, but in restoring figures like Pearse, Connolly, and Erskine Childers to the streets, he is placing them on the ground from which monuments are erected in the first place. Ryan's medley of impressions, insights, and judgments do not provide us with fully rounded characters but instead portray the self as agent—even secret agent—that created the conditions for the Irish revolution. As Ruth Dudley Edwards has astutely noted:

> Oddly enough, the only serious attempt to add some shade to Pearse's portrait was made by his first hagiographer. Desmond Ryan is a highly intelligent man who in maturity had had second thoughts. In a volume of memoirs, *Remembering Sion*, in 1934, although he wrote of him with love and admiration, he also admitted a darker side: his recklessness, his essential provincialism, his strong Napoleonic complex, and the glorification of war for its own sake. The book was ignored.[49]

Joyce's narrative methods provided the means of reflecting upon memory itself, and the "many facets, some tarnished and dull, some a-flame and a-glitter" (*RS*, 10), that make up the past. One of the distinctive aspects of John Devoy's memoir, *Recollections of an Irish Rebel*, according to Ryan, is that it possessed the Fenian trait of an autobiography without an ego: "the man who wrote the *Recollections* is no egoist, for he writes not of himself but of a movement." Yet he notes that Devoy's personality permeated all his public transactions, in keeping with an individual who shaped the course of Irish history: "Devoy grows slowly through his own words of others and the history of the movement to which he gave a long life of poverty and struggle and exile."[50] Ryan's memoir relays the colloquies that make up the self, showing that even in inner reveries, there is dialogue with many of the voices that made other worlds possible in modern Ireland, not least those imagined by James Joyce. If, according to Michael Löwy, "the absolute and radical rejection of the world in the tragic vision knows only a single temporal dimension: the present," then hope can only lie in "the underground tunnel" that leads to the future.[51] Joyce's vision "holds a prophecy," wrote Eimar O'Duffy, once a leading figure in the Irish Volunteers: "who knows that certain Irishmen may not yet get their way, and leave (to posterity) nothing of Ireland but what is enshrined in the pages of *Ulysses*."[52]

Acknowledgments

As the Decade of Centenaries relating to commemorations of the Irish revolution draws to close, it is fitting that its final years coincided with the centenary of the publication of James Joyce's *Ulysses*. Literary approaches have not featured prominently in accounts of the tumultuous formative years of early twentieth-century Ireland, but the days are thankfully gone when a historian could write that recourse to literature is only made "to conceal gaps in argument or the absence of supporting evidence." This literalist put-down was directed at Hannah Arendt's magisterial analysis of the rise of fascism in Europe, as if narrative, or indeed disjunctions in narrative, could be avoided in accounting for the seismic political upheavals of the twentieth century. In Joyce's *Ulysses*, narrative structure and closure are themselves in contention, in keeping with the perception that it was never finished as a work of art, only abandoned to meet the deadline of his "lucky day," his fortieth birthday on February 2, 1922.

The task of bringing things to an end besets any critical writing on Joyce, and in helping this book on its way, I have benefited greatly from many friends and colleagues. The debt I owe to the incisive intelligence and stylistic brio of the late Seamus Deane is evident throughout this work, and conversations with him were like concentrated courses on many of the issues discussed in the book, with, it must be added, equal measures of conviviality and humor. Joe Cleary, David Lloyd, Emer Nolan, and Clair Wills have also been abiding friends and interlocutors, their own work on literature and history setting the highest standards for other toilers in the field. Morris Beja, Valérie Bénéjam, Patrick Bixby, Joe Brooker, Katie Brown, Gregory Castle, Vincent Cheng, Luca Crispi, Ronan Crowley, Enda Duffy, Maud Ellmann, Catherine Flynn, Anne Fogarty, Finn Fordham, Darina Gallagher, Andrew Gibson, Vivien Igoe, Ellen Carol Jones, Declan Kiberd, Terence Killeen, Karen Lawrence,

Vicki Mahaffey, Julie McCormick-Weng, John McCourt, Barry McCrea, Katherine O'Callaghan, Laura O'Connor, Christine O'Neill, Sam Slote, Clare Wallace, and Siân White have also been part of continuous conversations in Joycean and modernist studies. Others have helped me to draw on their work in Irish studies and related cultural fields: Dudley Andrew, Ruth Barton, Desmond Bell, Mariana Bolfarine, Mary Burgess, Gabriel Byrne, Lisa Caulfield, Jeff Chown, James Coleman, Denis Condon, Claire Connolly, Marguérite Corporaal, Michael Cronin, Michael G. Cronin, Fergus Daly, Terry Eagleton, Orla Fitzpatrick, Renée Fox, Oona Frawley, Ann Gallagher, Laura Izarra, Gerry Kearns, Sinéad Kennedy, Colin Graham, Ailbhe Greaney, John Hill, Heather Laird, Joep Leerssen, Conor McCarthy, Niamh McNally, Margo McNulty, Angus Mitchell, Chris Morash, Willa Murphy, Caoilfhionn Ní Bheacháin, Barbara Novak, Barbara O'Connor, Brian O'Doherty, Cormac O'Malley, Stephen Rea, Katharina Rennhak, Ann Rigney, Kevin Rockett, Hedwig Schwall, Bruce Shapiro, Frank Shovlin, Aoife Spillane-Hinks, Margaret Spillane, Karen Till, John P. Waters, Katherine Waugh, and Robert Young.

In his after-dinner speech in Joyce's "The Dead," Gabriel Conroy celebrates: "We are met here as friends, in the spirit of good-fellowship, as colleagues, also to a certain extent, in the true spirit of *camaraderie*." Much of a similar spirit has been created by friends who provided support and the best of company over many years: Elizabeth O'Connor Chandler, Jim Chandler, Pia Conti, Farrel Corcoran, Ruth Deasy, Mary Doran, the late Bairbre Dowling, Rachael Dowling, Sheila Duddy, the late Tom Duddy, Michael Foley, Tadhg Foley, John Horgan, Marjorie Howes, Mary Jones, Anne Bernard Kearney, Richard Kearney, Christina Kennedy, Roisín Kennedy, Tanya Kiang, the late Siobhán Kilfeather, Kathryn Kozarits, Trish Lambe, Seona MacReamoinn, Brendán MacSuibhne, Paschal Mahoney, Stephanie McBride, Sinéad McCoole, Pauline McManus, Joseph McManus, Catherine Morris, Mary O'Connell, the late Áine O'Connor, Maureen O'Connor, and Niamh O'Sullivan. My late parents, Hugh and Josephine Gibbons, and the extended Gibbons family and their partners in Ireland, Wales, and the United States, have been a constant source of encouragement and debate, as has the Coyle family in Roscommon and elsewhere. If work takes place in what Joyce termed "the interval between friends," this applies even more in the case of one's own family: I cannot thank Dolores, Laura, and Barry enough for the heart-work that turns the slow ordeal of writing into a labor of love.

I would like to express my deepest thanks to Alan Thomas at the University of Chicago Press for taking this publication on board. The editorial guidance of Randy Petilos was invaluable, and Erin DeWitt's fastidious and scholarly copyediting made working on the manuscript a particular pleasure, redressing my own shortcomings time and again. I also wish to extend my thanks to the anonymous readers whose meticulous, perceptive reports greatly enhanced the final work.

※

I am grateful to the editors and publishers that printed earlier versions of expanded chapters in this book: chapter 1, "'Old Haunts': Joyce, the Republic, and Photographic Memory," in *Memory Ireland*, vol. 4: *James Joyce and Cultural Memory*, ed. Oona Frawley and Katherine O'Callaghan (Syracuse, NY: Syracuse University Press, 2014); chapter 4, "The Easter Rising as Modern Event: Media, Technology, and Terror," in *Science, Technology and Irish Modernism*, ed. Kathryn Conrad, Coilin Parsons, and Julie McCormick Weng (Syracuse, NY: Syracuse University Press, 2019); chapter 8: "On Another Man's Text: Ernie O'Malley, James Joyce, and Irish Modernism," in *Modern Ireland and Revolution: Ernie O'Malley in Context*, ed. Cormac O'Malley (Dublin: Irish Academic Press, 2016); and portions of the introduction and chapter 2, which appeared in "'Have You No Homes to Go To?': James Joyce and the Politics of Paralysis," in *Semi-Colonial Joyce*, ed. Derek Attridge and Marjorie Howes (Cambridge: Cambridge University Press, 2000), and "'Where Wolfe Tone's Statue Was Not': Joyce, Monuments, and Memory," in *History and Memory in Modern Ireland*, ed. Ian MacBride (Cambridge: Cambridge University Press, 2001). I am indebted to these publishers for allowing me to rehearse the ideas in this book first in their publications.

Notes

Preface

1. James Joyce, *Finnegans Wake* (1939), introduction by John Bishop (London: Penguin, 1999), 593. Henceforth *FW*, with page numbers followed by line numbers in text and notes.

2. James T. Farrell, "On Some Marxist Critics of Joyce" (1936), in *On Irish Themes*, ed. Dennis Flynn (Philadelphia: University of Pennsylvania Press, 1982), 93.

3. James T. Farrell, "Observations of the First Period of the Irish Renaissance," in *On Irish Themes*, ed. Flynn, 41.

4. William Irwin Thompson, *The Imagination of an Insurrection* (Oxford: Oxford University Press, 1967). For the Abbey Theatre's contribution to the Easter Rising, see Fearghal McGarry, *The Abbey Rebels of 1916: A Lost Revolution* (Dublin: Gill and Macmillan, 2015); for the view that the Abbey acted as a brake on revolution, see Lionel Pilkington, *Theatre and the State in Twentieth-Century Ireland* (London: Routledge, 2001).

5. Jim Moran, *Staging the Rising: 1916 as Theatre* (Cork: Cork University Press, 2005), 8.

6. John Francis Byrne, *Silent Years: An Autobiography with Memoirs of James Joyce and Our Ireland* (1953; repr., New York: Octagon Books, 1975), 127.

7. Thomas MacDonagh, "Of Ireland," in *Nineteen-Sixteen: An Anthology*, compiled by Edna C. Fitzhenry (Dublin: Browne and Nolan, 1966), 13.

8. One immediate aim, that of breaking complicity with empire in the event of conscription for the Great War, could be said to have succeeded. Another aim, that of placing Irish independence on the negotiating table during a postwar settlement, was not achieved at Versailles, laying the ground for the Anglo-Irish War and Civil War.

9. Michael Denning, *Culture in the Age of Three Worlds* (London: Verso, 2004), 37.

10. "William G. Fallon, 1881–1958," in *The Joyce We Knew: Memoirs of Joyce*, ed. Ulick O'Connor (Dublin: Brandon, 2004), 48. It is in this sense, Joyce wrote in his early talk on James Clarence Mangan, that poetry "is often found at war with its age . . . and sets store by every time less than the pulsation an artery, the time in which its intuitions start forth, holding it equal in its period and value to six thousand years." James Joyce, "James Clarence Mangan" (1902), in *Occasional, Critical, and Political Writing*, ed. Kevin Barry (Oxford: Oxford University Press, 2000), 59. Henceforth *OCPW*, followed by page numbers in text and notes.

11. Theodor Adorno, *Aesthetic Theory* (1970), trans. C. Lenhardt (London: Routledge & Kegan Paul, 1986), 366. For the view that the defeated may not fit in with the

laws of development at their time, but may speak to future generations, see Theodor W. Adorno, *Minima Moralia: Reflections from Damaged Life* (1951), trans. E. F. N. Jephcott (London: New Left Books, 1974), 151. As Adorno sees it, aesthetic autonomy, the modernist refusal of realist ties to what is represented, releases art from the pressures of the present, even in dark times.

12. Susan Sontag, "Unextinguished: The Case for Victor Serge," in Susan Sontag, *At the Same Time: Essays and Speeches*, ed. Paolo Dilonardo and Anne Jump (London: Hamish Hamilton, 2007), 83–84.

13. John Eglinton, "Irish Letter," *Dial* 86 (May 1929), reprinted in *James Joyce: The Critical Heritage*, vol. 2, *1928–1941*, ed. Robert H. Deming (London: Routledge & Kegan Paul, 1970), 624–26. Henceforth *JJCH*, followed by volume and page numbers in text and notes.

14. James Joyce, *A Portrait of the Artist as a Young Man* (1916), ed. with introduction by Seamus Deane (London: Penguin, 1982), 199. Henceforth *P*, followed by page numbers in text and notes.

15. Cited in Richard Greeman, "Translator's Foreword," in *Conquered City* (1932), by Victor Serge, trans. Richard Greeman (New York: New York Review Books, 2011), xvii–xviii. Serge is writing of Boris Pilniak's novel *Naked Year* (1922).

16. M. M. Bakhtin, "Forms of Time and the Chronotope of the Novel," in *The Dialogical Imagination: Four Essays*, ed. Michael Holquist, trans. Caryl Emerson and Michael Holquist (Austin: University of Texas Press, 1981), 249. In the glossary supplied at the end, the chronotope is described as "an optic for reading texts as x-rays of the forces at work in the culture system from which they spring" (425–26).

17. James Joyce, "Ibsen's New Drama" (1900), in *OCPW*, 45. Ibsen's words are from his letter to George Brandes (1870), cited in James T. Farrell, "Joyce and Ibsen," in *On Irish Themes*, ed. Flynn, 68.

18. Declan Kiberd, "Modernism in the Streets: Pearse and Joyce," in *Parnell and His Times*, ed. Joep Leerssen (Cambridge: Cambridge University Press, 2021), 221.

19. Joe Cleary, "The Book in the World: 100 Years of Ulysses," *Dublin Review of Books*, February 2022.

20. Unsigned review of Simone Téry, *L'île des bardes: Notes sur la littérature irlandaise contemporaine: Yeats, Æ, Synge, Stephens, Moore, Joyce* (Paris: Flammarion, 1925), in *Sligo Champion*, August 29, 1925, cited in John McCourt, *Consuming Joyce: 100 Years of "Ulysses" in Ireland* (London: Bloomsbury, 2022), 41.

21. "Politics and the Novel," *Los Angeles Times*, August 13, 2000.

22. Piers Brendon, *The Decline and Fall of the British Empire, 1781–1997* (London: Vintage, 2008), 290. For the international impact of the Easter Rising, see *1916 in Global Context: An Anti-Imperial Moment*, ed. Enrico dal Lago, Róisín Healy, and Gearóid Barry (London: Routledge, 2018).

23. Valéry Larbaud, "The Ulysses of James Joyce," *Criterion* 1, no. 1 (October 1922), reprinted in *JJCH*, vol. 1: *1907–1927*, 253.

Introduction

1. Daniel Bensaïd, *Marx, mode d'emploi* (Paris: Zones, 2009), cited in Enzo Traverso, *Left-Wing Melancholia: Marxism, History, and Memory* (New York: Columbia University Press, 2016), 217.

2. Tom Stoppard, *Travesties* (London: Faber and Faber, 1975), 44.

3. Desmond Ryan, "Still Remembering Sion," *University Review* 5, no. 2 (Summer 1968): 245.

4. Henri Troyat, *Tolstoy*, trans. Nancy Amphoux (Harmondsworth, UK: Penguin, 1970), 384. Prefiguring the future may be part of Stoppard's humorous conceit in *Travesties* since Joyce had not written *Ulysses* by 1917.

5. James Joyce, *Ulysses* (1922), ed. Hans Walter Gabler (New York: Vintage Books, 1993), 8.527, 9.89. Henceforth *U*, followed by chapter and line numbers in text and notes.

6. Paul K. Saint-Amour, "Rising Timely and Untimely: On Joycean Anachronism," in *The Edinburgh Companion to Irish Modernism*, ed. Maud Ellmann, Siân White, and Vicki Mahaffey (Edinburgh: Edinburgh University Press, 2021), 40.

7. Desmond Ryan, *The Man Called Pearse* (Dublin: Maunsel, 1919), in *Collected Works of Pádraic H. Pearse*, ed. Desmond Ryan (Dublin: Phoenix, 1924), 188. Henceforth *CWPP*, followed by page numbers in the notes. Pearse reiterated this in the address to his court-martial for treason: "We have kept faith with the past, and handed on a tradition to the future." *The Letters of P. H. Pearse*, ed. Séamus Ó Buachalla (Gerrards Cross: Colin Smythe, 1980), 279.

8. Collins's position in the Dáil, December 19, 1921, was that the Treaty provided "not the ultimate freedom that all nations desire and develop to, but the freedom to achieve it." It was left to the Donegal TD, P. J. Ward, to formulate the stepping-stone theory: "I will only vote for this Treaty as a stepping stone to put this country into such a position at some future time—when the opportunity does come—that it will claim the total separation that it is entitled to as a separate nation." Dáil Éireann debate, January 7, 1921, accessed at https://www.oireachtas.ie/en/debates/debate/dail/1922-01-07/2/.

9. John Eglinton, "Irish Books," in *Anglo-Irish Essays* (Dublin: Talbot Press, 1917), 89.

10. Anthony Collins, "The Richmond District Asylum and the 1916 Easter Rising," *Irish Journal of Psychological Medicine* 30 (2013): 280–81, cited in Brendan Kelly, *"He Lost Himself Completely": Shell Shock and Its Treatment at Dublin's Richmond War Hospital, 1916–1919* (Dublin: Liffey Press, 2014), 27–29.

11. David J. Morris, *The Evil Hours: A Biography of Post-Traumatic Stress Disorder* (New York: Mariner, 2015), 61. Citing Roger Luckhurst, Morris writes that "cinema's claim on the imagination is so strong that it serves to 'shape the psychological and general cultural discourse of trauma into the present'" (61). Hugo Münsterberg's *The Photoplay: A Psychological Study* (1916) was the earliest systematic account of crossovers between film techniques and mental life, including the flashback (which he termed "cut-back"). See also Roger Luckhurst, *The Trauma Question* (Abingdon: Routledge, 2013), esp. chap. 5, "Flashbacks, Mosaics and Loops: Trauma and Narrative Cinema," 177–208.

12. Maureen Turim has noted how scientific research into visual recall unavoidably involved "terminology [that] is borrowed from literary usage. This points to the circularity of literary and scientific influences." Maureen Turim, *Flashbacks in Film: Memory and History* (New York: Routledge, 1989), 209. Early psychological symptoms of shell shock such as nightmares, both asleep and semi-awake, crystallize into the disturbing flashbacks experienced in Regent's Park by the war veteran Septimus Smith of his dead comrade, Evans, in Virginia Woolf's *Mrs. Dalloway*: "There was his hand; there the dead. White things were assembling behind the railings opposite. But he

dared not look. Evans was behind the railings!" Virginia Woolf, *Mrs. Dalloway* (1925), in *The Mrs. Dalloway Reader*, ed. Francine Prose (Orlando, FL: Harcourt, 2003), 215.

13. Eric T. Dean Jr., *Shook Over Hell: Post-Traumatic Stress, Vietnam, and the Civil War* (Cambridge, MA: Harvard University Press, 1999); Jonathan Shay, *Achilles in Vietnam: Combat Trauma and the Undoing of Character* (New York: Simon and Schuster, 1996).

14. Morris, *The Evil Hours*, 69–77. For precursors of stress neuroses due to disruptive tempos of life, see Wolfgang Schivellbusch, *The Railway Journey: The Industrialization of Time and Space in the Nineteenth Century* (Berkeley: University of California Press, 1987).

15. According to Ruth Leys, "The term flashback implies the cinematic possibility of literally reproducing or cutting back to a scene from the past and hence expressing the idea that the trauma victim's experiences are exact 'reruns' or 'replays' of the traumatic incident." Ruth Leys, *Trauma: A Genealogy* (Chicago: University of Chicago Press, 2000), 241.

16. Walter Benjamin, "The Work of Art in the Age of Its Technological Reproducibility, Third Version" (1936), trans. Edmund Jephcott, in *Selected Writings: 1938–1940*, vol. 4, ed. Howard Eiland and Michael W. Jennings (Cambridge, MA: Harvard University Press, 2003), 266. Henceforth *BSW*, followed by volume and page number in text and notes.

17. Sergei Eisenstein, "Dickens, Griffith, and the Film Today," in *Film Form*, trans. Jay Leyda (London: Dennis Dobson, 1963), 195–256. As Benjamin noted, "The history of every art form has critical periods in which the particular form strains after effects which can be easily achieved only with a changed technical standard" (*BSW*, 4:266).

18. Kenneth Burke, "Literature as Equipment for Living," in *The Philosophy of Literary Form: Studies in Symbolic Action*, 3rd ed. (1941; Berkeley: University of California Press, 1974), 293–304.

19. James Joyce [perhaps to Mlle Guillermet], August 5, 1918, *Letters of James Joyce*, ed. Stuart Gilbert (New York: Viking Press, 1957), 118, cited and translated in Dominic Manganiello, *Joyce's Politics* (London: Routledge & Kegan Paul, 1980), 162. Original letter in French.

20. Fredric Jameson, *A Singular Modernity: Essay on the Ontology of the Present* (London: Verso, 2002), 103–5.

21. Douglas Goldring, *Odd Man Out: An Autobiography of a "Propaganda Novelist"* (London, 1935), 143, cited in Guy Woodward, "Douglas Goldring: 'An Englishman' and 1916," *Literature & History* 26, no. 2 (2017): 199. Goldring had already used this image in 1918: "The whole episode of the Rebellion has indeed struck through the black fog of politics which formerly interposed itself between our eyes and Ireland, and in an unforgettable lightning flash has shown us Ireland's bleeding heart and our own the sword transfixing it. And it did more, this terrible revealing lightning—it showed us ourselves as we never thought to see ourselves." "An Englishman" [Douglas Goldring], *Dublin: Explorations and Reflections* (Dublin: Maunsel, 1917), 14–15.

22. "An Englishman" [Douglas Goldring], *A Stranger to Ireland* (Dublin/London: Talbot Press, T. Fisher Unwin, 1918), 6. Goldring wrote from London in 1922 about Joyce in the Russian journal *Sovremennyi Zapad* (The Contemporary West), having already introduced *Ulysses* to Spanish readers in 1921: Emily Tall, "The Reception of James Joyce in Russia," in *The Reception of James Joyce in Europe*, ed. Geert Lernout and Wim Van Mierlo (London: Thoemmes Continuum, 2004), 244.

23. Shane Leslie, *Long Shadows: Memoirs of Shane Leslie* (London: John Murray, 1966), 187. For all the perceived compromises of the Anglo-Irish Treaty in December 1921, it succeeded in mitigating the force of the term "empire" by introducing the first official usage of the more loosely knit term "British Commonwealth of Nations."

24. Seamus Deane, "Introduction" to *P*, viii.

25. Nicholas Allen, *Modernism, Ireland, and Civil War* (Cambridge: Cambridge University Press, 2009), 3.

26. Georg Lukacs, *The Evolution of Modern Drama* (1909), cited in Terry Eagleton, *Marxism and Literary Criticism* (Methuen: London, 1976), 20; Adorno, *Aesthetic Theory*, esp. 202–33.

27. John Eglinton, "The Beginnings of Joyce," in *Irish Literary Portraits* (London: Macmillan, 1935), 133. Notwithstanding the demise of the visionary turn in the conservative new Irish state, Eglinton continued: "There was a moment nevertheless when it seemed possible that this might be the turn events would take" (134).

28. Adorno, *Aesthetic Theory*, 135. An artwork's refusal to be constrained by the present offers, in effect, a promissory note to the future: "By their negation [of the existent], even as total negation, artworks make a promise, just as the gesture with which narratives once began or the initial sound struck on a sitar promised what was yet to be heard, yet to be seen" (134).

29. Marc Bloch, *The Historian's Craft* (1949/53), 63–64, cited in Carlo Ginzburg, *Threads and Traces: True False Fictive*, trans. Anne C. Tedeschi and John Tedeschi (Berkeley: University of California Press, 2012), 3.

30. Aesthetic value is not the sole issue here, as underlying narrative or rhetorical tropes in documents invite interpretative skills and attention to nuances associated with criticism.

31. Síobhra Aiken notes how "modernist techniques are evident in a number of narratives that address the complexities of the revolutionary period—such as writings by Dorothy Macardle, Frank Gallagher, Ernie O'Malley, Elizabeth Bowen and . . . Francis Stuart," and rightly questions whether this should be seen as eschewing "narrative possibility" altogether. Síobhra Aiken, *Spiritual Wounds: Trauma, Testimony and the Irish Civil War* (Newbridge: Irish Academic Press, 2022), 28. As Joyce's reworking of Lessing's *Laocoön* (1766) indicates (see 240n45, below), and the analysis of Joseph Frank below suggests (78–79), one of the distinctive aspects of Irish modernism is the retention of time and narrative in the face of fragmentation, imagism, and spatial form.

32. Cited in Georges Didi-Huberman, *The Surviving Image: Phantoms of Time and Time of Phantoms: Aby Warburg's History of Art*, trans. Harvey L. Mendelson (University Park: University of Pennsylvania Press, 2017), 258.

33. Aby Warburg, "Dürer and Italian Antiquity" (1905), in *Renewal of Pagan Antiquity* (1932), trans. David Britt (Los Angeles: Getty Research Institute, 1999), 558. For a succinct account, see Georges Didi-Huberman, "Field and Vehicle of the Surviving Movement: The *Pathosformel*," in *The Surviving Image*, 115–25.

34. Aby Warburg, "Sandro Botticelli's *Birth of Venus* and *Spring*" (1893), in *Renewal of Pagan Antiquity*, 89–156.

35. Carlo Ginzburg, *The Cheese and the Worms: The Cosmos of a Sixteenth-Century Miller*, trans. Anne C. Tedeschi and John Tedeschi (Baltimore: Johns Hopkins University Press, 1980). In Joyce's writing, clashes between Catholicism, classical antiquity, and Irish vernacular culture are cross-cut by the even more profane forces of empire and modernity.

36. Didi-Huberman, *The Surviving Image*, 128. For Warburg, the danger and shape of snakes symbolized lightning, a view reinforced by his attendance at snake rituals among Hopi Indians bound up with controlling weather in its most fearful manifestations, such as lightning—not to mention forces of inner life. See David Freedberg, "Pathos at Oraibi: What Warburg Did Not See," https://arthistory.columbia.edu/sites/default/files/content/faculty/pdfs/freedberg/Pathos-at-Oraibi.pdf.

37. Cited in Ernst H. Gombrich, *Aby Warburg: An Intellectual Biography* (London: Warburg Institute, 1970), 248.

38. For a recent view of aesthetic form as charging texts with (counter-)currents that resist stasis, preventing unity and closure, see Susan J. Wolfson, *Formal Charges: The Shaping of Poetry in British Romanticism* (Stanford, CA: Stanford University Press, 1997), 230–31.

39. Didi-Huberman, *The Surviving Image*, 154.

40. Didi-Huberman, 178.

41. Cited in Bartholomew Ryan, "Mythologising the Exiled Self in James Joyce and Fernando Pessoa," *Pessoa Plural* 4 (Fall 2013): 79.

42. James Joyce, "James Clarence Mangan" (1907), in *OCPW*, 127.

43. The allusion in *Finnegans Wake* to shell shock/trauma occurs in the context of a passage relating to the Croke Park Bloody Sunday shootings (November 1920), Robert Emmet's execution, and the Royal Irish Artillery. For an insightful reading of associations with lightning, see Finn Fordham, "Lightning Becomes Electra: Violence, Inspiration, and Lucia Joyce in *Finnegans Wake*," *James Joyce Quarterly* 50, nos. 1/2 (Fall 2012–Winter 2013): 335–57. Henceforth references to journal are *JJQ* in the text and notes.

44. William James first introduced the term in *The Principles of Psychology*, vol. 1 (New York: Henry Holt, 1890), esp. 224–91.

45. Joseph Warren Beach, *The Twentieth Century Novel: Studies in Technique* (New York: Century, 1932), 529, cited in Franco Moretti, *Modern Epic: The World System from Goethe to Garcia Márquez*, trans. Quentin Hoare (London: Verso, 1996), 171.

46. Stephen Greenblatt, *Will in the World: How Shakespeare Became Shakespeare* (London: Jonathan Cape, 2004), 302, citing *Julius Caesar*, 2.1.68–69.

47. Saint-Amour, "Rising Timely and Untimely," 38.

48. Mary Colum, *From These Roots: The Ideas That Have Made Modern Literature* (London: Jonathan Cape, 1938), 317.

49. Umberto Eco, *The Middle Ages of James Joyce*, trans. Ellen Esrock (London: Hutchinson Radius, 1989), 42.

50. Woodward, "Douglas Goldring," 204. In T.S. Eliot's review, Goldring is considered to have written "unquestionably a brilliant novel," and the second half is singled out for special praise: *The Egoist* 5 (January 1918): 10.

51. Though often attributed to Mies van der Rohe, it sums up Warburg's approach, cited in Didi-Huberman, *The Surviving Image*, 351n305; see also Carlo Ginzburg, "Clues: Roots of an Evidential Paradigm," in *Myth, Clues, Emblems*, trans. John Tedeschi and Anne C. Tedeschi (London: Radius, 1990), 96.

52. Identified primarily as a female malady, under Freud's and Breuer's influence hysteria presented itself as a portal of the unconscious, before it eventually diversified into conditions associated with trauma, depression, and other disorders.

53. Sigmund Freud, "Totem and Taboo" (1912–13), trans. James Strachey, in *The Origins of Religion: The Pelican Freud Library*, vol. 13 (Harmondsworth, UK: Pen-

guin, 1985), 130. For Freud's contemporary, the psychologist Kurt Goldstein (in Oliver Sacks's summary), "Symptoms are not isolated expressions of local damage but attempted solutions of healing." Oliver Sacks, foreword to *The Organism*, by Kurt Goldstein (New York: Zone Books, 1995), 14.

54. Didi-Huberman, *The Surviving Image*, 180.

55. J. F. Byrne, cited in Patricia Hutchins, *James Joyce's World* (London: Methuen, 1957), 53. For a fuller account, see J. B. Lyons, "George Sigerson: Charcot's Translator," *Journal of the History of the Neurosciences* 6, no. 1 (April 1997): 50–60.

56. J.-M. Charcot, *Lectures on the Diseases of the Nervous System*, vols. I–II, trans. George Sigerson (London: New Sydenham Society, 1877, 1881). According to Lyons, Sigerson published six important neurological papers apart from his translations of Charcot, the first of which appeared in the French journal *Le Progrès médical*, closely associated with Charcot's institution, the Salpêtrière. Lyons, "George Sigerson," 54.

57. This was during a visit to attend the annual meeting of the British Medical Association in Cork in 1879. Lyons, "George Sigerson," 53.

58. Speech given on the occasion of his being made an honorary Fellow of the Royal College of Physicians of Ireland in 1918: *Irish Times*, March 16, 1918, cited in Lyons, 59. Gladstone's reading in proof stage of Sigerson's *History of Irish Land Tenure* (1871) influenced the passing of the first Irish Land Act (1870).

59. See Norbert Elias, *The Civilizing Process* (1939), rev. ed. (Oxford: Blackwell, 2000); and Mikhail Bakhtin, *Rabelais and His World* (Cambridge, MA: MIT Press 1968).

60. W. E. H. Lecky, *Ireland in the Eighteenth Century* (1892), vol. 1 (London: Longmans, 1913), 407–8.

61. Lecky's book went into eighteen editions and was translated into several languages: Donal McCartney, *W. E. H. Lecky: Historian and Politician, 1838–1903* (Dublin: Lilliput Press, 1994), 34. The discussions of modernity and tradition in *Stephen Hero* bear the hallmarks of Lecky, as Stephen comes across Moynihan in the National Library, preparing for his inaugural address at the Literary and Historical Society, with "some bulky volumes of Lecky by his side." James Joyce, *Stephen Hero* (1907), ed. Theodore Spencer (London: Paladin, 1991), 154. Henceforth *SH*, followed by page numbers in text and notes.

62. William McGrath, *Freud's Discovery of Psychoanalysis: The Politics of Hysteria* (Ithaca, NY: Cornell University Press, 1986), 79.

63. Peter Stallybrass and Allon White, *The Politics and Poetics of Transgression* (London: Methuen, 1986), 182.

64. Stallybrass and White, 193.

65. Georges Didi-Huberman, "Artistic Survival: Panofsky vs. Warburg and the Exorcism of Impure Time," *Common Knowledge* 6, no. 2 (Spring 2003): 276.

66. Giorgio Agamben, "Aby Warburg and the Nameless Science" (1975), in *Potentialities: Collected Essays in Philosophy*, trans. Daniel Heller-Roazen (Stanford, CA: Stanford University Press, 1999), 93.

67. Didi-Huberman, "Artistic Survival," 275.

68. Georges Didi-Huberman, *The Eye of History: When Images Take Positions*, trans. Shane B. Lillis (Cambridge, MA: MIT Press, 2018).

69. Hayden White, "The Burden of History," *History and Theory* 5, no. 2 (1966): 127, 111–13.

70. Seamus Deane, *Celtic Revivals: Essays in Modern Literature* (London: Faber and Faber, 1985), 130.

71. *BSW*, 2:301. Ironically, Benjamin here sees Joyce in apolitical terms of restricted interior monologue as opposed to Dadaist determinations to disrupt daily life, notwithstanding the fact that Joyce drew much more public opprobrium and political censorship than his Dada contemporaries.

72. David Carr, *Time, Narrative, and History* (Bloomington: Indiana University Press, 1991), 70. Conceptions of life in narrative terms is central to the work of many contemporary philosophers, among them Hannah Arendt, Julia Kristeva, Paul Ricouer, Alasdair MacIntyre, Charles Taylor, Richard Rorty, and Martha Nussbaum: see Hanna Meretoja, "Narrative and Human Existence: Ontology, Epistemology, and Ethics," *New Literary History* 45, no. 1 (Winter 2014): 89–109.

73. Josef Breuer and Sigmund Freud, *Studies on Hysteria* (1895), trans. James Strachey (New York: Basic Books, 1957), 160.

74. As Gordon Graham writes, "Once attention has been drawn to considerations of relevance and purpose as well as truth and accuracy, we have also admitted a space for the structure of narrative." Gordon Graham, *The Shape of the Past: A Philosophical Approach to History* (Oxford: Oxford University Press, 1997), 23; see also 158–65.

75. Carr, *Time, Narrative, and History*, 76.

76. J. M. Synge, "The Playboy of the Western World" (1907), in *Four Plays and The Aran Islands*, ed. Robin Skelton (London: Oxford University Press, 1967), 145.

77. Bloch, *Historian's Craft*, 63–64, cited in Ginzburg, *Threads and Traces*, 3.

78. Ginzburg, *Threads and Traces*, 3.

79. Joyce aligned himself with socialism in his early Italian years, and though the Labour movement is absent by comparison with nationalist politics in *Ulysses*, Connolly's Irish Socialist Party features in "A Painful Case," and a Connolly-type figure contests the municipal elections in "Ivy Day in the Committee Room," in *Dubliners*.

80. Emer Nolan, *James Joyce and Nationalism* (London: Routledge, 1995), 134.

81. As Peter Burke notes in a related context, the "high proportion of public themes, whether religious or political," in dreams in the early modern period is echoed in the social cast of German dreams in the Nazi era but not in the personal dreams of Americans, even "at the very time when the atom bomb was dropped on Japan." Peter Burke, "The Cultural History of Dreams," in *Varieties of Cultural History* (Cambridge: Polity Press, 1997), 42, 34.

82. Apart from Freud's analyses of group psychology, and works such as *The Future of an Illusion* (1927) and *Civilization and Its Discontents* (1930), Karl Jaspers's *General Psychopathology* (1913), Harold Lasswell's *Psychopathology and Politics* (1930), Wilhelm Reich's *The Mass Psychology of Fascism*, and work by the Frankfurt school represented different aspects of this trend.

83. Daniel Bensaïd, *Marx for Our Times: Adventures and Misadventures of a Critique*, trans. Gregory Elliott (London: Verso, 2002), 112.

84. Daniel Bensaïd, *Le pari mélancolique* (Paris: Fayard, 1997), 294–97, cited in Michael Löwy, foreword to *The Hidden God: A Study of Tragic Vision in the Pensées of Pascal and the Tragedies of Racine* (1964), by Lucien Goldmann (London: Verso, 2016), xxiv.

85. Walter Benjamin, "The Crisis of the Novel" (1930), in *BSW*, 2:300–301.

86. M. M. Bakhtin, "Forms of Time and the Chronotope of the Novel," in *The Dialogical Imagination: Four Essays*, ed. Michael Holquist, trans. Caryl Emerson and Mi-

chael Holquist (Austin: University of Texas Press, 1981), 243, 255. Bakhtin expands on this: through literary form "graphically visible markers of historical time are concentrated and condensed ... fused into unity markers of the epoch. The epoch become not only graphically visible [space], but narratively visible [time]" (247).

87. See Luke Gibbons, "'Spaces of Time through Times of Space': Haunting the 'Wandering Rocks,'" in *Joyce's Ghosts: Joyce, Modernism, and Memory* (Chicago: University of Chicago Press, 2015), 165–87.

88. Camille Bourniquel, *Ireland*, trans. John Fisher (London: Vista Books, 1960), 99.

89. Dorothy Macardle, "The City," in *Nineteen-Sixteen: An Anthology*, compiled by Edna C. Fitzhenry (Dublin: Browne and Nolan, 1966), 16.

90. Walter Benjamin, "On the Concept of History" (1940), in *BSW*, 4:295–97; Benjamin, "Little History of Photography" (1931), in *BSW*, 2:510.

91. The item is picked up again in the high parody of "Ithaca," where the throwaway handout appears as the tablets given to Moses, bearing "the secret of the race [i.e., Israelites as well as the Gold Cup], graven in the language of prediction" (*U*, 17.340–41).

92. Shiv Kumar, *Bergson and the Stream of Consciousness Novel* (New York: New York University Press, 1963), 143.

93. James Joyce to Grant Richards, May 5, 1906, in *James Joyce: Letters*, vol. 2, ed. Richard Ellmann (New York: Viking Press, 1966), 134. Henceforth *JJL*, followed by volume and page numbers in the notes.

94. Roger Casement to Alice Stopford Green, April 20, 1907, cited in *The Amazon Journal of Roger Casement*, ed. Angus Mitchell (Dublin: Lilliput Press, 1997), 280; emphasis added. It is possible to see in this the moral equivalent of what Freud termed *Nachträglichkeit* (belatedness), the reconstitution of one's own past in the light of the present, which is discussed below in chapter 5.

95. Allessandro Ferrara, *The Force of an Example: Explorations in the Paradigm of Judgment* (New York: Columbia University Press, 2008), 129.

96. Ariela Freedman, "Global Joyce," *Literature Compass* 7, no. 9 (2010): 799.

97. Ernst Bloch, "Upper Middle Classes, Objectivity and Montage," in *Heritage of Our Times* (1935), trans. Neville and Stephen Plaice (Cambridge: Polity Press, 1991), 205. Henceforth *HT*, followed by page numbers in the notes.

98. Ernst Bloch, "Spoken and Written Syntax: Anacoluthon," in *Literary Essays*, trans. Andrew Joron et al. (Stanford, CA: Stanford University Press, 1998), 504.

99. Bloch, *Literary Essays*, 104.

100. James Joyce, *Exiles* (1918), introduction by Padraic Colum (London: Four Square, 1962), 129. With withering irony, Joyce wrote in his notes on the play: "Why the title *Exiles*? A nation exacts a penance from those who dared to leave her payable on their return" ("Notes by the Author," 150).

Chapter One

1. Eimar O'Duffy, "'Ulysses,' by James Joyce," *Irish Review* 1, no. 4 (December 9, 1922): 13, reprinted in the *Journal of Irish Literature* 7, no. 1 (January 1978): 12–14.

2. Mary Colum, *Life and the Dream* (New York: Doubleday, 1947), 386.

3. Padraic Colum and Mary Colum, *Our Friend James Joyce* (New York: Doubleday Dolphin, 1958), 111.

4. Colum and Colum, 111.

5. James Joyce to T. W. Pugh, August 6, 1934, *JJL*, 3:314.

6. *The James Joyce/Paul Leon Papers*, ed. Catherine Fahy (Dublin: National Library of Ireland, 1992), 115. Unfortunately, it seems only one of the photographs have survived (241). See also letter from James Joyce to T. W. Pugh, September 22, 1934, *JJL*, 3:326.

7. James Joyce to George (Giorgio) Joyce, August 13, 1934, *JJL*, 3:318–19. Though clearly designed for promotional use, Joyce's eagerness for depicting authentic locations in *Ulysses* is evident. Requests for "photographs of the country," and magazines and books from Ireland, featured regularly in his correspondence with his brother Stanislaus and aunt Josephine: Richard Ellmann, *James Joyce* (Oxford: Oxford University Press, 1982), 236. Henceforth *JJ*, followed by page numbers in text and notes.

8. James Joyce to T. W. Pugh, August 6, 1934, *JJL*, 3:314. It is worth noting that Joyce considers the human figure capable of possessing an Irish countenance.

9. The *Evening Telegraph* cuttings Pugh sent to Joyce are in the [Herbert] Gorman Papers, The Harley K. Croessmann Collection, Southern Illinois University, Carbondale, Illinois, USA.

10. James Joyce, *Ulysses*, illustrated and signed by Henri Matisse (New York: Limited Editions Club, 1934).

11. Herbert Gorman, *James Joyce: A Definitive Biography* (London: John Lane, The Bodley Head, 1941), 348. Richard Ellmann wrote back to Pugh, "thanking him for the explanations supplied and in some cases confirming Pugh's suggestions": Catalogue, Mealy's Rare Book Sale, December 4, 2018. Joyce's letters to Pugh were auctioned at this sale.

12. In his textual wanderings in *Stephen Hero* through city streets, Stephen "read all the street-ballads which were stuck in the dusty windows of the Liberties. He read the racing names and prices scrawled in blue pencil outside the dingy tobaccoshops, the windows which were adorned with scarlet police journals. He examined all the book-stalls which offered old directories and volumes of sermons and unheard-of treatises..." (*SH*, 150).

13. Vincent Byrne, *Bureau of Military History*, Witness Statement No. 425, 3. Henceforth *BMH*, followed by witness statement and page number in text.

14. Seamus de Burca, *The Soldier's Song: The Story of Peadar O Cearnaigh* (Dublin: P. J. Bourke, 1957), 224. De Burca's biography of O Cearnaigh is dedicated to Thomas W. Pugh. The Pugh glassworks closed in 1890: see Mary Boydell, "The Pugh Glasshouse in Dublin," in *The Glass Circle* 2 (1975): 37–41.

15. Peter Francis, "Franz Tieze (1842–1932) and the Reinvention of History on Glass," *Burlington Magazine* 136, no. 1094 (May 1994): 291.

16. Seamus de Burca, "Obituary: Thomas W. Pugh," *Irish Times*, November 29, 1968; "Thomas W. Pugh," trans. Tim Quinlan, in A. P. Caomhánach, *Iris Cuimhneacháin: 1916–1966/Commemoration Journal: 1916–1966* (Dublin: St Joseph's, Fairview, 1966/2016), 31–32.

17. Peadar O Cearnaigh, "A Personal Narrative of Easter Week," in de Burca, *Soldier's Song*, 119.

18. Thomas Pugh, *BMH*, no. 397, 2; "Thomas W. Pugh," in Caomhánach, *Commemorative Journal: 1916–1966*, 32. Before the Easter Rising, Pugh worked in the Post Office Engineering Department in which Mulcahy was also employed.

19. Pugh, *BMH*, no. 397, 3.

20. De Burca, *Soldier's Song*, 114.
21. See chapter 2, 45.
22. Seosamh de Brún, *BMH*, no. 312, 9.
23. Pugh, *BMH*, no. 397, 8.
24. Thomas Leahy, *BMH*, no. 660, 20.
25. Seán O'Mahoney, *Frongoch: University of Revolution* (Dublin: FDR Teoranta, 1987), 106.
26. Cited in account of Pugh's autograph book by Kevin Markey, "In Frongoch," in Caomhánach, *Commemorative Journal: 1916–1966*, 48.
27. As Pugh wrote to the Military Pensions Board: "I was 'well got' as the saying is with the general body." "Subject Information," Thomas Pugh, File no. MSP34REF17155, Military Service Pensions Collection; Statement, "Thomas W. Pugh (17155)," Grade I, 13th December 1937.
28. De Burca, *Soldier's Song*, 26.
29. De Burca, 226.
30. Seamus Heaney, "Gravities," in *Death of a Naturalist* (London: Faber and Faber, 1966), 43.
31. Kenneth Reddin, "Obituary: James Joyce," *Irish Times*, January 14, 1941, reprinted in *A Bash in the Tunnel: James Joyce by the Irish*, ed. John Ryan (Brighton, UK: Clifton Books, 1970), 246.
32. "William G. Fallon," in *The Joyce We Knew: Memoirs of Joyce*, ed. Ulick O'Connor (Dingle: Brandon, 2004), 53–54, 49.
33. Graham Smith, *Light That Dances in the Mind: Photographs and Memory in the Writings of E. M. Forster and His Contemporaries* (Oxford: Peter Lang, 2007), 155.
34. For the classic account, see Roger Brown and James Kulik, "Flashbulb Memories," *Cognition* 5 (1977): 73–99. See also *Flashbulb Memories*, ed. Martin Conway (Hove, UK: Lawrence Elbaum Associates, 1995); and Charles Fernyhough, *Pieces of Light: The New Science of Memory* (London: Profile, 2012), 202–5, 249–53.
35. John S. Rickard, *Joyce's Book of Memory: The Mnemotechnic of "Ulysses"* (Durham, NC: Duke University Press, 1999), 1.
36. Quintilian, *Institutio Oratoria*, xi, ii, 17–122, cited in Francis A. Yates, *The Art of Memory* (1966; repr., London: Pimlico, 1992), 38.
37. Anne Whitehead, *Memory* (London: Routledge, 2009), 31; Carle Bonafous-Murat, "Disposition and Pre-Disposition: The Art of Involuntary Memory," in *Classic Joyce*, Joyce Studies in Italy, 6, ed. Franca Ruggieri (Roma: Bulzoni Editore, 1999), 357; Jacques Mailhos, "The Art of Memory: Joyce and Perec," in *Transcultural Joyce*, ed. Karen E. Lawrence (Cambridge: Cambridge University Press, 1998), 152.
38. Fredric Jameson, "'Ulysses' in History," in *James Joyce and Modern Literature*, ed. W. J. McCormack and Alister Stead (London: Routledge & Kegan Paul, 1982), 137.
39. Daniel Ferrer, "*Loci Memoriae*: Joyce and the Art of Memory," in *Classic Joyce*, 357; emphasis added.
40. Wendy Steiner, *Pictures of Romance: Form against Context in Painting and Literature* (Chicago: University of Chicago Press, 1988), 129.
41. James Joyce, "The Sisters," in *Dubliners* (1914), introduction by Terence Brown (London: Penguin, 1992), 4. Henceforth *D*, followed by page numbers in text.
42. Joseph Prescott, "Stylistic Realism in Joyce's *Ulysses*," in *A James Joyce Miscellany*, ed. Marvin Magalaner (Carbondale: Southern Illinois University Press, 1959),

22. Prescott notes how, in drafts of the opening chapter in *Ulysses*, the view of a calm Dublin Bay from the Martello Tower is changed to include a "smokeplume," and then the source of the smoke is added: "of the mailboat" (52).

43. For Warburg, see 234n36, above.

44. Georgina Binnie, "'Photo girl he calls her': Re-reading Milly in *Ulysses*," *Journal of Modern Literature* 42, no. 4 (Summer 2019): 49.

45. *Stephen Hero* relates of Stephen that "the treatises which were recommended to him he found valueless or trifling; the Laocoon of Lessing irritated him" (*SH*, 38), and in *Portrait* Stephen's criticism is that Lessing confined himself to writing of statues (*P*, 211).

46. James Joyce, "Paris Notebook" (1903), in *The Critical Writings of James Joyce*, ed. Ellsworth Mason and Richard Ellmann (London: Faber and Faber, 1959), 145. Stephen in *Portrait* explains how Aristotle and Aquinas extol stasis, but this is "a stasis called forth, prolonged, and at last dissolved by what I call the rhythm of beauty"—rhythm forming the "first formal esthetic relation of part to part in any esthetic whole" (*P*, 223).

47. As Christa-Maria Lerm Hayes notes, Joyce was among the first to grasp the innovative nature of Alexander Calder's "mobiles," sending his daughter Lucia to be taught by him. Christa-Maria Lerm Hayes, *Joyce in Art* (Dublin: Lilliput Press, 2004), 19–20.

48. Henri Bergson, *Matter and Memory* (1896), trans. N. M. Paul and W. S. Palmer (New York: Zone Books, 1991), 86–87.

49. Henri Bergson, *Creative Evolution*, trans. Arthur Marshall (Mineola, NY: Dover, 1998), 4, cited in Cleo Hanaway-Oakley, *James Joyce and the Phenomenology of Film* (Oxford: Oxford University Press, 2017), 36. For Harry Levin, "Bloom's mind is neither a *tabula rasa* nor a photographic plate, but a motion picture, which has been ingeniously cut and carefully edited to emphasize the close-ups and fade-outs of flickering emotion, the angles of observation and the flashbacks of reminiscence." Harry Levin, *James Joyce: A Critical Introduction* (1941; repr., London: Faber and Faber, 1960), 82.

50. Bergson, *Matter and Memory*, 138. See treatments of time by photographer Uta Barth in *The Long Now*, texts by Jonathan Crary, Russell Ferguson, Holly Myers et al. (New York: Gregory R. Miller and Co., 2010).

51. Geoffrey Batchen, *Forget Me Not: Photography and Remembrance* (New York: Van Gogh Museum/Princeton Architectural Press, 2004), 16.

52. Mailhos, "The Art of Memory," 152; emphasis added.

53. George Morrison, *An Irish Camera* (London: Pan Books, 1979), 8–9.

54. Damien Sutton, *Photography, Cinema, Memory: The Crystal Image of Time* (Minneapolis: University of Minnesota Press, 2009), 88. Sutton is recalling Walter Benjamin's classic account of Atget in "Little History of Photography," *BSW*, 2: 518–29.

55. Hayden White, "Truth and Circumstance: What (If Anything) Can Be Properly Said about the Holocaust," in *The Holocaust and Historical Methodology*, ed. Dan Stone (New York: Berghahn, 2012), 197–98.

56. For an extended survey of the Irish reception of *Ulysses*, see John McCourt, *Consuming Joyce: 100 Years of "Ulysses" in Ireland* (London: Bloomsbury, 2022).

57. John Nash, *James Joyce and the Act of Reception: Reading, Ireland, Modernism* (Cambridge: Cambridge University Press, 2006) 101; Peter Costello, "James Joyce and the Remaking of Modern Ireland," *Studies* 93, no. 370 (2004): 125. Bulmer Hob-

son, a leading republican who opposed the Easter Rising, purchased a copy from O'Hegarty's bookshop: McCourt, *Consuming Joyce*, 44.

58. Joyce, however, turned down invitations from both FitzGerald and Yeats to give his stamp of approval to the Free State (see 41).

59. O'Duffy, "'Ulysses,' by James Joyce," 12–13; [P. S. O'Hegarty], "Mr Joyce's *Ulysses*," *The Separatist*, September 2, 1922; Lawrence K. Emery [A.J. Rosenthal], "The Ulysses of Mr. James Joyce," *Klaxon* (Winter 1923–24): 14–20; Domini Canini [Shane Leslie], "*Ulysses*," *Dublin Review*, clxxi (September 1922): 112–19; C. C. Martindale, S.J., "*Ulysses*," *Dublin Review*, clxxi (September 1922): 273–76.

60. Nash, *Act of Reception*, 146; Costello, "James Joyce and the Remaking of Modern Ireland," 124.

61. James Joyce to Carlo Linati, September 21, 1920, *JJL*, 1:146.

62. C. S. Andrews, *Man of No Property* (Dublin: Mercier Press, 1982), 18–19.

63. Andrews, 18.

64. Born in 1889 at Lisnamaghery in the Clogher Valley, Co. Tyrone, Walsh graduated from St Mary's University College in Dublin (later incorporated into University College) with a degree in languages (Irish, French, German, and English). She joined Cumann na mBan, perhaps under the influence of Louise Gavan Duffy, and acted as a contact for prisoners from the Easter Rising interned in Reading Jail while based in London in 1916: Cathal O'Shannon, "Homecoming for Christmas—1916," *Irish Times*, December 24, 1949.

65. J. Bowyer Bell, *The Secret Army: The IRA* (Piscataway, NJ: Transaction Books, 1997), 81.

66. "The Library Conference: A Confusion of Ideals: 'Nationalism' or Culture?" *Irish Times*, June 6, 1936.

67. "'Irish Language Will Not Survive': Defence of Anglo-Irish Writers," *Irish Times*, December 13, 1940. For more on Walsh, see Kate O'Malley, "Róisín Walsh's Report of a Visit to American Libraries, Universities and Other Institutions 1939," *Analecta Hibernica* 44 (2013): 121–243.

68. Uinseann MacEoin, *Survivors*, 2nd ed. (Dublin: Argenta, 1987), 302; Ernie O'Malley, *The Singing Flame* (Dublin: Anvil, 1977), 172.

69. C. S. Andrews, *Dublin Made Me* (Dublin: Mercier Press, 1979), 216.

70. Andrews, 260. Andrews further remarks: "It was the first indication I had of Lemass's contempt for what he regarded as intellectuals." Robert Brennan (1881–1964), a leading republican activist, journalist, and future Irish ambassador to the United States, had met Joyce in the National Library years earlier and, visiting the nearly blind Joyce in later years in Paris, noted, "We talked of Dublin and it was rather pathetic to see how eager he was for details of his old friends." Robert Brennan, *Allegiance* (Dublin: Browne and Nolan, 1950), 17–18.

71. Andrews, *Dublin Made Me* 258; "Seán Dowling of Dublin: Surviving Staff Cmmdt I.R.A.," in MacEoin, *Survivors*, 193.

72. Samuel Beckett to Thomas MacGreevy, June 9, 1936, in *The Letters of Samuel Beckett, 1929–1940*, ed. Martha Dow Fehsenfeld and Lois More Overbeck, vol. 1 (Cambridge: Cambridge University Press, 2009), 342. Beckett refers contemptuously to Seán Ó Faoláin and Dowling as writing for "*Ireland Today*, the latest rag."

73. "Seán Dowling," in MacEoin, *Survivors*, 412. Dowling fought alongside Cathal Brugha, Todd Andrews, Mary MacSwiney, and Linda Kearns in the Tramway office near Nelson's Pillar in the Civil War.

74. Dennis Flynn, "Introduction," in Farrell, *On Irish Themes*, 21.

75. Fritz Senn, *Joycean Murmoirs: Fritz Senn on James Joyce*, ed. Christine O'Neill (Dublin: Lilliput Press, 2007), 37. Gerry O'Flaherty has recounted how a copy of *Ulysses* circulated among republican prisoners in Kilmainham Jail: "Living with Ulysses: Under Plain Cover," *Irish Independent*, James Joyce Centenary Supplement, February 2, 1982, cited in McCourt, *Consuming Joyce*, 22.

76. Mrs. McCarvill (Eileen McGrane), *BMH*, no. 1752, 1. See also Eileen MacCarvill, "Thomas MacDonagh," *National Student*, May 1936. Eileen MacCarvill's name (as she wrote it) is spelled variously as "Mc" or as "Carville," and is printed as it is presented in a particular document referring to her, rather than adding "[sic]" on each occasion.

77. "Women in Intelligence—Part 2: Eileen MacCarvill née McGrane," Military Service (1916–1923) Pensions Collection, https://militarypensions.wordpress.com/2018/06/29/women-in-intelligence-part-2-eileen-maccarvill-nee-mcgrane/; Marika MacCarvill, "The Story of Captain Eileen McGrane, Michael Collins's Right Hand Woman," RTÉ, August 21, 2020, https://www.rte.ie/history/the-ban/2020/0513/1138205-most-effective-women-the-story-of-eileen-mcgrane/.

78. Maine Jellett, *The Artist's Vision: Lectures and Essays on Art*, ed. with a foreword by Eileen MacCarvill and introduction by Albert Gleizes (Dundalk: Dundalgan Press, 1958), 90, 99–101.

79. The material is now in the Zurich James Joyce Foundation archive, whose founder and leading Joycean scholar, Fritz Senn, befriended MacCarvill in the 1960s. Patricia Hutchins's *James Joyce's Dublin* (London: Grey Walls Press, 1950), and *James Joyce's World* (London: Methuen, 1957), were among the first full-length Irish critical works, and the new generation of Joyce enthusiasts and experts, mainly Dublin based, included Brian O'Nolan, Niall Montgomery, Niall Sheridan, John Garvin, Gerry O'Flaherty, Arland Usher, Roger McHugh, and later, Vivian Igoe, Maurice Harmon, David Norris, and Peter Costello, among others. The literary magazine *Envoy*, James Joyce Special Number, vol. 5, no. 17 (April 1951), was notable for its disparagement of the then-expanding body of scholarship on Joyce, largely perceived as American: see Bruce Stewart, "Another Bash in the Tunnel: James Joyce and the *Envoy*," *Studies* 93, no. 370 (Summer 2004): 133–45.

80. William Brockman, "Learning to Be Joyce's Contemporary? Richard Ellmann's Discovery and Transformation of Joyce's Letters and Manuscripts," Special issue: Joyce and the Joyceans, *Journal of Modern Literature* 22, no. 2 (Winter 1998/99): 257. As Brockman relates, "MacCarvill attempted to assert primacy, noting her permission to publish from the Joyce estate, and offered in a conciliatory way to change the book's title and to eliminate over a dozen items to avoid competition with Ellmann's and Mason's book. But Ellmann prevailed, and her collection was never published." Ellsworth Mason's and Richard Ellmann's edition of *The Critical Writings of James Joyce* was published by Viking Press, New York, and Faber and Faber, London, in 1959.

81. "Similar Themes in Joyce and Mangan," *Irish Times*, August 27, 1968; "Place as Source and Aid to Joyce," *Irish Times*, August 28, 1968; "Joyce's References to the Liffey Explained," *Irish Times*, August 29, 1968.

82. See John MacCourt, "Reading Alternative Irelands Through Joyce's *Ulysses* in the 1920s," *JJQ* 56, nos. 1–2 (Winter 2019): 99–113.

83. [O'Hegarty], "Mr Joyce's *Ulysses*," 4.

84. O'Duffy, "'Ulysses,' by James Joyce," 13.

85. [O'Hegarty], "Mr Joyce's *Ulysses*," 4.

86. It later transpired that the nomination was blocked by a less sympathetic government minister, Richard Mulcahy: *Niall Montgomery Dublinman: Selected Writings*, ed. Christine O'Neill (Dublin: Ashfield Press, 2015), 53.

87. James Joyce to Stanislaus Joyce, March 20, 1922, in *JJL*, 3:61.

88. Ezra Pound to Homer Pound (his father), March 21, 1921, in *Ezra Pound to His Parents: Letters 1895–1929*, ed. Mary de Rachewiltz, A. David Moody, and Joanna Moody (New York: Oxford University Press, 2011), 481.

89. C. S. Andrews remarked of the prison camp at the Curragh in which he was interned in 1921: "I was more than amused to see the supercilious Desmond Fitzgerald walking around the compound in deep conversation" with Captain Keating, whom the British had appointed liaison officer with the prisoners. Andrews, *Dublin Made Me*, 177.

90. Ezra Pound to Homer Pound, January 17, 1926, in *Ezra Pound to His Parents*, 586.

91. Ezra Pound to James Joyce, December 21, 1931, in *JJL*, 3:237. The two final verses are even more mocking in tone, beginning: "'We must prothect out virchoos,' / Lowsy Esmong says to me, / 'And be chaste, begob, and holy / As our Lord was wont to be.'" For Pound's extended if uneasy friendship with FitzGerald, see Mary FitzGerald, "Ezra Pound and Irish Politics: An Unpublished Correspondence," *Paideuma: Modern and Contemporary Poetry and Poetics* 12, nos. 2/3 (Fall & Winter 1983): 377–417.

92. Nash, *Act of Reception*, 147–48.

93. Nash, 143.

94. Alluding to the passage in *Portrait* in which "the dim fabric of the city lay prone in haze. Like a scene on some vague arras, old as man's weariness, the image of the seventh city of christendom was visible to him across the timeless air, no older nor more weary nor less patient of subjection than in the days of the thingmote" (*P*, 181).

95. John Bishop, *Joyce's Book of the Dark: Finnegans Wake* (Madison: University of Wisconsin Press, 1986), 58.

96. This is accompanied on the page by a marginal gloss on a crude slogan alluding to Michael Collins's replacement, following his assassination, by Richard Mulcahy as the leader of anti-Treaty forces, "Move up, Mick, make way for Dick!": "Move up, Mackinerny! Make room for Muckinurney!" (*FW*, 264.2–5).

97. "William G. Fallon," in *The Joyce We Knew*, ed. O'Connor, 53.

98. Ulick O'Connor, introduction to *The Joyce We Knew*, 15.

99. *Sunday Press*, April 14, 1963.

Chapter Two

1. Shane Leslie, *The Celt and His World: A Study of the Relation of the Celt and the Teuton in History* (New York: Scribner's, 1917), 80.

2. Christopher Ricks, *Keats and Embarrassment* (Oxford: Oxford University Press, 1974), 51–52.

3. James Joyce, "Ireland: Island of Saints and Sages," in *OPCW*, 115. For Joyce, the "ridiculous" nature of Robert Emmet's uprising in 1803 was that it lacked the organization of later separatist movements such as the Fenians: James Joyce, "Fenianism: The Last Fenian," in *OCPW*, 138–39.

4. Pádraic H. Pearse, "Theobald Wolfe Tone," address at Bodenstown, June 22, 1913, in "Political Writings and Speeches," *CWPP*, 53.

5. C. J. Woods, *Bodenstown Revisited: The Grave of Theobald Wolfe Tone, Its Monuments and Its Pilgrimages* (Dublin: Four Courts Press, 2018), 41. The citizen is, of course, mistaken in locating Tone's resting place in Arbour Hill along with the Sheares brothers.

6. Friedrich Nietzsche, "On the Utility and Liability of History for Life" (1874), in *The Nietzsche Reader*, ed. Keith Ansell Pearson and Duncan Large (Oxford: Blackwell, 2006), 131–40.

7. Enda Duffy, "Disappearing Dublin: *Ulysses*, Postcoloniality, and the Politics of Space," in *Semicolonial Joyce*, ed. Derek Attridge and Marjorie Howes (Cambridge: Cambridge University Press, 2000), 54.

8. Michael J. F. McCarthy, *Five Years in Ireland: 1895–1900* (London: Simpkin, Marshall, Hamilton, Kent, 1901), 396.

9. Cited in Garry Owens, "National Monuments in Ireland c. 1870–1914: Symbolism and Ritual," in *Ireland: Art into History*, ed. Brian P. Kennedy and Raymond Gillespie (Dublin: Town House, 1994), 105.

10. Joseph A. Buttigieg, *A Portrait of the Artist in Different Perspective* (Athens: Ohio University Press, 1987), 31. As John S. Rickard describes it, drawing on Buttigieg's formulation, the past here operates not "as a protective barrier against the present, but as a painful and disturbing stimulus," opening up parts of people's lives they have been trying to escape from, restoring agency of a kind, if only by disrupting the force of habit. John S. Rickard, *Joyce's Book of Memory: The Mnemotechnic of "Ulysses"* (Durham, NC: Duke University Press, 1999), 72.

11. Benedict Anderson, *Imagined Communities: Reflections on the Origin and Spread of Nationalism* (London: Verso, 1991). For a perceptive critique of this aspect of Anderson's analysis, see Selina Guinness's argument that "there are reasons to suppose that the nation [in 1898] was a far less stable concept than this monumental emblem proposes." Selina Guinness, "The Year of the Undead, 1898," in *New Voices in Irish Criticism*, ed. P. J. Mathews (Dublin: Four Courts Press, 2000), 22.

12. Patrick R. O'Malley, *Liffey and Lethe: Paramnesiac History in Nineteenth-Century Anglo-Ireland* (Oxford: Oxford University Press, 2017), esp. 183–203.

13. Carle Bonafous-Murat, "Disposition and Pre-Disposition: The Art of Involuntary Memory," in *Classic Joyce*, Joyce Studies in Italy, 6, ed. Franca Ruggieri (Roma: Bulzoni Editore, 1999), 365.

14. Bonafous-Murat, 368.

15. Emmet's last words prohibited writing an epitaph for him as an individual until national identity is secured: "When my country takes her place among the nations of the earth, then, and not till then, let my epitaph be written. I have done."

16. Cited in Timothy J. O'Keefe, "The 1898 Efforts to Celebrate the United Irishmen: The '98 Centennial," *Eire-Ireland* 23, no. 2 (1988): 72.

17. Paul Frederick Lerner, *Hysterical Men: War, Psychiatry and the Politics of Trauma in Germany, 1890–1930* (Ithaca, NY: Cornell University Press, 2008), 215.

18. Alfred Tennyson, "In Memoriam" (1850), ed. Matthew Rowlinson (Peterborough, ONT: Broadview Editions, 2014), 125. In view of perceptions of hysteria as primarily a female malady, it is striking that Tennyson's lines predate Matthew Arnold's feminization of the Celt in *On the Study of Celtic Literature* (1867). For Shane Leslie's view of the "hysterical Celt," see above, 160.

19. F. S. L. Lyons, *Culture and Anarchy in Ireland, 1890–1939* (Oxford: Clarendon Press, 1979), 92.

20. F. S. L. Lyons, foreword to *The Letters of Patrick Pearse*, ed. Seamus Ó Buachalla (Gerrards Cross: Colin Smythe, 1960), ix.

21. Robert Hogan, *Eimar O'Duffy* (Lewisburg, PA: Bucknell University Press, 1972), 30–31. W. B. Yeats's depiction of "[Arthur] Griffith staring in hysterical pride" in Sir John Lavery's painting in the Hugh Lane/Municipal Gallery is another example: "The Municipal Gallery Revisited," in *The Collected Poems of W. B. Yeats* (New York: Macmillan, 1963), 316. As Colum Kenny suggests, this seems particularly ill-fitted to Griffith's practical political and economic temperament: Colum Kenny, "Friendly Enemies," *Dublin Review of Books*, November 2020, accessed at https://drb.ie/friendly-enemies/.

22. Eimar O'Duffy, *The Wasted Island* (Dublin: Martin Lester, 1919), 381.

23. Marjorie Howes, *Yeats's Nations: Gender, Class, and Irishness* (Cambridge: Cambridge University Press, 1998), 23; Sophie Bryant, "The Celtic Mind," *Contemporary Review*, July/December 1897, cited in Howes, *Yeats's Nations*, 192n25; James Murphy, *Abject Loyalties: Nationalism and Monarchy in Ireland during the Reign of Queen Victoria* (Cork: Cork University Press, 2001).

24. Fearghal McGarry, *The Rising: Ireland, Easter 1916* (Oxford: Oxford University Press, 2010), 71–72.

25. Michael T. Foy, *Tom Clarke: The True Leader of the Easter Rising* (Dublin: History Press, 2016), 160.

26. Foy, 236.

27. Fr. Columbus Murphy, O.F.S.C., "My Experiences in the 1916 Rising" (July 1916), ed. Conor Mulvagh and John McCafferty, *Analecta Hibernia*, no. 47 (2016): 174.

28. George Sigerson, *Bards of the Gael and Gall*, 2nd ed. (London: T. Fisher Unwin, 1907), 395.

29. Anderson, *Imagined Communities*, 24–36.

30. M. M. Bakhtin, "Epic and Novel," in *The Dialogical Imagination: Four Essays*, ed. Michael Holquist, trans. Caryl Emerson and Michael Holquist (Austin: University of Texas Press, 1981); Georg Lukacs, *The Theory of the Novel* (1914–15), trans. Anna Bostok (London: Merlin Press, 1971).

31. In Aristotle's *Poetics*, epic differed from tragedy in that it was not confined to the constraints of the stage and hence possessed "less unity": "in Epic poetry, owing to the narrative form, many events simultaneously transacted can be presented . . . diverting the mind of the hearer, and relieving the story with varying episodes." *The Poetics of Aristotle*, trans. S. H. Butcher (London: Macmillan, 1922), 111, 93. This allows for encyclopedic or episodic structures in which details accumulate, even of an irrational kind, and order is ultimately derived, not from narrative coherence but from nemesis, fate, or destiny.

32. Lukacs, *Theory of the Novel*, 60.

33. Franco Moretti, *Modern Epic: The World System from Goethe to Garcia Márquez*, trans. Quentin Hoare (London: Verso, 1996), 38. Moretti sees early precursors in Goethe's *Faust* (1831–32) and Melville's *Moby Dick* (1861), before later achievements such as Wagner's Niebelung cycle (1876), Ezra Pound's *Cantos* (1915–62), and T. S. Eliot's "The Waste Land" (1922).

34. Fredric Jameson, "'Ulysses' in History," in *James Joyce and Modern Literature*, ed. W. J. McCormack and Alister Stead (London: Routledge & Kegan Paul, 1982), 134.

35. Ernst Cassirer, *The Myth of the State* (New Haven, CT: Yale University Press, 1946), 28; Theodor W. Adorno, *Minima Moralia: Reflections from a Damaged Life* (1951), trans E. F. N. Jephcott (London: New Left Books, 1974), 152.

36. Cassirer, *Myth of the State*, 282.

37. Hermann Broch, "James Joyce and the Present Age" (1932), trans. Eugene and Maria Jolas, in *Geist and Zeitgeist: Six Essays*, ed. John Hargreaves (New York: Counterpoint, 2002), 67, 69. Henceforth *GZ*, followed by page numbers in text and notes.

38. *GZ*, 79. For Broch, the paradox is that a totality can only be seen as complete from the outside; but if there is an outside, it is no longer a totality. By the same token, if "the observer is always in the midst of it," there can only be a series of partial views.

39. Hannah Arendt, "Hermann Broch: 1886–1951," trans. Richard Winston, in *Men in Dark Times* (New York: Harvest Book, 1983), 133, 136.

40. Thomas Flanagan, *The Irish Novelists, 1800–1850* (New York: Columbia University Press, 1958), 100–101. Flanagan elaborates: "The English novelist was concerned with social choice and personal morality, which are the great issues of European fiction. But to the Irish novelist these were subordinated to questions of race, creed, and nationality—questions which tend of their nature to limit the range and power of fiction. Yet for the Irishman these were the crucial points by which he was given social identity" (35).

41. For the novel outside its Gothic setting, see Emer Nolan, *Catholic Emancipations: Irish Fiction from Thomas Moore to James Joyce* (Syracuse, NY: Syracuse University Press, 2007).

42. As Ciaran O'Neill notes of schoolboy fiction of the period, "adherence to social convention more or less guarantees social mobility for the boy hero in the English novels, whereas the same adherence in the Irish novels results in frustrated ambition and internal struggle," prompting a break with English models. Ciaran O'Neill, "The Irish Schoolboy Novel," *Éire-Ireland* 44, nos. 1–2 (Spring/Summer 2009): 150.

43. John Eglinton, "Living Nations and Regenerate Patriotism," in *Some Essays and Passages by John Eglinton*, selected by W. B. Yeats (Dundrum: Cuala Press, 1905), 7–8.

44. Caryl Emerson, "Boris Gudonov: Tragedy, Comedy, Carnival, and History on Stage," in *All the Same the Words Don't Go Away: Essays on Authors, Heroes, Aesthetics, and Stage Adaptations from the Russian Tradition* (Boston: Academic Studies Press, 2011), 163.

45. Standish O'Grady, *History of Ireland: Critical and Philosophical* (London: Sampson, Low & Co., 1881), 58. Henceforth *HI*, followed by page numbers in text.

46. Standish O'Grady, *All Ireland* (Dublin: Sealy, Bryers and Walker, 1898), 8.

47. Standish O'Grady, *History of Ireland: Cuculain and His Contemporaries*, vol. 2 (London: Sampson, Low et al., 1880), 19. Henceforth *CC*, followed by page numbers in text. O'Grady's spelling of "Cuculain" is retained in quotations from his texts.

48. "[I]ts real greatness lying in the promise of the future, not the actualities of the past.... That far off mythic age is a prophecy" (*HI*, 59).

49. *HI*, 45. O'Grady was aware that "my epic series, in which the literature has been toned and condensed into the uniformity and homogeneity of a single integral composition" may fail in its aim to have "full justice done to the subject"; yet he insists that the "wonderful glory" of the heroic age can only be seen "*through* the shifting chaos of the obscure epic tale, and the broken fragments of antique ruined verse" if brought to an imaginative completion of the tales (*HI*, 202–3; emphasis added).

50. *HI*, 145. The lack of definition and incompleteness of the Irish past was an abiding concern in the period. Thomas Kettle, a friend of Joyce's, described Irish history as that of "a people plunged into an unimaginable chaos of races, religions, ideas, appetites, and provincialism; brayed in the mortar without emerging as a consolidated whole; tenacious of the national idea but unable to bring it about; riven and pillaged by invasion without being conquered." Introduction to *Contemporary Ireland*, by L. Paul-Dubois (Dublin: Maunsel, 1908), vii.

51. Standish O'Grady, "The Great Enchantment," in *Selected Essays and Passages*, ed. Ernest A. Boyd (Dublin: Talbot Press, n.d.), 174.

52. *HI*, 62–63. O'Grady has in mind here the medieval redactions of Christian scribes, in the full knowledge it also applies to his own practice.

53. Standish O'Grady, "Ireland at the Hour," in *Selected Essays and Passages*, 222.

54. A footnote attests to the existence of Dublin (founded by the Vikings c. AD 888) as a wooden city and trading port in the second century, presenting Tacitus as his source, the historian cited by the citizen in the "Cyclops" chapter of *Ulysses*. Recent archaeological excavations have found evidence of housing predating the Vikings, including a Roman-era comb.

55. Standish O'Grady, preface to *Cuculain: An Epic* (London: Sampson, Low, Searle, Marston & Rivington, 1882), 1; emphasis added.

56. Thomas Kinsella, introduction to *The Táin: From the Irish Epic Táin Bó Cúailnge* (Oxford: Oxford University Press, 1970), xiii.

57. T. S. Eliot, "*Ulysses*, Order and Myth," *The Dial* lxxv, no. 5 (November 1923): 480–83.

58. Walter Benjamin, "Paris, Capital of the Nineteenth Century," in *The Arcades Project*, ed. Rolf Tiedeman, trans. Howard Eiland and Kevin McLaughlin (Cambridge, MA: Belknap Press, 1999), 14. T. S. Eliot also saw tradition as assembled through effort: "Tradition is a matter of much wider significance. It cannot be inherited, and if you want it you must obtain it by great labour." Even at that, order prevails, though it may be "if ever so slightly, altered" through innovation. T. S. Eliot, "Tradition and the Individual Talent" (1919), in *The Sacred Wood: Essays on Poetry and Criticism* (London: Methuen, 1920), 44.

59. Eleanor Hull, "Irish Heroic Sagas," in *The Glories of Ireland*, ed. Joseph Dunn and P. J. Lennox (Washington, DC: Phoenix Limited, 1914), 276.

60. Maria Tymoczko, *The Irish "Ulysses"* (Berkeley: University of California Press, 1994), 143.

61. Michael Bell, *Literature, Modernism and Myth* (Cambridge: Cambridge University Press, 1997), 78–79.

62. M. M. Bakhtin wrote that in its unified form, "the world of the epic is the national heroic past," but failed to note that a nation in an "inconclusive present" required the resuscitation of a more "contemporized" epic. M. M. Bakhtin, "Epic and Novel," in *The Dialogical Imagination*, 13, 27, 21.

63. Sigerson, *Bards of the Gael and Gall*, 2nd ed., 2. The first edition (1897) had already noted how passages in early Gaelic poetry "offer a certain modernity of thought and expression," and "where such attention was given by minds so keen and subtle to verse-Structure, it is little wonder that they anticipated many of the modern methods": "The modernity of the Irish bard's teaching is due to its antiquity; mankind has moved around on its tracks." Sigerson, *Bards of the Gael and Gall* (London: T. Fisher Unwin, 1897), 28, 48, 212. Joyce includes the first edition in his list of reading in an

early notebook: Luca Crispi, "A Commentary on James Joyce's National Library of Ireland 'Early Commonplace Book': 1903–1912 (MS 36,639/02/A)," *Genetic Joyce Studies* 9 (Spring 2009): 11.

64. Sigerson, *Bards of the Gael and Gall*, 2nd ed., 2.

65. Sigerson, 25.

66. Elsa D'Esterre-Keeling, review of *Bards of the Gael and the Gall* by George Sigerson, *Dublin Review*, October 1898, 275.

67. Pádraic H. Pearse, "Some Aspects of Irish Literature" (1912), in *CWPP*, 143, 142, 146.

68. Thomas MacDonagh, *Literature in Ireland: Studies Irish and Anglo-Irish* (1916; repr., Dublin: Talbot Press, 1919), 116, 92. Henceforth *LI*, followed by page numbers in text and notes.

69. Cited in Philip O'Leary, *The Prose Literature of the Gaelic Revival, 1881–1921: Ideology and Innovation* (University Park: Pennsylvania State University Press, 1994), 223.

70. Moretti, *Modern Epic*, 38.

71. Joyce sees language not just in formal structural terms but "on account of the public to which one can appeal": "Writing in English is the most ingenious torture ever devised for sins committed in previous lives. The English reading public explains why." James Joyce to Mlle Guillermet, September 5, 1918, in *JJL*, 1:119.

72. John Eglinton, "National Drama and Contemporary Life," in *Literary Ideals in Ireland*, by John Eglinton, W. B. Yeats, A.E., and W. Larminie (London/Dublin: T. Fisher Unwin/Daily Express Office, 1899), 27.

73. John Eglinton, "Mr. Yeats and Popular Poetry," in *Literary Ideals in Ireland*, 43. See Julie McCormick Weng, "John Eglinton: An Irish Futurist," in *Science, Technology, and Irish Modernism*, ed. Kathryn Conrad, Cóilín Parsons, and Julie McCormick Weng (Syracuse, NY: Syracuse University Press, 2019), 34–52.

74. Eglinton, "Mr. Yeats and Popular Poetry," 42.

75. Ernst Bloch, "Upper Middle Classes, Objectivity and Montage," in *HT*, 337, 225.

76. Theodor W. Adorno, "Art and the Arts," in *Can One Live After Auschwitz? A Philosophical Reader*, trans. R. Livingstone (Stanford, CA: Stanford University Press, 2003), 285.

77. Eugene McNulty and Róisín Ní Ghairbhí, "Introduction: Stages of the Rising," in *Patrick Pearse and the Theatre: Mac Piarais agus an Téatar*, ed. Eugene McNulty and Róisín Ní Ghairbhí (Dublin: Four Courts Press, 2016), 22.

78. Georges Didi-Huberman, *The Eye of History: When Images Take Positions*, trans. Shane B. Lillis (Cambridge, MA: MIT Press, 2018), 13.

79. Didi-Huberman, 51–54.

80. Didi-Huberman, 81. Didi-Huberman is citing Brecht's essay (titled in French translation) "Sur l'art ancient et l'art nouveau" (1920–33).

81. Moretti, *Modern Epic*, 188.

82. Bertolt Brecht, *Journals*, 137, in Didi-Huberman, *The Eye of History*, 89.

83. Ernst Bloch, "Transitions: Berlin. Functions in Hollow Space," in *HT*, 202; emphasis added.

84. John Wilson Foster, *Fictions of the Literary Revival: A Changeling Art* (Syracuse, NY: Syracuse University Press, 1987), 43.

85. W. B. Yeats, "Dramatis Personae: 1896–1902," in *Autobiographies*, ed. William H. O'Donnell and Douglas N. Archibald (New York: Scribner, 1999), 314.

86. As Andrew Gibson points out, it was against "transmigrations" of Victorian epics in Standish O'Grady, T. W. Rolleston, and others that Joyce set himself in "Cyclops," but which have often been mistaken for parodies of the forces behind the Easter Rising (in keeping with O'Grady's "infection" of Pearse). Andrew Gibson, *Joyce's Revenge: History, Politics and Aesthetics in "Ulysses"* (Oxford: Oxford University Press, 2002), 103–27.

87. Fr. Francis Shaw, S.J., "The Canon of Irish History: A Challenge," *Studies* LXI, 242 (Summer 1972): 130. The essay by Fr. Shaw (1907–1970), a former student of Eoin MacNeill's, was deemed too controversial for publication during the Golden Jubilee of the Easter Rising in 1966 and was not published until after his death.

88. O'Leary, *The Prose Literature of the Gaelic Revival*, 255.

89. O'Leary, 240.

90. Walter Benjamin, "What Is Epic Theatre?," in *Understanding Brecht*, trans. A. Bostock (London: Verso, 1998), 3–4.

91. John Wilson Foster, "The Artifice of Eternity: Medieval Aspects of Modern Irish Literature," in *Medieval and Modern Ireland*, ed. Richard Wall (Totowa, NJ: Barnes & Noble Books, 1988), 131.

92. Cited in Oliver MacDonagh, *Ireland: The Union and its Aftermath* (1977; repr., Dublin: University College Dublin Press, 2003), 27.

93. Moretti, *Modern Epic*, 189. Sigerson notes that while official court poetry filled ancient manuscripts "the genuine poetry . . . was relegated to the margins and blank spaces of the vellum manuscripts": "a monk in St. Gall pauses from his copying to write a couple of purely poetic stanzas to the blackbird." Sigerson, *Bards of the Gael and Gall*, 2nd ed., 11.

94. Moretti, *Modern Epic*, 50–51.

95. Bloch, "Montage, Direct," in *HT*, 203.

96. Foster, *Fictions of the Literary Revival*, 6.

Chapter Three

1. Desmond Ryan, *BMH*, no. 724, 1.

2. F. Scott Fitzgerald, in an interview with the *Richmond Times-Dispatch* (1923), cited in Ronald Berman, "Fitzgerald's Intellectual Context," in *A Historical Guide to F. Scott Fitzgerald*, ed. Kirk Curnutt (Oxford: Oxford University Press, 2004), 69. For Fitzgerald, Conrad's *Nostromo* was "the great novel of the past fifty years," whereas Joyce would be "the most profound literary influence in the next fifty years."

3. "Karl Radek on Joyce's Realism," *Contemporary World Literature and the Tasks of the Proletariat*, a report delivered to the Congress of Soviet Writers, August 1934, reprinted in *JJCH* 2:624–26.

4. Alfred Döblin, "'Ulysses' von Joyce," *Das Deutsche Buch* 8 (1928): 84, cited in Joyce Wexler, *Violence without God: The Rhetorical Despair of Twentieth-Century Writers* (London: Bloomsbury, 2017), 114.

5. Siegfried Kracauer, "History of German Film" (1942), cited in *Culture in the Anteroom: The Legacies of Siegfried Kracauer*, ed. Gert Germünden and Johannes von Moltke (Ann Arbor: University of Michigan Press, 2012), 2.

6. Enda Duffy, *The Subaltern "Ulysses"* (Minneapolis: University of Minnesota Press, 1994), 126–28. Duffy further elaborates on foreshadowings of the Rising in *Ulysses* in "Disappearing Dublin: *Ulysses*, Postcoloniality, and the Politics of Space,"

in *Semicolonial Joyce*, ed. Derek Attridge and Marjorie Howes (Cambridge: Cambridge University Press, 2000), 37–57; and "Setting: Dublin 1904/1922," in *The Cambridge Companion to "Ulysses,"* ed. Sean Latham (Cambridge: Cambridge University Press, 2014), 81.

7. See Diarmaid Ferriter, "'The Right to Speak for Ireland': Conn Curran and the *Nation*, 1917–22," in C. P. Curran, *James Joyce Remembered: Edition 2022* (1922; repr., Dublin: UCD Press, 2022), 153–68.

8. For more on the "Castle Document," see 253n53, below.

9. Luke Gibbons, *Joyce's Ghosts: Ireland, Modernism, and Memory* (Chicago: University of Chicago Press, 2015), ch. 6, 165–87.

10. *Irish Freedom*, November 1914, cited in John Ellis, "The Degenerate and the Martyr: Nationalist Propaganda and the Contestation of Irishness, 1914–1918," *Eire-Ireland* 35, nos. 3/4 (Fall 2000): 30.

11. Ronan McGreevy, "Seán Mac Diarmada: Single-Minded Separatist," *Irish Times*, March 9, 2016; Seán Mac Diarmada, "Letter to John Daly, 11 May 1916," in *Last Words: Letters and Statements of the Leaders Executed After the Rising at Easter 1916*, ed. Piaras F. Mac Lochlainn (Dublin: Stationery Office, 1990), 171.

12. Thomas MacDonagh, "Address to the Court-Martial, 2 May, 1916," in *Last Words*, ed. Mac Lochlainn, 56.

13. Wyndham Lewis, *Time and Western Man* (London: Chatto and Windus, 1927), 109.

14. James Joyce, "A Portrait of the Artist" (1904), in *The Workshop of Daedalus: James Joyce and the Raw Materials for "A Portrait of the Artist as a Young Man,"* ed. Robert Scholes and Richard M. Kain (Evanston, IL: Northwestern University Press, 1965), 60.

15. Susan de Sola Rodstein, "Back to 1904: Joyce, Ireland and Nationalism," in *Joyce: Feminism/Post/Colonialism*, ed. Ellen Carol Jones (Amsterdam: Rodopi, 1998), 150.

16. Pól Ó Dochartaigh, "The Source of Hell: Professor Pokorny of Vienna in 'Ulysses,'" *JJQ* 41, no. 4 (Summer 2004): 825–29.

17. "Workings of a Child's Mind," *Irish Times*, November 17, 1921. The use of the term contradicts Harald Beck's contention that it was not available to Joyce at the time: see "A Doctor but Not Dr. Freud," *James Joyce Online Notes*, http://www.jjon.org/joyce-s-allusions/freud. The *Irish Times* report was of a "largely-attended conference" held at the Synod Hall, Dublin, November 16. Dr. Smyly was one of the first Irish doctors to study war neurosis, lecturing on "Shell-Shock" at the Dublin University Biological Association, February 1, 1917.

18. Joan W. Scott, "The Incommensurability of Psychoanalysis and History," in *Psychology and History: Interdisciplinary Explorations*, ed. Christian Taleagá and Jovan Byford (Cambridge: Cambridge University Press, 2014), 44.

19. Joyce's acquaintance with the Wolf Man followed the publication of *Ulysses*. Notebooks (1925–26) for chapter XVI of *Finnegans Wake* contain references to "Little Hans" and "The Wolf Man." See Daniel Ferrer, "The Freudful Couchmare of /\d: Joyce's Notes on Freud and the Composition of Chapter XVI of *Finnegans Wake*," *JJQ* 22, no. 4 (1985): 367–82; Wim Van Mierlo, "The Freudful Couch Revisited: Contextualizing Joyce and the New Psychology," *Joyce Studies Annual* 8 (Summer 1997): 115–63.

20. Sigmund Freud, "From the History of an Infantile Neurosis," vol. 17, *Standard*

Edition of the Complete Works of Sigmund Freud (New York: Vintage, 2001), 119; emphasis added.

21. Peter Brooks, "Fictions of the Wolf-Man: Freud and Narrative Understanding," in *Reading for the Plot: Design and Intention in Narrative* (Cambridge, MA: Harvard University Press, 1992), 277.

22. J. F. Boyle, *The Irish Rebellion of 1916: A Brief History of the Revolt and Its Suppression* (London: Constable, 1916). For other proleptic and coded references to events beyond 1914, and particularly the 1916–21 period, see de Sola Rodstein, "Back to 1904," 145–86, and Paul K. Saint-Amour, "Rising Timely and Untimely: On Joycean Anachronism," in *The Edinburgh Companion to Irish Modernism*, ed. Maud Ellmann, Siân White, and Vicki Mahaffey (Edinburgh: Edinburgh University Press, 2021), 35–50.

23. A Captain Tompkins was in charge of a British army company off O'Connell Street, near the GPO, the headquarters of the Rising: Max Caulfield, *The Easter Rebellion* (London: Four Square Books, 1965), 300.

24. James Fairhall, *James Joyce and the Question of History* (Cambridge: Cambridge University Press, 1995), 47.

25. As well as HCE, "Eireweeker" would thus be Eire/Easter week; "bludyen" alludes to bloody and is also an anagram of Dublin. "O rally" refers to The O Rahilly (Michael Joseph O'Rahilly), the 1916 leader who died in combat, but also to orality, followed by the traditional tune, "Planxty O Reilly," composed by the last of the Irish bards, Turlough O'Carolan (1670–1738). The opening lines "Calling all downs. Calling all downs to dayne" (*FW*, 593.2) could be seen as mimicking radio broadcasts made by the rebels, though it is not clear that Joyce knew of the rebels' broadcasts during the Rising.

26. John Wyse Nolan is based on the real-life John Wyse Power, whose wife, Jenny, ran a restaurant on Henry Street that provided the room in which the seven signatories of the 1916 Proclamation convened a few days before the Rising. Bloom also frequented the establishment: as Nosey Flynn recounts, "I met him the day before yesterday and he coming out of that Irish farm dairy John Wyse Nolan's wife has in Henry street" (*U*, 8.949–51). See "John Wyse Nolan's Wife," Joyce Project, http://m.joyceproject.com/notes/080015nolanswife.html.

27. It may have been such a casual use of the phrase in 1904 by Mary Ellen Butler, in a conversation with Arthur Griffith, that led to its adoption as the name of a political movement. Margaret Ward, *In Their Own Voice* (Dublin: Attic Press, 1996), 14–15.

28. Perceptions of the "preordained" failure of the Easter Rising falls into this category, a foregone conclusion contested, as noted above, by Thomas MacDonagh: "It will be said our movement was doomed to failure. It had proved so. Yet it might have been otherwise. . . . That we had such a chance none knows so well as your statesmen and military experts." MacDonagh, "Address to the Court-Martial," 56.

29. H. R. Trevor-Roper, "History and Imagination," in *History and Imagination: Essays in Honour of H. R. Trevor-Roper*, ed. H. Lloyd Jones et al. (London: Duckworth, 1981), 364.

30. Ezra Pound, "At Last the Novel Appears," *The Egoist* iv, no. 2 (February 1917), in *JJCH*, 1:83.

31. The account of medical facts is that of Dr. George Milbry Gould, the "poetical ophthalmologist" whose diagnoses of the links between eyestrain and genius led Pound to recommend him as an eye surgeon to Joyce. *Pound/Joyce: The Letters of Ezra*

Pound to James Joyce, with Pound's Essays on Joyce, ed. Forrest Read (New York: New Directions, 1967), 96–97.

32. H. G. Wells, "James Joyce," review of *A Portrait of the Artist as a Young Man*, *Nation*, xx (February 24, 1917), in *JJCH*, 1:88.

33. *JJ*, 620. Wells's further elaboration throws light on his political sympathies: "And while you were brought up under the delusion of political suppression I was brought up under the delusion of political responsibility. It remains a fine thing for you to defy and break up. To me not in the least" (620–21). For Pound's and Wells's approaches to Joyce, see Joseph Brooker, *Joyce's Critics* (Madison: University of Wisconsin Press, 2004), 9–18.

34. Arthur Power, *Conversations with James Joyce*, ed. Clive Hart (London: Millington, 1974), 32.

35. Ezra Pound, "Thomas MacDonagh as Critic," *Poetry* 8, no. 6 (September 1916). For MacDonagh's subsequent critical reputation in the United States, see chapter 7, below.

36. Chris Baldick, *The Social Mission of English Criticism* (Oxford: Clarendon Press, 1987), 87.

37. For the role of literature and creative practice in such shifts in sentiment, see Raymond Williams, "Structures of Feeling," in *Marxism and Literature* (Oxford: Oxford University Press, 1977), 129–35.

38. Alasdair MacIntyre, *After Virtue: A Study in Moral Theory* (London: Duckworth, 1981), 211–12.

39. Michael André Bernstein, *Foregone Conclusions: Against Apocalyptic History* (Berkeley: University of California Press, 1994), 11, 4; emphasis added.

40. Among the early factors that contributed to the revolution were the founding of the Sinn Féin party in 1905, the return of the IRB organizer Tom Clarke from the United States to Dublin in 1907, Sinn Féin's participation in the North Leitrim by-election in 1907, and Patrick Pearse's opening of St. Enda's School in 1908. There was little prescience of the kind shown by Karl Kraus when he identified Germany as early as 1921 as a country "where the swastika rises alone above the ruins of the global conflagration," but as noted by John Eglinton above (230n13), social transformation was in the air, and as MacDonagh was at pains to emphasize: "This Rising did not result from accidental circumstances" ("Address to the Court-Martial," 55). For Kraus, see Edward Timms and Fred Bridgham, "Introduction: Falsehood in Wartime," in *The Last Days of Mankind: The Complete Text*, by Karl Kraus, trans. Fred Bridgham and Edward Timms (New Haven, CT: Yale University Press, 2015), xix–xx.

41. Moritz J. Bonn, *Modern Ireland and Her Agrarian Problem*, trans. T. W. Rolleston (Dublin: Hodges Figgis & Co., 1906), 11.

42. Fearghal McGarry, *The Rising: Ireland, Easter 1916* (Oxford: Oxford University Press, 2010), 116. As late as Wednesday, April 19, 1916, six days before the Rising, informers assured Dublin Castle there was no knowledge of impending arms importations into Ireland, though German intelligence to this affect had been intercepted. León Ó Broin, *Dublin Castle and the 1916 Rising: The Story of Sir Matthew Nathan* (Dublin: Helicon, 1966), 80–81.

43. Cited in Sean Enright, *After the Rising: Soldiers, Lawyers and Trials of the Irish Revolution* (Sallins: Merrion Press, 2016), 15.

44. A recent study, Brian Ward, *Imagining Alternative Irelands in 1912: Cultural Discourse in the Periodical Press* (Dublin: Four Courts Press, 2017), being true to its

subject, has no entry for the Easter Rising: it was not on the cards, even as an alternative future.

45. Gary Saul Morson, "Sideshadowing," in *Narrative and Freedom: The Shadows of Time* (New Haven, CT: Yale University Press, 1994), 117–72.

46. James Joyce, "The Shade of Parnell," in *OCPW*, 195.

47. Seymour Chatman, "What Novels Can Do That Films Can't (and Vice Versa)," in *On Narrative*, ed. W. J. T. Mitchell (Chicago: University of Chicago Press, 1981), 121–24.

48. Perhaps some details are meaningless but if so, they could be removed from the novel without any loss—a hazardous venture in the case of *Ulysses*.

49. Joseph Frank, *The Idea of Spatial Form* (New Brunswick, NJ: Rutgers University Press, 1991), 20.

50. Frank, 124; emphasis added.

51. It is striking that leaders of the Easter Rising considered it in terms of alternative currents: "In this ceaseless struggle," declared Thomas MacDonagh on being sentenced to death in 1916 for his part in the Rising, "there will be, as there has been, and must be, an alternative ebb and flow." MacDonagh, "Address to the Court-Martial," 55.

52. Greg Winston, *Joyce and Militarism* (Gainesville: University Press of Florida, 2012), 239.

53. Sean Enright shows that advance information (or warnings) pieced together by the Royal Commission after the Rising had not been found convincing beforehand by Sir Augustine Birrell, or Sir Matthew Nathan, Under Secretary at the Castle. Enright, *After the Rising*, ch. 2, 15–28. The so-called Castle Document, directing the mass arrest of volunteers and leaders of the nationalist community, some of which was considered to be a forgery, was based on such information (22).

54. Dublin Metropolitan Police Report, June 1, 1915 (NAI, CSO/JD/2/1), accessed at https://www.nationalarchives.ie/wp-content/uploads/2019/03/CSO_JD_2_1.pdf. J. J. Walsh, who owned a newspaper shop selling "seditious" literature, was later sentenced to ten years for his part in the Rising and became Minister for Posts and Telegraphs in the new Irish Free State.

55. Marcus de Búrca, *Michael Cusack and the GAA* (Dublin: Anvil Books, 1989), 181; *SH*, 66. See "An Stad: North Frederick Street," *Come Here to Me! Dublin Life & Culture*, March 26, 2015, https://comeheretome.com/2015/03/26/an-stad-north-frederick-street/.

56. Chester Anderson relates "The Irish fellows in Clarke's" (*P*, 228) to Tom Clarke, as do Shari and Bernard Benstock. James Joyce, *A Portrait of the Artist as a Young Man*, ed. Chester G. Anderson (New York: Viking Press, 1968), 535; Shari Benstock and Bernard Benstock, *Who's He When He's at Home: A James Joyce Directory* (Urbana: University of Illinois Press, 1980), 67.

57. Winston, *Joyce and Militarism*, 89–90.

58. For a concise view of the wide range of contested readings of the Casement "Black Diaries" relating homosexual encounters that drew on Casement the charge of being a "moral degenerate," see Duffy, *Subaltern "Ulysses,"* 102–4.

59. Frank Budgen, *James Joyce and the Making of "Ulysses"* (Bloomington: Indiana University Press, 1960), 122–23.

60. Frank Henderson, *BMH*, no. 249, 20.

61. Frank Kermode, *Genesis of Secrecy: On the Interpretation of Narrative* (Cambridge, MA: Harvard University Press, 1979), 49–73.

62. Robert M. Adams, *Surface and Symbol: The Consistency of James Joyce's "Ulysses"* (New York: Oxford, 1962), 218, 245–46, cited in Kermode, *Genesis of Secrecy*, 53.

63. Joyce improvised on five to eleven sets of proofs during the final preparation of the novel for the printer: as Luca Crispi notes, "*Ulysses* grew approximately one-third longer during the various proof stages." Luca Crispi, *Joyce's Creative Process and the Construction of Characters in Ulysses: Becoming the Blooms* (Oxford: Oxford University Press, 2015), 285.

64. John S. Rickard, *Joyce's Book of Memory: The Mnemotechnic of "Ulysses"* (Durham, NC: Duke University Press, 1999), 58.

65. "News item or rather phrase of conversation from ex-govt. official: 'The censorship was very much troubled by it (*Ulysses*) during the war. Thought it was all code.'" Ezra Pound to James Joyce, [July 1920], in *Pound/Joyce: The Letters of Ezra Pound to James Joyce*, 182.

66. For more on O'Malley, see chapter 8, below.

67. Ernie O'Malley, *Rising Out: Seán Connolly of Longford* (Dublin: University College Press, 2007), 109. It is no wonder the director of intelligence in Dublin Castle, Sir Ormonde Winter, expressed reservations about the use of eavesdropping on prisoners' conversations: "I might mention that among the various methods of obtaining information, listening sets installed in cells gave poor results, as they were found to be unsuited to the Irish brogue." Cited in Nicholas Allen, *Modernism, Ireland and Civil War* (Cambridge: Cambridge University Press, 2009), 28n34.

68. Kevin Bermingham, *The Most Dangerous Book: The Battle for James Joyce's "Ulysses"* (London: Head of Zeus, 2014), 115.

69. Duffy, *Subaltern "Ulysses,"* 108.

70. As John F. Boyle noted, Pearse "made no secret of his intentions, and from a hillside near his school it was openly stated, in his presence, some weeks before the revolt, that a rising would take place. Secrecy played little part in the preparations so far as Pearse, at any rate, was concerned." Boyle, *The Irish Rebellion of 1916*, 191.

71. Slavoj Žižek, "Psychoanalysis and Post-Marxism: The Case of Alain Badiou," *South Atlantic Quarterly* 97, no. 2 (Spring 1998): 240.

72. Patrick O'Farrell, *Ireland's English Question: Anglo-Irish Relations, 1534–1970* (New York: Schocken, 1971), 276.

73. Fred Moten, *The Universal Machine* (Durham, NC: Duke University Press, 2018), 235.

74. Fritz Senn, "Charting Elsewhereness: Erratic Interlocations," in *Joyce's "Wandering Rocks,"* ed. Andrew Gibson and Steve Morrison (Amsterdam: Rodopi, 2002), 165.

75. Stanley Fish, "Transmuting the Lump: Paradise Lost, 1942–1982," in *Literature and History: Theoretical Reflections and Russian Case Studies*, ed. Gary Saul Morson (Stanford, CA: Stanford University Press, 1986), 48.

76. Morson, "Sideshadowing," 118.

77. Morson, 119.

78. John Francis Byrne, *Silent Years: An Autobiography with Memoirs of James Joyce and Our Ireland* (1953; New York: Octagon Books, 1975), 115.

79. Joe Good, *Inside the GPO: A First Hand Account* (1946; repr., Dublin: O'Brien Press, 2015), 60.

80. R. M. Fox, *A History of the Irish Citizen Army* (Dublin: James Duffy, 1943), 189. As Franc Myles has noted of this urban warfare: "The type of street fighting that was

developing around the republican-held strongpoints was completely beyond the ken of anything previously experienced by the British High Command ... They had little experience of dealing with irregular forces in urban contexts." Franc Myles, "Beating the Retreat: The Final Hours of the Easter Rising," in *Making 1916: Material and Visual Culture of the Easter Rising*, ed. Lisa Godson and Joanna Brück (Liverpool: Liverpool University Press, 2016), 40. Crown forces learned quickly to adopt similar tactics but with drastic consequences, breaking through houses on North King Street, Dublin, and killing fifteen civilians in the vicinity.

81. Ivan Maisky, future Soviet ambassador to Britain, accompanied Kerzhentzev. Kerzhentzev had made an acquaintance with Padraic and Mary Colum while in political exile in New York and went on to write a Marxist history, *Revolutionary Ireland* (1918), inspired by Connolly's writings. See Maurice J. Casey, "Red Easter: Platon Milhailovich Kerzhentsev, the First Soviet Historian of Ireland," *History Ireland* 24, no. 5 (September/October 2016).

82. W. B. Yeats, "Easter 1916" (1920), in *Collected Poems of W. B. Yeats* (New York: Macmillan, 1963), 179; Ernie O'Malley, *On Another Man's Wound* (1936), rev. ed. (Dublin: Anvil Books, 2002), 51

83. Fredric Jameson, "Modernism and Imperialism," in *Nationalism, Colonialism and Literature*, ed. Seamus Deane (Minneapolis: Field Day/University of Minnesota Press, 1990), 64.

84. In cubism, as Braque explained, the permeability of objects and space was bound up with "the fragmentation [that] enabled me to establish the space and the movement within space, and I was unable to introduce the object until I had created the space." Cited in Stephen Kern, *The Modernist Novel* (Cambridge: Cambridge University Press, 2011), 76.

85. Wyndham Lewis, "Spatialization and Concreteness," in *Time and Western Man*, 179–80.

86. Wyndham Lewis, *The Apes of God* (1930; repr., Harmondsworth, UK: Penguin, 1963), 435; emphasis added.

87. Lewis, *Time and Western Man*, 93, 95.

88. Scott W. Klein, *The Fictions of James Joyce and Wyndham Lewis: Monsters of Nature and Design* (Cambridge: Cambridge University Press, 1994), 133–36.

89. Lewis, *The Apes of God*, 249, 345. For rooms and walls as barriers against invasion in Lewis's writing, see Klein, *Fictions of James Joyce and Wyndham Lewis*, 113–51.

90. "The room that began in Lewis as a physical containment of psychic energies, thus returns as the aggressive and already invaded site of politics." Klein, *Fictions of James Joyce and Wyndham Lewis*, 149.

91. Lewis, *Time and Western Man*, 120, 119.

92. Fredric Jameson, "'Ulysses' in History," in *James Joyce and Modern Literature*, ed. W. J. McCormack and Alister Stead (London: Routledge & Kegan Paul, 1982), 140.

93. Wexler, *Violence without God*, 112–13.

94. Ronald Bogue, *Deleuze's Way: Essays in Transverse Ethics and Aesthetics* (London: Routledge, 2007), 3.

95. Kristin Ross, *The Emergence of Social Space: Rimbaud and the Paris Commune* (London: Verso, 2008), 35.

96. Ross, 38. See Benjamin's *Arcades Project*, especially introductory account of the Parisian arcades operating as street furniture both inside and outside public

and private spaces: *The Arcades Project*, ed. Rolf Tiedeman, trans. Howard Eiland and Kevin McLaughlin (Cambridge, MA: Belknap Press, 1999), 7–15.

97. Boyle, *The Irish Rebellion of 1916*, 88.

98. James Connolly, "Labour in Irish History" (1910), in *Labour in Ireland* (Dublin: At the Sign of the Three Candles, 1949), 159.

99. Peter Hart, "What Did the Easter Rising Really Change?" in *Turning Points in Twentieth-Century History*, ed. Thomas Hachey (Dublin: Irish Academic Press, 2011), 8.

100. Duffy, "Disappearing Dublin," 50, 54.

101. "Only Lenin's Bolsheviks, the Serbs and the Irish remained true to the resolutions of the Second International to oppose the war": C. Desmond Greaves, *The Life and Times of James Connolly* (London: Lawrence and Wishart, 1972), 397.

102. Ruth Dudley Edwards, *James Connolly* (Dublin: Gill and Macmillan, 1981), 120.

103. James Connolly, "What Is Our Programme," *Workers' Republic*, January 22, 1916, in *Labour and Easter Week: A Selection from the Writings of James Connolly* (Dublin: At the Sign of the Three Candles, 1949), 139.

104. As Richard Aldington wrote in 1914 of the assertive Englishness of Lewis's modernist magazine *Blast*, even before the rush of patriotism in the Great War: "the paper is an effort to look at art from an Anglo-Saxon point of view instead of from a borrowed foreign standpoint" and is one in which "the admirable, unique and dominating characteristics [of the English are] piously blessed." Richard Aldington, "BLAST," *The Egoist*, July 15, 1914, 272.

105. Modris Eksteins, *Rites of Spring: The Great War and the Birth of the Modern Age* (London: Bantam Press, 1989), 119.

106. Döblin, "'Ulysses' von Joyce," cited in Wexler, *Violence without God*, 115–16; emphasis added.

107. Winston Churchill, Speech in Defence of the Anglo-Irish Treaty, December 1921, cited in Paul Bew, *Churchill and Ireland* (Oxford: Oxford University Press, 2016), xiii.

Chapter Four

1. Cited in Richard Carr, *Charlie Chaplin: A Political Biography from Victorian Britain to Modern America* (New York: Routledge, 2017), 91.

2. L. G. Redmond-Howard, *Six Days of the Republic: A Narrative and Critical Account of the Latest Phase in Irish Politics* (Dublin/London: E. Ponsonby/Maunsel, 1916), 22–23.

3. Ernie O'Malley, *On Another Man's Wound* (1936), rev. ed. (Dublin: Anvil, 2002), 40.

4. Redmond-Howard, *Six Days of the Republic*, 15. Similar incidents were also noted by the *Illustrated Sunday Herald*: "When the fighting started all the hooligans of the city were soon drawn to the spot in search of loot. Half the shops in Sackville Street were sacked. Children who have never possessed two pence of their own were imitating Charlie Chaplin with stolen silk hats in the middle of the turmoil and murder." Cited in Donal Fallon, "The 'Denizens of the Slums' and Looting During the Easter Rising," *Come Here to Me! Dublin Life & Culture*, October 4, 2015, https://

comeheretome.com/2015/10/04/the-denizens-of-the-slums-and-looting-during-the-easter-rising/.

5. Denis Condon, "Creating Great Trouble in a Most Laughable Manner: Chaplin in Dublin in 1914," *Film Ireland*, February 4, 2015, http://filmireland.net/2015/02/04/early-irish-cinema-creating-great-trouble-in-a-most-laughable-manner-chaplin-in-dublin/.

6. Siegfried Kracauer, "Chaplin's Triumph" (1931), trans. John MacKay, *Yale Journal of Criticism* 10, no. 1 (Spring 1997): 118.

7. Wes D. Gehring, *Charlie Chaplin and "A Woman of Paris": The Genesis of a Misunderstood Masterpiece* (Jefferson, NC: McFarland, 2021), 46. Chaplin was very conscious of his mother's Irish background and that his parents may have met while performing an Irish melodrama. Later in life, he stayed for extended periods in Waterville, County Kerry, where a statue commemorates his visits.

8. Susan Buck-Morss, *The Dialectics of Seeing: Walter Benjamin and the Arcades Project* (Cambridge, MA: Harvard University Press, 1989), 74. Benjamin's thinking on this was influenced by Georg Simmel's concept of "the ur-phenomenon," derived from Goethe, in which things exhibit the principles that inform them: "The highest thing would be to grasp that everything factual is already theory" (72).

9. Alasdair MacIntyre, *After Virtue: A Study in Moral Theory* (London: Duckworth, 1981), 212.

10. Laura O'Connor, "The 1916 Rising in the Story of Ireland," in *The Oxford Handbook of Modern Irish Fiction*, ed. Liam Harte (Oxford: Oxford University Press, 2020), 424.

11. The film was originally made in the United States in 1914, but exhibition in Ireland was disrupted due to the Great War and Easter Rising until January 1917, when it was billed for "one week only," though it was banned after two days. This led the critic Joseph Holloway to wonder in his diary (January 5, 1917) of an actual free Irish nation, whether we "would ever have it in reality—for 'one week only' even." Cited in Denis Condon, "'Would We Ever Have It in Reality?' Ireland a Nation 'For Two Days Only' in January 1917," Early Irish Cinema, https://earlyirishcinema.com/2017/01/25/would-we-ever-have-it-in-reality-ireland-a-nation-for-two-days-only-in-january-1917/. By the time the film was eventually exhibited in Ireland in 1922, actual news footage of post-1916 scenes noted above had been added, out of kilter with the early staged melodramatic historical scenes.

12. A column in an Irish newspaper seems to have had this possibility in mind: "'Ireland will never be fit to take its place among nationalities, big or small, until it is recast or remade. . . . What picture of the process of remolding will the historian of the future give his generation?' 'Why, a moving picture, of course. . . .'" Cited in Denis Condon, "*The Birth of Nation* in Ireland, Autumn 1916," in *Early Irish Cinema: What's on in Irish Cinemas—100 Years Ago*, September 14, 2016, https://earlyirishcinema.com/category/film-directors/d-w-griffith/. The question was asked by US senator Patrick J. Maguire in relation to the impact of *The Birth of a Nation* and answered by the *Evening Herald*'s "Man About Town."

13. R. F. Foster, *The Irish Story: Telling Tales and Making It Up in Ireland* (London: Allen Lane, 2001), 20.

14. Marshall McLuhan, *Understanding Media: The Extensions of Man* (New York: Signet, 1964), 263. McLuhan's claim has been challenged, and perhaps the first *news*

broadcast would be more accurate. See Cathal Brennan, "Radio and the Easter Rising," Timeline: Genealogy in Ireland, https://timeline.ie/radio-and-the-1916-rising/.

15. Walter Benjamin, "The Work of Art in the Age of Its Technological Reproducibility, Third Version" (1936), in *BSW* 4:251–67.

16. "The Confession of Faith of an Irish Nationalist," in *The Voice of Freedom: A Selection from 'Irish Freedom' 1910–1913* (Dublin: Freedom Office, 1913), 100, 111.

17. R. R. Madden, *The United Irishmen, Their Lives and Times*, 3rd series, 2nd ed. (London, 1860), 287, 478, cited in W. B. Stanford, *Ireland and the Classical Tradition* (Dublin: Allen Figgis, 1976), 216.

18. John Mitchel, cited in Stanford, *Ireland and the Classical Tradition*, 219.

19. Stanford, 220.

20. Padraic Colum, *The Road Around Ireland* (New York: Macmillan, 1926), 465. Colum was a close friend of MacDonagh's.

21. Pádraic H. Pearse, "The Spiritual Nation," in "Political Writings and Speeches," in *CWPP*, 329. The Pearse household was well versed in classic republicanism: a pamphlet published by James Pearse, Patrick's father, in defense of Irish legislative independence, was peppered with quotations from Caius Graccus, Tiberius Sempronius, and Polybius.

22. Edith Hall and Henry Stead, *A People's History of Classics: Class and Graeco-Roman Antiquity in Britain and Ireland, 1689 to 1939* (London: Routledge, 2020), 207. Hall and Stead further note that "when Irish radicals came to England during the Chartist unrest of the 1840s and 1850s, the classical expertise of even those from poorer backgrounds often caused astonishment" (207).

23. Eimar O'Duffy, *The Wasted Island* (Dublin: Martin Lester, 1919), 43, 41, 44.

24. O'Duffy, 44.

25. O'Duffy, 460.

26. Lennox Robinson, *The Lost Leader: A Play in Three Acts* (Dublin: T. Kiersey, 1918), 39–40. As Joseph M. Greenwood notes, the "double" who recalls Parnell in the play evokes the mistaken identities of Sydney Carton and Charles Darnay in Dickens's story: Joseph M. Greenwood, "'Recalled to Life': Postmodernism in Lennox Robinson's *The Lost Leader* (1918)," *Estudios Irlandeses*, no. 14 (March 2019–February 2020): 89.

27. Desmond Ryan, *The Man Called Pearse* (Dublin: Maunsel, 1919), 70–71.

28. Mary Brigid Pearse also adapted Dickens's *The Cricket on the Hearth* for the Leinster Stage Society at the Abbey Theatre, February 23–25, 1911: Róisín Ni Gairbhi, *Willie Pearse* (Dublin: O'Brien Press, 2015), 138, 100. Joyce, based in Trieste, also wrote an essay on Dickens in Italian to mark the occasion. James Joyce, "The Centenary of Charles Dickens" (1912), in *OCPW*, 183–86. See also the essay by Darrell Figgis, later a leading Irish Volunteer: "Charles Dickens," *Nineteenth Century and After* LXXI (February 7, 1912).

29. I am grateful to Brian Crowley, former director of the Pearse Museum at Rathfarnham, Dublin, for bringing these to my attention.

30. Gustave Flaubert, "Dictionary of Accepted Ideas," in *Bouvard and Peuchet*, trans. Mark Polizzotti (Champaign, IL: Dalkey Archive Press, 2005), 320.

31. Stephen Watt, *Joyce, O'Casey, and the Irish Popular Theatre* (Syracuse, NY: Syracuse University Press, 1991), 134.

32. Jim Cooke, "The Dickens Fellowship of Ireland," in *Charles Dickens's Ireland: An Anthology* (Dublin: Woodfield Press, 1999), 198. The reworking of Christianity

in a French Republican setting also prefigures sacrificial narratives cross-cutting the 1916 Rising.

33. R. F. Foster, *W. B. Yeats: A Life*, vol. 1: *The Apprentice Mage, 1865–1914* (Oxford: Oxford University Press, 1997), 618n126.

34. Foster, 413. Characteristically, recoil from the modern "Abyss" is registered in distinctively modern terms of "jarred" and "broken." Stephen Watt also cites Shakespearean echoes in an 1899 review of *The Only Way*: "The consummating sacrifice of his [Sydney Carton's] life for the life of his successful rival is an episode as dramatic, as heart-moving, as any in all of literature, outside the magic pages of Shakespeare himself" (Watt, *Joyce, O'Casey*, 135). The Easter Rising also had its Shakespearean associations: its timing coincided with the 400th anniversary of the playwright's death.

35. Watt, *Joyce, O'Casey*, 137.

36. The English republican hero Algernon Sidney was sentenced to death in 1683 by the notorious Judge Jeffreys, to whom Carton is compared in his early drunken career. Andrew Sander, introduction to *A Tale of Two Cities*, by Charles Dickens (Oxford: Oxford University Press, 1998), x, 83.

37. "The Last Howley of Killowen," *Household Words*, July 15, 1854; "Old Stories Retold: The Battle of Vinegar Hill," *All the Year Round*, February 23, 1867. For coverage of Irish material in Dickens's periodicals, see Cooke, *Charles Dickens's Ireland*, chs. 4, 8–10, and esp. ch. 12 ("Stories of Irish Rebellion").

38. Claire Tomalin, *The Invisible Woman: The Story of Nelly Ternan and Charles Dickens* (London: Penguin, 1991), 125–26. It was while helping Collins write *The Frozen Deep* that Dickens first conceived the main idea of *A Tale of Two Cities*.

39. On the harp as the central image in the story, see Robert Boyle, SJ, "'Two Gallants' and 'Ivy Day in the Committee Room,'" *JJQ* 1, no. 1 (Fall 1993). Joyce emphasized the importance of the harp, writing to his brother Stanislaus: "And after all *Two Gallants*—with the Sunday crowds and the harp in Kildare Street and Lenehan—is an Irish landscape" (*JJL*, 2:166).

40. Walter Benjamin, "The Flâneur," in *The Arcades Project*, ed. Rolf Tiedeman, trans. Howard Eiland and Kevin McLaughlin (Cambridge, MA: Belknap Press, 1999), 435.

41. Rex Ingram, *A Long Way from Tipperary*, 188, cited in Ruth Barton, *Rex Ingram: Visionary Director of the Silent Screen* (Lexington: University of Kentucky Press, 2015), 24. John Martin-Harvey starred eventually in the film version *The Only Way*, directed by Herbert Wilcox in 1926.

42. Not noted for her irony, the compromised hero and Sydney Carton figure is called "Desmond Ryan," the name of Patrick Pearse's secretary and a prominent Easter Rising combatant, who is the subject of chapter 9, below.

43. Eimar O'Duffy, review of *The Walk of a Queen*, by Annie P. Smithson, *Irish Review* 1, no. 6 (January 6, 1923): 70–71, reprinted in the *Irish Journal of Literature*, Eimar O'Duffy Issue, VII, no. 1 (January 1978): 14–15. Alexander Dumas's story "The Corsican Brothers," popularized by the Irish playwright Dion Boucicault in his melodramatic adaptation in 1852, prefigures Dickens's *Tale*: see Joss Marsh, "Mimi and Matinée Idol; Martin-Harvey, Sydney Carton and the Staging of *A Tale of Two Cities*, 1860–1939," in *Charles Dickens, "A Tale of Two Cities" and the French Revolution*, ed. Colin Jones, Josephine McDonagh, and Jon Mee (Basingstoke, UK: Palgrave, 2009), 130, 138.

44. Kevin Rockett, "Emmet on Film," *History Ireland* 11, no. 3 (Autumn 2003).

45. W. J. McCormack, *Dublin 1916: The French Connection* (Dublin: Gill and Macmillan, 2012), 12–13.

46. Sergei Eisenstein, "Dickens, Griffith, and the Film Today" in *Film Form*, trans. Jay Leyda (London: Dennis Dobson, 1963), 213.

47. Michael Farrell, *Thy Tears Might Cease* (1963; repr., London: Arrow, 1968), 263, 267. Michael Farrell (1899–1962) was a veteran of the War of Independence and was imprisoned in Mountjoy Prison for his activities. His finely achieved novel was published posthumously and ranks with O'Duffy's *The Wasted Island* as the most insightful fictional treatment of the slow gestation of events leading to the Easter Rising.

48. Ronan McGreevy, "Irishman's Diary," *Irish Times*, July 20, 2020. For the opposition of German autocratic values in war rhetoric to French republicanism, see Willi Jasper, *Lusitania: The Cultural History of a Catastrophe* (New Haven, CT: Yale University Press, 2016), 153–65. By contrast, for James Connolly, the more advanced state of socialism in Germany (as the scale of post–Great War revolutions showed) was the crucial factor in determining its more progressive politics.

49. Farrell, *Thy Tears Might Cease*, 265. It is noteworthy that Martin does not notice, or suppresses, the invocation of God in the Proclamation.

50. Roisín Higgins, "'The Irish Republic Was Proclaimed by Poster': The Politics of Commemorating the Easter Rising," in *Remembering 1916: The Easter Rising, the Somme and the Politics of Memory in Ireland*, ed. Richard S. Grayson and Fearghal McGarry (Cambridge: Cambridge University Press, 2016), 51.

51. Max Caulfield, *The Easter Rebellion* (London: Four Square Books, 1965), 272.

52. Eugene Cadava, *Words of Light: Theses on the Photography of History* (Princeton, NJ: Princeton University Press, 1997), 61.

53. Orla Fitzpatrick, "Photography, Dublin and 1916," in *Reflecting 1916: Photography and the Easter Rising*, ed. Trish Lambe and Tanya Kiang (Dublin: Gallery of Photography, 2016), 22.

54. Patrick J. Kelly, *BMH*, no. 781, 63.

55. Fintan Cullen, *Ireland on Show: Art, Union, and Nationhood* (Farnham: Ashgate, 2012), 97–124; Kevin Rockett and Emer Rockett, *Magic Lantern, Panorama and Moving Slide Shows in Ireland, 1786–1909* (Dublin: Four Courts Press, 2011), 70–71.

56. Catherine Morris, *Alice Milligan and the Irish Cultural Revival* (Dublin: Four Courts Press, 2012), 256–60.

57. W. B. Yeats, *Memoirs*, ed. Denis Donoghue (New York: Macmillan, 1973), 42.

58. See Roland Barthes's comments on the "eyes raised heavenwards" in a famous half-profile shot of John F. Kennedy: "The Photographic Message," in *Image/Music/Text*, trans. Stephen Heath (London: Fontana, 1977), 22.

59. Elaine Sisson, "Masculinity and Citizenship: Boyhood and Nationhood at St Enda's," in *The Life and After-Life of P. H. Pearse: Pádraic Mac Piarais: Saol agus Oidhreacht*, ed. Roisín Higgins and Regina Uí Choilleatáin (Dublin: Irish Academic Press, 2009), 215.

60. Joanna Lowry, "History, Allegory, Technologies of Vision," in *History Painting Re-assessed: The Representation of History in Contemporary Art*, ed. David Green and Peter Seddon (Manchester: Manchester University Press, 2000), 9.

61. James W. Harkins Jr. *Sydney Carton: A Tale of Two Cities* (Mount Holyoke, MA: Shea Dramatic Series, 1900), 81.

62. See Dickens's letter (in French) from Paris to his friend John Forster in the year

of revolutions, 1848: "I find that I like the Republic so much that I must renounce my own language and only write in the language of the French Republic—the language of gods and angels—the language, in a word, of the French people." Cited and translated in Gareth Stedman Jones, "The Redemptive Powers of Violence? Carlyle, Marx and Dickens," in *Charles Dickens, "A Tale of Two Cities" and the French Revolution*, ed. Jones, McDonagh, and Mee, 57.

63. Jones, 56.

64. Dickens, *A Tale of Two Cities*, 359–60.

65. For Ernest Bloch, "Visual montage is an appropriate vehicle for representing utopianism since its juxtaposition of fragments allows for a blossoming of allegory—providing multiple jumping off points in the present from which to imagine a better future." Ernst Bloch, *The Utopian Function of Art and Literature*, cited in Maud Lavin, "Photomontage, Mass Culture, and Modernity: Utopianism in the Circle of New Advertising Designers," in *Montage and Modern Life, 1919–1942*, ed. Maud Lavin et al. (Cambridge, MA: MIT Press, 1992), 53.

66. Hayden White, "The Modernist Event," in *Figural Realism: Studies in the Mimesis Effect* (Baltimore: Johns Hopkins University Press, 1999), 81.

67. Steve Coleman, "Mobilized Sound: Memory, Inscription, and Vision in Irish Traditional Music," *Irish Journal of Anthropology* 13, no. 1 (2010): 28.

68. Walter Benjamin, "[On the Theory of Knowledge, Theory of Progress]," in *The Arcades Project*, 461. Writing on Dickens and film, Eisenstein argues that structures of montage are situated in the society they articulate: "The question of montage imagery is based on a definite structure and system of thinking; it derives and has been derived only through collective consciousness, appearing as a reflection of a new (socialist) stage of human society and as a thinking result of ideal and philosophic education, inseparably connected with the social structure of that society": Eisenstein, "Dickens, Griffith, and the Film Today," 245.

69. Benjamin, "[On the Theory of Knowledge, Theory of Progress]," 461.

70. Sean Healy, BMH, no. 1479, 35.

71. Charlie Chaplin, *My Autobiography* (London: Penguin, 2003), 280–81; Manus O'Riordan, "Larkin in America: The Road to Sing Sing," in *James Larkin: Lion of the Fold*, ed. Donal Nevin (Dublin: Gill and Macmillan, 1998), 72–73; ["On Larkin: A Miscellany"], "Charlie Chaplin and the Slippers," in *James Larkin*, ed. Nevin, 473.

Chapter Five

1. Theodor W. Adorno, "The Position of the Narrator in the Contemporary Novel" (1954), in *Notes to Literature*, vol. 1, trans. Shierry Weber Nicholson (New York: Columbia University Press, 1991), 31. Adorno continues: "A narrative that presented itself as though the narrator had mastered this kind of experience would rightly meet with impatience and skepticism on the part of its audience."

2. Cited in William Irwin Thompson, *The Imagination of an Insurrection* (Oxford: Oxford University Press, 1967), 107.

3. V. I. Lenin, "The Irish Rebellion of 1916," in *1916: The Easter Rising*, ed. O. Dudley Edwards and Fergus Pyle (London: Macgibbon & Kee, 1968), 194.

4. Conor Mulvagh, "How Loss of Ireland Signaled the End of the British Empire," *Irish Independent*, January 21, 2019.

5. Cited in Deirdre MacMahon, "Ireland and the Empire-Commonwealth, 1900–1948," in *The Oxford History of the British Empire*, vol. IV, *The Twentieth Century*, ed. Judith M. Brown and Wm. Roger Louis (Oxford: Oxford University Press, 1999), 146.

6. Queneau also includes the famous tenor "John Mac Cormack" among the rebels, whom Joyce greatly admired and with whom he shared a singing platform at a concert in Dublin, 1904. MacCormack's singing teacher Vincent O'Brien agreed with his Italian teachers in Dublin that "after MacCormack, Joyce's voice was the 'closest in quality'" to that of the great tenor. John Scarry, "James Joyce and John McCormack," *Revue Belge de Philologie et d'Histoire*, 52, no. 3 (1974): 525.

7. Raymond Queneau, *We Always Treat Women Too Well*, trans. Barbara Wright (London: Oneworld Classics, 2011), 124.

8. Queneau, 51.

9. Queneau, 45–46. In a joke footnote, echoing Karl Radek's critique of *Ulysses* in 1934, the incongruity of mentioning Joyce's name is pointed out: "There is a slight anachronism here, but Caffrey, being illiterate, could not have known in 1916 that *Ulysses* had not yet appeared" (46).

10. Jay Winter, *Sites of Memory, Sites of Mourning: The Great War in European Cultural History* (Cambridge: Cambridge University Press, 1995).

11. Paul Fussell, *The Great War and Modern Memory* (Oxford: Oxford University Press, 1975); Samuel Hynes, *A War Imagined: The First World War and English Culture* (London: Bodley Head, 1990).

12. Cited in Georges Didi-Huberman, *The Eye of History: When Images Take Positions*, trans. Shane B. Lillis (Cambridge, MA: MIT Press, 2018), 57.

13. Didi-Huberman, 63.

14. Fussell, *The Great War*, 21–23. This was not confined to literature but extended also to medical treatment: as noted in the introduction above, doctors and psychologists struggled to make sense of war neurosis or "shell-shock," leaving hospitals such as Craiglockhart or Dublin's Richmond War Hospital to deal with the walking wounded.

15. Fussell, 174.

16. Hynes, *A War Imagined*, 343.

17. Fussell, *The Great War*, 183, 310; emphasis added. Pro-forma postcards were distributed to soldiers, in which soldiers simply filled in blanks to convey feelings that defeated personal expression (185–86).

18. Thomas MacGreevy, *Jack B. Yeats: An Appreciation and an Interpretation* (Dublin: Victor Waddington, 1946), 26. For modernist responses in this context, see David Lloyd, "Republics of Difference: Yeats, MacGreevy, Beckett," *Field Day Review* 1 (2005): 43–66.

19. Geert Buelens, *Everything to Nothing: The Poetry of the Great War, Revolution and the Transformation of Europe*, trans. David McKay (London: Verso, 2015), 76–77.

20. Buelens, 77.

21. Citing a real-life equivalent of Joyce's use of the technique, Mary Colum notes a stenographic report taken down verbatim of a wounded criminal in New York, "incapable of imposing any logic on what he was saying," and strongly resembling Molly Bloom's soliloquy in all but its added punctuation. Mary Colum, *From These Roots: The Ideas That Have Made Modern Literature* (London: Jonathan Cape, 1938), 319.

22. Walter Benjamin, *The Writer of Modern Life: Essays on Charles Baudelaire*, ed. Michael Jennings (Cambridge, MA: Harvard University Press, 2006), 172.

23. Buelens, *Everything to Nothing*, 77.

24. Buelens, 146.

25. "A Dyspeptic Portrait," *Freeman's Journal*, April 7, 1917, in *JJCH*, 1:98.

26. As Kraus's translators Fred Bridgham and Edward Timms note, "This medley of authentic detail and imaginative fantasy may remind readers of Joyce's *Ulysses*": Kraus, *The Last Days of Mankind: The Complete Text* (New Haven, CT: Yale University Press, 2015), 591.

27. Elaine Sisson, "'A Note on What Happened': Experimental Influences on the Irish Stage: 1919–1929," in Forum Kritika: Radical Theatre on Ireland (Part 2), 133, *Kritika Kultura*, no. 15 (2010): 132–48, https://ajol.ateneo.edu/kk/articles/59/562.

28. Bloch, "Revue Form in Philosophy" (1928), in *HT*, 334.

29. *The Prison Letters of Countess Markievicz* (London: Virago, 1987), 156.

30. *Prison Letters*, 192.

31. *Prison Letters*, 229.

32. See Paige Reynolds, "Modernist Martyrdom: Scripting the Death of Terence MacSwiney," in *Modernism, Drama, and the Audience for Irish Spectacle* (Cambridge: Cambridge University Press, 2011), 116–55.

33. Cited in Nicholas Allen, *Modernism, Ireland, and Civil War* (Cambridge: Cambridge University Press, 2009), 54.

34. Virginia Woolf, diary entry, October 25, 1920, in *A Writer's Diary: Being Extracts from the Diary of Virginia Woolf*, ed. Leonard Woolf (San Diego: Harvest, 1982), 28.

35. Wyndham Lewis, *The Lion and the Fox: The Role of the Hero in the Plays of Shakespeare* (1927; repr., London: Methuen, 1966), 322.

36. John Wyse Jackson and Peter Costello, *John Stanislaus Joyce: The Voluminous Life and Genius of James Joyce's Father* (London: Fourth Estate, 1998), 98.

37. Ezra Pound to John Quinn, October 31, 1920, in *The Selected Letters of Ezra Pound to John Quinn, 1915–1924*, ed. Timothy Materer (Durham, NC: Duke University Press, 1991), 199.

38. Instead of an armed uprising in Dublin, republican units nationwide systematically burned over one hundred tax offices and two hundred police barracks throughout the country to cripple financial and local administration.

39. Extensive sections were initially published in the *Freeman's Journal*, August 23, 1920, but Gallagher was not happy with the formatting. Declan Jackson, "The 'Indivisible' Truth: The Public and Private Writings of Frank Gallagher, 1911–65" (PhD thesis, University of Limerick, 2014), 109.

40. Jackson, 199–200. As Jackson notes, the staccato, abbreviated form is also found in Gallagher's unpublished diaries, suggesting that even the exigency of a shortage of paper may also have contributed to the compression of language (141).

41. Jackson, 204.

42. Journal entry, December 2, 1928, in *Lady Gregory's Journals, 1916–1930*, ed. Lennox Robinson (London: Putnam, 1946), 249. Lady Gregory's review in the *Nation and Athenaeum*, December 15, 1928, is reprinted in Lucy McDiarmid, "The Demotic Lady Gregory," in *High and Low Moderns: Literature and Culture, 1889–1939*, ed. Maria di Battista and Lucy McDiarmid (New York: Oxford University Press, 1996), 232–34.

43. Ernst Bloch, "Preface to the 1935 Edition," in *HT*, 3.

44. Ernst Bloch, "Upper Middle Classes, Objectivity and Montage," in *HT*, 224.

45. Walter Benjamin, "[On the Theory of Knowledge, Theory of Progress]," in *The Arcades Project*, ed. Rolf Tiedeman, trans. Howard Eiland and Kevin McLaughlin (Cambridge, MA: Belknap Press, 1999), 475.

46. Frank Gallagher, *Days of Fear: Diary of a 1920s Hunger Striker* (1928; repr., Cork: Mercier Press, 2008), 30, 67; ellipses in original. Henceforth *DF*, followed by page numbers in text and notes.

47. David Hogan [Frank Gallagher], *The Four Glorious Years* (Dublin: Irish Press, 1954), 44. Leeann Lane notes that characters in Dorothy Macardle's prison stories from the same period in her collection *Earth-Bound* (1924) look not to heaven for fortitude but to the Irish past: in "'The Prisoner,' the unrequited ghost appears from the betrayal of Lord Edward Fitzgerald in the 1798 rebellion." Leann Lane, *Dorothy Macardle* (Dublin: University College Dublin Press, 2019), 69–70.

48. Michael Biggs, "The Rationality of Self-Inflicted Sufferings: Hunger Strikes by Irish Republicans, 1916–1923," Sociology Working Papers, Paper no. 2007-03, University of Oxford, 8–9, https://users.ox.ac.uk/~sfos0060/SWP2007-03.pdf.

49. Hogan [Gallagher], *Four Glorious Years*, 44.

50. Hogan [Gallagher], 189. Gallagher had already described an early version of this graphic picture in words in *Days of Fear*: "I see them—that blue transparency in their faces which fasting gives, big wide eyes with a steady stare in them, lips pressed tightly together" (*DF*, 111).

51. C. S. ("Todd") Andrews was admitted to Mountjoy at the same time as Salkeld and shared a cell with him. C. S. Andrews, *Dublin Made Me* (Dublin: Mercier Press, 1979), 137–43.

52. For this artistic movement, see Matthew Gale and Katy Wan, *Magic Realism: Art in Weimar Germany 1919–33* (London: Tate, 2018).

53. Joseph Lennon, "The Starvation of a Man: Terence MacSwiney and Famine Memory," in *The Famine and the Troubles: Memory Ireland*, vol. 4, ed. Oona Frawley (Syracuse, NY: Syracuse University Press, 2014), 70.

54. At the age of five, Weil gave up sugar in sympathy with French soldiers surviving on rations in the Great War. Though France in World War Two did not undergo the widespread starvation experienced in the Soviet Union and Eastern Europe (and the Netherlands during the 1944–45 *Hongerwinte*), systematic requisitioning of goods for German consumption ensured calorie intake dropped to just over one-half of its prewar rate, with consequent increases in mortality. Cormac Ó Gráda, "The Famines of WWII," CEPR policy portal, VoxEU.org, September 2, 2019, https://voxeu.org/article/famines-wwii.

55. Siobhan Campbell, "Biographical Note," to Kathleen Coyle, *The Magical Realm: An Irish Childhood* (1943; repr., Dublin: Wolfhound Press, 1997), 269. Coyle recounts her acquaintance with the Joyces in "My Last Visit with James Joyce," *Tomorrow* 10, no. 2 (October 1950): 15–17.

56. Simone Weil, "London Notebook," in *First and Last Notebooks*, trans. Richard Rees (Oxford: Oxford University Press, 1970), 364.

57. Richard Rees, foreword to *First and Last Notebooks*, by Weil, xiii.

58. Kathleen Coyle, *A Flock of Birds* (New York: Dutton, 1930), 14. Henceforth *FB*, followed by page numbers, in text and notes.

59. Simone Weil, "Pre-War Notebook (1933–1939)," in *First and Last Notebooks*, 3.

60. "If the lower part of the soul is laid bare and exposed through the destruction of the discursive part, and if in this way perpetual duration is traversed with a finite lapse of time ... eternal light will have pity and envelope the entire soul within its eternity." Simone Weil, "New York Notebook, 1942," in *First and Last Notebooks*, 292.

61. *FB*, 252. As Gerardine Meaney notes, "This sense of dislocation, of living in an afterwards drained of significance, is very strong in the women's fiction from this period dealing with wars global and local, from the perspective, as Coyle puts it, of the woman thinking 'it out for a very long time afterwards.'" Gerardine Meaney, "Fiction, 1922–1960," in *A History of Modern Irish Women's Literature*, ed. Heather Ingman and Cliona Ó Gallchoir (Cambridge: Cambridge University Press, 2018), 196.

62. *FB*, 42. "Russell" is possibly George Russell (1867–1935), whose interventions in the Dublin Lock-Out of 1913 were valued by socialists. It may also refer to Coyle's fellow socialist Charles Russell, whose pamphlet *Should the Workers of Ireland Support Sinn Féin?* (1919) echoes the sentiments of her *Sinn Féin and Socialism* (1919) publication, discussed below.

63. The difficulties in dating the action are noted by John Cronin and John Wilson Foster, with Foster opting for 1918: John Cronin, "Kathleen Coyle (1886–1952): *A Flock of Birds*," in *The Anglo-Irish Novel*, vol. 2, *1900–1940* (Belfast: Appletree Press, 1990), 135; John Wilson Foster, *Irish Novels, 1890–1940: New Bearings in Culture and Fiction* (Oxford: Oxford University Press, 2008), 478.

64. *FB*, 164. In an extended passage in *Portrait*, the wheeling of a flock of birds in the air outside the National Library relieves Stephen of his present anxieties as if pointing to the future, indicating why birds were auguries in antiquity (*P*, 243–44).

65. Cited in Gabriella Fiori, *Simone Weil: An Intellectual Biography*, trans. Joseph R. Berrigan (Athens: University of Georgia Press, 1989), 10; emphasis added.

66. Anne Fogarty, "'A World of Hotels and Gaols': Women Novelists and the Spaces of Irish Modernism, 1930–32," in *Modernist Afterlives in Irish Literature and Culture*, ed. Paige Reynolds (London: Anthem Press, 2016), 19.

67. *FB*, 256. In their last meeting, Christy informs Catherine that Cicely, his politically sympathetic girlfriend, had recounted to him the incident about the flock of birds in his childhood: "'I did not know you had told her that. It is a long time since I heard it . . . when I was a little child . . .' 'When you were a little child.' 'Mother! It will only be a flock of birds . . . it will pass.' 'I know it will pass.' It's meaning would never pass" (*FB*, 254).

68. Gabriel Marcel had asked Vladimir Nabokov to step in at the last moment to deliver a lecture on Pushkin that was attended by Joyce: "Pushkin, or the Real and the Plausible," *New York Review of Books*, March 31, 1988.

69. Cronin, *The Anglo-Irish Novel*, 2:135. See also Foster, *Irish Novels, 1890–1940*, 477.

70. Coyle, "My Last Visit with James Joyce," 17.

71. For Eliot, speaking at Washington State University in 1953, "The *point de repère* usually and conveniently taken as the starting-point of modern poetry is the group denominated 'imagists' in London about 1910." Cited in Peter Jones, ed., *Imagist Poetry* (London: Penguin, 1972), 14. The first "Tour Eiffel"/Imagist meeting took place on March 25, 1909, with T. E. Hulme extending invitations to F. S. Flint, Joseph Campbell (who was addressed by the misspelt Gaelic version of his name, Seosamh MacCathmoil), Edward Storer, and "4 or 5 other 'versers.'" Helen Carr, *The Verse Revolutionaries: Ezra Pound, H.D. and the Imagists* (London: Jonathan Cape, 2009), 165.

72. Carr, *Verse Revolutionaries*, 174.

73. Hugh Kenner, *The Pound Era* (Berkeley: University of California Press, 1971), 182.

74. Alex Davis, "Joseph Campbell and the London Avant-Garde," in *The Irish Revival Reappraised*, ed. Betsey Taylor FitzSimon and James H. Murphy (Dublin: Four Courts Press, 2004), 151, 153.

75. William Pratt, introduction to *The Imagist Poem: Poetry in Miniature* (New York: Dutton, 1961), 22, 29.

76. Alex Davis, "Joseph Campbell and the London Avant-Garde," 47–48.

77. Pratt, introduction to *The Imagist Poem*, 24.

78. Carr, *Verse Revolutionaries*, 196.

79. See the opening stanza in "Deep Ways and Dripping Boughs," which anticipates Poundian imagery: "Deep ways and dripping boughs, / The fog falling drearily; / Cowherds calling on their cows, / And I crying wearily, / Wearily, wearily, out-a-door, / Houseless, hearthless, coatless, kindless, / Poorest of the wandering poor." The poem goes on to depict the "beggar Christ" as a wanderer and outcast, a measure of his own dissenting Christianity. *The Poems of Joseph Campbell*, ed. Austin Clarke (Dublin: Allen Figgis, 1963), 103–4.

80. Joseph Campbell, "I Am the Mountainy Singer," in *Poems of Joseph Campbell*, 77.

81. James Joyce, "Gas from a Burner" (1912) in *The Portable James Joyce*, ed. Harry Levin (New York: Penguin, 1985), 661.

82. Ezra Pound to James Joyce, March 1, 1917, in *Pound/Joyce: The Letters of Ezra Pound to James Joyce, with Pound's Essays on Joyce*, ed. Forrest Read (New York: New Directions, 1967), 94. Campbell's marriage to Nancy Maude in 1910 led to estrangement from her English military family background, though her great-grandmother, Emily, was half-sister to Lord Edward Fitzgerald.

83. Joseph Campbell, *"As I Was among the Captives": Joseph Campbell's Prison Diary, 1922–1923*, ed. Eiléan Ní Chuilleanáin (Cork: Cork University Press, 2001), 111. Henceforth *JCPD*, followed by page numbers in text and notes.

84. Michael Hopkinson, *Green Against Green: A History of the Irish Civil War* (Dublin: Gill and Macmillan, 1988), 268–71.

85. Eiléan Ní Chuilleanáin, "Introduction," *JCPD*, 7.

86. Eugene Sheehy, "My School Friend James Joyce," in *James Joyce: Interviews and Recollections*, ed. E. H. Mikhail (London: Macmillan, 1990), 14.

87. Francis Stuart, *Black List, Section H* (1971; repr., London: Penguin, 1995), 95.

88. Stuart, 96, 101.

89. Samuel Beckett, "MacGreevy on Yeats," in *Disjecta: Miscellaneous Writings and a Dramatic Fragment*, ed. Ruby Cohn (London: John Calder, 1983), 97.

Chapter Six

1. Roger Casement, "The Romance of Irish History," in *The Glories of Ireland*, ed. Joseph Dunn and P. J. Lennox (Washington, DC: Phoenix Limited, 1914), 6. This book was in the Zentralbibliothek, Zurich, used frequently by Joyce.

2. *OCPW*, 110. For discussions of Joyce and the Phoenicians, see Elizabeth Butler Cullingford, "Phoenician Genealogies and Oriental Geographies: Joyce, Language and Race," in *Semicolonial Joyce*, ed. Derek Attridge and Marjorie Howes (Cambridge: Cambridge University Press, 2000), 219–39; Carol Shloss, "Joyce in the Context of Irish Orientalism," *JJQ* 35, nos. 2/3 (1998): 264–71; Joseph Lennon, *Irish Orientalism: A Literary and Intellectual History* (Syracuse, NY: Syracuse University Press, 2008),

207–14. Joyce's interest in Phoenician connections may have been rekindled by his reading of the early works of the Italian historian Guglielmo Ferrero: see Salvatore Pappalardo, "Waking Europa: Joyce, Ferrero and the Metamorphosis of Irish History," *Journal of Modern Literature* 34, no. 2 (Winter 2011): 154–77.

3. Having been regarded as discredited, the indebtedness of Celtic languages to Phoenician outposts on the Atlantic, and particularly the Phoenician alphabet, has taken on a new momentum through the recent linguistic and archaeological researches of John T. Koch, Barry Cunliffe, and others. See John T. Koch, "Phoenicians in the West and the Break-up of the Atlantic Bronze Age and Proto-Celtic," in *Celtic from the West 3: Atlantic Europe in the Metal Ages: Questions of Shared Language*, ed. John T. Koch and Barry Cunliffe (Oxford: Oxbow Books, 2016), 431–77. The implications of Koch's and Cunliffe's theories for questioning uniform notions of mythic "Celts" are noted in J. P. Mallory, *The Origins of the Irish* (London: Thames and Hudson, 2013), 246–52, and Alice Roberts, *The Celts: Search for a Civilization* (London: Heron Books, 2015), 225–75. Barry Cunliffe provided the foreword to Bob Quinn's iconoclastic *The Atlantean Irish: Ireland's Oriental and Maritime Heritage* (Dublin: Lilliput Press, 2005).

4. As Vincent Cheng points out, Joyce had a copy of *Britisches gegen Deutsches Imperium* (1915), with a foreword by Roger Casement, in his Trieste library. Vincent Cheng, *Joyce, Race, and Empire* (Cambridge: Cambridge University Press, 1995), 130.

5. Roderick O'Flaherty, *Ogygia: Seu Rerum Hibernicarum Chronologia* [*Ogygia: Or a Chronological Account of Irish Events*] (1685). W. B. Stanford comments: "As his title indicates, he believed that Ireland was the Ogygia described by Plutarch as an island west of Britain visited by Greeks (including Hercules), where the God Cronos lay imprisoned in a cave." Stanford, *Ireland and the Classical Tradition* (Dublin: Allen Figgis, 1976), 205–6.

6. Pádraic and Mary Colum record that Joyce was "deeply impressed" by Bérard's work, attended his funeral, and gave Bérard's translation of the *Odyssey* as a gift to friends. *Our Friend James Joyce*, 89, cited in Michael Seidel, *Epic Geography: James Joyce's "Ulysses"* (Princeton, NJ: Princeton University Press, 1976).

7. James Joyce to Louis Gillet, September 8, 1938, in *JJL*, 1:401, translation in Seidel, *Epic Geography*, 19. For Irish aspects relating to Bérard, see Maria Tymoczko, *The Irish "Ulysses"* (Berkeley: University of California Press, 1994), 36–43.

8. Helen's stay in Phoenicia ties Troy and Phoenicia in ancient epic accounts, and the love of Dido of Carthage for Aeneas of Troy adds a further link (Dido was originally a Phoenician princess before fleeing to Carthage).

9. *The Graphic* (1878), cited in Rachel Bryant Davies, "'A Subject Which Is Peculiarly Adapted to All Cyclists': Popular Understandings of Classical Archaeology in the Nineteenth Century," in *Victorian Culture and the Origins of Disciplines*, ed. Bernard Lightman and Bennet Zon (London: Routledge, 2020), 178.

10. Cited in Angus Mitchell, *Roger Casement* (Dublin: O'Brien Press, 2013), 167.

11. Roger Casement to Wilfred Scawen Blunt, May 14, 1914, cited in Séamas Ó Siocháin, *Roger Casement: Imperialist, Rebel, Revolutionary* (Dublin: Lilliput, 2008), 377.

12. John Redmond was always "more conscious than any of his Irish colleagues of Britain as the centre of a great empire, where for white men at least, self-government was a natural and reasonable objective." F. S. L. Lyons, *Ireland since the Famine* (London: Weidenfeld and Nicholson, 1971), 261. There were notable dissenters from this

view in the Irish Parliamentary Party, among them James J. O'Kelly: see Paul A. Townend, *The Road to Home Rule: Anti-Imperialism and Irish National Movement* (Madison: University of Wisconsin Press, 2016).

13. Joseph Farrell, "Walcott's *Omeros*: The Classical Epic in a Postmodern Word," in *Epic Traditions in the Contemporary World: The Poetics of Community*, ed. Margaret Beissinger, Jane Tylus, and Susanne Wofford (Berkeley: University of California Press, 1999), 287.

14. Joep Leerssen, *Remembrance and Imagination: Patterns in the Historical and Literary Representation of Ireland in the Nineteenth Century* (Cork: Cork University Press, 1996), 72–73, 245. The Roman historian Varro placed the Celts alongside the Phoenicians and Carthaginians in antiquity, and Leerssen traces the modern origins of the Phoenician model to the mid-seventeenth-century linguistic research of the French scholar Samuel Bochart, which passed into Irish culture through the influence of the native Irish scholar Seán Ó Neachtain and, as noted above, later in the eighteenth century by Charles Vallancey.

15. See Pappalardo, "Waking Europa," 172; and also R. J. Schork, "Awake, Phoenician Too Frequently," *JJQ* 27, no. 4 (Summer 1990): 767–76.

16. Sir William Betham, *The Gael and Cymbri; or, An Inquiry into the Origin and History of the Irish Scoti, Britons, and Gauls* (Dublin: William Curry, Jun, and Co., 1834); Thomas Moore, *History of Ireland*, 3 vols. (London: Longman, Brown, and Green, 1838–46). In addition to Moore, Catholic apologists such as the Rev. Charles O'Conor, Dr. John Lanigan, and John D'Alton also defended Phoenician ancestry. For the controversies surrounding O'Brien's boundless scholarship, see Leerssen, *Remembrance and Imagination*, 113–20.

17. For Ireland, the Cyclops, and history painting, see Luke Gibbons, "'In the Cyclops Eye': James Barry, Historical Portraiture, and Colonial Ireland," in *A Shared Legacy: Essays on Irish and Scottish Art and Visual Culture*, ed. Fintan Cullen and John Morrison (Aldershot, UK: Ashgate, 2005), 35–60.

18. Doctore Joachimo Laurentio Villanueva, *Phœnician Ireland*, translated and illustrated with Notes, Plates, and Ptolemy's Map of Erin made Modern, by Henry O'Brien (London: Longman & Co. 1833), 78–79.

19. Villanueva, *Phoenician Ireland*, 78–79. This rehabilitation of the Cyclops is not without foundation in the mythological sources: in Hesiod's version of the origins of the Cyclops, they were imprisoned by their father, Uranus, in Tartarus and worked subsequently in subterranean forges under Mount Etna where they made thunderbolts for Zeus.

20. Cited as a gloss on Abbé Melchior Cesarotti's *Critical Observations of the First Book of Fingal*, in *The Poems of Ossian in Original Gaelic*, with a literal translation into Latin, by the late Robert MacFarlan, A.M., vol. 1 (London: W. Bulmer, 1807), cc.

21. Lennon, *Irish Orientalism*, 205–14. As late as 1922, Robert Dunlop's *Ireland from the Earliest Times to the Present Day*, published by Oxford University Press, upheld the Phoenician origins of the Irish (Cullingford, "Phoenician Genealogies," 231). As noted above (222n2, 267n3, and 268n14), recent research on Atlantic ancestry has problematized the standard nineteenth-century model of central European origins of the Celts. As John T. Koch avers, "Despite repeated debunkings and general signs of exhaustion... the standard narrative of the Celts still begins in Iron Age central Europe": "I think there has been a tendency to ignore the Iberian material... and that's because there

is a conflict with this standard model if we have evidence of a very early Celtic presence out of the Atlantic west." Cited in Roberts, *The Celts*, 249, 248.

22. Norman Vance, *Irish Literature: A Social History* (Oxford: Blackwell, 1990), 201. See also Vance, "Celts, Carthaginians and Constitutions: Anglo-Irish Literary Relations, 1780–1820," *Irish Historical Studies* 22, no. 87 (March 1981): 216–38.

23. Colum Kenny, *The Enigma of Arthur Griffith: "Father of Us All"* (Newbridge: Merrion Press, 2020).

24. See Dermot Keogh and Andrew McCarthy, *Limerick Boycott 1904: Anti-Semitism in Ireland* (Cork: Mercier Press, 2005), 65–68.

25. Gerald Y. Goldberg, "'Ireland Is the Only Country': Joyce and the Jewish Dimension," *The Crane Bag* 6, no. 1 (1982): 7.

26. Marcus de Búrca, *Michael Cusack and the GAA* (Dublin: Anvil Books, 1989), 47. See also John Garvin, *James Joyce's Disunited Kingdom, and the Irish Dimension* (Dublin: Gill and Macmillan, 1976), 92.

27. In Joyce's mock-heroic version, the boulder is converted into a biscuit tin and, in an early draft of the chapter, is directly attributed to Cusack's prowess in the shot put: "Out runs Cusack and the bloody biscuit tin in his hand and little Alf trying to hold him and roaring:—Where is he till I murder him!—It was the mercy of God that the sun was in his eyes. Anyway he made a swipe in the air and let fly. God, he near sent it to the county Longford. The bloody tin fell on the cobblestone with a {clatter} that would waken the dead. You know he's a powerful fellow Cusack. Best man in Ireland in his time at putting the fifty six pound shot. That's a fact. He won prizes and cups and medals. O, Cusack was a famous man in his day, faith." Scene 4, Draft V.A.8, in Philip F. Herring, "Material for 'Cyclops,'" in *Joyce's Notes and Early Drafts for "Ulysses": Selections from the Buffalo Collection* (Charlottesville: University of Virginia Press), 165.

28. Marcus de Búrca, *Michael Cusack and the GAA* (Dublin: Anvil Books, 1989), 180.

29. De Búrca, 15.

30. Herring, "Material for 'Cyclops,'" 153–55; *Celtic Times*, April 16, 1887, 6; April 9, 1887, 2; April 2, 1887, 4; May 7, 1887, 4; June 18, 1887, 3.

31. De Búrca, *Michael Cusack and the GAA*, 153.

32. James Joyce to Stanislaus Joyce, September 18, 1906, in *JJL*, 2:167.

33. For overlaps between the citizen's and Joyce's views as expressed in his journalism, see Emer Nolan, *Joyce and Nationalism* (London: Routledge, 1995), 96–113.

34. As Maria Tymoczko notes: "Part of the irony of the chapter is that much of the automated thinking of the nationalists also derives from the discourses of the English, the hated 'Sassenach': trite, late Victorian views of death, chivalry, and science, expressed in a language of romantic literature, the English press, and the like." Maria Tymoczko, "Joyce's Postpositivist Prose: Cultural Translation and Transculturation," in *Irish Studies in Brazil*, ed. Munira H. Mutran and Laura P. Z. Izarra (São Paulo: Associação Editorial Humanitas, 2005), 209. See also Andrew Gibson, *Joyce's Revenge: History, Politics and Aesthetics in "Ulysses"* (Oxford: Oxford University Press, 2002), 124–25; and the extended discussion in Enda Duffy, *The Subaltern "Ulysses"* (Minneapolis: University of Minnesota Press, 1994), 114–29.

35. Herring, "Material for 'Cyclops,'" 179.

36. Frederick Ryan, "Empire and Liberty," *Dana*, no. 4 (August 1904): 114. *Dana*,

coedited by Eglinton and Ryan, turned down publication of Joyce's essay "A Portrait of the Artist" but published an early poem.

37. C. P. Curran, *James Joyce Remembered* (London: Oxford University Press, 1968), 80.

38. Arthur Griffith, "The Death of Fredrick Ryan," *Sinn Fein*, April 12, 1913, reprinted in "Constructing the Canon: Versions of National Identity," in *The Field Day Anthology of Irish Writing*, ed. Seamus Deane, vol. 2 (Derry: Field Day Publications/ London: Faber and Faber, 1991), 1003. Sheehy Skeffington's riposte to Griffith is also published in this section.

39. For the tensions between insular and outward-looking nationalist currents in "Cyclops," see Cheng, *Joyce, Race, and Empire*, 180–84.

40. See Sam Slote, "Epic Modernism: *Ulysses* and *Finnegans Wake*," in *The Oxford Handbook of Modern Irish Fiction*, ed. Liam Harte (Oxford: Oxford University Press, 2020), 159–161.

41. M. Keith Booker, *"Ulysses," Capitalism, and Colonialism* (Westport, CT: Greenwood Press, 2000), 99.

42. Booker, 98–99.

43. John Nash, "'Hanging over the Bloody Paper,' Newspapers and Imperialism in *Ulysses*," in *Modernism and Empire*, ed. Howard J. Booth and Nigel Rigby (Manchester: Manchester University Press, 2000), 190.

44. Emer Nolan, *James Joyce and Nationalism* (London: Routledge, 1995), 103.

45. *OCPW*, 119. The Anglo-Belgian Indian Rubber Company was one of the chief beneficiaries of the rubber trade in the Congo Free State.

46. E. D. Morel, *Red Rubber: The Story of the Rubber Slave Trade*, with an introduction by Sir Harry H. Johnston (1906; repr., New York: Nassau Print, 2006).

47. See Patrick R. Mullen, *The Bugger's Tool: Irish Modernism, Queer Labour and Postcolonial History* (Oxford: Oxford University Press, 2012).

48. Herring, "Material for 'Cyclops,'" 141. Herring provides valuable background on the Alake's visit, including the fact that Queen Victoria had sent his father, through Lord Chichester, "two bound volumes of the Word of God, saying that that book was the secret of England's greatness" (140).

49. For the Alake's espousal of modernizing policies, see Nash, "'Hanging over the Bloody Newspaper,'" 188–91. In a gloss on this episode, Robert Adams reports that having received a communication from an anthropologist who visited him in 1961, "the Alaki [*sic*] still survives, remembers well his London visit, and is gratified to learn that a record of it is preserved in *Ulysses*." Robert M. Adams, *Surface and Symbol: The Consistency of James Joyce's "Ulysses"* (New York: Oxford University Press, 1962), 202. This raises questions not unlike Alf Bergan's spotting Paddy Dignam after the latter's funeral, for the Alake would appear to have died in 1920. It must refer to his successor, the 7th Alake. See "Oba GBADEBO I, 6th Alake of Abeokuta 1892/1920, born 1854, declared Paramount Ruler of Egbaland circa 1914, married and had issue. He died 28th May 1920," in "Nigeria Ogun State (Abeokuta)," *Hive Blog*, https://hive.blog/new/@denisani/nigeria-ogun-state-abeokuta.

50. R. B. McDowell, *Alice Stopford Green: A Passionate Historian* (Dublin: Allen Figgis, 1968), 63, 65.

51. Cited in Ben Kiernan, "From Irish Famine to Congo Reform: Nineteenth-Century Roots of International Human Rights Law and Activism," in *Confronting*

Genocide, ed. R. Provost and P. Akhavan (Ius Gentium: Comparative Perspectives on Law and Justice 7) (Dordrecht: Springer, 2011), 40.

52. McDowell, *Alice Stopford Green*, 74.

53. Casement, "The Romance of Irish History," 1.

54. Nolan, *James Joyce and Nationalism*, 119.

55. Alice Stopford Green, "The Trade Routes of Ireland," in *The Old Irish World* (Dublin: Gill, 1912), 66. Joyce mentions the wool trade in his "Ireland: Island of Saints and Sages" lecture (*OCPW*, 119). Joyce's familiarity with Green is evident in his listing of her book *Irish Nationality* (1911) in his "Early Commonplace Book": see Luca Crispi, "A Commentary on James Joyce's National Library of Ireland 'Early Commonplace Book': 1903–1912 (MS 36,639/02/A)," *Genetic Joyce Studies* 9 (Spring 2009): 24. Several of Green's works on Irish history were in the Zentralbibliothek, Zurich, used by Joyce.

56. Tacitus, *The Agricola and Germania*, trans. H. Mattingly and S. A. Hanford (Harmondsworth, UK: Penguin, 1970), 81.

57. Patrick R. Mullen, "Ruling Passion: James Joyce, Roger Casement, and the Drama of Universal Love," in *The Bugger's Tool*, 94–116.

58. Roger Casement, "The Keeper of the Sea" (1911), in *The Crime Against Europe: The Writings and Poetry of Roger Casement*, ed. Herbert O. Mackey (Dublin: C.J. Fallon, 1958), 22. The essay was originally published in Roger Casement, *Ireland, Germany and Freedom of the Seas: A Possible Outcome of the War of 1914* (New York: Irish Press Bureau, 1914). These essays echo Alice Stopford Green's histories of the crushing of Irish trade under colonialism, much of which is echoed by the citizen.

59. *The Amazon Journal of Roger Casement*, ed. Angus Mitchell (Dublin: Lilliput Press, 1997), 173, 179; emphasis added.

60. Sharon Sliwinski, "The Childhood of Human Rights: The Kodak on the Congo," *Journal of Visual Culture* 5, no. 3 (2006): 334.

61. Rosa Luxemburg, *The Junius Pamphlet: The Crisis in Social Democracy* (1915), in *The Rosa Luxemburg Reader*, ed. Peter Hurdis and Kevin B. Anderson (New York: Monthly Review Press, 2004), 339. Luxemburg cited Casement's "English Blue Book Report" in *The Accumulation of Capital* (1913; repr., London: Routledge, 2003), 339n6.

62. James Connolly, "Belgian Rubber and Belgian Neutrality," *Irish Worker*, November 14, 1914.

63. "Then and Now," *Irish War News: The Irish Republic* 1, no. 1, Tuesday April 25, 1916, 2.

64. Antony Taylor, *"Down with the Crown": British Anti-Monarchism and Debates about Royalty since 1790* (London: Reaktion, 1999), 21.

65. Taylor, 22.

66. Jordan Goodman, *The Devil and Mr Casement* (London: Verso, 2010), 166.

67. Goodman, 179.

68. "That the citizen would point to Casement as Irish in 1914 ... begins to suggest a post-1916 understanding of Casement in the chapter": Mullen, *The Bugger's Tool*, 99.

69. Roger Casement, "The Ballymoney Meeting," *Times*, October 31, 1913, cited in Tracey Schwartz, "'Fabled by the Daughters of Memory': Roger Casement, James Joyce and the Nationalist Hero," in *Memory Ireland: James Joyce and Cultural Memory*, ed. Oona Frawley and Katherine O'Callaghan (Syracuse, NY: Syracuse University Press, 2014), 79–80.

70. Samuel Moyn, *The Last Utopia: Human Rights in History* (Cambridge, MA: Belknap Press/Harvard University Press, 2010), chap. 3. On joining the Council of Europe in 1949, Ireland, through its Minister for External Affairs Sean MacBride, tried to include a "national right to self-determination" as a preamble to its code of rights. William Schabas, "Ireland: The European Convention on Human Rights and the Personal Contribution of Sean MacBride," in *Judges, Transition, and Human Rights*, ed. John Morison, Kieran McEvoy, and Gordon Anthony (Oxford: Oxford University Press, 2006), 256.

71. Casement, "The Keeper of the Sea," 19.

72. Mitchell, *Roger Casement*, 180–81.

73. *The Amazon Journal of Roger Casement*, 280.

74. Hannah Arendt, *The Origins of Totalitarianism* (1951; repr., New York: Schocken, 2004), 380–81. Henceforth *OT*, followed by page numbers in text.

75. Marjorie Howes, "Joyce, Colonialism, and Nationalism," in *The Cambridge Companion to James Joyce*, ed. Derek Attridge, 2nd ed. (Cambridge: Cambridge University Press, 2004), 254–71.

76. Wyndham Lewis, *Pale-Face: The Philosophy of the Melting Pot* (London: Chatto, 1929), 33, citing—and deprecating—W. E. B. Du Bois's novel, *Dark Princess: A Romance* (New York: Harcourt, Brace, 1928). For the African threat to classical Hellenism, see David Adams, *Colonial Odysseys: Empire and Epic in the Modernist Novel* (Ithaca, NY: Cornell University Press, 2003), 13–45.

77. Casement accepted as "careless" his use of the term "Irish Putumayo" to describe a typhus outbreak and near-famine conditions in Connemara in 1913. As Angus Mitchell explains, "In linking this local incident to the Putumayo atrocities and ultimately to the meta-narrative of Atlantic history he was suggesting that the process of 'colonialism' was a transnational and historical continuum, achieved through deliberate acts of violence and wars of attrition." Angus Mitchell, "'An Irish Putumayo': Roger Casement's Humanitarian Relief Campaign among the Connemara Islanders, 1913–14," *Irish Economic and Social History* 31 (2004): 43–44, 41–60.

78. For destructive rivalry in a far-from-abstract world system in which dominant powers pursue their own national/imperial interests, see Richard Lachmann, *First Class Passengers on a Sinking Ship: Elite Politics and the Decline of Great Powers* (London: Verso, 2020).

79. Joyce had originally placed anticipation of the coming war in O'Madden Burke's mouth in "Cyclops," but deleted it in published version: "[T]here's a war coming for the Sassenachs and the Germans will give them a hell of a gate of going. What the imperial yeomanry got from the Boers is only what you might call a hors d'oeuvre." Herring, *Joyce's Notes and Early Drafts for "Ulysses,"* 180. Myles Crawford also forecasts the war in "Aeolus," speaking of the house of Hapsburg: "Going to be trouble there one day. [. . .] Don't you forget that!" (*U*, 7.543–44).

80. Hermann Broch, "James Joyce and the Present Age" (1932), in *GZ*, 77.

81. Robert K. Weininger, *The German Joyce* (Gainesville: University of Florida Press, 2012), 47–48.

82. Sliwinski, "The Childhood of Human Rights," 356.

83. Hannah Arendt, "What Remains? The Language Remains," in *Essays in Understanding, 1930–1954* (New York: Schocken, 1994), 12; Arendt, *Eichmann in Jerusalem: A Report on the Banality of Evil* (New York: Viking Press, 1965), 268–69; emphasis added.

84. Nicolas Guilhot, "Limited Sovereignty or Producing Governmentality? Two Human Rights Regimes in U.S. Political Discourse," *Constellations* 15, no. 4 (December 2008): 506–7. See also International Commission of Jurists, eds., *Development, Human Rights, and the Rule of Law: Report of a Conference Held in The Hague* (Oxford: Pergamon Press, 1981).

85. Moyn, *The Last Utopia*, 12, 30–31, 42.

86. Herbert O. Mackey, *The Life and Times of Roger Casement* (Dublin: C.J. Fallon, 1954), 119. The rule of English law in Ireland, Casement affirms, "dare not rest on the will of the Irish people, but . . . is a rule derived not from right, but from conquest" (120).

87. A. Dirk Moses, "The Holocaust and World History: Raphael Lemkin and Comparative Methodology," in *The Holocaust and Historical Methodology*, ed. Dan Stone (New York: Berghahn, 2012), 276, 280.

88. Rebecca Solnit, *A Book of Migrations: Some Passages in Ireland* (London: Verso, 2011), 40.

89. Roger Casement, "The Elsewhere Empire" (1914), in *The Crime Against Europe*, ed. Mackay, 82.

90. Casement, "The Romance of Irish History," 6.

Chapter Seven

1. "Memorial to Irish Poets: Pearse, MacDonagh and Plunkett Lauded by Writers Here," *New York Times*, June 29, 1916.

2. Robert Schmuhl, "Peering through the Fog: American Newspapers and the Easter Rising," *Irish Communications Review*, no. 12 (2010): 37.

3. Woodrow Wilson, "Appeal for Support of the League of Nations," Colorado, September 25, 1919, in *Woodrow Wilson: Essential Speeches and Writings of the Scholar-President*, ed. Mario R. Di Nunzio (New York: New York University Press, 2006), 412. Theodore Roosevelt had earlier popularized the term—and animus against— "hyphenated" Americans in his 1915 speech, "Americanism": "There is no such thing as a hyphenated American who is a good American."

4. Shane Leslie, *The Irish Issue in Its American Aspect* (London: T. Fisher Unwin, 1919), 90. Earlier he had noted: "The Celt does not admit compromise. . . . He may be hysterical, but hypocritical—never!" Leslie, *The Celt and His World: A Study of the Relation of the Celt and the Teuton in History* (New York: Scribner's, 1917), 194.

5. F. Scott Fitzgerald to Mars Richard Taylor, June 10, 1917, in *The Letters of Scott Fitzgerald*, ed. Andrew Turnbull (Harmondsworth, UK: Penguin, 1968), 434.

6. Fitzgerald intended to dedicate *This Side of Paradise* to Leslie, but relations cooled following Fay's death and Fitzgerald's marriage. In a later memoir, Leslie wrote of an early draft of the novel that "the manuscript was pushed into my hands by the weeping Fay, who was writing Irish laments and keenings for Fitzgerald." Maggie Gordon Froehlich, "Passionate Discretion: Fitzgerald in the Unpublished Correspondence of Sigourney Fay, Shane Leslie, and William Hemmick," *F. Scott Fitzgerald Review* 10, no. 1 (September 2012): 15.

7. [F. Scott Fitzgerald], review of *The Celt and His World*, by Shane Leslie, *Nassau Literary Magazine* (Princeton), 73 (May 1917), reprinted in *F. Scott Fitzgerald on Authorship*, ed. Matthew J. Bruccoli, with Judith S. Baughmann (Columbia: University of South Carolina Press, 1996), 24–25.

8. F. Scott Fitzgerald, *This Side of Paradise* (1920), introduction by Patrick O'Donnell (London: Penguin, 2000), 23. Henceforth *TSP*, followed by page numbers in text. Leslie's opinions are in the background here: "Sinn Fein is a fever . . . something between the psychology of a race riot and of a religious revival. The riffraff and the rowdy of Ireland are of it, but so also are the radiant and the righteous of soul, and of the best that a nation can contain." Leslie, *The Irish Issue*, 80.

9. Froehlich, "Passionate Discretion," 14–15.

10. F. Scott Fitzgerald to Edmund Wilson, Fall 1917, in *Letters of Scott Fitzgerald*, 341.

11. Froehlich, "Passionate Discretion," 8. Froehlich suggests that both Leslie and Fay "were deeply interested in the role the Church might play influencing international politics, whether in relationship to Irish nationalism or the Great War" (12).

12. F. Scott Fitzgerald to Edmund Wilson, Fall 1917, in *Letters of Scott Fitzgerald*, 341.

13. O'Donnell, "Notes," in *TSP*, 266.

14. Sir Shane Leslie, review of *Ulysses*, *Quarterly Review* 238 (October 1922), in *JJCH*, 1:207. In response to *Ulysses*, Alfred Noyes devoted a full review to what he castigated as "the literary Bolshevism of the Hour": "Rottenness in Literature," *Sunday Chronicle*, October 29, 1922, 2, reprinted as "Alfred Noyes on Literary Bolshevism," in *JJCH*, 1:274–75.

15. Laura O'Connor, *Haunted English: The Celtic Fringe, the British Empire, and De-Anglicization* (Baltimore: Johns Hopkins Press, 2006), 219n25. Moore was also reading Francis Hackett's more supportive views on the Rising in *New Republic*.

16. Brian O'Doherty, "Once Upon a Space: Paintings and Poetry in New York," *University Review* 1, no. 10 (Autumn 1956): 26.

17. Marianne Moore, "Sojourn in the Whale," in *New Collected Poems*, ed. Heather Cass White (London: Faber and Faber, 2017), 35.

18. David Armitage, "The Elephant and the Whale: Empires and Oceans in World History," in *Foundations of Modern International Thought* (Cambridge: Cambridge University Press, 2013), 48; Michelle M. Strong, *Education, Travel, and the 'Civilisation' of the Working Classes* (Basingstoke, UK: Palgrave Macmillan 2014), 167n2.

19. Moore, "Sojourn in the Whale," 35.

20. Leslie, *The Irish Issue*, 14.

21. O'Connor, *Haunted English*, 162, 155.

22. Marianne Moore, "Henry James as a Characteristic American" (1934), in *Complete Prose of Marianne Moore*, ed. Patricia Willis (London: Faber, 1987), 321–22.

23. Leslie, *The Irish Issue*, 73, 87.

24. Ezra Pound, "Thomas MacDonagh as Critic," *Poetry* 8, no. 6 (September 1916): 309.

25. Corbin Henderson, "Too Far from Paris," cited in MacDonagh, *LI*, 15.

26. *The Letters of Ezra Pound to Alice Corbin Henderson*, ed. Ira B. Nadel (Austin: University of Texas Press, 1993), 152.

27. Ezra Pound to John Quinn, August 11, 1916, in *Selected Letters of Ezra Pound to John Quinn, 1915–1924*, ed. Timothy Materer (Durham, NC: Duke University Press, 1991), 80.

28. [Harriet Monroe and Alice Corbin Henderson], introduction to *The New Poetry: An Anthology* (New York: Macmillan, 1918), ix. The spirited enthusiasm for things Irish knew few limits: "One may, for example, believe Synge to be the greatest poet-playwright in English since Shakespeare, and one of the great poets of the world; but a few more decades must pass before such ranking can have authority" (x).

29. A.C.H., "On the Movement," *Poetry* 14, no. 3 (June 1991): 160.

30. *A Modern Book of Criticism*, ed. Lewis Lewisohn (New York: Boni and Liveright, 1919), reissued by the Modern Library, New York (n.d.).

31. Hackett's brother Dominick was a close friend of Thomas MacDonagh's, and the Easter Rising proved instrumental in transferring Francis Hackett's sympathies, as an editor of the *New Republic* based in Chicago in the United States, from Home Rule to Sinn Féin sympathies.

32. Randolph Bourne, "Trans-national America," *The Atlantic*, June 1916, reprinted in *The Radical Will: Selected Writings, 1911–1918*, ed. Olaf Hansen (Berkeley: University of California Press, 1977), 249.

33. *Modern Book of Criticism*, iv. Lewisohn shared his New York publisher, Benjamin Huebsch, with James Joyce and befriended Joyce in Paris, co-drafting the protest against Samuel Roth's piracy of *Ulysses* signed by over one hundred eminent world figures, including Albert Einstein, T. S. Eliot, D. H. Lawrence, Virginia Woolf, and André Gide.

34. Padraic Colum, "Youngest Ireland," *Seven Arts* 2, no. 5 (September 1917): 618.

35. *Modern Book of Criticism*, 135, 137.

36. *Modern Book of Criticism*, 137.

37. *Modern Book of Criticism*, 138.

38. Johann Norstedt, *Thomas MacDonagh: A Critical Biography* (Charlottesville: University Press of Virginia, 1980), 151–52.

39. H. L. Mencken, "The Books of the Irish," *Smart Set* 51, no. 3 (March 1917): 138–44, reprinted as "The Irish Renaissance," in H. L. Mencken, *Smart Set Criticism*, ed. William H. Nolte (Washington, DC: Gateway Editions, 1987), 311, 313

40. H. L. Mencken, *The American Language* (1919; repr., New York: Alfred A. Knopf, 1949), 161–62.

41. Mencken, "Books of the Irish," 311.

42. Mencken, 313, 312.

43. Mencken, 312–13.

44. Ernest Boyd, *H. L. Mencken* (New York: Robert M. McBride, 1925), 74, 44. For Boyd's early championing of the distinctive Irish nature of Joyce's achievements, see John McCourt, *Consuming Joyce: 100 Years of "Ulysses" in Ireland* (London: Bloomsbury, 2022), 39–41, 65–66; and Luke Gibbons, *Joyce's Ghosts: Ireland, Modernism, and Memory* (Chicago: University of Chicago Press, 2015), 83–85.

45. Van Wyck Brooks, "On Creating a Usable Past," *Dial* 64, no. 764 (April 11, 1918): 337–41. The concept of a usable past has generated an extensive literature, including Henry Steele Commager, *The Search for a Usable Past and Other Essays in Historiography* (New York: Alfred A. Knopf, 1967); Russell Reising, *The Unusable Past: Theory and the Study of American Literature* (London: Methuen, 1986); and Casey Nelson Blake, *Beloved Community: The Cultural Criticism of Randolph Bourne, Van Wyck Brooks, Waldo Frank, and Lewis Mumford* (Chapel Hill: University of North Carolina Press, 1990).

46. Tara Stubbs, *American Literature and Irish Culture, 1910–55: The Politics of Enchantment* (Manchester: Manchester University Press, 2015), 3.

47. Van Wyck Brooks, "Ireland 1916," *Dial* 61, no. 780 (November 30, 1916): 458.

48. Brooks, 459.

49. Brooks, 459–60.

50. Van Wyck Brooks, "The Critics and Young America" (1917), in Irving Babbit

et al., *Criticism in America: Its Function and Status* (New York: Harcourt, Brace & Co., 1924), 117.

51. Brooks, 118.

52. Van Wyck Brooks, review of *A Portrait of the Artist as a Young Man*, *Seven Arts* 2, no. 7 (May 1917): 122, reprinted in *JJCH*, 1:107. Brooks's assertion of American autonomy took on a distinctively conservative turn in his later years, attacking Joyce, ironically, for deprecating the great English literary tradition that he had done so much to distance American literature from in his early years. See Jeffrey Segal, *Joyce in America: Cultural Politics and the Trials of "Ulysses"* (Berkeley: University of California Press, 1993), 72.

53. Colum, "Youngest Ireland," 617–18.

54. Stubbs, *American Literature and Irish Culture*, 11. The vernacular turn toward Native American or pre-Columbian culture in American modernism, represented by Alice Corbin Henderson's and Mabel Dodge Luhan's literary circles in New Mexico, can be seen as an attempt to provide the New World with a rediscovered "usable" antiquity, opening itself to precisely the Indigenous culture that the first immigrants, as colonists, chose to ignore on Randolph Bourne's estimation (see 275n32, above).

55. Stubbs, 11.

56. *TSP*, 192. For connections between *Portrait* and *This Side of Paradise*, see Patrick O'Donnell, introduction, to *TSP*, xxi. Joyce's *Portrait* was third on Fitzgerald's list of "10 Best Books I Have Read" (1923), reprinted in *F. Scott Fitzgerald on Authorship*, 86.

57. Ron Ebest, *Private Histories: The Writings of Irish Americans, 1900–1935* (Notre Dame, IN: University of Notre Dame Press, 2005), 98, 101.

58. Alain Locke, "The New Negro," in *The New Negro: An Interpretation*, ed. Alain Locke (New York: Albert and Charles Boni, 1925), 7.

59. The poem anticipates sentiments of the "Cyclops" chapter in *Ulysses* in its juxtaposition of England's conquering with the Bible and gun: "Why then put by the guns and whips / Take them, and play the champion's part . . . / You, with a prayer on your lips / And murder in your heart": Louis Untermeyer, "To England (Upon the Executions of the Three Irish Poets—Pearse, MacDonagh and Plunkett—After the Uprising in Dublin," *The Masses*, August 1916, 11; *The Crisis* 12, no. 5 (September 1916): 232.

60. "Ireland," *The Crisis* 12, no. 4 (August 1916): 166–67.

61. "Sir Roger Casement—Patriot, Martyr," *The Crisis* 12, no. 4 (August 1916): 215–16.

62. Tyrone Tillery, *Claude McKay: A Black Poet's Struggle for Identity* (Amherst: University of Massachusetts Press, 1992), 49–51.

63. Dunbar's "Circumstances Alter Cases," for instance, adopts Irish brogue in the manner of F. Scott Fitzgerald's' Monsignor Darcy in *This Side of Paradise*: "Ah, wouldn't I send him away with a whirl, / O chone! / They say the gossoon is decent and dirty / . . . You'll be sure he's no match for my little colleen, / O chone!" See Jean Wagner, *Black Poets of the United States: From Paul Laurence Dunbar to Langston Hughes* (Champaign: University of Illinois Press, 1973), 107.

64. Cited in Michael North, *The Dialect of Modernism: Race, Language, and Twentieth-Century Literature* (New York: Oxford University Press, 1994), 132. Henceforth *DM*, followed by page numbers in notes.

65. Lee M. Jenkins, "'Black Murphy': Claude McKay and Ireland," *Irish University Review* 33, no. 2 (Autumn–Winter 2003): 285.

66. Claude McKay, "How Black Sees Green and Red," *Liberator* 4, no. 6 (June 1921): 19.

67. McKay, 21.

68. McKay, 19–21.

69. McKay, 20.

70. "The slogan of the art world is 'Return to the Primitive.' . . . Homage is rendered to dead Negro artists, while the living must struggle for recognition." Claude McKay, "The Negroes in America," in *DM*, 114.

71. *The Passion of Claude McKay: Selected Poetry and Prose, 1912–1948*, ed. Wayne F. Cooper (New York: Schocken, 1973), 151, cited in *DM*, 115.

72. Claude McKay, *Constab Ballads* (London: Watts & Co., 1912), 7. This impatience with discipline is not without its own ironies, given that his own poetry was criticized for adhering too closely to standard English metrical forms such as iambic pentameter, and genres such as the sonnet.

73. Sydney Olivier, *White Capital and Cultured Labor*, ed. Ramsey MacDonald (London: Independent Labor Party, 1906), 104, cited in Michael Malouf, *Transatlantic Solidarities: Irish Nationalism and Caribbean Poetics* (Charlottesville: University of Virginia Press, 2000), 87. Olivier, a friend of George Bernard Shaw's, was a Fabianist governor of Jamaica. Malouf perceptively explains how his land-reform policies drew on the parallels between the land question in Ireland and Jamaica by his Irish predecessor, Henry Blake (87, 223).

74. McKay's "hybrid" practice, as Lee Jenkins points out (see 276n65, above), is not to reject standard (Western) notions of either class or poetic form but rather to appropriate and recast them in different idioms, much as MacDonagh sought not to reject English but rewrite it in the "Irish mode." The suggestion that Irish militancy may drive a wedge into capital/labor conflict in Britain is close to Karl Marx's own view.

75. Kipling, cited in *DM*, 130.

76. Cited in Alan J. Ward, *Ireland and Anglo-American Relations, 1899–1921* (Toronto: University of Toronto Press, 1969), 170.

77. Cited in Bruce Nelson, *Irish Nationalists and the Making of the Irish Race* (Princeton, NJ: Princeton University Press, 2012), 222.

78. "Speech by Marcus Garvey," September 25, 1921, in *The Marcus Garvey Papers*, ed. Robert A. Hill, vol. 4 (Berkeley: University of California Press, 1985), 83. Garvey's use of "dominions" also throws Canada, South Africa, Australia, and New Zealand into the mix, but in his support for the Anglo-Irish Treaty, he was prepared for settle for Dominion status in the end.

79. F. Scott Fitzgerald, *The Great Gatsby* (1926; repr., London: Penguin, 1950), 19. "Goddard" is an amalgam of "Grant" and "Stoddard." See Mick Gidley, "Notes on F. Scott Fitzgerald and the Passing of the Great Race," *Journal of American Studies* 7, no. 2 (August 1973): 171–81.

80. Benjamin T. Spencer's paraphrasing of Richard Grant White, *The Quest for Nationality* (*DM*, 131).

81. I.O. [C. J. C. Street], *Ireland in 1921* (London, 1922), cited in Francis Costello, *The Irish Revolution and Its Aftermath, 1914–123* (Dublin: Irish Academic Press, 2003), 58.

82. Owen Dudley Edwards, "The Lost Teigueen: F. Scott Fitzgerald's Ethics and Ethnicity," in *Scott Fitzgerald: The Promises of Life*, ed. A Robert Lee (London: Vision Press, 1989), 201.

83. Joe Cleary, "Irish American Modernism," in *The Cambridge Companion to Irish Modernism*, ed. Joe Cleary (Cambridge: Cambridge University, 2014), 183. Cleary's discussion also traces the modernist leanings of Eugene O'Neill's and Flannery O'Connor's displaced Irish and Catholic backgrounds in the innovations they brought to American literature.

84. Claude McKay, *Banjo: A Story without a Plot* (New York: Harper and Brothers, 1929), 201.

85. Ernie O'Malley to Helen Merriam Golden, May 1930, in *Broken Landscapes: Selected Letters of Ernie O'Malley, 1924–1957*, ed. Cormac K. H. O'Malley and Nicholas Allen (Dublin: Lilliput Press, 2011), 71. Henceforth *BL*, followed by page numbers in the notes.

86. Ernie O'Malley to Sheila Humphreys, March 13, 1931 (*BL*, 85).

87. Ernie O'Malley to Harriet Monroe, January 10, 1935 (*BL*, 108).

Chapter Eight

1. Ernie O'Malley, writing about the English painter John Piper, "Painting: The School of London," *The Bell* 14, no. 3 (July 1947), reprinted in *BL*, 418.

2. [Alice Corbin Henderson], "Larkin–O'Malley Offerings Win Praise from El Zaguan Audience," *Santa Fe New Mexican*, August 20, 1930, 8. Ernie O'Malley Papers, box 21, folder 32, Archive of Irish America 060 (henceforth EOM AIA 060), Tamiment Library and Robert F. Wagner Labor Archives, New York University Library; emphasis added. The young poet Francis Ledwidge (1887–1917) did not participate in the Easter Rising but lost his life in the Great War at Ypres, July 1917; his sympathy for his fellow poet, and leader of the Rising, Thomas MacDonagh, was memorialized in one of his finest poems, "Lament for Thomas MacDonagh."

3. "O'Malley to Read Joyce on Tuesday," *Santa Fe New Mexican*, undated clipping [November 1930], O'Malley Papers, box 21, folder 32, EOM AIA 060.

4. "O'Malley to Make Last Talk Tuesday Evening," *Santa Fe New Mexican*, undated clipping [late November 1930], O'Malley Papers, box 21, folder 32, EOM AIA 060.

5. There is a possibility that O'Malley may have met Joyce in Paris in 1926, where he reconnected with his former IRA colleague Seán MacBride. Personal communication from Cormac K. H. O'Malley.

6. Richard Miller, "Ernest O'Malley Concludes Talks on Irish Literature," *Santa Fe New Mexican*, undated clipping [late November 1930], O'Malley Papers, box 21, folder 32, EOM AIA 060.

7. Miller, "Ernest O'Malley Concludes Talks on Irish Literature."

8. Miller, "Ernest O'Malley Concludes Talks on Irish Literature."

9. Ernie O'Malley to Harriet Monroe, August 7, 1934 (*BL*, 105).

10. Ernie O'Malley to Dorothy Brett, March 11, 1930 (*BL*, 69). Writing about "the Irish understanding of actuality," O'Malley noted: "Living is so fantastic and strange and un-understandable that they accept the supernatural or that which cannot be explained as the actual, and with the actual they reverse the effect. The dead are almost closer to us at home than the living, and things called 'miracles' seem to fit into life like toast and cream." Ernie O'Malley to Helen Hooker, May 8, 1935 (*BL*, 117).

11. Ernie O'Malley, *On Another Man's Wound* (1936), rev. ed. (Dublin: Anvil, 2002). Henceforth *OAMW*, followed by page numbers in text and notes. Ernie O'Malley, *The Singing Flame* (Dublin: Anvil, 1977). Henceforth *SF*, followed by page numbers in text.

12. Yeats was responding to Seán Ó Faoláin's and Frank O'Connor's proposal of O'Malley. See Frank O'Connor, *My Father's Son* (London: Pan, 1971), 99, cited in Richard English, *Ernie O'Malley: IRA Intellectual* (Oxford: Clarendon Press, 1998), 49. English points out that Yeats, in fact, supported O'Malley's election.

13. John McGahern, "In Pursuit of a Single Flame," in *Love of the World: Essays*, ed. Stanley van der Viel (London: Faber and Faber, 2010), 259.

14. Hart Crane to Malcolm Cowley, June 2, 1931, in *The Letters of Hart Crane, 1916–1932*, ed. Brom Weber (Berkeley: University of California Press, 1965), 371.

15. Ernie O'Malley to Edward Weston, February 15, 1931 (*BL*, 83).

16. Ernie O'Malley to Paul Strand, July 13, 1932, reporting conversation with Sykes and Clurman, January 10, 1932 (*BL*, 88).

17. Ernie O'Malley to Harriet Monroe, October 22, 1935 (*BL*, 109).

18. Writing to Kelleher, O'Malley listed among the studies of Joyce in his possession: "—a book on *Finnegans Wake* by two Americans whose name I forget [Joseph Campbell and Henry Morton Robinson, *A Skeleton Key to Finnegans Wake* (New York: Harcourt Brace & Co., 1944)]—a recently published book here by Faber but not a good book [perhaps T. S. Eliot, *Introducing James Joyce: A Selection of Joyce's Prose* (London: Faber, 1942, 1945)]—Frank Budgen: *James Joyce*, 1934—Harry Levine [Levin, *James Joyce: A Critical Introduction* (London: Faber, 1944)]—Louis Goeding [Louis Golding], *James Joyce* (London: Thornton Butterworth), 1933—Charles Duff: *James Joyce and the Plain Reader*, 1932—S. Foster Damon, *Odyssey in Dublin*, Hound and Horn, Fall, 1929—Bernard Bandler II: *Joyce's Exiles*, Hound and Horn, Jan. 1933." Ernie O'Malley to John V. Kelleher, October 22, 1947 (*BL*, 257).

19. O'Malley visited the newly opened Gotham Book Mart on his first day in New York and noted "a dollar edition of [D. H.] Lawrence" on sale: Diary, October 12–16, 1928 (*BL*, 49). Nos. 8, 13, 15, 19–20, 24, 25, 26, and 27 of *transition* were in his possession, but his notebooks contain passages from many more issues. In 1939, he thanked James Johnson Sweeney for sending issues from New York: Ernie O'Malley to James Johnson Sweeney, December 14, 1939 (*BL*, 179).

20. Ernie O'Malley, Notebook #10-1, box 9, folder 20, O'Malley Papers, EOM AIA 060.

21. Ernie O'Malley, Diary, Coolidge, New Mexico, December 4, 1929, box 42, folder 34, 34-9, O'Malley Papers, EOM AIA 060.

22. English, *Ernie O'Malley*, 73. O'Malley may have delivered some talks from notes rather than completed scripts—as he wrote of a lecture given at Harvard in 1935: "As usual I worked so much on it that I nearly wrote a book of notes on Sunday and Monday and had enough material for 8 lectures. I really should write out lectures fully for then I would have a series of small booklets." Ernie O'Malley to Helen Hooker, April 23, 1934 (*BL*, 114).

23. Walter Benjamin, *The Arcades Project*, ed. Rolf Tiedeman, trans. Howard Eiland and Kevin McLaughlin (Cambridge, MA: Belknap Press, 1999).

24. Hannah Arendt, "Introduction: Walter Benjamin 1892–1940," in Walter Benjamin, *Illuminations*, trans. Harry Zohn (London: Fontana, 1973), 47.

25. Many of the original sources consulted by O'Malley are reprinted, sometimes in part, by Robert Deming in *James Joyce: The Critical Heritage*, vol. 1: 1907–1927; vol. 2: 1928–1941.

26. O'Malley, Notebook #10-71, box 11, folder 19, O'Malley Papers, EOM AIA 060. Excerpts from *Ulysses* will be given as O'Malley wrote them even when, as occasion-

ally happens, they are abbreviated or contain minor errors in transcription: page references to original passages in *Ulysses* where appropriate will follow in parentheses.

27. James Fitzharris (aka "Skin-the-Goat") was imprisoned for driving the decoy cab that helped the Invincibles escape from the Phoenix Park following the assassination of Lord Frederick Cavendish and Thomas Henry Burke, May 6, 1882.

28. The quotation, slightly amended, is from Gilbert Seldes, "The Moods of Satire," a review of Alfred Budd's *The Oxford Circus: A Novel of Oxford and Youth*, *The Dial* 76, no. 2 (February 1924), 188. Seldes discusses Joyce in the context of satire.

29. Stuart Gilbert, "The 'Aeolus' Episode in *Ulysses*," *transition* 18 (November 1929): 138.

30. For the opposition of the press and the church to the Republic before the Treaty was signed, see Desmond Ryan, *Unique Dictator: A Study of De Valera* (London: Arthur Barker, 1936), 275.

31. John M. Regan, "Kindling the Singing Flame: The Destruction of the Public Record Office (30 June 1922), as a Historical Problem," in *Modern Ireland and Revolution: Ernie O'Malley in Context*, ed. Cormac K. H. O'Malley (New Bridge: Irish Academic Press, 2016), 107–23.

32. Gilbert, "The 'Aeolus' Episode in *Ulysses*," 138.

33. Gilbert, 137. As Joyce spells Manannán as both "Mananaan" and "Mananaun," I have retained his misspellings.

34. *The Topographical Poems of John O'Dubhagain and Giolla na Naomh O'Huidhrin*, ed. John O'Donovan (Dublin: Irish Archaeological and Celtic Society, 1862), xlii.

35. O'Malley wrote to Paul Strand on August 6, 1953: "Burrishoole has in ways been associated with our name since the 10th century, and I was anxious to bring the children up related to land and sea until they grew up" (*BL*, 311).

36. O'Malley notes the association of Clew Bay with the fabled Children of Lir in local memory: "On Inisglora the bewitched Children of Lir took human shape; here they were buried. Within living memory sails were dipped when boats passed Inisglora as was the custom off Caher." Ernie O'Malley, "County of Mayo," *Holiday* (London), October 28, 1946 (*BL*, 403).

37. O'Malley, Notebook #10-128, Book II, notes on Ernst R. Curtius's "Technique and Thematic Development in Joyce," *transition*, nos. 16–17 (June 1929), O'Malley Papers, EOM AIA 060.

38. Curtius, "Technique," 312.

39. Seán Ó Faoláin, review of *On Another Man's Wound*, *Ireland Today* 1, no. 5 (October 1936): 67. This view is echoed in Anne Dolan, "The Papers in Context," in *No Surrender Here!: The Civil War Papers of Ernie O'Malley, 1922–24*, ed. Cormac K. H. O'Malley and Anne Dolan, introduction by J. J. Lee (Dublin: Lilliput Press, 2007), xlviii–xlix.

40. Earnán O'Malley, "Ireland," *Architectural Digest* (London) 17, no. 7 (July 1947): 172–74 (*BL*, 422). He adds, in a gloss on revolutionary "extremism": "The sense of expediency or of compromise, which are commonplace in English politics, are not easy to apply to such fundamental issues."

41. Donald L. Carveth, *The Still Small Voice: Psychoanalytic Reflections on Guilt and Conscience* (London: Karnac Books, 2013), 91.

42. Carveth, 103–4. O'Malley's condition was diagnosed by Dr. Frank Johnson in New York, 1934, in relation to his application for a military service pension: Eve Morrison, "Witnessing the Republic: The Ernie O'Malley Notebook Interviews and

the Bureau of Military History Compared," in *Modern Ireland and Revolution: Ernie O'Malley in Context*, 124.

43. *OAMW*, 373. Insofar as conscience weighed heavily, it was for abject failures, such as the inability to hold the Four Courts at the outset of the Civil War. He wrote of the gun battle that led to his capture in November 1922: "I would not surrender as I thought I should wipe out the disgraceful surrender of the Four Courts." "Details of Military Service, 1916–1924 and List of Wounds," in *No Surrender Here!*, lvi.

44. Stuart Gilbert, "An Irish *Ulysses*: 'Hades' Episode," *Fortnightly Review* cxxxii (July 1929): 48.

45. Ernie O'Malley to Paul Strand, December 28, 1934 (BL, 107).

46. O'Malley, Notebook #10-128, Book II, notes on Maurice Murphy, "James Joyce and Ireland," *The Nation*, cxxix (October 16, 1929), 426, O'Malley Papers, EOM AIA 060.

47. O'Malley, "Ireland" (BL, 423). There are clear echoes here of Joyce's comparison, drawing on Oscar Wilde, of Irish readers and audiences to the "rage of Caliban" (U, 1.143) seeing himself in a mirror for the first time.

48. As O'Malley wrote to his future wife Helen Hooker before they left the United States for Ireland in 1935: "The problem of reality in my country has yet to be faced. It is a bitter country and one without pity.... I mention this because I don't want any romantic idea of the country to obscure its reality." Cited in English, *Ernie O'Malley*, 185.

49. O'Malley, Notebook #10-128, Book II, notes on Cyril Connolly, "The Position of Joyce," *Life and Letters* 2, no. 11 (April 1929): 273–90, O'Malley Papers, EOM AIA 060.

50. Cyril Connolly, "The Position of Joyce," 277–78, O'Malley, Notebook #10-128, Book II, EOM AIA 060.

51. Anti-Treaty Pamphlet, 1922, Capuchin Archive, South Dublin County Libraries, http://source.southdublinlibraries.ie/handle/10599/9051.

52. *OAMW*, 52. See *P*, 280.

53. English, *Ernie O'Malley*, 151.

54. Letter to Sheila Humphreys, December 25, 1923, in *No Surrender Here!*, 473.

55. *OAMW*, 143. O'Malley continues: "Areas of country had a habit of going to sleep. They would wake up after a century or more and step into a gap. This unexpected quality was there in what I knew to be a bad area. It might awaken of itself; the times and situation might start the spark" (*OAMW*, 144).

56. Robert K. Weininger, *The German Joyce* (Gainesville: University of Florida Press, 2012), 24–64, 180–93.

57. O'Malley, Notebook #10-127, Book III, O'Malley Papers, EOM AIA 060; Frank Swinnerton, *The Georgian Literary Scene* (London: Heineman, 1935), 433.

58. Peter Bürger, *Theory of the Avant-Garde*, trans. Michel Shaw (Minneapolis: University of Minnesota Press, 1984), ch. 2. See also Andreas Huyssen, *After the Great Divide: Modernism, Mass Culture and Postmodernism* (London: Macmillan, 1986), vii–ix, chs. 1, 2.

59. Benjamin Gilbert Brooks, "Shem the Penman: An Appreciation of James Joyce," *Nineteenth Century and After* 29 (March 1941): 273.

60. As noted in chapter 3 above, O'Malley also notes how the obscurity of *Finnegans Wake* could be deployed in cryptic communications in prison to evade surveillance.

61. O'Malley is recalling Joseph Dunn's archaic translation of the *Táin*, which, ac-

cording to his friend John V. Kelleher, was also the version most likely to have been used by Joyce. "Identifying the Irish Printed Sources for *Finnegans Wake*," in *Selected Writings of John V. Kelleher on Ireland and Irish-America*, ed. Charles Fanning (Carbondale: Southern Illinois Press, 2002), 69.

62. O'Malley, Notebook #10-127, Book III, O'Malley Papers, EOM AIA 060; Joseph Warren Beach, *The Twentieth Century Novel: Studies in Technique* (New York: Century, 1932), 411.

63. McGahern, "In Pursuit of a Single Flame," 254.

64. *OAMW*, 343. The importance of "minute knowledge of their areas" (*OAMW*, 343) is stressed throughout: "I had to study the layout of the town or village closely, its streets, by-paths and back gardens.... I had to learn to efface myself, to merge into the customs, speech and dress; to withdraw myself from my own work in such a way that my movements and talk would seem natural" (*OAMW*, 148). Echoes of the artist in Joyce's *Portrait*, hiding behind his "handiwork," are striking (*P*, 233).

65. Convinced of his guilt but without evidence, British authorities framed Moran for the Mount Street shootings. In fact, Moran was involved in the Gresham Hotel shootings, but this was not discovered at the time. May Moran, *Executed for Ireland: The Patrick Moran Story* (Cork: Mercier Press, 2010), 62–90.

66. An earlier notebook draft had "Never sleep with another man's pipe": see entry for N25 (VI.B.15): 150(i), in *James Joyce Digital Archive*, ed. Danis Rose and John O'Hanlon, https://jjda.ie/main/JJDA/F/flex/pa/lexpa.htm.

67. *OAMW*, 403. O'Malley's book opens with a slightly different version, echoing the "once upon a time" formula that opens Joyce's *Portrait*: "Our nurse, Nannie, told my eldest brother and me stories and legends. Her stories began: 'Once upon a time and a very good time it was,' and ended with, 'They put on the kettle and made tay, and if they were not happy that you may'" (*OAMW*, 15). The next sentence in O'Malley's book, relating deeds of "Fionn and his giant strength; the epic of Cuchulainn" is condensed by Joyce into "Fine again, Cuohoolson! Peace, O wiley!" (*FW*, 332.8–9), alluding also to major casualties of the Easter Rising, Patrick Pearse and the O'Rahilly, and the fictional "Persse O'Reilly" in *Finnegans Wake*.

Chapter Nine

1. Desmond Ryan, *Remembering Sion* (London: Arthur Barker, 1934), 43. Henceforth *RS*, followed by page numbers in text and notes.

2. Ernie O'Malley to Desmond Ryan, December 22, 1936 (*BL*, 136). O'Malley is perhaps recalling Robert Sage's estimate of Joyce: "He has telescoped time, space, all humanity and the universe of gods and heroes." Robert Sage, "Before Ulysses—and After," in Samuel Beckett et al., *Our Exagmination Round His Factication for Incamination of "Work in Progress"* (1929; London: Faber and Faber, 1972), 155.

3. O'Malley to Ryan, December 22, 1936 (*BL*, 136).

4. Desmond Ryan, *BMH*, no. 725, 8.

5. Pádraic H. Pearse, "The Story of a Success" (1917), in *CWPP*, viii.

6. Desmond Ryan, *The Man Called Pearse* (Dublin: Maunsel, 1919).

7. Desmond Ryan, *James Connolly*, foreword by H. W. Nevinson (Dublin: Talbot Press, 1924); James Connolly, *The Workers' Republic; Socialism and Nationalism; Labour and Easter Week*, ed. Desmond Ryan (Dublin: Sign of the Three Candles, 1948).

8. "Dalcassians" refers to Dal-Cais in Munster, the region from which Brian Boru sought to establish a unified Ireland under his rule in the eleventh century.

9. Desmond Ryan, "Still Remembering Sion," *University Review* 5, no. 2 (Summer 1968): 248. Henceforth "SRS," followed by page numbers in text and notes.

10. "SRS," 251. Ryan's was not the only contemporary book in which Pearse appeared alongside Joyce: Padraic Colum's *The Road Around Ireland* (1926) devoted extensive sections, based on firsthand acquaintance, to Pearse, Joyce, and Thomas MacDonagh, as did Mary Colum's later memoir, *Life and the Dream* (New York: Doubleday, 1947).

11. Patrick Lynch, introduction to *The Fenian Chief: A Biography of James Stephens*, by Desmond Ryan (Dublin: Gill and Sons, 1967), xii.

12. According to Ryan, Partition "was imposed upon Michael Collins and Arthur Griffith by trickery, in the House of Commons not one Irish representative, Ulster, Unionist, or Nationalist voted for it in 1920." Desmond Ryan, *Ireland, Whose Ireland?* (London: Key Books, 1946), 51.

13. Fergus FitzGerald, "Foreword," revised by Garret FitzGerald, in *Desmond's Rising: Memoirs 1913 to Easter 1916*, by Desmond FitzGerald (Dublin: Liberties Press, 2006), 7. Desmond FitzGerald, as noted in chapter 5 above, was familiar with the early modernist scene, being a member, along with fellow republican Joseph Campbell, of the original Imagist poetry movement, and a friend of Ezra Pound.

14. Desmond Ryan, *The Invisible Army: A Story of Michael Collins* (London: Arthur Barker, 1932), 17–18; ellipses in original. Henceforth IA, followed by page numbers in text.

15. Samuel Beckett, "Recent Irish Poetry" (1934), in *Disjecta: Miscellaneous Writings and Dramatic Fragments*, ed. Ruby Cohn (London: John Calder, 1983), 71.

16. Daniel Corkery, *Synge and Anglo-Irish Literature* (1931; repr., Cork: Mercier Press, 1966), 3.

17. Corkery, 5.

18. Peter Goldie, *On Personality* (London: Routledge, 2004), 105, 109.

19. Roy Pascal, *The Dual Voice: Free Indirect Speech and Its Functioning in the Nineteenth-Century European Novel* (Manchester: Manchester University Press, 1977).

20. In later years, Ryan edited, with William O'Brien, a two-volume edition of the extensive correspondence of the exiled Fenian, *John Devoy's Post-Bag* (Dublin: Fallon, 1948, 1953).

21. Cited in Frances Flanagan, *Remembering the Revolution: Dissent, Culture, and Nationalism in the Irish Free State* (Oxford: Oxford University Press, 2015), 168.

22. These are based on the summary executions of the republican leaders Rory O'Connor, Liam Mellows, Joe McKelvey, and Dick Barrett, in December 1922.

23. Ryan, *Ireland, Whose Ireland?*, 44.

24. Ryan, 51.

25. Ryan, 44.

26. Lynch, introduction to Ryan, *Fenian Chief*, xii.

27. Micheál Ó Dubhshláine reports that some "people were of the opinion that it was much more than a friendship" between Pearse and Nicolls: *A Dark Day on the Blaskets: The Drowning of Domhnall Ó Criomhthain and Eibhlín Nic Niocaill on the Blasket Islands* (Dingle: Brandon, 2003), 121. Nicolls drowned off the Blasket Islands while attempting to save Cáit Ní Criomhthain, who had gotten into difficulties while

swimming with her. Cáit survived but her young brother, Domhnall, also drowned when he went to their aid. The Ó Criomhthain's father, Tomás, recounted the tragedy in his famous 1929 memoir, *An tOileánach* (The Islandman).

28. Brendan Walsh, *The Pedagogy of Protest: The Educational Thought and Work of Patrick H. Pearse* (Oxford: Peter Lang, 2007), 15.

29. Walsh, 183–84.

30. Ruth Dudley Edwards, *Patrick Pearse: The Triumph of Failure* (London: Faber and Faber, 1977), 106.

31. Colum, *Life and the Dream*, 152, 153.

32. *An Claideamh Solais*, August 21, 1909, cited in Ó Dubhshláine, *A Dark Day on the Blaskets*, 120. Pearse continued; "If she had been asked to choose the manner of her death she would surely have chosen in thus. . . . Greater love than this no man hath than he give his life for a friend" (123).

33. As Margaret Pearse saw Ryan and ten others march from St. Enda's on the morning of the rebellion to assemble in the GPO, she enjoined them, bearing in mind that her husband James Pearse was English, to remember that "if you ever are free, it is the son of an Englishman who will have freed you" (*RS*, 130).

34. H. G. Wells, "James Joyce," review of *A Portrait of the Artist as a Young Man*, *Nation* xx (February 1917), in *JJCH*, 1:86–87. Irish readers decades later were no less vehement in their condemnations of "filthy" preoccupations with the water-closet and the brothel: see the exchange of letters in the *Irish Times*, November/December 1949, following Maria Jolas's protest at the official snub of a Joyce exhibition in Paris by Seán MacBride, Minister for External Affairs.

35. Lindsey Tucker, *Stephen and Bloom at Life's Feast: Alimentary Symbolism and the Creative Process in James Joyce's "Ulysses"* (Columbus: Ohio State University Press, 1984). See also John McCourt, "An Odyssey in the Sewer: *Ulysses* in Ireland in the 1920s," in McCourt, *Consuming Joyce: 100 Years of "Ulysses" in Ireland* (London: Bloomsbury, 2022), 19–46.

36. Desmond Ryan, *"Ulysses,"* unpublished essay, Ryan Papers, LA 10/414 UCD Archives, 2. It is striking that in the amended version of *Ulysses* in *Remembering Sion*, Stephen is "obsessed" rather than haunted by his mother's death, and Bloom is "overshadowed by the loss of his young son, Roddy [sic]" (*RS*, 45).

37. C. D. C. Reeve, *Love's Confusions* (Cambridge, MA: Harvard University Press, 2005), 43.

38. Reeve, 61–62.

39. James Joyce, "Drama and Life" (1900), in *OCPW*, 29.

40. Arthur Power, *Conversations with James Joyce*, ed. Clive Hart (London: Millington, 1974), 98.

41. E. M. Forster, *Howards End* (1910; repr., London: Penguin, 2000), 220, cited in Reeve, *Love's Confusions*, 71.

42. W. B. Yeats, "The Stare's Nest by My Window," in *The Collected Poems of W. B. Yeats* (New York: Macmillan, 1963), 204.

43. Reeve, *Love's Confusions*, 62. It is for this reason, Reeve points out, that "by encouraging us to disclose more and more of what we would otherwise hide, intimate love—almost paradoxically—give rise to many of the anxieties for which it promises to be the cure" (63).

44. Ryan's unpublished notes on *Ulysses* cite Joyce's own words on interior monologue in Édouard Dujardin: the reader "is posted within the mind of the protagonist

and it is the continuous unfolding of his thoughts which, replacing normal objective narrations, depicts to us his actions and experiences." Ryan, "*Ulysses*," 4.

45. Lynch, introduction to Ryan, *Fenian Chief*, xv.

46. Ryan, "*Ulysses*," 3.

47. Desmond Ryan, "When a Sceptre Haunted Cork," *The Bell* XII, no. 4 (July 1946): 317–24.

48. Desmond Ryan, "Sinn Féin Policy and Practice, 1916–1926," in *The Irish Struggle, 1916–1926*, ed. Desmond Williams (London: Routledge & Kegan Paul, 1966), 31.

49. Ruth Dudley Edwards, "Confessions of an Irish Revisionist," in *The Troubled Face of Biography*, ed. Eric Homberger and John Charmley (London: Macmillan, 1988), 65.

50. Desmond Ryan, *The Phoenix Flame: A Study of Fenianism and John Devoy* (London: Arthur Barker, 1937), 316–17.

51. Michael Löwy, foreword to *The Hidden God: A Study of Tragic Vision in the Pensées of Pascal and the Tragedies of Racine* (1964), by Lucien Goldmann (London: Verso, 2016), xviii, xx.

52. Eimar O'Duffy, "'Ulysses,' by James Joyce," *Irish Review* 1, no. 4 (December 9, 1922), reprinted in the *Journal of Irish Literature* 7, no. 1 (January 1978): 12.

Index

Note: Page numbers followed by an *f* indicate a figure.

Abbey Theatre, 37, 168, 258n28; constraint on revolution, xiii, 4–5, 37–38; role in Easter Rising, xiii, 229n4, 259n28

Abeokuta, Alake of, 144–47, 151; and Congo Reform Association, 147, 270n49; perceived nobility of, 151; perceived servility of, 145–47, 270n48; real-life figure, 370n49

accent: Dublin, 21–22; Irish, 128, 167, 197, 212; modernism and, 128, 167

Adams, Robert Martin, 82, 270n49

Adorno, Theodor W., 5, 20, 53, 111, 261n1; art as epiphany, xv; art as possibility, xv, 6; autonomy and form, 5, 20, 233n26, 233n28; fascism and hero-worship, 53, 246n35; future orientation of art, xv, 6, 229n11, 233n28; on Joyce's rebellion against realism, 111; *Ulysses* as epic under imperialism, 53; universality of art, 20

advertising, 46, 55, 103–4

Æ (George Russell), xiv, 20, 166, 181, 192, 265n62

Aeneas, 267n8

Africa, 65; Egypt, 72, 79, 89, 112, 135, 137, 138, 141, 144, 177, 178; Nigeria, 145; North, xviii, 135–38, 184; South, 98 (*see also* Boer War); Zulu, 145

African American, 175, 276n38, 277n70; African Black Brotherhood, 174; Harlem Renaissance, 173–75; Jim Crow era, 178–79; responses to Easter Rising, 173–78

African Blood Brotherhood, 174

Agricola, 148

Aiken, Frank, 37, 184, 190

Aiken, Síobhra: narrative and trauma, 233n31

Aldington, Richard, 40, 256n104

Allen, Nicholas, 5, 200

America. *See* United States

Anderson, Benedict, 49, 53, 244n11

Anderson, Chester, 80, 253n56

Andrews, C. S. ("Todd"): on Desmond FitzGerald, 243n89; knowledge of Joyce, 35–36; in Mountjoy, 264n51; and *Ulysses*, 35, 241n70

Anglo-Belgian Rubber Company, 152, 270n45

Anglo-Irish, cultural and national leadership, 36, 37, 56, 58, 153, 181, 194–95, 241n67

Anglo-Saxonism, xv, 137, 167, 170, 172, 176, 177, 178, 256n104

An Stad, 80, 253n55

anti-Semitism, 141–42; Arthur Griffith and Oliver St. John Gogarty, 141–42

Antrim, County: Ballymoney, 153

Aquinas, St. Thomas, 240n46

"Araby" (*Dubliners*), 20

Aran Islands, 92–93, 136–37

Arendt, Hannah: on Benjamin, 187; and Broch, 155; critique of abstract universal human rights, 154, 156; "entailed inheritance" (Burke), 154; human diversity and rights, 156; and primitivism, 154, 156; "right to have rights," 154; rise of fascism, 225; statelessness, 156
Argos, 74
Aristotle, 34, 71, 240n46, 245n31
Arnold, Matthew, 144, 244n18
Ascot Gold Cup, 18
Asculum, Battle of, 74
Ashe, Thomas: filming of funeral, 106
"As I Was among the Captives": Joseph Campbell's Prison Diary, 1922–1923 (Campbell): exchanges with Francis Stuart, 131; hunger strike, 131; influence of Joyce, 132; and literary figures, 131; stream-of-consciousness technique, 130–33; tunneling in prison camp, 132
Atget, Eugène, 240n54
Atkinson, Robert: and Irish language, 61; parodied in *Finnegans Wake*, 61
Austen, Jane, 55
Australia, 98
avant-garde, xv, xix, 3; and aesthetics, xix; everyday life, 3, 6, 8–9, 49–50, 77, 87, 129, 194–95, 197; in London, 129; not elitist, xix, 39, 167–68; politics and war, xix, 39, 115–16, 123–24, 129, 167–68, 194–97, 198

Babbit, Irving, 170
Bakhtin, Mikhail: carnivalesque, 12; "Chronotope," xvi, 17, 230n16, 236n86; epic and novel, 53, 247n62
Bandler, Bernard, II, 279n18
Barker, Thomas Jones: ambiguity of painting, 151; Orange Lodge banners, 151; *The Secret of England's Greatness*, 151–52, 152f
Barrett, Dick, 283n22
Barry, Denis, 131
Barry, Kevin (Volunteer), 126
Barthes, Roland, 107, 260n58
Batchen, Geoffrey, 33

Baudelaire, Charles: shocks of modernity, 115, 194
Beach, Joseph Warren, 198
Beach, Sylvia, 29, 34
Beck, Harald, 250n17
Beckett, Samuel, 37, 133, 185, 190, 207, 241n72, 282n2
Behan, Brendan, 25
Belgium: atrocities in Congo, 19, 146–47, 270n45; imperialism, 144, 146, 150, 152, 156; "Little Belgium," 151
Bell, The (magazine), 38, 185
Benet, Stephen, 162
Benjamin, Walter, 42; *Arcades Project*, 88, 92, 187, 255n96, 257n8; art as anticipation, 3; "aura," xiv, 94, 97; avant-garde and popular culture, 3, 232n17; closing gap between image and event, 92; crystalizing event, 110; on epic, 17, 64–65; left-wing melancholia, xiv; media technology, 4, 14, 232n17; montage, 92, 100, 109–10, 121; montage in modern city, 14, 100, 109–10, 236n71, 257n8, 261n68; "now-time" (*Jetztzeit*), 18; optical unconscious, 18; photography, 240n54; popular culture, 3, 232n17; public and private space in arcades, 88, 255n96
Bensaïd, Daniel, 1; history as nightmare, 16
Benstock, Bernard, 253n56
Benstock, Shari, 253n56
Bérard, Victor: Joyce on, 136, 267n6; Phoenician origins of *Odyssey*, 17, 136
Bergson, Henri: memory as cinematographic, 32–33; photograph as antithesis of memory, 33; on time, 69, 86–87, 129; Wyndham Lewis's critique of time-philosophy, 86–88
Bernstein, Michel André: probability and necessity in history, 77
Best, Richard, 192
Betham, Sir William, 138
Bible: book of Job, 131; and empire, 145–46, 149–51, 276n59; Ezekiel, 132
Biggs, Michael, 122
Birrell, Sir Augustine, 78

Bishop, John, 42
Black and Tans, 93
Blanqui, Louis Auguste, 88
Blast (magazine), 256n104
Bleibtreu, Herr (*Ulysses*), 71
Bloch, Ernst, xvii, 5, 116; clash of old and new in Joyce, 65; Joyce as Protean figure, 20; montage on the streets, 62–63; "objective montage" in *Ulysses*, 20; stream of consciousness as disruption, 20, 120–21; technical, cultural, and visual montage, 64, 261n65
Bloch, Marc, 6, 15
Bloody Sunday shootings (1921), xiii, 73, 234n43
"Bloomsday," 38
Blunt, Wilfred Scawen, 267n11
"Boarding House, A" (*Dubliners*), 170
Bochart, Samuel, 268n14
Boer War, 145–46, 155, 272n79; Arthur Griffith on, 144; Jameson Raid, 144; Transvaal War, 144
Boland, Harry, 106
Bolshevism: Bolshevik delegation to Dublin, 86; and Easter Rising, 4, 256n101; F. Scott Fitzgerald on, 162; Joyce's work as literary Bolshevism, 163, 274n14
Bonafous-Murat, Carle, 49
Bonn, Moritz, 78
Booker, M. Keith, 145–46
Borges, Jorge Luis, 51
Boru, Brian, 143
Botticelli, Sandro: *Birth of Venus*, 7, 32
Boucicault, Dion: *The Corsican Brothers*, 259n43; *Robert Emmet*, 101
Bourne, Randolph, 166; Anglo-Saxon domination, 167; Native American culture, 167, 276n54; "Trans-national America," 167, 276n54
Bourniquel, Camille, 18
Boyd, Ernest: introducing Joyce to US, 170; Irishness of Joyce, 275n44; "Ku Klux Kriticism," 170; Mencken on *Ireland's Literary Renaissance*, 169; relationship to Mencken, 169, 170; Van Wyck Brooks on, 171

Boyd, Thomas, 209
Boyle, John F.: *The Irish Rebellion of 1916*, 72–73; local knowledge used by rebels, 88; Pearse and secrecy, 254n70
Braque, Georges, 255n84
Bray, County Wicklow, 23
Brecht, Bertolt, xvii, 5, 196; on Charlie Chaplin, 113; Didi-Huberman on *Arbeitsjournal*, 63–64, 248n80; epic theater, 63–64; jumps and leaps in history, 63; montage in reality, 63; on *Ulysses*, 63, 112
Brennan, Robert, 36, 241n70
Brett, Dorothy, 182, 185, 278n10
Breuer, Josef, 234n52
Bridgham, Fred, 263n26
Briggs, Cyril: and Irish independence, 174
Britain, Great: British Cotton Growing Association, 147; Commonwealth, 137, 233n23; Edward VII, 73–74; Empire, xiii, xvi, xvii, xviii, 4, 5, 16, 51, 62, 89, 93, 111–12, 141, 144–45, 146–47, 151, 156, 177, 196, 229n8; Gothic Revival, 63; monarchy, 146; Prince of Wales, 163; return to Camelot, xiv, 63; Victorian, xiv, 4, 15, 87, 143, 151–52, 219, 269n34
Brittain, Vera, 185
Broch, Hermann, xvii, 5; and allegory in *Ulysses*, 155; Arendt on, 55; on epic, 54–55; escapes Nazis, 155; exile, 155; human rights, 155; simultaneity, 54; theoretical physics, 54; on *Ulysses*, 54–55, 155, 246n38; world literature, 54
Brooks, Benjamin Gilbert, 197, 199
Brooks, Peter: overlapping temporalities, 72
Brooks, Van Wyck, xviii, 18, 159, 166; criticisms of Joyce, 276n52; criticism in US, 159, 170–71; Easter Rising, 170–71; on Ernest Boyd, 171; Hiberno-English, 172; influence of pragmatism, 270; Irish Revival and criticism, 170–73; and John B. Yeats, 172; MacDonagh and Joyce's *Por-*

Brooks, Van Wyck (*continued*)
  trait, 172, 276n52; and Mary Colum, 272; and Padraic Colum, 171; on Thomas MacDonagh, 171–72; US, Ireland, and national criticism, 171; "usable past," 170
Browning, Robert, 37
Bruno, Giordano, 29
Brutus (*Julius Caesar*), 9
Budgen, Frank, 81, 279n18
Buelens, Geert, 114–16
Bunyan, John, 132
Bürger, Peter, 197
Burke, Edmund: "entailed inheritance," 154; *Reflections on the Revolution in France*, 7, 108
Burke, Kenneth, 3
Burke, O'Madden (*Ulysses*), 272n79
Burke, Peter, 236n81
Burke, Richard, 215–16
Burke, Thomas Henry, 11, 105
Burn, W. L., 65
Butler, Mary Ellen, 251n27
Byrne, John Francis: and "Castle Document," 69; "Cranly" in *Portrait*, 68; "The Irish Grievance," 85–86; on MacDonagh, xiv; tunneling in urban warfare, 85
Byrne, Vincent, 24

Cadava, Eugene, 103
Caesar, Julius, 74
Cahill, P., 132
Caius Graccus, 258n21
Calder, Alexander, 240n47
Campbell, Joseph, 7, 18, 40, 116, 166; "Deep Ways and Dripping Boughs," 266n79; and Desmond FitzGerald, 129; and Ezra Pound, 128–29; "I Am the Mountainy Singer," 129; imagism, 128, 265n71; imprisonment during Civil War, 130–33; international literary interests, 129; and MacDonagh, 128–29; marriage to Nancy Maude, 129, 132, 266n82; opposition to conscription, 130; rhythm and movement in poetry, 129; in War of Independence, 129–30; Wicklow County Council, 130. See also *"As I Was among the Captives"*
Campbell, Joseph (critic), 279n18
Campbell, Thomas, 138
Carew, Sir George, 123
Caribbean: British rule, 177, 277n73; class in colonial context, 175–76; epic and modernism, 137, 175
Carlyle, Thomas, 108
Carolan, Michael: IRA intelligence, 38; and *Ulysses*, 35
Carr, Helen, 129
Carson, Edward, 112, 153, 162
Carthage, 138, 141, 267n8
Carton, Sidney. See *Tale of Two Cities, A*
Casement, Roger, 5; *Amazon Journal*, 150; anti-imperialism, xviii, 147, 148, 153; Black Diaries, 253n58; *Britisches gegen Deutsches Imperium*, 267n4; and Connemara, 272n77; "crimes against humanity," xviii, 149–50; cross-cultural solidarity, xviii, 19, 148, 154–55, 157; Easter Rising, xviii, 5, 19, 137, 153, 156, 166, 174, 200; "The Elsewhere Empire," 157; and ethical memory, 19, 153–54; execution, 9–10, 19, 147, 149, 165, 174, 270n47, 271n57; exposing atrocities in Belgian Congo, 19, 146–47; Ezra Pound on, 165; homosexuality, 147, 149; vs. insular nationalism, 148; Irishness of, 146, 153; "Irish outlaw," 156; Irish vs. English law, 273n86; John Quinn on, 165; "The Keeper of the Sea," 271n58; living between two worlds, 156–57; on the *Odyssey*, 135, 157; political humanitarianism, 153–54; Putumayo, 150, 151, 154, 272n77; "The Romance of Irish History," 137
Casey, Joseph: attempted rescue at Clerkenwell, 204
Casey, Peter: Clerkenwell rescue, 204; and Joyce family, 204
Cassirer, Ernst, 7; myth and fascism, 33
Catholicism, Roman, 107; censorship, 40–41, 205, 212, 213, 214; control of education, 208, 209; and education

of F. Scott Fitzgerald, 160–63; as imperium, 189; and Joyce, 76, 141, 193, 233n35; messianism, 94, 111, 127, 217; modernization, 13; and nationalism, xvii, 4, 35, 103, 111, 139; republicanism, 35, 95, 96, 102; superstition, 12–13
Caulfield, Max, 103
Cavalcanti, Guido, 18
Cavendish, Lord Frederick, 11, 105
celebrity culture, xviii; "matinee idol," 97; stage, 96, 97
Celticism: absence of Hell, 71; *Celtic Times*, 143; Celtic Twilight, xiii, 9, 15, 64, 93, 163, 169, 194; Easter Rising, 91; and Ezra Pound, 128–29; feminization, 244n18; and F. Scott Fitzgerald, 162, 173, 178; Hallstatt origin, 136; hysterical Celt, 50, 160, 244n18, 273n4; Joyce on, 135, 137; La Tène origin, 136; Leerssen on, 137; and MacDonagh, 175; Marianne Moore on, 164; *Odyssey*, 45; Phoenician origins of Celtic languages, 135–36, 137–38, 140, 267n3, 268n14, 268n21; renaissance, 166, 170, 171, 173, 175; romanticism, 169, 210; psychology, 52, 65–66; Victorian, 4, 143. *See also* Phoenicians
censorship: prison, 117; US Post Office and *Ulysses*, 83. *See also* Catholicism, Roman
Cesarotti, Abbé Melchior, 139
Cézanne, Paul, 113
Chaplin, Charlie, 94, 103; Benjamin on, 3; Brecht on, 113; Easter Rising and *The Vagabond*, 92; and family of Jim Larkin, 119; impersonation competitions, 92, 92f; impersonations during Easter Rising, 91, 110, 256n4; and the Irish question, 91, 92, 257n7; John Redmond as, 92; Joyce learning from, 197; Kracauer on, 92; and popular culture, 3, 92, 113; popularity in Dublin, 92; visiting Jim Larkin in prison, 110
Charcot, Jean-Martin: hysteria, 9–11; *Lectures on the Diseases of the Nervous System*, 10; on rational reform, 13; and Sigerson, 10–11, 235n56; visit to Ireland, 10
Chatman, Seymour: on narrative, 78
Chesterton, G. K., 130
Chichester, Lord, 270n48
Childers, Erskine, 214, 223
Churchill, Winston, 90, 160
Cicero, 29, 95
cinema: Bergson on, 33; Eisenstein on Dickens, 3, 102, 108, 110; film techniques and narrative, 3, 62–63, 78, 100–102, 207–8; and national narratives, 93, 101, 106, 108–10; popularity in Dublin, 91–93; technology, 3. *See also* image, moving image
civilization: Arendt on, 154–56; civilizing process, 11–12, 136, 141, 172; and empire, 40, 145–46, 149–51, 153, 179, 276n59
Civil War, Irish, xiii, 5, 13, 36–37, 38, 39, 106, 130, 144, 184, 185, 186, 190, 192, 194, 195, 197, 199, 200, 214, 229n8, 254n67, 265n63; burning of Four Courts, 184, 200, 281n43; comparison with Easter Rising, 195; destruction of Public Records Office, 190; role of church and the media on public opinion, 190
Civil War, US, 174, 175; and shell shock, 3
Clancy, George: "Davin" in *Portrait*, 69; killed by Black and Tans, 69
Clare, County: Carron, 142; Dal-Cais, 283n8
Clarke, Austin, 24, 37, 181
Clarke, Tom, 79–80; Easter Rising as awakening, 51; returning from US, 80, 252n40; tobacconist shop, 80, 253n56
Cleary, Joe: *Ulysses* as revolutionary, xvi; WASP anxieties in *The Great Gatsby*, 178
Clerkenwell explosion, 73, 204
Clurman, Harold, 185
Cluseret, Gen. Gustave: James Connolly on, 89; proposed commander of Fenian insurrection, 88–89; tunneling walls in Paris Commune, 88

Cohalan, Daniel, 162
Coleman, Steve, 109
Coliseum Theatre, 80, 104*f*; advertisement, 103, 104*f*; 1916 bombardment, 103–4
Collins, Michael: Desmond Ryan's *The Invisible Army*, 206–7; Easter Rising as Greek tragedy, 111; and Eileen McGrane, 38; filming of Thomas Ashe's funeral, 106; future vindication of treaty, 2, 231n8; hit squad, 35; loyalty toward, 26–27, 204–5; parody in *Finnegans Wake*, 243n96; and Partition, 283n12; photos of, 106; and Pugh, 26–27
Collins, Wilkie: *The Frozen Deep* and Dickens, 99, 259n38
Collopy brothers (Bill and Dick), 43–44
Colum, Mary, 21; on Celtic Twilight, 9; *Life and the Dream*, 217; meeting Platon Kerzhentsev, 255n81; meeting with Pugh, 21–22; on stream of consciousness, 9, 262n21; on *Ulysses*, 9; and Van Wyck Brooks, 172; on Victor Bérard and Joyce, 267n6
Colum, Padraic, 21–22, 166, 181; Diarmuid and Gráinne, 172; influence of Abbey Theatre, 168; Joyce, Pearse, and MacDonagh in *The Road around Ireland*, 258n20, 283n10; speaker at Joyce conferences, 38; St. Enda's, 164; US responses to Easter Rising, 159; on Victor Bérard and Joyce, 267n6; "Youngest Ireland," 167, 171
Columbus, Fr., 52
commemoration, 48, 50, 103, 225; Easter Rising, 103, 225; Emmet rebellion, 46–47, 50, 93, 97–98, 101, 102, 193, 234n43, 243n3; 1798 rebellion, 45–49, 99–100
Condon, Denis: *Birth of a Nation* in Ireland, 257n12; *Ireland a Nation*, 257n11; popularity of Charlie Chaplin in Dublin, 92
Congo, Belgian, 19, 137, 146–47, 148, 151–52, 153, 154, 156, 174, 270n45; Congo Reform Association, 144, 147, 150; and "Little Belgium," 150–51

Conmee, Rev. John, S.J., 84
Connolly, Alistair, 26
Connolly, Cyril, 194
Connolly, James: on Belgian Congo, 150–51; and Daniel de Leon, 213; on German social reforms, 260n48; on Gustave Cluseret and Fenian insurrection, 89; influence on Bolshevik history of Ireland, 255n81, 256n101; influence on Pearse, 217; Ireland as weak link in empire, 89, 153; in Joyce's writings, 236n79; and Paris Commune, 88–89; respected by opponents, 212–13; threats of contemporary famine, 154–55; urban warfare, 15, 69, 85–86, 88–89, 128, 204, 205, 223, 256n101; use of magic lantern in protest, 106
Connolly, Seán, xiii
Conrad, Joseph, 249n2
Cooney, Andy, 37
Co-operative movement, 16
Cork, 26, 110, 117, 118, 119, 121, 126, 141, 222
Corkery, Daniel, 36, 210, 212, 222
Costello, Maurice, 100
Costello, Peter, 35, 215
Cowley, Malcolm, 185
Cox, Eleanor Rogers, 159
Coyle, Kathleen, 7, 116; comparisons with Virginia Woolf, 128; and Desmond Ryan, 128; "Hiberno-Marxism," 128; and Lucia Joyce, 128; marriage to Charles Meagher, 128; meeting Joyce, 128, 264n55; and Rebecca West, 127; *Sinn Féin and Socialism* (as Selma Sigerson), 128; and socialist activism, 128. See also *Flock of Birds, A*
Craig, Gordon, 97
Crane, Hart, 179; on O'Malley, 185
"crimes against humanity," xviii, 19, 149, 151, 154, 155–56
Crisis, The, 174
Cromwell, Oliver, 145–46, 150
Cronos, 267n5
Crowley, Brian, 258n29
Crusader, The, 174

Cúchulainn, 58; *Boy Deeds of Cuchulain*, 107; cult of at St. Enda's, 107; in *Finnegans Wake*, 282n67; love triangle, 61; in *On Another Man's Wound*, 283n67; parody of in *The Singing Flame*, 198; paroxysms as hysterical fits, 52; in *This Side of Paradise* (Fitzgerald), 161, 173
Cullen, Tom, 38
culture, popular: American magazines, 130; jazz, 65; replacing church influence, 111–12. See also cinema
Cumann na mBan, 16, 38, 241n64
Cunliffe, Barry, 267n3
Curran, Constantine P., 23; on Fred Ryan and Joyce, 144; in *Ulysses*, 68; writing for *The Nation*, 68
Curran, Sarah, 97, 98, 101
Curtius, Ernst Robert, 186, 191
Cusack, Michael, 80, 141; athletic prowess, 143, 269n27; caricature in "Cyclops," 141–42; *Celtic Times*, 143; and County Clare, 142; Gaelic Athletic Association (GAA), 141–42; socialist leanings, 142; supporting native industries, 143
Cuzzi, Paolo, 71
Cyclops: Irish ancestry, 138–39, 268n17, 268n19

D'Alton, John, 268n16
Daly, P. T., 50
Damon, S. Foster, 279n18
David, Jacques-Louis: *Oath of the Horatii*, 107
Davis, Alex, 129
Davis, Thomas, 122; classical republicanism, 95
Davitt, Michael, 143
Deane, Seamus: imaginary and actual, 14; inadequacy of Celtic Revival, 4–5, 19
De Búrca, Marcus, 142–43
De Burca, Seamus, 27, 238n14
Deleuze, Gilles, 88
Denning, Michael, xiv
De Valera, Éamon, 93, 162, 184, 190, 204, 280n30

Devlin, Denis, 186
Devoy, John, 50, 206, 221, 223–24, 283n20
Dewey, John, 170
Dickens, Charles, xviii, 3, 48, 96–102, 108; *David Copperfield*, 98; Dickens Fellowship of Ireland, 97; Eisenstein on Dickens's prefiguring cinematic style, 3, 102; *Household Words*, 99; Joyce on, 258n28; relationship with Ellen Ternan, 99; stories on 1798 rebellion, 98–99, 259n37; sympathy with republicanism, 108, 261n62; tour of Ireland, 99. See also *Tale of Two Cities, A*
Dickinson, Emily, 172
Didi-Huberman, Georges: on Aby Warburg, 8–9, 13–14, 234n36, 234n51, 235n65; form as historical ebb and flow, 13–14; form as transindividual, 8; on Joyce, 112; Joyce and montage, 248n78, 248n80; modernist crisis in representation, 112; modernist form and war experience, 262n12; narrative, 14; return of the repressed, 10
Dido, Queen, 138, 267n8
Dilthey, Wilhelm, 166
Dilworth, Margaret, 26
Dineen, F. B., 80
disillusionment, xiv, 195, 201, 203
Döblin, Alfred, xvii, 5, 68, 249n4; art and new objectivity, 90
Dolan, Anne, 280n39
Doolittle, Hilda (H.D.), 40, 165
Dostoevsky, Fyodor, 126; precursor to Joyce, 131
Dowden, Edward, 97, 171
Dowling, Frank, 36, 107
Dowling, Seán, 36–38; art critic for *Ireland Today*, 37; end to Civil War, 37, 241n73; IRA director of operations, 36; and Joyce, 37; meeting James T. Farrell, 37; protégé of MacDonagh, 37; pupil at St. Enda's, 36
Druids, as Egyptian (Joyce), 135, 266n2
Dublin: bombardment of, 2, 26, 34, 69, 74, 85, 103, 189–90, 206, 280n31; Dublin Metropolitan Police, 79; and

Dublin (*continued*)
Empire, 15, 45, 51, 145–46; founding of, 58–59, 247n54; linked to countryside, 16; local knowledge of, 87, 88–89, 199–200; lock-out 1913, 15, 203, 265n62; modernity of, 5, 8, 92; overlapping histories (*Portrait*), 32; reservoir of memory, 49; sites of negative topography, 47; statues, xvi, 26, 46–47, 48, 84, 193, 223; walking the streets, 18, 24, 30–32, 48–50, 53, 67, 82, 84–85, 86–87, 89, 115

Dublin, buildings: Barney Kiernan's, 22, 24, 35, 58, 129, 142, 144, 147, 148, 151, 189; Belvedere College 31, 42; Bohemian Picture Theatre, 92; Cabman's Shelter, Loopline Bridge, 105, 105*f*; Camden Theatre, 100; Clare Street, 10; Coliseum, 80, 103, 104; Coombe, 22; Croke Park, 80; Dublin Bakery Company (DBC), 67; Duke's Lawn, 100; Findlaters's Church, 80; Glasnevin Cemetery, 29, 48; Gresham Hotel, 282n65; Grosvenor Hotel, 81; Hely's stationers, 29, 38, 45, 49; Holles Street Hospital, 22; Lafayette's photography, 31; Jacob's factory, 26; Kelly's Gun and Ammunition shop, 85; Kildare Street club, 99; Leinster House, 100; Martello Tower, Sandycove, 22; Masterpiece Theatre, 92; Mendicity Institution, 47; Moira House, 47–48; Municipal Gallery, 245n21; National Library, 28, 35, 81; National Museum, 81, 92; Nelson's Pillar, 28, 84, 241n73; Pigeon House, 136; Red Bank restaurant, 81; Richmond Asylum, 2; Richmond Barracks, 26; Royal College of Surgeons, 73; Royal Hibernian Academy (RHA), 26; Star of the Sea Church, 22; St. Joseph's, Marino, 25; St. Michan's Church, 47; St. Patrick's Hospital, 2; Synod Hall, 250n17; Tramway Office, 241n73; Trinity College, 35; University College, Dublin, 186

Dublin, places: Abbey Street, 86; Ailesbury Road, 184; Amiens Street, 28; Arbour hill, 244n5; Bachelor's Walk, 85; Ballsbridge, 184; Blessington Street, 80; Cabra Park, 34; Cecilia Street, 186; Coombe, 213; Cork Hill, 106; Cypress Grove, Templeogue, 35; Dame Street, 106; Dawson Street, 34, 38; Dollymount Strand, 31; Eccles Street, 29; Fairview, 18, 81; Fingal, 11; Fitzwilliam Street, 28; Grafton Street, 45, 213, 214; Haddington Road, 80; Henry Street, 27, 103; Holles Street, 22; Island Street, 48; James Street, 213; Kildare Street, 99, 259n39; Liffey, 106; Liffey Street, 24; Loopline Bridge, 105, 105*f*; Marino, 26; Martello Tower, Sandycove, 22–23, 240n42; Merrion Square, 100; Middle Abbey Street, 74; "The Monto," 213; Mount Street, 103, 104*f*, 200, 282n65; North Frederick Street, 253n55; North King Street, 255n80; O'Connell Street/Sackville Street, 27, 67, 80, 84–85, 193, 251n23, 256n4; Parliament Street, 106; Parnell Street, 79; Phibsboro, 92; Potter's Alley, 24; Rathfarnham, 95; Royal Canal, 81; Rutland Square, 80, 106; Sandycove, 22; Sandymount Strand, 18, 22; St. Stephen's Green, 26, 45; Talbot Street, 24, 27, 28, 80, 92; Templeogue, 35; Thomas Street, 47–48, 99; Westland Row, 103, 213; Westmoreland Street, 31; Windsor Villas, 81

Dublin Castle, 38, 77, 79, 83–84, 106, 112, 179, 252n42; "Castle Document," 69, 81, 250n8, 253n53

Dubliners (Joyce): "After the Race," 45, 145; akin to shock of war front, 116; "Araby," national memory, 99; "The Dead," 182, 220, 228; dispelling illusions, xiv, xvii; elliptical style, 81; "Grace," 106; "Ivy Day in the Committee Room," 236n79; military presence in Dublin, 79; paralysis, 31–32, 52; photographic style, 29;

possible prevention of Easter Rising, 75; prevention of publication, 73–74, 130; "The Sisters," 10, 30, 31, 32, 81, 32, 239n41; "Two Gallants," 99–100
Dublin Magazine, 178, 181
Dublin Opinion, 35
Dublin Review, 35
Dubois, L. Paul, 138
Du Bois, W. E. B., xviii, 5; and Easter Rising, 174; and Irish racism, 174; on Roger Casement, 174
Dudley, Earl of (Lord Lieutenant), 45, 48, 59
Dudley, Lady, 45, 49, 59
Duff, Charles, 279n18
Duffy, Enda: Casement's Black Diaries, 253n58; on the citizen, 269n34; "double-timing" in *Ulysses*, 68, 249n6; negative topography, 47; shocks linking *Ulysses* and Easter Rising, 89; shock tactics and revolutionary writing, 83
Duffy, Louise Gavan, 241n64
Dujardin, Édouard, 284n44
Dumas, Alexander, 259n43
Dunbar, Paul Laurence, 175; "Circumstances Alter Cases," 276n63
Dunlop, Robert, 268n21
Dunn, Joseph, 281n61

Easter Rising (1916): affinities with *Ulysses*, xiii, xvi, xviii, 1, 3, 4, 9, 16, 17–18, 20, 34, 52, 65, 71, 73–75, 76, 79–85, 87, 89–90, 94, 111–12, 203, 219, 222–23, 249n86, 254n80; as awakening, 51; barricades, 18, 88; blow to empire, 4, 65, 112; Catholic messianism, 94, 111, 127, 217; and Charlie Chaplin, 91–92, 256n4; checkpoint, 104*f*; and cinema, 91–92; and classical republicanism, 94–95; as commemorative event, 103; contemporary perceptions of, 94; destined not to fail, xiv, 251n28, 253n51; Dublin Castle and intelligence, 79–84; Edward Carson on, 112; and Emmet, 102; "first radio broadcast" of news, 94; "forged" documents, 69, 81, 250n8, 253n53; and French Revolution, 96, 102; vs. German monarchical rule, 102; and Great War, xvii–xviii, 4, 74–75, 112; as Greek tragedy (Michael Collins), 111; heterogeneity of causes, 4, 15–16, 73, 94, 252n40; international dimension, 4, 5, 16, 20, 65, 110, 144, 157, 159–60, 161, 162, 163–64, 165, 166–68, 169–72, 173–79; Lenin on, 112; and local knowledge, 87, 88–89, 199–200; looting, 51; mandate from the future, 1–2, 70; modern event, xviii, 92–94; nightmare of history, 51–52; and Paris Commune, 88–89; parody of (Queneau), 3, 112, 262nn6–9; plans conceived as a novel, 67; "poet's rebellion," 15, 159, 273n1, 276n59, 278n2; prefigurings of (in *Ulysses*), 1–2, 72–75; preparations for, 81, 203; relating past to future, 2; Republican self-sacrifice, 95; romantic idealism, 111; rupturing reality, 64; and Russian Revolution, 4; Sir Henry Wilson on, 112; spatial form, 17–18, 32–33, 79–83, 84–86, 87–89; subjective participation in, 83–84, 256n99; tricolor, 102; tunneling through walls, 17, 84–85; unexpected nature of, 78; use of Jacob's biscuits tins, 24
Eco, Umberto: on stream of consciousness, 9
Edwards, Ruth Dudley, 223
Eglinton, John (W. G. Magee), 71; future orientation in Joyce, 2, 6, 231n9; individualism and nation, 55–56; on Joyce as idol, xv, 233n27; modern epic and technology, 62; objects acquiring aesthetic form, 62
Egoist, The, 82
Eiland, Howard, 163
Einstein, Albert, 32, 275n33
Eisenstein, Sergei: "dissolve" in *A Tale of Two Cities*, 102, 108; on D. W. Griffith and Dickens, 3, 101; montage, 109–10, 113, 185, 261n68

Eksteins, Modris, 89–90
Elias, Norbert, 12
Eliot, T. S., 9, 165, 275n33; *Introducing James Joyce*, 279n18; review of *Ulysses*, 59, 247n57; on tradition, 247n58; *The Waste Land*, 245n33
Ellmann, Maud, 2, 20
Ellmann, Richard, 17, 23, 25, 38, 148; and Eileen MacCarvill, 242n80; and Pugh, 238n11
Emerson, Caryl, 56
Emmet, Robert: affinities with Sidney Carton, 101; Boucicault's play *Robert Emmet*, 101; classical republicanism, 95; Easter Rising, 102; execution, 47–48, 50; in insurrection, 46, 47–48, 50; *Ireland a Nation*, 93; Irish theater and film, 101; Joyce on, 243n3; last words, 244n25; Sarah Curran, 97, 101
English, Richard, 196
Enright, Seán, 253n53
Envoy, 242n79
epic, 40, 144; ancient, 17, 53; Aristotle, 245n31; Bakhtin on, 53; Broch on, 54; Eglinton on modern epic and technology, 62; epic theater, 64; foundational form, 56; heroism, 52; Irish, 45, 54, 59, 64–65; Lukacs on, 53; vs. lyric, 61; modern epic, 17, 53, 59, 60–65; and novel, 53, 60–61; O'Grady on, 56–60; ordered cosmos of classical epic, 53; paratactical nature of, 53; relation to history (Greece), 56; romantic, 56–60; Sigerson on, 60–62
epiphany: Adorno on, 48; MacDonagh on, 61
Etna, Mount, 268n19
Evans, Caradoc, 221
Evening Mail, 35
Evening Telegraph, 24, 238n9
executions: of British hostages, 193; Civil War, 214, 283n22; Easter Rising and War of Independence, xiv, 4, 19, 26, 52, 73, 76, 101, 124, 126–27, 129, 147, 149, 159, 164, 165, 169, 173–74, 189, 200, 203; 1798 rebellion and Emmet's insurrection, 50, 98–99, 234n23; in *A Tale of Two Cities*, 97–98, 108–9

Fallon, William, 30; Joyce and the future, xiv; Joyce and rugby, 42–43; Joyce's photographic memory, 28; in *Portrait*, 30
Famine, Great, 13, 49, 161, 199; contemporary threats of famine, 154, 272n77; famine memory, 119, 122–23, 210; relation to hunger strike, 119, 122–23, 264n53
Farr, Florence, 128–29
Farrell, James T.: Abbey Theatre as constraint on insurrection, viii; introducing Victor Serge to English readership, xv; meeting IRA sympathizers, 37; *Ulysses* and Irish revolution, viii
Farrell, Michael: GPO and French Revolution in *Thy Tears Might Cease*, 102, 260n47
fascism: Arendt on, 225; Mussolini, 131; and myth (Adorno and Cassirer), 53
Fay, Monsignor Sigourney, 160–62, 273n6, 274n11
Fay, William, 186
Fenianism: 15, 51, 73, 77, 82, 89, 174, 189, 204, 206, 211, 212, 221, 222, 223, 243n3, 283n11, 285n50, 285n85. *See also* Irish Republican Brotherhood
Ferrer, Daniel, 30, 229
Ferrero, Guglielmo, 267n2
ffrench-Mullan, Madeline, 73
Fielding, Henry, 55
Figgis, Darrell, 258n28
Fingal, 11; 268n20
Finnegans Wake (Joyce), 38; capture of O'Malley, 200; Easter Rising, xii, 73; empire, 154; erasing English language, 62; and *Foras Feasa* (Keating), 38; history and hysteria, 11, on lightning, 8; Lough Neagh, 25; Michael Collins and Richard Mulcahy, 243n96; *Mime of Mick, Nick and the*

Maggies, 23; moving pictures in, 42; on O'Rahilly, 74, 251n25; Parnell, 11; parody of *On Another Man's Wound*, 201, 283n67; parody of *Portrait*, 41–42; on Partition, xvii, 119; Persse O'Reilly, 251n23, 283n67; Phoenicians, 136, 138, 140; Phoenix Park, 11, 138, 140; Piggott and forgery, 24–25; Pugh family, 24–25; Robert Atkinson satirized, 61; rugby, 42–43; on shock, 8; Sigerson, 11, 60, 61; Sinn Féin, 74; on *Ulysses*, 60; United Ireland, 43

Fish, Stanley, 85

Fitzgerald, David, 36

FitzGerald, Desmond: early purchaser of *Ulysses*, 34; friendship with Campbell and Ezra Pound, 40, 283n13; Imagist movement, 40, 283n13; Joyce and Tailteann Games, 41, 241n38; memoir, 283n13; minister for publicity, 40; Pound's verses on, 40–41; proposing Joyce for Nobel Prize, 40

Fitzgerald, F. Scott, xviii, 5; on Celticism, 160, 162; Home Rule and Easter Rising, 160–61; Irishness in *Great Gatsby*, 160, 162, 173; review of *The Celt and His World*, 160; and Shane Leslie, 160–61, 273n6; on *Ulysses*, 67, 249n2; white supremacy in *Great Gatsby*, 178, 277n79. See also *This Side of Paradise*

Fitzgerald, Lord Edward: capture and shooting, 47–48; Carton House, 98–99; Duke's Lawn in "Two Gallants," 100; haunting of history in Dorothy Macardles's "The Prisoner," 264n47, 266n82

Fitzgerald, Michael, 93, 119

Fitzharris, James ("Skin-the-Goat"), 105, 155, 188, 280n27

Flanagan, Thomas, 55, 246n40

flashbacks: cinematic device, 2–3, 231nn11–12; flashbulb memory, 28; fusing past and present, 2–3; and shell shock, 2–3, 8; in Woolf's *Mrs. Dalloway*, 231n12

Flaubert, Gustave, 97

Flint, F. S., 128, 165, 265n71

Flock of Birds, A (Coyle), 124–29; deprivation of food, 124; Dostoevsky, 126; echoes of *Portrait* (Joyce), 127; Einstein theory, 124; execution of Kevin Barry, 126; indeterminacy of time, 125–26; and Joyce, 125, 127; mother-daughter relations, 125, 127; mother-son relations, 124–27; Nietzsche, 126, 127; Simone Weil on, 124, state execution, 124–28; Terence MacSwiney, 126

folk culture, 165, 169, 175; Dionysian 7, 233n23; pagan, 7, 11, 14, 59; superstition, 12, suppression of, 12, tales, 201, 282n67

form, aesthetic: akin to electric charge, 7–8; autonomy of, 6; breaking into the real, 17, 18, 24, 49, 62, 84–85, 86, 87–88, 92, 115, 230n18, 238n12; composure of, 7–8; disruptive, 62, 77, 86, 88, 115; dynamic, 7–8, 9, 234n38; everyday life, 3, 6, 8–9, 49–50, 77, 87, 194–95; experiments in style, 93, 116–33; and history, 6–7, 15, 16–17; reading skills, 6–7; repressed content, 10; search for adequate expression in Great War, 113, 114–16; as symptom, 9–10; transindividual, 10

Foster, John Wilson, 64, 65

Forster, E. M., 220

Forster, John, 260n62

Foster, R. F.: Joyce subverting narratives of the nation, 93

Foucault, Michel, 63

France, 2, 40, 43; civic republicanism vs. German autocracy, 102; Exposition Universelle, 107; French delegates to 1798 centenary commemorations, 45, 48; French Revolution, 7; Great War, 149, 159, 264n54; and Irish insurgency, 96; Nazi occupation, 124; Pearse and, 107; republic, 102; and Roman garb, 94; and self-sacrifice, 95, 108–9; tricolor, 102; in *The Wasted Island* (O'Duffy), 96

Frank, Joseph: narrative excess and *Ulysses*, 79; spatial form stepping outside narrative time, 79, 85, 253n50; unity of spatial form, 79; visual nature of spatial form, 79
free indirect discourse, 119, 212–13
Freeman's Journal, The, 32, 203, 210, 211
French, Lord, 106
Freud, Sigmund, 10; dream-work, 16; familiarity with "Viennese school" in Ireland, 71, 250n17; hysteria and reminiscences, 10, 234n52; influence of Lecky on, 13; melancholia, xv; *Nachträglichkeit* (belatedness), 71–72, 237n94; on narrative and real life, 14–15; overlapping temporalities, 72, 79; psychoanalysis and history, 18; *Psychopathology of Everyday Life*, 9, 16, 71; rationalism, 13; the "Wolf Man," 72, 250n19
Friend, Major General, 78
Fuseli, Henry: *Oath of the Three Confederates on the Rutli*, 107
Fussell, Paul: inadequacy of poetry in Great War, 113–14; modernist forms and war trauma, 114; unreliability of firsthand accounts, 114, 262n17
futurism, 115

Gabler, Hans Walter, 38, 192
Gaelic Athletic Association (GAA), 50, 141, 142
Gaelic League, 50, 182
Galileo: "It still moves," 32
Gallagher, Frank, 7, 116; *Days of Fear*, 119–24, 131; on hunger strike in Mountjoy prison, 120–24, 264n50; Lady Gregory on, 120; modernist techniques in real life, 124; in Sinn Féin's publicity department, 120; stream-of-consciousness narration, 120–24
Galway, County: Connemara, 136, 154, 272n77; Gort, 142
Garibaldi, 131
Garvey, Marcus, xviii; Ireland as catalyst in world decolonization, 177–78, 277n78

Gehring, Wes D., 92
General Post Office (GPO), 73
George, David Lloyd, 93
George, Henry, 143
George III, King, 131
Germany, 12
Gibbons, Luke, 237n87, 268n17, 275n44
Gibson, Andrew, 49, 249n86
Gide, André, 275n33
Gilbert, Stuart, 2, 168, 186, 190, 191; "An Irish *Ulysses*," 193
Gillet, Louis, 124, 136
Gillet, Louisette, 124
Ginzburg, Carlo, 7, 15
Gladstone, W. E. H., 144
Goethe, J. W., 245n33; on the *Laocoön*, 7
Gogarty, Oliver St. John: anti-Semitism, 141–42; gold medal for poetry, 41
Gogol, Nikolai, 91, 130; *Dead Souls*, 131
Goldie, Peter, 211, 215–16
Golding, Louis, 279n18
Goldring, Douglas: *The Fortune*, 4, 9, 234n50; linking Easter Rising with Russian Revolution, 4, 232nn21–22; visit to Dublin after Easter Rising, 4, 232n21
Gore-Booth, Eva, 181
Gorman, Herbert, 23
Gotham Book Mart, 186, 279n19
Gould, George Milbry, 251n31
"Grace" (*Dubliners*): Mrs. Kernan, 14, 156; Tom Kernan, 47–49, 99
Graham, Gordon, 236n74
Grant, Madison, 178, 277n79
Grattan, Henry, 24, 157
Graves, Robert, 185
Great War, 5; advanced social system in Germany (James Connolly), 260n48; bleakness of *Dubliners* compared to No Man's Land, 116; conscription, 130, 229n8; Defence of the Realm Act, 105; and Easter Rising, 4, 196; and English national integrity, 90; German autocracy, 260n48; and imperialism, 89, 150–51, 154–55; Irish America and, 159–60, 177; and modernism, xvii, 5, 89–90, 113–16; photography and, 105; shell shock and

trauma, 2–3, 8, 231nn11–12; *Travesties*, 1
Greaves, C. Desmond: Dublin as revolutionary center, 89
Greece, classical, 56, 95, 135, 136, 173, 267n5
Green, Alice Stopford: Congo Reform Association, 147; cross-cultural solidarity, 147–49; *Irish Nationality*, 271n55; Joyce's familiarity with writings, 271n55; medieval Irish trade, 148–49, 271n55, 271n58
Greenblatt, Stephen, 9
Greenwood, Joseph M., 258n26
Gregory, Lady, 97, 113–14, 166, 263n42
Griffith, Arthur, 5, 74, 80; clarification of anti-Semitic views, 141–42; on Fred Ryan, 144; "hysterical pride," 245n21; Limerick boycott, 140; and Partition, 283n12; "Shanganagh," 145; and Sinn Féin, 251n27; support of Zionism, 140; *United Irishman*, 140, 145–46
Griffith, D. W., 3, 178
Grimm brothers, 12
Grosvenor Sanatorium, Kent, 124
Group Theatre (New York), 185
Guinness, Selina, 244n11

Hackett, Dominic, 199, 275n31
Hackett, Francis, 166, 274n15, 275n31
Hall, Edith, 96
Harkins, James W., Jr., 108
harp: Aeolian, 100; symbol of United Irishmen, 99–100
Hart, Peter, 89
Hassell, John, 108
H.D. (Hilda Dolittle), 40
Healy, Seán, 110
Heaney, Seamus: "Gravities," 27
Helen of Troy, 267n8
Henderson, Alice Corbin: on Celtic diction, 166; cofounder *Poetry* magazine, 165; and Irish Revival, 165–66; and MacDonagh, 165; *The New Poetry: A Study Outline*, 165–66, 274n28; and O'Malley, 179–78, 183; "Too Far from Paris," 165; vernacular modernism, 165–66, 276n54

Henderson, Frank: on Volunteers appearing out of nowhere, 81
Hercules, 267n5
Herring, Philip, 147
Hesiod, 268n19
Higgins, Róisín, 103
history: and actuality, 74; contingency, 74; vs. inevitability, 68, 74; and possibility, 18, 74, 77
history, Irish: event and narrative, 83; fragmented, 16, 171–73; lacking narrative coherence, 82; and narrative, 78–84, 91–93; nightmare of (*Ulysses*) 16, 52; not fully formed, 57, 247n50; posing problems for artistic representation, 16, 114
Hobson, Bulmer, 39
Hoffmansthal, Hugh Von, 166
Hogan, David: on Cecil Ffrench Salkeld, 123; Four Glorious Years, 122. *See also* Gallagher, Frank
Hogan, Robert, 51
Holloway, Joseph, 257n11
Holocaust, 111, 153, 240n55, 273n87
Holyhead, 80
Homer, 3, 144; and Greece, 56; *Iliad*, 62; Ireland as Calypso's isle, 17; *Odyssey*, xviii, 9, 16–17, 24, 45, 56, 62, 136, 155, 190, 267n6; Ogygia as Ireland, 136; Phoenician origins of *Odyssey*, 17, 137
Home Rule, 56, 75, 78, 93, 143, 160, 268n12; political shift to Sinn Féin, 112, 148, 275n31
Hone, Evie, 185
Howes, Marjorie, 51
Huebsch, Benjamin, 275n33
Hull, Eleanor, 149
Hulme, T. E., 40, 128–29, 265n71
human rights, 150; Amnesty International, 150; Arendt on, 154–56; collective vs. individualistic, 153, 156; cultural inheritance, 154; dignity, 156; extending beyond national sovereignty, 156; human diversity, 156; Human Rights Watch, 150; national self-determination, 153; political nature of, 153, 154–56; social and economic rights, 156; transcendental,

human rights (*continued*)
156–57; United Nations declaration, 155; universal, 156–57
hunger strike, 93; and Great Famine, 119, 122–23; and modernism, 117, 124; Republican protest in 1920, 119–24; and social solidarity, 119
Hunt, Leigh, 132
Hyde, Douglas, 166, 182
Hynes, Samuel: Eliot's "The Waste Land" and Great War experience, 114
hysteria: and body politic, 11–14, 50–52; as Celtic malaise, 50–51; and Charcot, 10–14; and Cúchulainn, 52; and Easter Rising, 50–51; female malady, 51; male hysteria, 50; and Pearse, 50; as revolutionary, 51; and Sigerson, 10–11, 52. *See also* paralysis

Ibsen, Henrik, xvi, 18
image: moving image, xvii, 7, 31–34, 41–42, 107–8, 113, 164, 239n42, 240n46, 240n47, 240n49, 257n12; and narrative, 78–81; still image, 31–32, 87, 240n46
Imagist movement, 128, 265n71
imperialism, xviii, 53, 148, 149, 150, 156, 175, 255n83; not an abstract system, 152, 155, 156
imprisonment, prison writing: Constance Markievicz, 115–17; Ernie O'Malley, 189, 198–99; Francis Stuart, 130, 132–33; Frank Gallagher, 116–19; Joseph Campbell, 130–33
India, 48, 89, 112, 150, 165; Ireland and, 137, 144, 157, 176, 177, 178, 224
Ingram, John Kells: "The Memory of the Dead," 46, 48, 99
interior monologue: inner speech mixed with external voices, 211; in *Remembering Sion*, 211; Woolfian inner self vs. Augustinian inner dialogue, 211. *See also* stream of consciousness
International James Joyce Symposium, 38

International Summer Course (Joyce), 38
Invisible Army, The (Ryan), 205; Civil War, 214–15; and Easter Week, 214; heroism of Collins, 208, 215; Mananaan MacLir, 215; montage and cinematic techniques in, 207–8
Ireland: abject loyalty, 15; Act of Union (1800), 55; and Caribbean, 177, 277n73; catalyst in decolonization, xvi, xvii, 4, 5, 16, 62, 89, 112, 137, 141, 155, 157, 177, 229n8, 233n23, 261n4; difficulties in representing Irish revolution, 114, 116; duration of the past, 33; economy and trade in Middle Ages, 148–49; fractured history, 57, 247n50; as "Hibernia," 139; history not fully formed, 57, 247n50; joining Council of Europe, 272n70; knowledge of classics in Irish culture, 96, 258n22; modernity, 5, 65, 93–94; "national right to self-determination," 272n70; persistence of the medieval, 65, 167, 172; shaking foundations of English politics (Churchill), 90; as social laboratory of the modern, 65, 249n92; story of, 93–94
Ireland a Nation (film), 93, 119, 257n11
Ireland, Socialist Party of, 25, 236n79
Irish Bookshop, 34
Irish Bulletin, 120
Irish Citizen Army (ICA), 25, 73
Irish Civil War, xviii, 4, 13; cessation of hostilities, 37
Irish College, Rome, 162
Irish Freedom, 35, 70, 95, 250n10, 258n16
Irish Free State, xvii, 4, 5, 34, 35, 37, 39–41, 184, 198, 201, 214, 241n58, 253n54
Irish Race Convention (Paris), 40
Irish Republican Brotherhood (IRB), 25, 39, 50, 51, 95, 166, 174, 252n40
Irish Review, 35, 237, 285
Irish Rugby Football Union (IRFU), 43
Irish School of Wireless, 94
Irish Times, 126, 200, 203–4, 284n34
Irish Volunteers: eighteenth century,

24; twentieth century, 24, 25, 69, 81, 83–84, 103, 106, 119, 206, 217, 224, 253
Irish War News, 151
Isle of Man, 191
Istanbul, 20

Jackson, Declan, 120
Jacob's biscuit factory: biscuit tin in *Ulysses*, 24; and Easter Rising, 24, 26
James, Henry, 91, 164
James, William, 170; stream of consciousness, 8, 234n44
James Joyce Institute, 39
James Joyce School, 39
Jameson, Fredric: dereification in *Ulysses*, 87; modernism in the periphery, 4; montage on the streets, 86; *Ulysses* as epic under imperialism, 53
Jarman, Francis, 99
Jeffreys, Judge, 259n36
Jenkins, Lee, 175, 277n74
John O'Leary Literary Society, 25
Jolas, Eugene, 186, 191
Jolas, Maria, 284n34
Jones, Gareth Steadman, 108
Jonson, Ben, 18
Joyce, Giorgio, 23, 238n7
Joyce, James: Adorno on Joyce's rebellion against realism, 111; aesthetic form akin to electric charge, 8; on ancient Druids, 23; *Anna Livia Plurabelle*, 186; appeal to republicans, 21–28, 34–39; on Calvinism, 141; on campaign against *Ulysses* in Ireland, 35; challenging consensus that led to Great War, 5; contributing as much to Ireland as the revolution, 36, 39–40, 194; on Cromwell, 146; and Desmond Ryan, 28; on Emmet, 243n3; on English liberalism, 143–44; *Exiles*, 20, 186; fluidity of the past, 70; and the Free State 35, 39–40; future orientation of, xiv, 57, 224; "Gas from a Burner," 129; on Great Famine, 119, 143; "Home Rule Comet," 143; "Ibsen's New Drama," 230n17; inadequacy of artistic form to Irish revolution, 3–4, 20, 72–73; "Ireland at the Bar," 79–80; "Ireland: Island of Saints and Sages," 10, 52, 135, 137, 138, 141, 143, 146, 243n3; Irishness of, 39; on Irish paralysis, xvii, 10; on *The Irish Rebellion* (Boyle), 72; "James Clarence Mangan," 229n10, 234n42; and John MacCormack, 262n6; and Kathleen Coyle, 55, 264n55; and Kenneth Reddin, 28; knowledge of Dublin, 21–22; "The Last Fenian," 243n3; love without illusions, 218–24; memorizing *The Lady of the Lake*, 29; *The Mime of Mick, Nick and the Maggies*, 22; "Paris Notebook," 240n46; and Patrick Touhy, 28; personal views on Irish politics, xvi, 3–4, 52; Phoenician origins of the Irish, 135–36, 141, 266n2; photographic memory, 28–34; on physical force in Irish politics, 52; political inadequacy of Irish Revival, 4; *Pomes Penyeach*, 186; "A Portrait of the Artist" (essay), 270n36; promoting Irish industry, 143; proposed for Nobel Prize, 40; and Pugh, 21–28; related to Terence MacSwiney, 118; "The Right Heart in the Wrong Place," 118; and rugby, 42–43; on sculpture as movement, 32; seeking photographs of locations in *Ulysses*, 22–23; "The Shade of Parnell," 51, 144, 253n46; singing ability, 262n6; Sinn Féin sympathies, xvi; statue of, xvii; *Stephen Hero*, 69, 80, 235n60, 238n12, 240n45; *Tales of Shem and Shaun*, 186; and time, 69–70; universal as local, 157; and William Fallon, 28, 42; and the "Wolf Man" in Freud, 250n19; *Work in Progress*, 186. See also *Dubliners*; *Finnegans Wake*; *Portrait of the Artist as a Young Man, A*; *Ulysses*
Joyce, John Stanislaus, 118, 263n36
Joyce, Lucia, 128, 240n47
Joyce, Stanislaus, 238n7, 259n39
Juvenal, 148

"Kathleen ni Houlihan," 94, 117
Kavanagh, Patrick, 185
Keane, Edward T., 34
Kearney, Peadar: combatant in Jacob's factory, 25–26; and Pugh, 25–28, 238n14; "The Soldier's Song," 25
Keating, Captain, 243n89
Keating, Geoffrey: *Foras Feasa ar Éireann*, 38
Keats, John, 7
Kelleher, John V., 186, 279n18, 282n61
Kelly, Patrick J., 106
Kennedy, John F., 260n58
Kenner, Hugh, 128
Kenny, Colum, 141, 245n21
Keogh, Jack, 131
Kermode, Frank, 82
Kerry, County, 190, 264n5; Valentia Island wireless station, 94; Waterville, 257n7
Kettle, Thomas, 247n50
Kerzhentsev, Platon, 86
Kiberd, Declan: on Easter Rising, xvi
Kildare, County, 46–47; Carton House, 98–99; Clongowes college, 18, 48; Curragh camp, 130, 132; Maynooth, 98–99
Kilkenny, 166; *Kilkenny People*, 34
Kilmer, Joyce: death in Great War in 1918, 159; "Easter Week: In Memory of Joseph Mary Plunkett," 159; "Poets Marched in the Van of Irish Revolt," 159
Kinsella, Thomas, 59
Kipling, Rudyard, 177
Klaxon, 35
Koch, John T. 268n21
Kracauer, Siegfried: camera's eye for detail, 68; on Charlie Chaplin, 92
Kraepelin, Emil, 50
Kraus, Karl, *The Last Days of Mankind*, 115, 252n40; compared to *Ulysses*, 263n26; prediction of rise of fascism, 252n40
Kumar, Shiv, 18

Laforgue, Jules, 194
Lamar, William H., 83
Land League, 49; Land War, 11, 13, 16, 176
Lane, Leeann, 264n47
Lanigan, John, 268n16
Lansing, Robert, 177
Larbaud, Valéry, xix, 222
Larkin, James: Dublin lock-out, 15, 205, 213, 265; on Easter Rising, 94, 175; visited by Charlie Chaplin in prison, 110
Lawrence, D. H., 165, 179, 182, 185, 275n33, 279n19
Lawrence, T. E., 185
Le Brocquy, Louis, 185
Lecky, W. E. H.: *History of the Rise and Influence of the Spirit of Rationalism in Europe*, 13, 235n61; influence on Freud, 13, 235n62; on Irish superstition, 12–13; Joyce's familiarity with, 236n61
Ledwich, Edward, 138
Ledwidge, Francis, 166, 181; "Lament for Thomas MacDonagh," 278n2
Leerssen, Joep: on Phoenician origins of the Irish, 137, 268n14
Leinster, Duke of, 100
Leitrim, County, 252n40; Carrick-on-Shannon, 200; Lough Allen, 200
Lemass, Seán, 36, 241n70
Lemkin, Raphael: candidates for genocide, 156
Lenin, Vladimir I., 4, 153, 256n101; on Easter Rising, 112
Lennon, Joseph, 123
Leon, Ferdinand, 100
Leopold, King, 19
Leslie, Shane: absence of Celtic Odyssey, 46; *The Celt and His World*, 45; co-dedicatee of *The Beautiful and Damned*, 160; diplomatic activity, 160; on Easter Rising as hysterical, 160; literary Bolshevism of Joyce's work, 163; mentoring of F. Scott Fitzgerald, 160–63; and Monsignor Sigourney Fay, 160–62; read by Marianne Moore, 163; recommending *This Side of Paradise* for publication, 160; review of *Ulysses*, 23; at St. En-

da's, 164; on Thomas MacDonagh and Padraic Colum, 164
Lessing, G. E.: *Laocoön*, 8, 17, 33, 37, 240n45
Lester, Seán, 205
Letts, Winifred, 166
Levant, xviii, 136
Levin, Harry, 240n49, 279n18
Lewis, Wyndham P., 5; animated still life in Joyce, 87; *The Apes of God*, 86, 87; *Blast* magazine, 256n104; criticisms of Joyce, 14, 86–88; critique of time-philosophy in Bergson and Whitehead, 86–87; dissolution of matter, 14, 86–88; English national integrity, 89; General Strike, 87; invisibility of Irish ethnic difference, 118; Irish rebellion, 86–77; Joyce, Yeats, and Irish insurgency, 87; Joyce and time, 69, 86–87; Joyce's vs. Proust's relation to past, 70; on solidity of objects, 86–87; on W. E. B. Du Bois, 154, 272n76
Lewisohn, Lewis, xviii; inclusion of Irish authors, 166; on Irish Revival, 167; and Joyce, 275n33; and MacDonagh, 167–68; *A Modern Book of Criticism*, 166–67; and multi-ethnic America, 167
lightning: Easter Rising, 75, 232n21; in Joyce, 8; as metaphor of literary form, 7–8; in Warburg, 7–8, 234n36
Lir, Children of, 280n36
Lir, Manannán Mac, 190–91, 216
Lissagaray, Prosper-Olivier: *History of the Paris Commune*, 89
Literature in Ireland (MacDonagh), 61, 164–65; and American criticism, 166; indirection in language, 61, 168–69; on "Irish mode," 61, 128–29, 167–68; lyric vs. epic in Irish cultural history, 61; medievalism in Ireland, 167, 172; modern lyric, 61; "Of Ireland," xiv; viewing tradition as broken, 172–73
Little Review, 82–83, 119
Locke, Alain, 173
Lord Lieutenant. *See* Dudley, Earl of

London: imagism and the avant-garde, 128–29, 265n71; Irish accents, 208, 212; Terence MacSwiney funeral, 40, 41, 61, 69, 87, 117–18, 171, 175–76, 205, 206, 209, 218, 241n64
Longford, County, 269n27
Lough Neagh, 25
Louth, County: Drogheda, 145
love, 31, 46, 115, 190; of country, 163, 165; divine love in the Bible, 144–46; without illusions, 18, 221–22; Joyce's love of Ireland, 39–40, 222; love stories, 101–2; maternal, 19, 125, 127, 183, 191, 217–18, 219–21; modern love, 61; opening on to wider world, 137, 144, 148, 163; passionate Irish, 176; paternal, 183, 219; and Pearse, 216, 217–18, 223; in politics, 190; romantic, 124; self-sacrifice, xviii, 96–98, 100–101, 108–9, 127
Lowell, Amy, 165
Löwy, Michael, 224
Luhan, Mabel Dodge, 179, 276n54
Lukacs, Georg: on aesthetic form, 5; epic and novel, 53
Lusitania, 260n48
Luther, Martin, 141
Luxemburg, Rosa: critique of imperialism, 150, 152; on "Little Belgium," 150; on Putumayo, 150
Lynch, Liam, 37
Lyons, F. S. L., 50
Lyons, J. B., 11, 235n56

Macardle, Dorothy: "The City," 18; "The Prisoner," 264n47
MacBride, John, 80
MacBride, Maud Gonne, 36, 97, 106; threat of contemporary famine in Ireland, 190
MacBride, Seán, 278n5, 284n34
MacCarvill, Eileen (née McGrane): Cumann na mBan, 38; editor of Mainie Jellett, 39; imprisonment, 381; intelligence work for Michael Collins, 38, 242n77; Joyce's unpublished writings, 38–39, 242n80; lecturer at UCD, 37, 242n76; modern-

MacCarvill, Eileen (née McGrane) (*continued*)
ist art, 39; NUI Senate, 38; papers at early Joyce conferences, 38, 242n81; reading *Ulysses* in prison, 37, 242n75; Swift scholar, 39
MacCarvill, Patrick, 38
MacCumhaill, Fionn, 64, 143, 215, 282n67
Mac Diarmada, Seán, 69; last words, 70; mandate from the future, 70; on shock benefit of Easter Rising, 51
MacDonagh, Thomas: address to court-martial, 253n31; associated with Joyce in responses to Easter Rising, xviii, 15, 76, 168; on avant-garde, 70, 129, 167; cites Henderson and *Poetry* magazine, 165–66, 179; and classical republicanism, 95, 258n20; commander at Jacob's factory, 24; on dialect, 175, 277n74; and Dominic Hackett, 275n31; Easter Rising as wake-up call, 70; Easter Rising not destined to fail, xiv, 251n28, 253n51; ebb and flow of history, 253n51; epiphany, 61; on French Revolution, 167; future mandate of Rising, 70; futurism, 168; importance of criticism and creativity for cultural movement, 171; among "last romantics," 113; lecturing at UCD, 37, 38, 242n76; in *Modern Book of Criticism* (Lewisohn), 167–69; and modernism, 168; and Padraic Colum, 258n20, 283n10; "poet's rebellion," 15, 159, 278n2, 276n59; against realism, 168; reviewed by Ezra Pound, 165; and Shane Leslie, 164; at St. Enda's, 164; training methods for Rising, 81, 164. See also *Literature in Ireland*
MacGreevy, Thomas: difficulties in representing Irish revolution, 114
MacIntyre, Alasdair: narrative as lived experience, 76, 93
MacManus, M. J., 34
MacNamara, Brinsley, 211
MacNeill, Eoin, 64, 69, 79, 103, 148, 249n87

MacSwiney, Peter Paul, 119
MacSwiney, Terence, 29, 93, 122; funeral noted by Wyndham Lewis, Virginia Woolf, 118; hunger strikes draws attention of Proust, 117; illustration in *Le Petit Journal*, 118; Joyce's poetic protest on his death, 118; martyr complex linked to Joyce (Pound), 119; relative of Joyce, 118; solidarity with Cork hunger-strikers, 119
Madden, R. R., 95
magical realism (Germany), 123
Maginni, Denis J.: in *Ulysses*, 84
Maguire, J. F., 164
Maguire, Patrick J., 257n12
Mahaffey, Vicki, 225
Mailhos, Jacques, 33
Maisky, Ivan, 86, 255n81
Mallarmé, Stéphane, 166
Manchester, 26, 145, 211
Mangan, James Clarence, 39, 229n10
Mansfield, Katherine, 130
Marcel, Gabriel, 265n68
Marinetti, Filippo, 115
Markham, Edwin, 159
Markievicz, Constance, 97; on pressures on language in prison writing, 117
Martindale, Rev. C. C., 222
Martin-Harvey, John, xvii, 98f; circulating in Irish literary and political circles, 97; among Dublin's favorite actors, 97; in film version of *The Only Way*, 259n41; and Gordon Craig, 97; house visited by Dickens Fellowship of Ireland, 97; idolized by Gerty MacDowell and Milly Bloom, 97; lectures at Trinity College, 97; matinee idol in *Ulysses*, 97; starring role as Sidney Carton in *The Only Way*, 97–98, 98f, 100–101, 108, 109f, 259n43; W. B. Yeats on his performance in *Hamlet*, 97–98
Marx, Karl: dominant ideas in society, 14; French Revolution, 261n62; revolutions clothing themselves in antique garb, 94
Mason, Ellsworth, 38, 242n80
Masses, The, 174

Matisse, Henri: illustrations of *Ulysses*, 23–24
Maude, Nancy, 129, 132, 266n82
Maunsel & Company, 73–74, 129
Maxwell, John, 51, 73
Mayo, County: Ballina, 132; Burrishrule, 280n35; Caher, 280n36; Castlebar, 191; Clew Bay, 191, 280n36; Foxford, 143; Inisglora, 280n36
McCartan, Michael, 80
McCartan, Patrick, 36
McCormack, John, 262n6
McCormack, W. J., 101
McDowell, R. B., 147
McGahern, John: on O'Malley, 184, 199
McGrath, William, 13
McGreevy, Ronan, 102
McHugh, Roger, 186
McKay, Claude, xviii, 5; affinities with MacDonagh, 171, 175, 277n74; agrarian protest, 176, 277n73; *Banjo*, Irish models, 179; Caribbean under British rule, 177; conception of class in colonial context, 175–76, 277n74; dialect and vernacular modernism, 175, 277n72, 277n74; on Irish racism, 175–76; MacSwiney's hunger strike, 175; participating with "Sinn Fein Communists," 175, 277n74; "primitivism," 176, 277n70
McKelvey, Joe, 283n22
McLoughlin, Prof., 186
McLuhan, Marshall: news of Easter Rising as first radio broadcast, 94, 257n14
McNeice, Louis, 185
Meaney, Geraldine, 265n61
Meath, County: Navan, 205; Tara, 80
medievalism, 65; fragmented remains, 59–61, 64; illuminations, 128; Irish international trade, 148; MacDonagh and Joyce, 172, 222; and the modern, 65; persistence in Ireland, 65, 172
Meillet, Leo, 89
melancholia, left-wing, xiv, 3, 6; contrasted with nostalgia, xiv, 141, 205; not letting go, xv, 33–34; regret contrasted with remorse, 191–93

Mellows, Liam, 177, 283n22
Melville, Herman, 130, 172, 245n33
memory: "akasic," 190; art of memory (Yates), 19–20; classical training, 19–20; contingency, 34, 48–49; counter-memory, 34, 48–49; and cultural unconscious 6, 16, 99–100; displacement in, 30; disrupting habit, 48–49, 244n10; ethical memory, 18–19, 138, 154–55; "fabled by the daughters of memory," 74; involuntary, 15, 18, 30, 31, 33–34, 50, 99–100; Joyce contrasted with Proust, 18, 70, 132; and loss, 3, 6, 33–34; mnemonic systems, 19–20, 29–30; negative topography, 47, photographic, xvii, 27–34, 42; related to buildings and architecture of city, 29–30; repressed in hysteria, 10. *See also* time
Mencken, H. L., xviii, 5, 166; *The American Language*, 169; *American Mercury*, 170; *American Spectator*, 170; biography by Ernest Boyd, 170; and Boyd, 169–70, 275n44; first US publisher of Joyce, 170; on Irish idioms, 169; on Irish Revival, 169; on MacDonagh, 168–69
Merriman, Brian, 222
Milligan, Alice, 106–7
Mise Éire, 109–10
Mitchel, John: and classical republicanism, 95
Mitchell, Angus, 272n77
modernism: collages, 62, 86, 89, 110; and contingency, 18, 49, 55; cubism, 115, 255n84; currents in Irish revolution, xiv–xv, 4–5, 10; futurism, 115, 168; and Great War, 113–16; peripheral modernism, 4, 55, 65, 176; revolutionary writing, 83; and simultaneity, 17, 54–55, 82, 85; and space, 165–68; surrealism, 37, 113; vernacular modernism, 54, 128, 165, 166–67, 175, 212, 233n35, 276n54; *vers libre*, 168; vorticism, 166. *See also* avant-garde; form, aesthetic; Imagist movement; montage; shock

Monroe, Harriet, 165, 168, 179, 183, 185
montage, xvii, 14, 116; and aesthetic form, 14, 63; cinematic techniques in, 102, 207–8; comic, 102, 113; disruptive, 62–63, 120–21, 207–8, 209; extreme situations, 121, 197–98; in history, 14, 16, 20, 109–10; of objects, 62, 92–93; street culture, 14, 62, 86, 92–93; time, 63–64, 100, 109, 207, 261n65; transformative power, 223
monuments: lacking in Irish culture, 48; Nietzsche, 47; proposed statue of Joyce, xvi–xvii; Wolfe Tone's statue, 26, 45–47 (*see also* Tone, Theobald Wolfe)
Mooney, Seán, 132
Moore, George, 36, 55, 166
Moore, Marianne, xviii, 5; claiming Celtic ancestry, 164; on Henry James, 164; and Shane Leslie, 163; "Sojourn in the Whale" influenced by Easter Rising, 163–64
Moore, Thomas, 138, 268n16
Moran, Patrick, 199–200, 282n65
More, Paul Elmer, 170
Morel, E. D.: *Red Rubber*, 147
Moretti, Franco: epic in the margins, 65, 249n93; epic as transnational, 65; on modern epic, 53, 65, 245n33; *Ulysses* not Irish, 65; universalism, 54
Morris, Catherine, 106
Morris, David, 231n11
Morrison, George, 33, 109–10
Morson, Gary: sideshadowing narratives, 85
Moten, Fred, 84
Moyn, Samuel: human rights linked to national rights, 153, 156
Mulcahy, Richard, 25, 238n18, 243n86; parody in *Finnegans Wake*, 243n96
Mullen, Patrick, 149
Munro, Harold, 40
Münsterberg, Hugo, 231n11
Murphy, Joseph, 119
Murphy, Maurice, 194
Murry, John Middleton, 130
Mussolini, Benito, 130
myth: "broken lights" (Joyce), 17; and Easter Rising, 111–12; and epic, 17; and fascism (Cassirer), 33; O'Grady, 56–60

Ná Bac Leis, 81
Nabokov, Vladimir, 265n68
Nachträglichkeit (belatedness), 71, 237n94
Napoleon Bonaparte, 22, 130, 164, 182, 222
narrative: alternative futures, 85; autobiography, 75; break with Victorian, 14, 15, 109; counter-narrative, 79, 85; discontinuity, 78–82; dislocation, 85–88; disruptive, 81–82; dissolution, 109; encrypted, 82–83; events, 77–78, 83–84; foreshadowing, 78–79; free indirect discourse, 21–22; of history vs. fiction (Aristotle), 34, 245n31; interior monologue, 119–20, 210–11, 215; limits of, 113–17, 121–23, 233n31; as lived experience, 14–15, 76, 94; modernist, 14; multiple, 14–15, 78–81; naming vs. asserting, 78; narrative excess, 79–81, 88; nineteenth century, 14; not omniscient, 15, 79–81; proleptic, 82, 85, 224; sideshadowing, 78–79, 85; vs. spectacle, 31–32, 48–49, 117, 151; third-party narration and misunderstanding, 221; time of narrative, 121; Woolfian vs. Augustinian interior monologue, 211–12. *See also* free indirect discourse; montage; stream of consciousness
Nash, John: on Alake parody in *Ulysses*, 146; circulation of *Ulysses* in Dublin, 34; spectacle in Joyce's writing, 41
Nathan, Sir Matthew, 252n42, 253n53
Nation, The, 48
Nation, The (London), 68
National Association for the Advancement of Colored People (NAACP), 174
New Delhi, 20
Newman, Cardinal John Henry, 18
Newman College, New Jersey, 160, 162
New Mexico, 185, 276n54

New Republic, 275n31
newspapers, 29–30, 147–48, 150, 167, 218; inaccuracy of, 40
New York City, 93, 94; and response to Easter Rising, 165
New York Times, 69, 130
New York World's Fair (1939), 191
Ní Chuilleanáin, Eiléan, 132
Nicolls, Eveleen, 216–17, 283n27
Ní Criomhthain, Cáit, 283n27
Nietzsche, Friedrich, 61, 65, 127, 128, 149; on monumental time, 47
Nolan, Emer: on Alake parody in *Ulysses*, 146; anti-imperialism in *Ulysses*, 148; on the citizen and Joyce, 269n33; on Easter Rising, 16, 90, 102
Nolan, Jenny Wyse, 251n26
Nolan, John Wyse, 251n26
Nordau, Max, 51
novel: bildungsroman in Ireland, 55; vs. epic, 53; Irishness in, 55; *Künstlerroman* in Ireland, 55–56; national tale in Ireland, 55; as plan for Easter Rising, 67; relative failure of novel form in colonial Ireland, 52–54, 55–56
Noyes, Alfred, 274n14

Oates, Joyce Carol: on *Ulysses*, xvii
O'Brien, Henry, 138–40; on Irish ancestry of Cyclops, 139; *Phœnician Ireland*, 137, 140f
O'Brien, Vincent, 262n6
O'Brien, William, 283n20
O'Carolan, Turlough, 251n25
O'Casey, Seán, 207; *The Plough and the Stars*, 221
O'Conaire, Padraic, 209
O'Connell, Daniel, 93, 136
O'Connor, Flannery, 278n83
O'Connor, Frank, 185, 279n12
O'Connor, Laura: on Marianne Moore, 164, 274n15; reconfiguring narratives of Easter Rising, 93
O'Connor, Rory, 283n22
O'Connor, Ulick, 42
O'Conor, Rev. Charles, 268n16
Ó Criomhthain, Domhnall, 283n27
Ó Criomhthain, Tomás, 283n27

O'Doherty, Brian: on Marianne Moore, 164
O'Donnell, Patrick, 162
O'Donnell, Peadar, 36, 185
O'Donnell, Thomas, M.P., 144
O'Donovan, Jim, 38
O'Donovan Rossa, Jeremiah, 51, 99, 106
O'Duffy, Eimar, 21, 39; on degeneration, 51; echoes of *A Tale of Two Cities*, 101, 259n42; hysterical nature of rebels, 51; on *Ulysses*, 21, 39, 224; *The Wasted Island*, 51, 96, 260n47
Ó Faoláin, Seán, 36, 185, 279n12
O'Farrell, Patrick, 84
O'Flaherty, Liam, 185
O'Flaherty, Roderick: *Ogygia*, 136, 277n5
Ogham, 11
O'Grady, Standish James, xiv, xvii, 4, 63, 72, 143, 249n86; anachronistic treatment of ancient Dublin, 58; Anglo-Irish empire, 56; aristocratic values, 56–57; on classical epic, 56; epic claims to history, 57–58; *History of Ireland: Critical and Philosophical*, 56–58; *History of Ireland: Cuculain and His Contemporaries*, 57, 58–59; *History of Ireland: The Heroic Period*, 57; imagination in history, 57; inchoate state of Irish past, 57, 247n50; and narrative order, 56–57; prophesizing Revival and insurrection, 64; putative influence on Pearse, 64; removal of shock, 57; on "revival," 57, 246n48, 246n49, 247n50, 247n52; and romantic epic, xiv, 56–60; supporting conscription during Great War, 130
Ogygia, 136, 267n5
O'Hegarty, P. S., 34, 38; on the avant-garde, 39; defending Joyce's sexual frankness, 39; early review of *Ulysses*, 39; editor of *The Separatist*, 39; on Joyce's Irishness, 40; on Joyce's love of Dublin, 39–40
O'Keeffe, Georgia, 179, 185
O'Kelly, James J., 268n12
O'Leary, John, 107; John O'Leary Literary Society, 25

O'Leary, Philip, 64
Olivier, Sidney, 277n73
O'Malley, Ernie, xviii, 7; abstentionist TD, 184; acquaintance with Joyce, 182, 278n5; affinities between Irish and Native American culture, 179; affinities with Joyce, 198–200; and Alice Corbin Henderson, 179–83; avant-garde in aesthetics and politics, 196–98; capture during Civil War, 197–98; Civil War, 179, 183, 184, 186, 190, 192–93, 194, 195, 197–200; conscience and remorse, 191; cryptic communication akin to *Finnegans Wake*, 81–82; and Desmond Ryan, 203, 282n2; Easter Rising, 86, 183–84; escape from Kilmainham, 184, 199–200; on executions, 191–93; in *Finnegans Wake*, 200–201, 254n67; and Hart Crane, 185; haunted by dead comrades, 182, 278n10; on hunger strike, 184; impersonations of Westerns, 91; imprisonment, 184, 196, 198–200; improvised form of Easter Rising, 86; Irish Academy of Letters, 184; lecturing on Irish Revival, 180, 185; lecturing on Joyce, 182, 185; lecturing on *Ulysses*, 182–85; links between Mananaan MacLir and O'Malley territory, 191; and local knowledge, 199–200, 282n64; on MacDonagh, 179; neurasthenia, 193, 280n42; *On Another Man's Wound*, xviii, 184, 195, 199–200; parody of *Táin Bó Cúailnge*, 198; and Patrick Moran, 199–200; published in *Poetry*, 179, 182; reading of Joyce, 181–93; on revolutionary "extremism," 280n40; *Rising Out*, 82–83; role in Irish revolution, 183–84; Santa Fe, 179–82; *The Singing Flame*, xviii, 184, 186, 197–98; stay in the United States, Mexico, Peru, 184; talk at Harvard, 279n22; Taos, 179–82; travels to Europe after Civil War, 184; UCD Dramatic Society, 186; War of Independence, 195, 199–200; and

W. B. Yeats, 184, 279n12; wounded in capture, 184, 197–98
O'Malley, Ernie, on Cyclops chapter: English "syphilisation," 189; GPO, 188; history as nightmare, 189; John F. Taylor's speech, 188; Joyce's demotic style, 197–98; Kevin Egan in Paris, 189–90; Mananaan MacLir, 190–91; newspapers influence on public opinion, 190; noting Irish topics, 188, 197; Rumbold and gallows, 189; Skin-the-Goat, 188
O'Malley, Ernie, *Notes on Joyce*: "akasic" memory, 190; akin to Benjamin's *Arcades Project*, 187; never written up for publication, 187; *Ulysses*, "agenbite of inwit," 189, 191–92
O'Malley, Helen Hooker, 36, 184, 191, 278n10, 279n22, 281n48
Ó Neachtain, Seán, 268n16
O'Neill, Ciaran, 246n42
O'Neill, Eugene, 278n83
O'Neill, Moira, 166, 181
O'Neill, Owen Roe, 131
O'Neill, Sir Felim, 131
Only Way, The (Wills), 98f; dramatization based on *A Tale of Two Cities*, 97, 108; film versions, 100–101, 259n41; Maurice Costello in, 100; popular success at Theatre Royal, 97; Rex Ingram on, 100–101; Shakespearean echoes, 259n34
O'Rahilly, Eoghan, 222
O'Rahilly, Michael Joseph, 251n25, 282n87
O'Reilly, Tom, 106
O'Riada, Seán, 109
Ossian, 139
"Ossorian," 144
O'Sullivan, Seamus, 166
Otis, Mr. and Mrs. Raymond, 182
O'Toole, L. J., 80
Owen, Wilfred, 166

"Painful Case, A" (*Dubliners*), 4, 213
paralysis: and aesthetic form, 8–9; failure to interiorize in Ireland, 52; as

Irish social condition, xvii, 10, 52–53; jolted by shock, 48–49, 53; and Joyce, 10–13; and Sigerson, 10–12, 52

Paris: Bastille, 108; and Easter Rising, 87–89; Eiffel Tower, 107; Exposition Universelle, 107; Paris Commune, xvii; "piercing the houses," 88; Sorbonne, 38; transforming public and private space, 88, 255n96; Versailles, 107

Parnell, Charles Stewart, xv, 11, 24–25, 47, 51, 78, 79, 96, 106, 144, 160, 188, 193, 258n26

past, the, xiii, 10, 12, 14, 24–25, 32, 35, 78, 83, 84, 120–24; anachronism, 125, 167, 176, 182, 183; cultural past, 124–25, 131, 134, 135, 136, 151; superimposition of past and present, 163–64, 184–87; "survivals," 183; unrequited pasts, xv, 12, 15, 16, 17, 20, 24–26, 65, 74–77, 132, 142, 145, 148–51, 186–87, 222–23. *See also* memory

Paul, Elliot, 186

Pearse, James, 258n21, 284n33

Pearse, Margaret, 284n33

Pearse, Mary Brigid, 96, 258n28

Pearse, P. H. (Patrick): attacks on Catholic hierarchy, 217; camera shy, 106–7; classical republicanism, 258n21; comforting a British soldier in GPO, 217; contradictions of, 213–15; Desmond Ryan on, 67, 215–17; dislike of Tolstoy, 217; doubts about Easter Rising, 216–17; feminism, 215; future vindication of Rising, 2, 231n7; as hysteric, 50; and Labour movement, 217; lack of self-absorption, 217; loss at Eibhlín Nic Niocaill's death, 216, 283n27, 284n32; Mary Colum on, 217; mastery of Gaelic epic literature, 64; modern element in epic past, 61, 64; opposition to corporal punishment, 217; on plans for Easter Rising as a novel, 67; putative influence of Standish O'Grady on, 64; reading the Proclamation, 42; on republican "virtus," 96; single-mindedness, 215–16; theater as Brechtian, 63; "Two Pearses," 216; on Wolfe Tone's burial place, 45. *See also* St. Enda's

Pearse, William, 96

Pessoa, Ferdinand: on *Ulysses*, 8

Phoenicians, 11, 19; Cadmus and invention of letters, 73, 138; Catholic apologists and Irish origins, 137–41, 268n14, 268n16; in *Finnegans Wake*, 11, 138; and General Vallancey, 135–36, 138, 268n14; Joyce and, 135, 266n2, 267nn6–7; origins of Celtic languages, 135–36, 137–38, 268n14; Tyre, 138; *Ulysses* as Phoenician seafarer, 17, 136

Phoenix Park: in "Aeolus," 94; assassinations, 24–25, 105, 155, 188, 280n27; in *Finnegans Wake*, 138, 140; and Phoenicians, 138, 140

photography: antithesis of memory (Bergson), 33; contingency, 33–34; glimpse of the future, 33; in Great War, 105; incidental details, 33; and Leopold Bloom's musings, 29, 31; and memory, 29; and Michael Collins, 106; and movement, 32, 41–42; national propaganda, 106; and Pearse, 106; "play of the possible" 33; prohibited at Boland funeral, 106; "Soldier's Kodak," 105; at St. Enda's, 106; still image, 41–42; and time, 103–5

Picasso, Pablo, 3, 62, 113

Pilniak, Boris, 230n15

Plautus: *Poenula*, 135

Plunkett, Count, 105; speech, 105*f*

Plunkett, Joseph Mary, 51, 69, 113, 159, 161, 167, 173, 276n59

Plutarch, 267n5

Poetry magazine, 120, 130, 165, 179

Poincaré, Henri, 69

Pokorny, Professor (*Ulysses*), 71

Polybius, 258n21

Pope, Alexander, 31

Portrait of the Artist as a Young Man, A (Joyce), 35, 68, 69; bat-like secrecy, 10; bird-girl episode, 31–32;

Portrait of the Artist as a Young Man, A (Joyce) (*continued*)
commemoration of 1798 rebellion, 45, 48; diary entries, 80; and Easter Rising, 75; forging conscience of the race, xvi, 3; movement in, 31; nets thrown around artist, 55; and *Pathosformel*, 32; photographic nature of, 28; published in 1916, xvii, 15; reviewed, xviii, 15; on Tone and Parnell, xv; walking the streets, 18, 28, 80; Wolfe Tone's burial place, 46

Pound, Ezra, xiv; and Alice Corbin Henderson, 165; on Desmond FitzGerald, 40–41; Imagist movement, 40; and Joyce, 15, 74–75, 243n91; on Joyce as akin to MacSwiney and Pearse in martyrdom, 119; on Joyce and MacDonagh, 15, 76, 165; on *Literature in Ireland* (MacDonagh), 165; and Marianne Moore, 164; on *Portrait* and Irish troubles, 15, 75, 252n33; on Roger Casement, 165; surveillance of Joyce, 82, 254n65; and Van Wyck Brooks, 172

Power, Arthur, 76, 221
Prescott, Joseph, 239n42
primitivism, 53, 139, 146; and Arendt, 154; and Claude McKay, 176, 277n70
prisons: Aylesbury, 117; Brixton, 117, 119; Clerkenwell, 73, 204; Cork Men's Gaol, 119; Curragh camp, 130, 132, 184, 198, 243n89; Frongoch, 26, 27, 205, 239nn25–26; Kilmainham, 37, 184, 189, 196, 199, 200, 242n75; Knutsford, 26; Mountjoy, 38, 120–24, 130, 132, 260n47, 264n51; Pentonville, 147; Reading, 241n64; Richmond Barracks, 26; Stafford, 106, 205; Sing-Sing, 110; Waltham, 38; Wormwood Scrubs, 205n26

private sphere: not a haven from public world, 52; implications of absence in Ireland for the novel, 52–53; lack of in Ireland, 11; transformations of public and private space, 88

"Proclaiming a Republic: The 1916 Rising" exhibition, 92

Prometheus, 20
Protestantism: antiquarians, 139; Orange lodges, 151; and Unionism, 47, 141, 153
Proteus, 20
Proust, Marcel, 18, 70, 132; *Le Côté de Guermantes*, 117; on MacSwiney's hunger strike, 117
Ptolemy, 140f, 148, 149, 268n18
public sphere, 47; contested, 76, 186–87, 216; counter-public sphere, 218; patriarchal, 67, 73, 93; and private sphere, 37, 50, 65, 67, 73, 107, 111, 168, 183, 186, 219
Pugh, Thomas W., xvi, xvii, 25f, 30, 34, 42; autograph book, 26; combatant in Jacob's factory, 24, 26–27; correspondence with Joyce, 238nn5–6, 236n8; in *Finnegans Wake*, 24–25; glass-making family, 24–25, 238n14; imprisonment, 26; and Joyce, xvii, 21–25; knowledge of Joyceana, 27; loyalty to Michael Collins, 26–27; marriage to Margaret Dilworth, 26; partial blindness, 24; and Peadar Kearney, 25–28; photographic memory, xvii, 27–28; Richard Mulcahy and IRB, 25, 238n18; as socialist, 25–26; sources for biographies, 25; trade unionist, 27, 239n27
Pushkin, Alexander, 265n68
Putumayo: and Roger Casement, 150, 152, 154, 272n77; and Rosa Luxemburg, 150
Pyrrhus, 74

Queneau, Raymond, 3, 262n6; *We Always Treat Women Too Well*, 112–13, 262n7, 262n9
Quinn, Bob, 267n3
Quinn, John, 4, 165
Quintilian, 29–30

racism: in Ireland, 142–44; Irish-American, 174, 175–76; imperial grounding of, 143, 154–57, 177
Radek, Karl: critique of *Ulysses*, 67, 68
Raleigh, Sir Walter, 132

Random House, edition of *Ulysses: How to Enjoy "Ulysses"* brochure, 22–23*f*; mistakes in, 22–23
Reddin, Kenneth, 30; on Joyce's photographic memory, 28
Redmond, John, 74, 148; as Charlie Chaplin, 92; and empire, 267n12; support of Great War, 70
Reeve, C. D. C., 219–21, 284n43
Remembering Sion (Ryan), xviii, 19, 203, 206, 283n9; vs. anti-Semitism, 213; and Arthur Griffith, 212–13; attacks critics of Joyce, 218–20; censorship and vigilance committees, 213; Christian Brothers' education, 208, 213; compared to Desmond Fitz-Gerald's memoir, 207; critique of Daniel Corkery, 210–11; disillusionment, 218–24; echoes of Stephen Dedalus, 211–12; exile and external perspective, 210–11; experimental style, 206–7; free indirect discourse, 212–13; Great Famine, 210; idioms and accents, 212; interior dialogue and external voices, 211–12; intimacy and knowledge, 220–21; and James Connolly, 213; Joyce and Gaelic tradition, 222; Joyce's love of Dublin, 203, 222–23; love without illusions, 200–201; on O'Casey, 221; opposition to Catholic control, 208, 212–14; on Pearse, 203–4, 205, 215–18, 223; romantic idealism, 209–10; "Still Remembering Sion," 208; on Synge, 221; on *Ulysses*, 1, 203, 222–23
Renaissance: Celtic, 166, 170, 171, 173, 175; Harlem, 173, 174–75; Italy, 7–9, 14, 168, 173
representation: aesthetic and political, xvii, 70, 129, 167, 194–97, 199; collapse of realism, xvii, 113–17; crises in artistic, 14, 86, 113–17, 194–98; and Irish revolution, 3–4, 114, 116, 194–98; modernist forms, 86, 113–17; and prison experience, 117, 123
republicanism: Dickens's affinities, 108; French influence on Ireland, 95–99, 106; Irish conversant with classical republicanism, 94–95; Irish republicans' interest in Joyce, xiv, xv, 4–5, 34–35, 37–38 (*see also entries on specific individuals*); in popular culture, 95–99, 107–9; self-sacrifice and public good, 94–95; "Virtus," 95, 107; in *The Wasted Island* (O'Duffy), 96
Richardson, Samuel, 55
Rickard, John, 8; on past and memory, 244n10; on proleptic memory in Joyce, 82
Ricks, Christopher, 46
Rinucinni, Cardinal, 131
Roberts, George, 74, 129
Robinson, Henry Morton, 279n18
Robinson, Lennox, 34; *The Lost Leader*, 96, 258n26
Rockett, Kevin, 101
Rolleston, T. W., 249n86
romanticism: epic, 56–59; idealization, 111–12, 209–10; Joyce smashes, 220; nostalgia, xiv; romantic Ireland, xiv, xvii, 4, 15, 102, 111–12, 114, 209–10, 223, 281n48
Rome, classical, 95, 107, 138, 173
Roosevelt, Theodore: hyphenated Americans, 159, 273n3
Roper, Hugh Trevor, 75
Roscommon, County, 83; Castlerea, 97; Lough Meelagh, 200
Ross, Kristen, 88
Roth, Samuel, 23, 275n33
Royal Irish Constabulary (RIC), 110
rugby, 42–43
Russell, Charles: *Should the Workers of Ireland Support Sinn Féin?*, 265n62
Russell, George (Æ), 84, 204
Russian Revolution, xv; Bolshevik delegation to Dublin, 86; Congress of Soviet Writers, 68; linked to Irish revolution, 4, 128
Ryan, Desmond, xviii, 5, 7, 259n42; anti-Partition League, 215, 283n12; biographer, 223; bomb-making for Easter Rising, 203; combatant in GPO, 203, 214–15; *Daily Herald*, 205–6; *Daily Worker*, 205; Dickens and Pearse

Ryan, Desmond (*continued*) household, 96; Easter Rising as a novel, 67; education, 205; executor of Pearse's will, 203; and Fenian movement, 222; *Freeman's Journal*, 205; imprisonment, 205; indebtedness to Joyce, xix, 204, 206; and Irish Volunteers, 205; James Stephens (IRB), 221; John Devoy, 221, 223; loyalty to Michael Collins, 204, 205, 215; *The Man Called Pearse*, 204; Marx and Engels, 222; meeting Joyce, 206; misgivings about treaty, 205–6, 214–15; and O'Malley, 203, 214, 282n2; pacifism, 203; and Pearse, 204, 215–17, 223; publications on Connolly, 204, 282n7; publications on Pearse, 203–4, 282nn5–6; *Saint Eustace and the Albatross*, 206; and socialism, 204, 205, 212–13; St. Enda's, 203, 205, 208; *The Torch*, 206; on *Ulysses* and Irish revolution, 1, 203, 222–23; "*Ulysses*" essay, 284n36; *Unique Dictator: A Study of De Valera*, 280n30; "When a Spectre Haunted Cork," 222. See also *Invisible Army, The*; *Remembering Sion*

Ryan, Frederick: Arthur Griffith on, 144; editing *Egyptian Standard*, 144; "Empire and Liberty," 144; outlook like Joyce's, 144

Ryan, W. P.: *The Irish Literary Revival*, 205; editor of *Irish Peasant*, 205

Sage, Robert, 282n2
Saint-Amour, Paul, 2; *Ulysses* and Easter Rising, 9
Saint Leger (horse race), 18
Salkeld, Cecil Ffrench, 123, 264n51
Sandow, Eugen, 29
Santa Fe New Mexican, 180–83
Sarsfield, Patrick, 131
Sassoon, Siegfried, 166, 185
Schliemann, Heinrich, 136
Scopas, 29
Scotland, 99
Scott, Walter, 55

Second World War, 15, 153, 206, 264n54
Senn, Fritz; "de-ported" in Joyce, 84; *Ulysses* read in prison, 38, 242n75
Separatist, The, 39–40
Serge, Victor, xvi, 185; admirer of *Ulysses*, xv; left-wing melancholy, xv; on modernist novel, xv–xvi; revolutionary potential, xv; on Russian Revolution, xv; Susan Sontag on, xv
Seven Arts, 167
Shakespeare, William, 71; and Easter Rising, 259n34; *Hamlet*, 19, 97–98, 193; *King Lear*, 131, *Merchant of Venice*, 213; *Timon of Athens*, 131
Shakespeare Press, 35
Shannon (river), 200
Shaw, Fr. Francis, 64, 249n87
Shaw, George Bernard, 36, 166, 277n73
Sheehy, John Joe, 37
shell shock, xviii, 8; and Easter Rising, 2, 262n14; and flashbacks, 2–3; Great War, 2–3, 250n17, 262n14; historical precedents, 3; Irish revolution, 193, 234n43, 250n17; relation to cinema, 2–3
Shields, Arthur, 26
shock, 52; disrupting habit, 48, 244n10; and Easter Rising, xvii, 2, 51–52, 77, 89, 93, 214; and Gaelic past, 57, 61, 208; Great War, xvii; Irish revolution, 124, 192–93, 195, 214, 234n43; and modernity, 48–49, 88–89, 113, 115, 262n22; as political awakening, 48–49; shock value of Joyce's writing, 8, 9, 35, 84, 116, 263n25
Sidney, Algernon, 98, 259n36
Sigerson, Dora, 181
Sigerson, George: *Bards of the Gael and Gall*, 60–61, 249n93; on Celtic modernity, 60–61, 247n63, 248n66; Cúchulainn and hysterical paroxysms, 52; in *Finnegans Wake*, 11, 60; Joyce's familiarity with, 10, 247n63; on land question, 10, 235n58; medical career, 10–11, 235n58; on modern epic, 60–61; "national epic has yet to be written" (in *Ulysses*), 60; on pa-

ralysis, 10–11, 52; translator of Charcot, 10, 235nn56–57
Sigerson, Selma: *Sinn Féin and Socialism*, 128. *See also* Coyle, Kathleen
Simmel, Georg, 257n8
Simonides, and art of memory, 29–30
simultaneity, 167–69, 172, 178; synchronicity, 165, 180
Sing-Sing prison, 110
Sinn Féin, 6, 35, 38, 46, 69; Bloom and origins of the term, 74, 251n27; communism and socialism, 127–28, 214, 255n62, 277n66; Easter Rising, 94, 175; Griffith and economic policy, 143; Joyce's sympathies with, xvi, 76; publicity department, 120; rise of, 74, 252n40; spread of following Rising, 68, 74, 76, 161, 205; takes over from Home Rule, 112, 148, 275n31
Sirr, Major, 48
Sisson, Elaine, 107, 116
"The Sisters" (*Dubliners*): blurring of life and death, 31; ellipses in, 81; paralysis, 31; walking the streets, 31
Skeffington, Francis Sheehy: and "Castle Document," 69, 144; on Fred Ryan, 270n38; "McCann" in *Portrait*, 69; murdered in Easter Rising, 69
"Skin-the-Goat." *See* Fitzharris, James
Sliwinski, Sharon, 150, 155
Slocum, John J., 186
Smart Set, The, 179
Smith, Graham E., 29
Smithson, Annie M. P.: *The Walk of a Queen*, 101, 259nn42–43
Smyly, Cecil: "Some Aspects of Psychoanalysis," 71, 250n17
Socialist Party of Ireland, 15, 128, 236n79
Socrates, 95
Solnit, Rebecca, 136
Sontag, Susan, xv
space: in chronotope, xvi; dissolution, xvii; in *Laocoön*, 17; mapping Dublin, 17–18, 94; private and public, 10–12, 52, 53, 83, 87–88, 212, 217, 255n96; sense of location, 18, 24, 46–48, 94, 88–89, 99–100, 126, 199–200, 254n74

spatial form: alternative futures, 85; counter-narratives in, 79, 85; and dislocation, 85–86; lateral movement, 85; and narrative excess, 79; sideshadowing, 85; stepping outside narrative time, 79, 85; unity of, 79, 86. *See also* Frank, Joseph
Spring-Rice, Cecil, 4
Stalin, Joseph; betrayal of socialism, xvi
Stanford, W. B., 95, 267n5
Stead, Henry, 96, 258n22
Steiner, Wendy, 30
St. Enda's School, 36, 64, 95, 96, 107, 161, 164, 203, 205, 208, 252n40, 260n59
Stephen Hero (Joyce), 2, 61
Stephens, James (Fenian leader), 89, 206, 221, 283n11
Stephens, James (writer), 166, 181
Stevens, Wallace, 165
St. Lucia, 20
Stoddard, Lothrop, 178, 277n79
Stoppard, Tom: *Travesties*, 1, 230n4
Storer, Edward, 265n71
Strabo, 139
Strachey, Lytton, 223
Stramm, August, 114–15
Strand, Paul, 179, 185, 193, 280n35
stream of consciousness: bearing witness to time of writing, 121; Bloch on montage elements in, 121; in Campbell's prison diary, 131; connected to external world, 121; Eco on, 9; Frank Gallagher's akin to Molly Bloom's, 122; not a smooth flow, 7–8; precursor in *Julius Caesar*, 9; and real life, 7–8, 262n21; and time, 121–22; Woolfian vs. Augustinian, 211–12
stream-of-consciousness narration, 120–24; in real life, 124; Terence MacSwiney, 93, 117–19
Street, C. J. C., 178
Strongbow, 131
Stuart, Francis, 116, 132; *Black List, Section H*, 132–33; on prison writing, 131–32; tunneling in Curragh Camp, 131
Stubbs, Tara, 170, 174

Suffragette movement, 16
surveillance: deficits in relation to Easter Rising, 78–80, 83–84; insurgent attempts to outwit, 81–83; and local knowledge, 83; and narrative, 78–84
Sweeney, James Johnson, 279n19
Swift, Jonathan, 141
Swinnerton, Frank, 197
Sydney Carton: A Tale of Two Cities (Harkins), 108
Sykes, Gerald, 185, 279n16
symptoms: vs. signs, 8, 12, 49, 51, 52, 235n53; symptomatic expressions, xvii, 8–10, 16, 75–76, 83, 231n12
Synge, J. M., 15, 97, 166, 181, 194, 221; compared to Shakespeare, 274n28

Tacitus, 148
Tailteann Games: invitation to Joyce, 41; Oliver St. John Gogarty and gold medal, 41
Táin Bó Cúailnge, 59, 198
Taine, Hippolyte, 108
Tale of Two Cities, A (Dickens), xviii, 260n62; Charles Darnay, 258n26; glimpses of future in, 108; influence in Ireland, 96–101; Lucie Manette, 99; Sidney Carton, xviii, 96–98, 100–101, 108–9, 258n26, 259n34, 259nn42–43
Taylor, Anthony, 151
Taylor, Mars Richard, 160
technologies: electric light, 93, 106; electric power, 8, 62, 91–93, 126–27, 136; magic lantern, 106–7; media, xviii (*see also* cinema; photography); mutoscope, 42; phonograph (gramophone), 29; radio, 42, 93–94; telegraph, 94, 117; transport, 93
Tennyson, Alfred: "In Memoriam," 50; "Ulysses," 61
Ternan, Ellen Lawless, 99; meets Dickens, 99; resemblance to Lucie Manette, 99, 259n38
Ternan, Thomas Lawless, 99
Téry, Simone, xvi
Thackeray, William M., 55, 131
This Side of Paradise (Fitzgerald), 160–62; and Bolshevism, 162; Cuchulin in, 161; Irish president's visit to the US, 162; and Irish question, 162; and Joyce's *Portrait*, 173, 276n56
Thomas, Edward, 166
Thom's Dublin Directory, 29
Tiberius Gracchus, 95
Tiberius Sempronius, 258n21
Tieze, Franz: master forger, 24
time, 165; anachronisms in O'Grady's *Cuculain*, 58–59; alternative futures, xv, 3, 6, 85, 93, 103, 125, 253n44; Broch on, 54–55, 82, 85; chronotopes, xvi, 17, 230n16, 236n86; in cinema, 33; clock time, 33; in cosmic space, 33; "double-timing" in *Ulysses*, 68–70; Dunsink time, 69; Einstein on, 32, 69, 125; flow, xvii, 13–14, 30–31, 33, 54, 79, 105, 117, 212, 253n51; fluidity of past, present, future, 2–5, 6, 7–8, 18–19, 55, 62, 70, 71–72, 75, 77, 82, 85, 102, 105–6, 107, 110, 114, 116, 122, 125, 126, 194, 229n11, 233n28, 237n94; GPO, 103; Greenwich mean time, 69; in *Laocoön*, 17; "long now," 33; and narrative, 69, 79–81; overlapping temporalities, 18, 32, 71–72, 186; in photography, 32–33, 103–4; police surveillance, 79–81; redirection of, 103–5; simultaneity, 17; and *Ulysses*, 63, 70–72, 251n22; unresolved pasts, 3, 18, 105, 170, 201, 264n47; usable pasts, 170–71. *See also* Bergson, Henri
Times, The (London), 11, 146, 153
Tipperary, County: Mullinahone, 37
Tokyo, 20
Tolstoy, Leo, 130; *Anna Karenina*, 131; *The Decembrists*, 1; *Resurrection*, 131; *War and Peace*, 1, 131
Tompkins, Captain, 252n23
Tone, Theobald Wolfe, 98, 122; burial place, 46, 244n4, 244n5; foundations of statue, 45–46, 50; site of absent statue, 26, 45
Touhy, Patrick, 28
trade unions: General Strike, 87, 117, 121; War of Independence, 17
tradition: continuous, xiv, 60, 63–64,

172–73, 174, 179; Irish, as broken, xv, 17, 173, 199, 246n49
transition (journal), 42, 186, 279n19
trauma, 2–3, 8, 28, 32, 52, 71–72, 231n11, 232n15, 233n31; Easter Rising and Irish revolution, 2, 132–33, 192–93, 234n43; and Great War, xvii, 2–3, 8, 50, 109, 113–14
Treaty, Anglo-Irish, 26, 39, 130, 184, 190, 195–96, 205–6, 213; Churchill on, 256n107; and Easter Rising, 195, 281n51; "empire" replaced by "commonwealth," 233n23; Joyce on, 119, 243n96; Marcus Garvey on, 277n78; role of press and church on public opinion, 190, 280n30; as stepping-stone, 2, 231n8; as subjection, 196
Trevor-Roper, Hugh, 75
Trieste, 16, 135, 143, 146, 258n28, 267n4
Trinity College, Dublin, 35, 41, 61, 171
Trotsky, Leon: refusal to repudiate Russian Revolution, xvi
Troy, 17, 135, 136, 138, 267n8; Priam's palace and Irish hovels, 136–37
Turgenev, Ivan, 157, 210
Turim, Maureen, 231n12
Twomey, Maurice, 37
Tymoczko, Maria, 59, 269n34

Ulster, 172
Ulysses (Joyce): affinities with Easter Rising, 6, 9, 73–74, 89; "Agenbite of inwit" (conscience as physical), 19, 189, 192; anachronisms in, 70–74; Belgian Congo, 145–46; brochure for readers, 22–23; censorship, 82; challenging omniscient narration, 17, 79–82; cinematic, 33, 119, 207, 240n49; combining classical, Christian, and Irish pasts, 14; cosmic space, 33; counter-narratives, 79; drowning in, 19, 191, 193; Dublin burning in, 73; encyclopedic, 60; enigmas in, 82; and ethical memory ("moral history"), 19–20, 138, 154; formal breakthroughs, 6; Free State responses, 34, 39–40; future orientation, 1–2, 6, 8–9, 14, 16–17, 57, 70–74, 224; importance of Dublin topography, 24; Irish campaign against, 34–35; Jacob's biscuit tin, 24; "a kind of retrospective arrangement," 48; limits of narrative coherence, 54–55, 82; as literary Bolshevism, 163, 274n14; local knowledge, 17–18, 48–49, 79, 88–89, 199–200; maternal love, 19, 125, 127, 183, 191, 217–18, 219–20; modern epic, 17, 53, 59, 60–62, 65; moving pictures in, xvii, 7, 9–10, 31, 78, 107–8, 113, 240n49, 259n42; *Nacheinander* and *Nebeneinander*, 32; narrative and contingency, 78–79; narrative excess, 79, 87; nightmare of history, 16, 51–52, 189; paternal love, 183, 219; personal identity, questioning of, 75; Pessoa on, 8; phantasmagoria of "Circe," 9; Phoenician background, 17, 136–37; and photography, 28, 31; and political revolution, xvi, xvii; prophesying Great War, 155, 272n79; reassembling Dublin, 20; relation to *Odyssey*, 16–17, 136–37, 155; republican responses to, xiv, xv, 4–5, 34–35, 37–38 (*see also individual figures*); "Sewer School" critics, 218–20; "shout in the street," 68; "striking of the match," 68; as subversive code, 79–81, 82–83; and surveillance, 82–83; totalizing designs of, 241n74; uncertainty principle in, 243n101; unexpected appearances in, 82–84; unweaving the past, 75; as world literature, 17, 20, 36, 157, 222
Ulysses, fictional characters: Alexander Keyes, 190–91; Alf Bergan, 189, 270n49; Bantam Lyons, 18; Ben Dollard, 48; Blazes Boylan, 82; Buck Mulligan, 23, 82, 188; Bumbold, 118–19, 149, 189; the citizen, 24, 46, 74, 131, 141–48, 150, 152, 189, 244n85, 247n54, 269n23 (*see also* Cusack, Michael); Cyril Sargent, 18; Denis J. Maginni, 84; Father Conmee, 84; Garrett Deasy, 68; Gerty MacDowell, 97; J.J. O Molloy, 146–47;

Ulysses, fictional characters (*continued*) John Wyse Nolan, 74; Kevin Egan, 49, 189, 204, 211; Leopold Bloom (see *Ulysses*, Leopold Bloom); Mananaan MacLir, 190–91, 215; man in brown macintosh, 62; Milly Bloom, 97, 240n4; Molly Bloom (see *Ulysses*, Molly Bloom); Paddy Dignam, 48, 82, 189, 193, 270n49; Private Carr, 69, 74; Rudy Bloom, 219; Sandwichmen, 45–46, 50; Stephen Dedalus (see *Ulysses*, Stephen Dedalus); throwaway, 18, 237n91; Tom Kernan, 47–48; Viceregal cavalcade, 45–46

Ulysses, Leopold Bloom, xvi, 23, 28–33, 35, 39, 40, 42, 45; advertisements, 103; anti-Semitism, 142–43; bourgeois nationhood, xvi; cinematic mind, 240n49; cosmic time, 33; "enemy of stopped action," 30–31, 47, 67, 79, 82; free association of thought, 9, 216; and memory, 18, 24, 28, 33–34; Molly's infidelity, 219; and mutoscope, 42; on nationhood, 46, 142; nihilism, 54; pacifism, 190; paternal love, 19, 183, 219; and photography, 31; and prophecy, 18; reflecting on death, 29; and Sinn Féin, 74, 251n26; walking through walls, 84

Ulysses, Molly Bloom: admirer of John Martin-Harvey, 97; external intrusions on soliloquy, 121–22, 262n21; frankness of soliloquy, 35, 40, 216; maternal love, 183; photographic portrait, 31, 36, 40

Ulysses, Stephen Dedalus, 53; cosmic time, 33; and distended time and space, 1–2, 17, 41–42; on gesture as structural rhythm, 9–10; global vision, xvi; haunted by dead mother, 183, 193, 219; Mananaan MacLir, 190, 211, 215; meditations, 14, 190, 211; moving houses, 30; nightmare of history, 16, 52, 189; shadows, 217; walking the streets, 18; word and image, 32, 22, 23

unconscious, in history, 6, 15, 18; aesthetic form, 15; and Celtic Twilight, 15; "optical unconscious" (Benjamin), 18

United Irishmen: Maiden Harp emblem of, 99–100; Napper Tandy, 46; Oliver Bond, 47; Sheares brothers, 46, 47; William Jackson, 47. *See also* Emmet, Robert; Fitzgerald, Lord Edward; Tone, Theobald Wolfe

United States: Anglo-Saxon ties following Great War, 177; censorship and surveillance of Joyce, 83; Civil War, 3; critical responses to Easter Rising, xviii, 159–60, 273n2; Great War, 177, 274n11; hyphenated Americans, 159–60, 273n3; Native American culture, 179, 276n54; Revolution, xvii; Versailles Peace Conference, 177

Universal Negro Improvement Association (UNIA), 177

Untermeyer, Louis, 159; "To England (upon the Executions of the Three Irish Poets—Pearse, Macdonough and Plunkett—After the Uprising in Dublin)," 175, 276n59

Uranus, 268n19

USSR, Congress of Soviet Writers, 68

Vallancey, Charles: Phoenician origins of Celtic languages, 135–36, 138, 268n14

Van Winkle, Rip, 131

Vico, Giambattista, 39; on Irish ancestry of Cyclops, 139

Victoria, Queen, 106, 145, 151, 189, 270n48

"Viennese school," in *Ulysses*, 71

Villaneuva, Joachimo: *Phœnician Ireland*, 138, 140f, 268n19

Wagner, Richard, 168, 245n33

Walden, Herwarth, 115

Walden, Nell, 115

Wales, 26, 163, 205

walls: Bloom walking through, 84; prison walls, 132–33; tunneling through in Easter Rising, 18, 84–85, 88, 103; walking through in *Apes of God*, 87–88

Walsh, Billy, 132

Walsh, J.J., 80–81, 253n54
Walsh, Maurice, 36
Walsh, Róisín, 35–36, 241n64; circulating *Ulysses* in Civil War, 35–36; and Dublin Public Library system, 35, 241n67; Saor Éire convention, 36
Warburg, Aby, 14, 20, 32; aesthetic form akin to lightning, 7–8; art and antiquity, 7–9; Botticelli's *Birth of Venus*, 7; Cassirer on, 7; clash of Christianity and pagan antiquity, 7, 14; Dionysian elements in culture, 7; dynamism of aesthetic form, 7–8, 9; form as symptom, 8–9; "God is in the details," 8, 234n51; on *Laocoön*, 7; *Pathosformel*, 7–9, 14, 17, 32
Ward, P. J., 231n8
Washington Post, response to Easter Rising, 159
Watt, Stephen, 259n34
Weil, Simone: fasting as protest, 124, 264n54, 264n60; on *A Flock of Birds* (Coyle), 124
Wells, H. G.: against Easter Rising, 76; Joyce and insurgent writing, 76, 252n33; *Portrait* as anti-English, 75–76; "Sewer School" of Joyce critics, 218–19
Westmeath, County, 171–72, 173
Weston, Edward, 179, 185
Wexler, Joyce, 87–88
White, Hayden: dissolution of narrative, 109; fiction and art of the possible, 34; history, absence of modernist techniques, 14, 109
Whitehead, Anne, 30
Whitfield, Muriel, 34
Whitman, Walt, 129, 166, 172
Widdemer, Margaret, 159
Wilcox, Herbert, 259n41
Wilde, Oscar, 281n47; *De Profundis*, 131; and Freeman Wills, 97; *The Picture of Dorian Gray*, 41
Williams, Raymond, 31, 77, 252n37
Williams, William Carlos, 165

Wills, Rev. Freeman: *The Only Way*, 97; and Wilde family, 97
Wilson, Edmund, 162
Wilson, Woodrow: Ireland and Versailles settlement, 177, 229n8; Irish as hyphenated Americans, 159–60, 273n3
Winston, Greg, 79
Winter, Jay, 113
Winter, Sir Ormond, 38, 254n67
Woods, Christopher, 46
Woodward, Guy, 9
Woolf, Virginia, 34, 231n12
Worker's Republic, 85
world literature, 17, 20, 36, 157, 222

Yates, Francis, 29–30
Yeats, Jack B., 106; innovations in Irish art, 114
Yeats, W. B., 166, 181, 220, 223; and Abbey Theatre, 4; achievement for Ireland, 36, 194; Æ as "poet of new inspiration," xiii–xiv; on Arthur Griffith, 245n21; as dreamer, 62; on Easter Rising, 114; encouraging Joyce to visit Ireland, 41, 241n58; hostility to commodity culture, 56; on John Martin-Harvey, 97; on John O'Leary, 107; among "last romantics," 113; and modernism, 14, 87; musical collaboration with Florence Farr, 129; O'Grady and anticipations of the Rising, 64; on O'Malley, 184, 279n12; romantic Ireland, 198; speaks on *Ulysses* at Trinity College, 41; subscriber of *Ulysses*, 34; "Who Goes with Fergus," 219
Yorktown, xvii
Young, Ella, 185

Zangwill, Israel, 221
Zeus, 268n19
Zionism, 159
Žižek, Slavoj, 81–82
Zurich, 24, 25